VISUALIZING THE SACRED
||||||||||||||||||||||||||||||||||||||||||||||||||||||||||||||||||||||||||||||||||||||||||||||||||||
THE LINDA SCHELE SERIES IN MAYA AND PRE-COLUMBIAN STUDIES

EDITED BY
George E. Lankford, F. Kent Reilly III, and James F. Garber

VISUALIZING THE SACRED

Cosmic Visions, Regionalism, and the Art of the Mississippian World

UNIVERSITY OF TEXAS PRESS | AUSTIN

This series was made possible through the generosity of William C. Nowlin, Jr., and Bettye H. Nowlin, the National Endowment for the Humanities, and various individual donors.

Copyright © 2011 by the University of Texas Press
All rights reserved
FIRST EDITION, 2011

Requests for permission to reproduce material from this work should be sent to:
Permissions
University of Texas Press
P.O. Box 7819
Austin, TX 78713-7819
www.utexas.edu/utpress/about/bpermission.html

Library of Congress Cataloging-in-Publication Data

Visualizing the sacred : cosmic visions, regionalism, and the art of the Mississippian world / edited by George E. Lankford, F. Kent Reilly III, and James F. Garber. — 1st ed

p. cm. — (The Linda Schele series in Maya and pre-Columbian studies)

Includes bibliographical references and index.
ISBN 978-0-292-72308-5 (cloth)
ISBN 978-0-292-73751-8 (paper)
ISBN 978-0-292-78465-9 (e-book)
1. Mississippian culture. 2. Mississippian art. 3. Indian cosmology—Mississippi River Valley—History—To 1500. 4. Indians of North America—Mississippi River Valley—Religion. 5. Visions—Mississippi River Valley—History—To 1500. 6. Regionalism—Mississippi River Valley—History—To 1500. 7. Mississippi River Valley—Antiquities. 8. Middle West—Antiquities. 9. Southern States—Antiquities. 10. East (U.S.)—Antiquities.
I. Lankford, George E., 1938– II. Reilly, F. Kent. III. Garber, James.
E99.M6815V57 2010   977—dc22
2010035076

Cover photograph by David H. Dye. Used by permission.
Design by Carrie House, HOUSEdesign llc

To the Lannan Foundation of Santa Fe, New Mexico, in thanks for the constant financial support that makes this volume and our workshop meetings possible.

⸻

For Antonio J. Waring, Jr., M.D., who pioneered the modern study of the symbolism and iconography of the Native American cultures of the Mississippian period, and for the many student volunteers from Texas State University–San Marcos and other institutions, who are the indispensable elements in the success of our research.

CONTENTS

Acknowledgments, x

Introduction, xi
F. Kent Reilly III, James F. Garber, and George E. Lankford

GENERAL STUDIES

CHAPTER 1
Regional Approaches to Iconographic Art
George E. Lankford
3

CHAPTER 2
The Cosmology of the Osage: *The Star People and Their Universe*
James R. Duncan
18

REGIONAL STUDIES: MIDDLE MISSISSIPPI VALLEY

CHAPTER 3
The Regional Culture Signature of the Braden Art Style
James A. Brown
37

CHAPTER 4
Early Manifestations of Mississippian Iconography
in Middle Mississippi Valley Rock-Art
Carol Diaz-Granados
64

REGIONAL STUDIES: LOWER MISSISSIPPI VALLEY

CHAPTER 5
Mississippian Ceramic Art in the
Lower Mississippi Valley: *A Thematic Overview*
David H. Dye
99

CHAPTER 6
The Great Serpent in the Lower Mississippi Valley
F. Kent Reilly III
118

REGIONAL STUDIES: CUMBERLAND VALLEY

CHAPTER 7
Iconography of the Thruston Tablet
Vincas P. Steponaitis, Vernon James Knight, Jr., George E. Lankford,
Robert V. Sharp, and David H. Dye
137

CHAPTER 8
Woman in the Patterned Shawl: *Female Effigy Vessels and
Figurines from the Middle Cumberland River Basin*
Robert V. Sharp, Vernon James Knight, Jr., and George E. Lankford
177

REGIONAL STUDIES: MOUNDVILLE

CHAPTER 9
A Redefinition of the Hemphill Style in Mississippian Art
Vernon James Knight, Jr., and Vincas P. Steponaitis
201

CHAPTER 10
The Raptor on the Path
George E. Lankford
240

CHAPTER 11
The Swirl-Cross and the Center
George E. Lankford
251

REGIONAL STUDIES: ETOWAH AND UPPER TENNESSEE VALLEY

CHAPTER 12
Iconography of the Hightower Region of Eastern
Tennessee and Northern Georgia
Adam King
279

CHAPTER 13
Dancing in the Otherworld: *The Human Figural Art
of the Hightower Style Revisited*
F. Kent Reilly III and James F. Garber
294

CHAPTER 14
Raptor Imagery at Etowah: *The Raptor Is the Path to Power*
Adam King and F. Kent Reilly III
313

Bibliography, 321
Contributors, 347
Index, 349

ACKNOWLEDGMENTS

With appreciation and thanks the editors of this volume recognize the two readers and reviewers of this work for both their perseverance and their very helpful comments: Randolph Widmer of the University of Houston and Virginia Fields of the Los Angeles County Museum of Art.

David Dye of the University of Memphis has contributed many of the photographs. Without David's contribution we would be unable to illustrate many of our iconographic conclusions. The Peabody Museum Press, Peabody Museum of Archaeology and Ethnology, Harvard University, Cambridge, Massachusetts, has also graciously granted permission for the use of copyrighted material.

We also acknowledge the support and aid of the Lannan Foundation of Santa Fe, New Mexico; the dean of Liberal Arts at Texas State University–San Marcos, Ann Marie Ellis; and the faculty and staff of the Anthropology Department at Texas State University–San Marcos and the Center for the Study of the Arts and Symbolism of Ancient America (CASAA), which is housed in this department.

Finally, neither the conferences that generate the intellectual ideas highlighted in this volume nor the volume itself would be possible without the organizational skills of Duncan McKinnon and Johann Sawyer, to whom we also convey our thanks and appreciation.

INTRODUCTION

F. Kent Reilly III, James F. Garber, and George E. Lankford

I began with the desire to speak with the dead.
STEPHEN GREENBLATT, "Towards a Poetics of Culture" (1989)

Linda Schele often said that the primary focus of those who study ancient cultures should be the revival of the voices of the ancient peoples who created those cultures. Agreeing with Linda, the contributors to this volume interpret the past not as a dead and static series of events but as an active and animated influence that has messages for both Native American and Euro-American cultures today. The primary means of listening to these ancient Native American voices has been the Mississippian Iconographic Workshop held at Texas State University in San Marcos since 1993. The workshop is sponsored by the Center for the Study of the Arts and Symbolism of Ancient America (CASAA) and hosted by the Department of Anthropology, Texas State University–San Marcos. No endeavor of this magnitude can be successful without adequate funding. Fortunately for the workshop, the Lannan Foundation of Santa Fe, New Mexico, has generously provided that funding, and the workshop participants will forever be indebted to that foundation.

Objects produced by Native American artists and craftspeople during the Mississippian period (AD 900–1600) in the Eastern Woodlands of the United States (Map 1) are the common currency of our workshop discussions. Created from copper, shell, stone, and clay, many of these objects are equal in beauty and craftsmanship to the objects produced in the ancient Andes or Mesoamerica. Unfortunately, even though this corpus of Mississippian artistic production has been the subject of two major art exhibitions in recent years (Brose et al. 1985; Townsend and Sharp 2004), it has not gained the recognition from the broader public that it so richly deserves. During the Mississippian period certain of these finely crafted objects, particularly those created from copper and shell, undoubtedly functioned as items of great ideological significance and, like many of their Mesoamerican counterparts, almost certainly were "employed as social currency in the realm of ritual regal gifts" (Reents-Budet 1994:4).

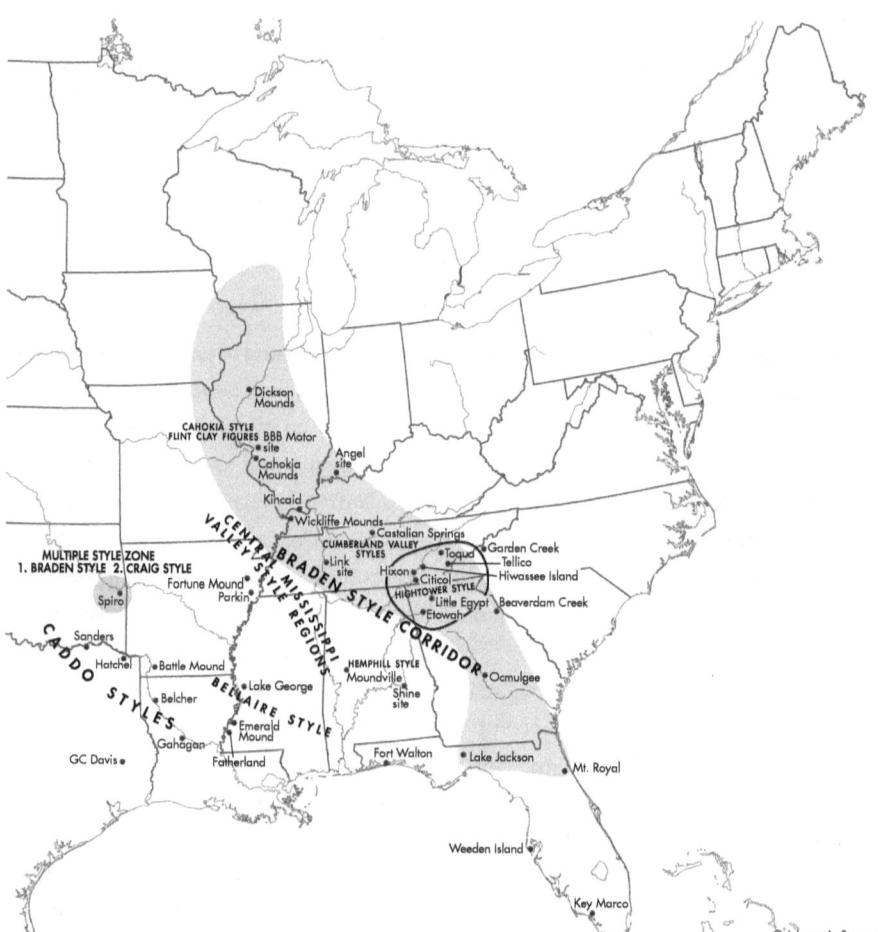

MAP 1. Mississippian archaeological sites were located over a large area of the central and southeastern United States. This geographical area is remarkable for its large number of rivers and streams and the rich alluvial lands that are the product of this riverine environment. The earliest archaeological sites that are clearly Mississippian are located in the vicinity of the ancient city of Cahokia in Illinois. This region is also the original location of the Braden style. The largest number of Braden style objects, however, is found at the Spiro site in Oklahoma. The area of eastern Tennessee and northwestern Georgia is the location of the Hightower style. Eastern Texas, western Louisiana, and southwestern Arkansas were the location of the Caddoan style. The symbols and motifs that are found at Moundville appear to be part of a style region that includes south-central Mississippi and southern Louisiana.

The participants in the Mississippian Iconographic Workshop are a diverse group of archaeologists, anthropologists, folklorists, art historians, and upon several occasions Native American religious practitioners. All of these individuals bring with them their enthusiasm and desire to communicate with the Native American past through an interdisciplinary approach. Each participant has his or her own set of questions or research agendas, but all are committed to the free flow of ideas through the interaction of different approaches. One methodology in particular, however, has emerged as being particularly rewarding.

Essentially, this methodology begins with the division of the participants into a series of subgroups. Each subgroup organizes itself around a particular structural or iconographic problem. The members of the subgroup amass a corpus of photographs and drawings of objects that are central to the problem that they are addressing. These drawings are grouped into categories. Each object is then examined through the process of structural analysis. This exercise reveals patterns of shared icons. These patterns are organized into groups of equally shared elements, symbols, motifs, and themes. Each category is examined and compared for commonalities of symbols as well as shared motifs and themes. A search of ethnographic literature is conducted to see if these iconographic patterns can be linked to general or specific aspects of Native American ideology and belief systems. Even in instances where no link can be revealed, the pattern stands as an area of potential future research.

This methodology is not new. It has been used to recover meaning from the symbol systems of both Mesoamerica and South America. When applied to the art and symbolism of the Mississippian peoples, this methodology has provided significant breakthroughs in regard to our understanding of both style and meaning. Among these breakthroughs is the recognition of a Greater Braden style that almost certainly originated in the region of Cahokia. Additionally, the importance of ethnographic sources from the Southeast, the Great Lakes, and the northern and southern Great Plains has become evident. In fact this recognition of the significance of ethnographic literature in the recovery of meaning from ancient Native American art has "proved to be the Rosetta Stone that led to many of the interpretations presented herein" (Steponaitis 2007). Finally, the recognition of style regions, the focus of this volume, is seen as the key to understanding Mississippian art and its associated sociopolitical landscape.

It is important to note, however, that there has never been a need within the workshop format for a consensus on any specific iconographic issue. In fact, disagreements and discussions generated by those disagreements have often led to an expansion of the methodological envelope in which we conduct our research. One telling difference of opinion is the lack of an agreed-upon label to apply to the iconographic corpus with which we conduct our research. When the workshop first began, this was referred to in the literature as the Southeastern Ceremonial Complex or SECC (see Chapter 1). At our annual meeting in 1998 one of this volume's editors (James F. Garber) conducted a discussion whose aim was to define the SECC. After an hour of fruitless dialogue, however, no consensus could be reached. No discussion in the last eight years has changed that impasse. But all the participants could agree that the material dated to the Mississippian period and that a large number of the symbols were first visualized in the art of the Ohio Hopewell culture (AD 1–400). Many participants also agreed that to identify the corpus as a southeastern phenomenon was a mistake, since its geographical range was recognized. Scholars also disagree about the use of the term "complex" as a description of what appears to be some form of interaction among related regional complexes. They recognize, however, that certain symbols not only cross the stylistic boundaries described in this book but can be found in distant cultural areas such as the American Southwest (Lankford 2006).

To date no common label has been forthcoming. But the corpus appears to be perceived in three ways. Some of the workshop participants prefer that no label be applied. Others wish to retain the old SECC designations because they are ingrained in the literature (King 2007b, 2007c) but acknowledge that it is not a single complex. Finally, a third group approves of the label "Mississippian Ideological Interaction Sphere (MIIS)" to describe the interrelated regional ideological complexes of the Mississippian tradition (Reilly and Garber 2007).

Reilly and Garber organized the annual Texas State workshop into smaller groups of conferees focused on different geographical areas for the task of examining the nature of the regional aspects of those putative culture zones and the resulting influences on the iconography. For several years the individuals in the groups studied particular sites and their art forms from the regional perspective, producing iconographic papers, and only then focused as a group on a comparative study of the regions in relation to each other.

This volume contains the papers resulting from this approach, clarified by dialogue and criticism within the group.

The chapters are loosely organized by area. They cannot truthfully be called "regions" at this point, for none of the discussions focused primarily on trying to define the boundaries in terms of geology, geography, style, culture, or iconographic corpus. The zones continue to have undefined boundaries, and no attempts have yet been made to identify types of unity or connectedness. Instead, the groups have focused on particular collections of art in an attempt to discern the nature of the corpus and to identify some of the rules governing the artists and their iconographic production as well as their distribution. They made a final attempt to compare the areas studied in terms of their polities, culture, and iconography, but the results are so tentative that they do not appear in this volume. The discussions that the comparisons have sparked have not yet matured enough to withstand public gaze, so they are better left for the future.

Instead of presenting large conclusions, this book offers a series of smaller studies focused on specific (local) art forms and their contexts. The closest thing to a general study is Chapter 1, which offers a historical overview of the academic tension between the general view of Mississippian iconography and the local view, so even that study is focused on the regional. In Chapter 2 James Duncan, operating on the widely accepted hypothesis that the Cahokia phenomenon was largely Siouan in origin, explores the historical religious beliefs of the Osage as a possible ethnographic path to understanding some of the iconography found far from Cahokia, such as at Spiro.

After Duncan's presentation of the Osage religion as it is currently understood by practitioners, the rest of the chapters are organized in a loose geographical way: the Middle Mississippi Valley (a term that will please no one, since it ignores the delineation of Central and Upper Mississippi Valley so dear to the hearts of many), the Lower Mississippi Valley, the Cumberland Valley, Moundville, and Etowah and the Upper Tennessee Valley.

Two chapters look at iconography in the Middle Mississippi Valley. In Chapter 3 James Brown provides a formal identification of the Braden art style as a regional art developing through time. This long-awaited study buttresses his argument that in the regional development of art in the Mississippian world the Braden style emerged as a (the?) major source of the corpus that became known as the SECC (Knight et al. 2001:131). In Chapter 4 Carol

Diaz-Granados follows the argument that the Braden style was seminal in Mississippian iconography. She examines the images of the rock-art of Missouri west of Cahokia that date from early Mississippian times. By identifying them with the Braden style, she lays a claim that the early corpus of the classic iconographic images was regional (local) despite its later appearance in many far-flung sites as the core of Mississippian iconography.

Farther south in the Mississippi Valley is an area that has traditionally been overlooked in iconographic studies of Mississippian art, largely because it was not a major participant in the imagery that was used in Antonio Waring's definition of the SECC. In Chapter 5 David Dye undertakes an assessment of the themes present in the Mississippian ceramic art of the well-populated floodplain of the Arkansas and Mississippi deltas and adjacent areas. His brief survey reveals the iconographic richness of the area, despite its exclusion from the "classic SECC" model, and illustrates the value of a more inclusive regional perspective. In Chapter 6 Kent Reilly underscores the point with a focused study of the imagery of the "Great Serpent" in the Lower Mississippi Valley.

The two Cumberland Valley studies are interesting examples of the larger research group approach, for both resulted from team discussion and lab examinations in Texas and Tennessee. In Chapter 7 the full team of Vin Steponaitis, Jim Knight, George Lankford, Robert Sharp, and David Dye presents a complicated analysis of a complex iconographic object, the famed Thruston Tablet found near Nashville in the nineteenth century. Their high-tech approach to the problem of separating layers of an artistic palimpsest is interesting in its own right, and their examination of the separated images offers insights into the meaning of "storyboard" iconographic art.

Three members of that team produced a separate study of female effigy vessels, which constitute one of the characteristic art forms of the Cumberland area. Basing their observations on a large corpus (with contributions of images by Cumberland scholars Kevin Smith and Ian Brown), Robert Sharp, Jim Knight, and George Lankford offer some new observations in Chapter 8 about the rules for producing the ceramic images and suggest some cultural interpretations.

Three chapters are concerned with Moundville art. Jim Knight and Vin Steponaitis, who have collaborated on a classic recent Moundville study (Knight and Steponaitis 1998), join forces again to produce a new style definition. In Chapter 9 they examine the traditional ceramic artifacts grouped as the "Hemphill Engraved" style, extract and clarify the rules governing the style, and add to the corpus from various media other than ceramics. The result is a new way of looking at a greatly expanded art style and its surprising diffusion. Chapter 10, which also deals with Moundville art, is an extension of an earlier study by George Lankford. He isolates the Raptor image and looks closely at its likely meaning in the Moundville context, arguing that in Moundville usage it took on a unique denotation and function, different from the Raptors of other locations. This study works well as a companion piece to Chapter 14, for the two regional Raptors together provide several provocative insights into the nature of artistic diffusion. In Chapter 11, another study on Moundville art, Lankford focuses on the "swirl-cross" motif emphasized at Moundville and demonstrates some ways in which comparative analysis of imagery in the full corpus can be used to reveal the meanings of such local and diffused iconographic images.

In Chapter 12 Adam King undertakes the characterization of an iconographic style region, termed the "Hightower." In the process he offers several new insights about relationships and the meaning of art forms. In Chapter 13 Kent Reilly and Jim Garber focus on one particular art theme from that area, a distinctive set of related Hightower-style engraved shell gorgets. By emphasizing theme over style in this case, they offer a provocative suggestion that the series constitutes a "storyboard" art display that calls for a different kind of iconographic analysis. In Chapter 14 King and Reilly probe the meaning of the Raptor as it is found in both imported and local art objects in the Hightower region. The contrast between their conclusions and Lankford's conclusions regarding the Moundville Raptor underscores the importance of small-scale comparative examination of similar iconography appearing in different sites and geographic areas.

Many of these regional studies highlight the problem of how to identify a basic meaning of an image while recognizing and honoring the nuances and redefinitions that took place in local usage. Another type of regional problem is exemplified in the Spiro site of the Arkansas River Valley, where an astounding number of imported art forms have dominated the discussion of iconography in the region. The articulation of local Caddo art forms with the imported iconographic materials has long been discussed, but without final resolution.

Each chapter in this volume represents a close study of an individual style, image, symbol, motif, or theme within the broader category of

Mississippian-period art. When taken as a whole, however, the contents of *Visualizing the Sacred* provide a cognitive window through which to view the aesthetics and beliefs of a broader yet specific period of the ancient Native American past. Like our preceding volume, *Ancient Objects and Sacred Realms*, this volume is first and last a collaborative effort. The rewards of collaborative work are both personal and intellectual in that revelations in meaning are tested, at the time of their inception, by a broader jury. Certainly each workshop participant at some point in the process realizes that these ancient objects are also a language whose interpretation allows an enlargement of the windows through which the ancient American past is viewed. Needless to say, we take great joy in sharing with our peers the revelations in meaning that occur in our workshop context.

Ultimately all of the participants understand that both the objects examined and the interpretations presented in our workshop and in these volumes are, in fact, the voices of the ancient inhabitants of this continent. Through this and future publications these ancient North Americans share their vision of their natural and supernatural environment with both the authors and the readers. In effect the readers of this volume should be left with the understanding that these wonderful works of art and the symbols they carried were created by an ancient and dynamic people whose Native American descendants continue to live in and create vibrant and meaningful cultural traditions.

GENERAL STUDIES

CHAPTER 1
Regional Approaches to Iconographic Art
George E. Lankford

The enigma of the Mississippian complicated art forms now usually called the Southeastern Ceremonial Complex (SECC) was recognized well over a century ago. As one spectacular piece of art after another came from the ground, it became obvious that the art itself called for an explanation of origins: who had made such art, and why? As the collections grew, a second aspect of the enigma became increasingly apparent, for the distribution of similar pieces was widespread: how had the distribution occurred, and what did it say about the societies who lived in those locations?

As time went by, the issues became crystallized in two polar problems. On the one hand, the art motifs, themes, and styles pointed to some sort of unity across ethnographic boundaries of all kinds, but the nature of that unity was a subject for debate. On the other hand, some of the art was clearly produced locally and some was exotic but not found universally, indicating that in some way the images had regional meanings—an aspect of diversity within the vast collection of art forms. This diversity-within-unity became a common tension in the discussion, as students of the spectacular art forms found themselves oscillating between the poles as they thought about the objects under scrutiny.

The unity side of the dialectic received most attention in the early years for two reasons. First, it was necessary to demonstrate that there really was some sort of unified phenomenon that needed explanation; the material was not that widely known. Second, the possibility of a prehistoric pan-Indian movement expressed in art forms could not be ignored: if true, it would be important for the reconstruction of the past. Whether the mechanism for such a phenomenon proved to be a migration of tribes, a direct connection with Mesoamerica, or a rapidly diffusing religious movement, it offered a major rewriting of prehistory.

"Cult" was one of the terms most frequently used to describe the phenomenon during the early years. At a special Society for American Archaeology symposium convened at the University of Michigan in 1947, Philip Phillips attributed the original use of the word to Herbert Spinden, a Mesoamericanist who had suggested in 1931 that the Southeastern art was the result of a "warrior cult" diffused from Mexico (Williams 1968:72). Spinden was apparently using the word with its ordinary meaning in religious studies: a group of people united by belief and ritual practice. "Cult" was the word of choice at that 1947 meeting, but Phillips indicated his unhappiness with the term. He had already offered "Eagle Warrior Complex" as a name for the phenomenon and suggested that the word "cult" be dropped: "I now feel that we have little or no conception of the true meaning of the material called 'Southern Cult'" (Williams 1968:74, 73). His phrasing ("material called 'Southern Cult'") indicated that the blurring of the word had already begun. Waring described his current work with Preston Holder, noting that "we concluded that we were dealing with a very special ceremonial phenomenon which we termed (cautiously and rather clumsily) 'a Southeastern ceremonial complex'" (quoted in Williams 1968:73). Despite their creation of the new label that was destined to last for decades, Waring and Holder themselves were strongly wedded to "cult," perhaps because Waring had also written a sequel to their classic 1945 presentation. Although it was not published until 1968, it bore the title "The Southern Cult and Muskhogean Ceremonial" (Williams 1968:30–69). Sensitive to the criticism of the use of "cult" at the 1947 meeting, however, Waring apparently rewrote his manuscript, promising to avoid the offending word—a promise not kept, as editor Stephen Williams wryly noted (Williams 1968:30).

The almost exclusive use of "cult" at the 1947 meeting and the discussion of its appropriateness make it clear that the unity side of the dialectic was the focus of attention. Even so, some aspects of the diversity issue were inserted into the symposium. Alex Krieger had published an article examining the putative connection of Mesoamerican art to the Southeastern "cult" and had found problems with the argument (Krieger 1945). He told the 1947 gathering that "wherever the 'Cult' occurred widely spread in the Southeast, there were significantly different style or subject emphases at the various centers. This strongly suggests that we are dealing with a series of related cults rather than a single 'Cult'" (Williams 1968:74).

W. C. McKern attempted to get to the definitional issues by asking: "What is implied in your use of this term?" James Griffin fairly impatiently referred him to Waring and Holder's 1945 article, where they "define the use of the term as it is now generally applied." A careful reading of that article, however, reveals that no definition was offered. The authors presented a "trait list," but it only indicated what they considered "in" the cult. The word was used most frequently as an adjective: "cult complex," "cult centers," "cult period," "cult material," and "cult sites" (Williams 1968:9, 22, 26, 29). This usage seems to be primarily a reference to the artistic material itself rather than to more abstract meanings: a "cult center" or "site" is a location where the art forms are found, "cult material" refers to the particular art forms that are surveyed and listed in the article, and the "cult period" is a temporal span identifiable by the presence of the art forms. In these cases "cult" thus seems to mean simply "this collection of art," a shorthand term with no larger implication intended. The best clues to the concept of "cult" were offered at the end of the paper, when the word became a noun. The authors indicated their agreement with a 1940 statement by Phillips: "We are evidently concerned with the transmission of a cult (or a group of associated cults) rather than culture in a more general sense" (Williams 1968:29). This "cult" gives no indication of being more tightly defined than a group of people united in ritual behavior related to one or more specified divinities—the sort of usage customary in religious studies ("cult" or "cultus"). Waring and Holder, however, had more in mind than that. In their conclusion they were more specific about how they saw the agency responsible for the art. They hypothesized "a highly-developed cult or cult complex . . . synthesized within the southeastern United States in a single community or restricted group of communities . . . [a process that] probably took place in the Middle Mississippi Basin. From this center the cult spread rapidly" (Williams 1968:29).

The notion of a rapidly spreading cult had been cited earlier as a way of explaining variation between sites (Williams 1968:23), and the concept called up various images of how the "cult" beliefs and practices could have been communicated. The authors offered one more insight into their presuppositions on the nature of the cult: it had "swept through the late prehistoric Southeast very much as the Ghost Dance swept from tribe to tribe across the Plains in the late nineteenth century" (Williams 1968:28). They were reiterating their position put forward a decade earlier at a 1937 gathering in Savannah (Williams 1968:6). It was not a surprising hypothesis, because scholars in the early twentieth century were still rocked by the recent Ghost Dance among the Plains tribes, an actual historical event in recent memory that was still being analyzed. From the vantage point of a later day, it is possible to recognize that they were using as a model a form of religious structure that anthropologists now call a revitalization movement, a specialized type of religious practice that is understood to be rooted in extreme cultural stress and to be focused on a "prophet" whose vision and charisma form the heart of the "cult." Even though the scholarly studies on this type of religious structure had not been completed in the 1940s (see Wallace 1956, a seminal work), these characteristics were already known, for many of the anthropologists of the day had lived through the Ghost Dance phenomenon and knew it well.

This sort of presupposition about the agency behind the prehistoric art was disturbing to some of the people at the 1947 symposium. Philip Phillips objected that "'cult' has the connotation of a single concept. It is apparent that our ceremonial complex consists of a series of concepts" (Williams 1968:76). Other scholars also expressed concern about the word. Frederica De Laguna warned that their thinking was "unduly influenced by the constant use of the term 'cult.' A cult is not a whole religion which dominates or connects with all of cultural life—it is much more restricted in emphasis. It appears that we are dealing with a major series of religious ideas and institutions here" (Williams 1968:77). McKern had the last word on the diversity problem: "we must remember that the same symbol might have different interpretations with different cultural manifestations. The thunderbird, for example, was a common symbol over a wide area, but had different mythological and religious significance in various cultural settings" (Williams 1968:77). These objections had their influence: by the time Waring's papers were published two decades later, it was possible for his editor to refer to the "Southeastern Ceremonial Complex (to give it its proper name)" (Williams 1968:7).

The shifting of labels was helpful in lessening the restrictive power of the presuppositions about the nature of the phenomenon contained in the "cult" label, but it did not directly address the problem of the unity-diversity tension. Waring and Holder had already begun to point out some of the issues in their 1945 synthesis, even though their primary focus was on the unity of the phenomenon. It was in the discussion of style that the tension became articulated:

The material from Spiro is in many ways radically different from that of Etowah and Moundville ... The bulk of material from each of the three great sites could not possibly be confused with another. Nevertheless, and this is an extremely important point, there exists at the core a basic group of elements and a basic stylistic similarity in all of the material. (Williams 1968:22)

Waring and Holder recognized that despite the frequently exotic origin of the raw material "the finished ceremonial object usually shows the characteristics of the stylistic subarea in which it is found, and, within limits, could not be confused with material from another area." They also pointed out that the distribution of similar artifacts is localized, and even "the motifs appear disproportionately from site to site." Moreover, they said, the intrasite distribution of material varies from site to site: some in graves, some in structures, and so on (Williams 1968:22). Despite these evidences of regionalization in the art styles and distribution patterns, Waring and Holder concluded with a hypothesis about the spreading cult, thus reaffirming their emphasis on the unity of the phenomenon. Within that spread, however, they left room for regionalization: "Local variations in the complex are explicable in terms of the previous ceremonial life and basic economics of the subareas under consideration" (Williams 1968:29).

Regionalization was the focus of the next Waring paper, "Southern Cult and Muskhogean Ceremonial," written in the 1940s (Williams 1968:30–69). In this lengthy and well-argued study, Waring presented an illustration of his point about the regionalizing power of "previous ceremonial life and basic economics" of the local site. The people under study were the historic Muskogee (Creeks). In an ingenious argument Waring examined the mythic tradition of the *hiyuyulgi*, the four "people" who brought to the ancestral Creeks the basics of their culture, including horticulture and medicines. In his analysis the story was interpreted as historical legend: the four visitors became more than just culture-bearers—they were the "cult-bringers" who were the agents of transmission of the Southeastern Ceremonial Complex. The major ceremonial offered as an example of a relic of the cult was the Green Corn ceremony (Busk) of the Creeks, and many details seemed to correlate well with the prehistoric art (Williams 1968:47–51). In 1968, when Waring's paper was finally published, James Howard's supportive study of the Muskogee ethnographic background in relation to the Southeastern Ceremonial Complex was also published (Howard 1968). This sort of examination, using the regional or local ethnographic material to interpret the art forms of the SECC, was a powerful model of how the images were to be interpreted, incorporating the important principle of regional creation, adaptation, and synthesis.

James Griffin, who was the chair of the 1947 symposium, had little trouble with the "cult" language. He had recently published an article speculating that the possible Mexican connection with the Southeastern "Cult" had come via the Tristán de Luna expedition of 1558, a position affirming the focus on the unity of the phenomenon and its late date (Griffin 1944). When he summarized the discussion, however, he was sensitive to the critique of the term, referring to "a ceremonial complex, which might be termed 'Cult' as a convenience." He recognized a need for attention to the regional dimension of the phenomenon in his concluding remark: "A common stratum of ideas from Spiro to Etowah merges with local cultures producing distinguishable local variations. The pressing needs at the present time are for a study of the cultural and chronological position of particular items of the complex, of the *various regional and site expressions of the complex*, and a searching study of the possibility of 'Cult' continuation into the ethnographic present" (Williams 1968:77; emphasis added).

A few years later Griffin published a survey of materials from Spiro, documenting their relationships to other sites and noting the absence of some SECC materials found at eastern sites. He backed away from the late dating, affirming that "the height of the Southern Cult was in existence during the De Soto entrada and would go back in time to at least 1300 or 1400. Few archaeologists now regard this Southern Cult as an efflorescence brought about by a cultural crisis and a phenomenon which spread with great rapidity throughout the southeast" (Griffin 1952:105). Observing that "many students have recognized the cultural divergence exhibited by sites and centers which possess common cult attributes," Griffin offered his hypothesis: the Southern Cult art "represents the ceremonial activities and religious mythological beliefs which achieved wide acceptance in the Southeast from the Caddoan area to the Atlantic Coast during the Mississippi period . . . The artistic expression of the socio-religious pattern of the Mississippi culture is available to archaeology in the form of the Southern Cult artifacts. These vary locally reflecting the individual artisans' ability and the particular mode of tribal interpretation of a widespread cosmology" (Griffin 1952:103, 105).

During those years the continuing archaeological examination of the key sites yielding SECC materials kept the issue of the nature and relationship of the larger complex to particular sites in the scholarly dialogue. Thus, for example, David Baerreis argued that the Spiro site had produced a "Spiro Ceremonial Complex" before the advent of the larger SECC (Baerreis 1957). His paper provoked disagreement from Griffin, who discussed the chronological problems in Caddoan archaeology and the artifacts from the Spiro site, concluding that there was no basis at that time for believing in an earlier artistic complex (Griffin 1961). Such discussions kept the issues, if not the general concept, of regionalism before the archaeological community, but the focus remained on the larger "cult." The enigma of the Spiro collection was largely seen as a problem of the nature of the general phenomenon rather than a local peculiarity. Thus Phillips and James Brown could later point out that "Spiro played an important part in the formation of the Cult. Without the Craig Mound finds there might not have been such a concept. Up to that point it was still possible to reconcile the similarities of art and ceremonial objects from major late Southeastern centers, Etowah, Moundville, Southeast Missouri, Tennessee-Cumberland (as it was then called), Walls-Pecan Point, etc., as expressions of a shared 'Middle Mississippi' culture" (Phillips and Brown 1978:169).

The attempt to change the label was still not successful well into the 1960s, as seen in Gordon Willey's use of "Southern Cult" in his survey of North American prehistory (Willey 1964:304–307). He noted that the hypothesis of a "messianic" movement had been refuted by the earlier dating of the art. "It is, however, still possible that a cult phenomenon was involved, although one wholly pre-Columbian. Such a cult, or widely shared religious ideology, could have been an expression of vitality rather than despair" (Willey 1964:306). In this brief summary, the "cult" was the sole concern.

In his review of the knowledge of the prehistory of the Southeast, William Sears also continued the use of "Southern Cult," although he defined it phenomenologically as "a complex of ceremonial artifacts, art styles, and representations ranging from ceremonial axes, through often elaborate ear spools, to representations of an eagle being and other natural and symbolic motifs, executed in copper and conch shell" (Sears 1964:279). His peculiar definition added terminological confusion to the discussion, for he made it clear that he wished to use "Southern Cult" to refer to the mental and material artifacts of the religious organization rather than the organization itself. Pointing out that its "most elaborate expressions" were at the non–Middle Mississippian sites of Spiro and Etowah, Sears suggested the roots of the "cult" were in the Caddoan societies and the early appearance of some Mesoamerican influence in that region. Again, his focus was on the single "cult" phenomenon, but with a reference to the Caddoan region as an ancestral hearth (Sears 1964:278–283).

It was not until 1976 that another major assault on the monolithic concept of the artistic phenomenon was launched. James Brown, collaborator with Phillips on the massive survey of Spiro engraved shell (Phillips and Brown 1978, 1984), issued a "call for critical re-examination of the original Cult concept as exposited by Waring and Holder (1945)" (Brown 1976:116). He focused on the trait list that was essentially the Waring and Holder "definition" of SECC, indicating that "their point of departure for generating the trait list was the detailed depiction of fully costumed falcon warriors in the famous Rogan plates from Etowah" (Brown 1976:118). Brown pointed out that the procedure had an arbitrary beginning, omitted many important traits, and ignored issues of cultural context. He called it "a retrogressive process aimed at eliminating artifact distributions with undesirable distributions as 'false' Cult traits" and wondered "how many other traits will have like fate so that the only sites included in 'good cult' standing will be the very sites the list is defined from. The problem here is that the 'culling' procedure is strictly circular in logic" (Brown 1976:118–119).

It was time to reconsider the whole concept, Brown argued, because

> stylistic analysis has finally caught up with the Southern Cult concept. The result has been the discovery and documentation of many style groups in the engraved shell alone (Muller 1966a, b). At least two major style systems have been isolated at Spiro . . . The recognition of style systems, moreover, leads to the discovery of many more motifs and designs, including so-called "pottery designs" that the trait-list does not associate. (Brown 1976:121)

Even more important than an inadequate trait list as a defining tool, however, was the contextless nature of the traits in the SECC formulation. "The effect of not recognizing the function connections among Mississippian Period artifacts and symbolism is a failure to unite conceptually significant parts of the ritual, paraphernalia and iconography of the period" (Brown 1976:123). Brown pointed out that the understanding of the structure of

Mississippian societies had come a long way since Waring and Holder and suggested that the societal context of religious belief, ritual, and art be examined as an avenue into the complexities of Mississippian art. When that is done, he predicted,

> the number of interrelated style elements will significantly increase and . . . the set of designs, motifs and basic elements will significantly increase and . . . the interrelated style elements will be found in many distinct themes. And lastly, the old notion of a "cult" that diffused from a center to the edge of complex Mississippian social systems will be replaced by a concept of interregional interaction. (Brown 1976:132)

As for a better understanding of the artistic phenomenon than was permitted by the term "cult," Brown and Phillips said it concisely in the Spiro engraved-shell volumes: "'Cult' is, however, a misnomer, a word of insufficient coverage. It would probably be more accurate to describe the phenomenon as an interconnected medley of cults, partly syncretized, on the way perhaps to becoming a pan-Southeastern ideology" (Phillips and Brown 1978:169).

In 1984 an important exhibition of Mississippian art objects was assembled at the Cottonlandia Museum in Greenwood, Mississippi. The accompanying conference provided the occasion for a number of papers on the art that were later published in a groundbreaking volume (Galloway 1989). The book itself demonstrated the growing unease with the SECC/cult terminology and concepts. The series editors pointed out that the "interpretive concept" of the SECC had been modified "so radically that many now argue it should be abandoned" (Galloway 1989:xi). In her introduction Patricia Galloway noted: "The increasing specification of chronologies and distributions, and indeed the better understanding of social process in the intervening thirty years, has served to further deconstruct the original concept—to modify it, and even to call for its abolition" (Galloway 1989:2). Since the major problems posed by the art corpus (distribution, meaning, function) had still not been resolved, she argued, "it is not entirely surprising that nineteen scholars—among them a prominent abolitionist or two—could be found to discuss at least the surviving shreds of the SECC" (Galloway 1989:2).

Those nineteen scholars produced an impressive array of articles, some of them classic studies. Two "definitional" chapters agreed on the use of

"Southern Cult" as the more appropriate term for the SECC materials. Jon Muller suggested that "Southern Cult" not be used in a "sociological sense," that it should be understood as plural, and that it would probably continue to be misleading, but he argued for retaining it for lack of a better term. He then devoted most of his chapter to providing a chronological sequence of periods of the "cult" to help clarify some of the confusion about regional styles and stylistic evolution. David Brose followed Muller's lead terminologically, but he focused on clarification of how the art and artifacts were related to the political and economic structure of the Mississippian polities.

The main collection of articles in the volume consisted of ten studies of "regional manifestations." The authors' task was to elucidate the nature of the SECC materials (apparently meaning the accepted Waring and Holder list) that had been found in geographic areas from the Great Plains to southern Florida. Many of these areas had received little iconographic scrutiny and are usually considered marginal to the center of the SECC diffusion, so these chapters provide useful summaries for the area. The treatment given each area was tempered by the local situation and probably by the author's conviction regarding the canonical list of SECC iconographic materials. The outcome is a set of studies that range from a description of the area and its archaeology (e.g., Dan Morse and Phyllis Morse's concise overview of the Central Mississippi Valley and the development of SECC symbols there) to a detailed study of the iconography of a few items from a location (e.g., Thomas Emerson's thorough paper on Cahokian water symbolism), with the other chapters falling on the continuum between those end points. The final collection of five "Interpretations" differs from the preceding section largely in that they are not tied to local areas. They include a classic update on "Style Divisions" of the SECC (James Brown), a hemispheric comparative study of symbols appearing in art and ritual in North, Central, and South America in prehistoric times (Robert Hall), an update on the parallels between Mississippian and Mesoamerican cultures (Malcolm Webb), and two focused examinations: the possible political rooting of the SECC "monsters" (V. J. Knight, Jr.) and a comparative study of the "Birdman" theme in the SECC (John Strong).

For several reasons this volume should be considered an important milestone on the road to unraveling the iconography. In terms of the regionalism-unity dialectic, it stood in the old tradition: while it offered valuable regional studies, it approached them from the view of the reified body of iconographic art. That is to say, the apparent invitation to the authors was to clarify the

SECC materials, thus establishing a class of objects for focus within the local area. The result was a useful survey of the locations of artifacts on the Waring-Holder list, from the Great Plains to south Florida. Geographical regions were emphasized, but the stylistic regions of Brown's perspective were subordinated to the examination of the old SECC corpus.

In a catalogue published in connection with a major exhibit of "Ancient Art of the American Woodland Indians" at the Detroit Institute of Arts in 1985, James Brown had an opportunity to demonstrate his willingness to do without the monolithic perspective of the SECC (Brose et al. 1985:93–145). In an article entitled "The Mississippian Period" he employed a different organization to approach the art of the era. First, he discussed the diversities of style, a topic already vetted in his "Southern Cult Reconsidered" paper (Brown 1976), the Spiro volumes (Phillips and Brown 1978, 1984:39–68), and his Cottonlandia essay (Brown 1989). As he put it: "Analyses of the corpus of Mississippian have disclosed an amazing diversity of styles, each—as we shall see—probably connected with a specific region" (Brown 1985:98). Brown followed this regional survey of the differences in the art with an extended discussion of the possible socioreligious organizations that were connected to the different themes present in the art. Thus he presented a functional perspective on much of the art of the period, emphasizing these rubrics: Mississippian ancestor cults, the iconography of chiefs, the serpent and fertility cults, and the serpent and the skull. In taking this approach he was able to survey the art without ever mentioning the "Southeastern Ceremonial Complex" as an entity, at the same time insisting that "forces were at work outside Mesoamerica that dictated the imagery and vehicles for artistic creation in the Southeast" (Brown 1985:140).

Brown's insistence on the importance of the diversity of the religious functions of the art forms was reinforced by an influential study of "The Institutional Organization of Mississippian Religion" (Knight 1986). V. J. Knight, Jr., had written his dissertation on Muskhogean culture of the late prehistoric era. That led him to point out in print that Mississippian religion was not monolithic (an idea that was embedded in some of the assumptions about the nature of the Southeastern Ceremonial Complex) but was instead composed of several quite different types of institutions and ritual traditions.

The next collection of iconographic papers was gathered in 1997 as the result of several years of an experiment in the workshop approach to interpreting the SECC imagery. The workshop was hosted by Kent Reilly and the

Department of Anthropology, Texas State University–San Marcos, beginning in 1993. The scholarly interactions proved synergistic: individual researchers produced papers for academic conferences (as early as 1997) and for publication, first in abbreviated fashion in the major exhibition catalog *Hero, Hawk, and Open Hand* by the Art Institute of Chicago (Townsend and Sharp 2004) and then in a workshop volume called *Ancient Objects and Sacred Realms* (Reilly and Garber 2007). The topics were of the authors' own choosing and reflected their scholarly interests, but the result was a useful collection of studies offering new insights, especially in the relation of ethnography and iconography.

Although the focus of those early workshop years was on the most widespread SECC artifacts and motifs, the very nature of the iconographic analytical process demanded a research focus on particular art objects from particular sites. The result was a tendency for the papers to be regional in original focus, often with an attempt to produce interpretations of the local materials that could be more generally applied. Thus four of the nine studies in *Ancient Objects* were focused on the Braden style, identified as originating in the Cahokia area (Brown 2007c). One study used ethnographic insights from the Osage to illuminate Cahokia archaeology (Kehoe 2007). Brown presented an examination of the "Birdman" from the Braden style in the light of Siouan ethnography (Brown 2007b). A study of the "petaloid" motif, based largely on Braden art from Spiro, argued that it served as a locative (locational symbol) for the celestial world (Reilly 2007c).

A focus on engraved shell gorgets from the Cumberland and Tennessee Valleys produced a set of cosmological interpretations with possible wider application to other regions (Lankford 2007d). Another chapter argued that a cluster of SECC motifs could be interpreted as war trophies; the conclusion was drawn from an examination of ceramic engraving in a small area of the Lower Mississippi Valley and Moundville (Dye 2007). Moundville imagery was the focus of three more articles. Two were linked in a study of the ethnographic and mythic background of mortuary beliefs expressed in a cluster of ceramic symbols (Lankford 2007b) and a survey of beliefs about the master of the Beneath World seen in engraved serpents at Moundville and beyond (Lankford 2007a). A tightly focused examination of a symbol found almost nowhere else but Moundville identified an unknown moth divinity and enlarged the corpus of the SECC, since the figure was not listed in the Waring and Holder trait list (Knight and Franke 2007).

The debates on style regions, geographic regions, and the most useful terminology for talking about these issues continued in the workshop group, but a separate conversation was also going on at the same time. The publication of a catalogue of engraved shell gorgets together with geographic distribution maps and chronology of sites (Brain and Phillips 1996) began a wide-scale renewal of the issues of dating the shell gorgets and thus the chronology of the whole corpus of Mississippian art. Adam King organized a symposium of papers focused on the dating problems (Southeastern Archaeological Conference, 2000), but the contributions inevitably offered far more than just chronological data and arguments. Once again, the nature of archaeological dating necessitated a regional focus for most of the papers, and many of them reflected the growing emphasis on style regions.

The resulting volume (King 2007a) is an important collection with contributions far beyond the dating issues. In a thorough introductory chapter and epilogue, King clarified many of the issues in a refreshingly clear way. Jon Muller (2007) wrestled with the terminological problems and produced some helpful suggestions for the continuing discussions about "cult" versus "SECC" versus "Mississippian Art and Ceremonial Complex" versus "Mississippian Ideological Interaction Sphere" versus "Southeastern Interaction Network." David Hally provided an extensive study of chronology and geographic distribution of engraved shell gorgets as factors in a regional study of art forms (Hally 2007). Several important studies have analyzed that art, including Lynne Sullivan's in the same volume (Kneberg 1959; Muller 1966a, 1966b; Sullivan 2001, 2007), but Hally brought them into a new synthesis that stands as a standard for regional examination.

The other excellent studies, from Cahokia to Florida, offer the same sort of chronology plus interpretive insights, making the volume a major contribution to the discussion of Mississippian iconographic art.

While the articles in the King collection were being readied for publication, debate continued in the San Marcos workshop. The continuing discussions made it clear that much of the debate hinged on unspoken assumptions about the SECC (the unity issues), so Knight led the drive to make those presuppositions apparent in order to address them in the dialogue. The statement produced by some of the conferees did not meet with universal agreement, so it was published as a position paper by three of the workshop attendees (Knight et al. 2001). The article included several observations that illustrated some of the issues that had been subjects of debate.

It is now clear that SECC images are expressed in a variety of divergent styles tied to specific geographic areas inhabited by a mosaic of ethnic and linguistic groups. Furthermore, the images are not distributed uniformly across the Southeastern culture area. Rather, major sites yield contrasting sets of SECC images and artifact genres (Krieger 1945), very likely associated with local variations in beliefs, worldviews, rituals, and social ranking. Moreover, the SECC materials have a much longer history than was originally envisioned, and evidence suggests that the meanings of particular images changed over time. On close inspection, then, the original complex begins to dissolve into a series of regional complexes, each to be understood as undergoing local development (Knight et al. 2001:129–130).

Other discussions within the workshop and outside of it articulated well with this emphasis on regionalism as a key to making sense of the SECC. One of the suggestions in the paper was to define the "SECC" as consisting of the artistic images contained in the "Classic Braden style" materials found at Spiro and elsewhere (Knight et al. 2001:131). This argument was consistent with the growing realization that Cahokia and the Braden style were most likely the result of the prehistoric culture of Siouan-speaking peoples and thus the expression of a particular linguistic and cultural ethnic group. If this identification is correct, then the SECC, defined as rooted in Classic Braden, was itself a regional formulation. It became increasingly clear to the workshop participants that a stronger focus on regional iconography was likely to lead to productive breakthroughs in understanding the nature and function of the artistic symbols. These various insights were taken to their logical conclusion by Knight in an article challenging the very use of the term expressing the concept of a unified iconographic art. The title of the article made the point: "Farewell to the Southeastern Ceremonial Complex" (Knight 2006). Without pointing specifically to regionalism as a new focus, Knight suggested some benefits of abandoning the "SECC" after so many years of its domination:

> Freeing ourselves of implausible assumptions about pan-Southeastern sameness of mythic expression, art, ritual, and elite access to power in the Mississippian world will result in a new clarity. For example, we can begin to ask more interesting questions about thematic differences in art between major sites and regions. We can begin to ask more interesting questions about the relationship between visual symbols

and elite statuses in different political environments, and at different times. New units and concepts can address art style, iconography, ritual, exchange, and social statuses, either separately or in conjunction. These new units and concepts can be framed at whatever scale suits us, whatever scale works. So as far as I am concerned, let us press forward with new classifications that will enhance our understanding of Mississippian art and its contexts. (Knight 2006:4)

In a curious coincidence, the 1997 collection (Reilly and Garber 2007) and the 2000 collection (King 2007a) were published in the same year, and all the participants finally had access to the double collection of articles. With those papers added to the conceptual and terminological articles in print (e.g., Knight 2006; Knight et al. 2001; Pauketat 2004, esp. 112–118, 143–144; Pauketat and Emerson 1991, 1997), the stage is set for a new season of clarifying discussion about Mississippian iconographic art. The scholarly community faces several challenges. (1) Did the Braden style have its origins in the Cahokia phenomenon? (2) How does ongoing discussion of the nature and history of Cahokian society affect the understanding of the evolution and proliferation of the Braden style? (3) How should the indigenous local art traditions and styles be understood? Is "style region" the most accurate or useful way to think of the Mississippian-era art map of the Eastern Woodlands and Plains? (4) How did Braden art impact the local traditions? (5) What other exotic iconographic art influenced the local regions? (6) What were the connections and influences among style regions, and which of them formed something like iconographic networks? (7) What new kinds of artistic syntheses emerged from those contacts?

When all these regional kinds of questions have been explored, it may be possible to raise the old unity questions in a whole new way. What kinds of social phenomena produced the patterns of art styles and iconographic meanings that left their footprints in the ground? And how many such phenomena did it take to accomplish the artistic mosaic of the Eastern Woodlands during those astounding Mississippian centuries?

CHAPTER 2

The Cosmology of the Osage
The Star People and Their Universe

James R. Duncan

During the first quarter of the twentieth century, John R. Swanton collected a corpus of southeastern oral traditions reflecting the cosmology of the Muskogeans and their neighbors, particularly the Natchez, the last Mississippian polity to survive the European intrusion (Reilly and Garber 2007:1). The importance of the Muskogean cosmology in deciphering the "Southern Cult" iconography was emphasized by Waring and Holder (1945) and reemphasized by Williams (1968). Recently George Lankford has added a new set of empirical meanings, a general cosmological model from central Algonkian sources (Lankford 2007d:15–16).

The purpose of this chapter is twofold: first, to compare the Dhegihan cosmology to the Muskogean and Central Algonkian cosmological models; and second, to determine which cosmology best fits the motifs and symbols employed in the Greater Braden art style (Brown 2004:112–114, 2007c:214; Hall 2004:97–98; Reilly 2004:133). The appeal of visual imagery remains a strong motivation among many of today's Osage—and their Dhegihan kin, the Omaha, Ponca, Kansa, and Arkansas (Quapaw)—in preserving illustrative materials, and this characteristic has been a great help in gathering ethnographic information from Dhegihan sources, principally the Osage.

In my collecting of ethnography through note-taking and videotaping among the Osage, my informants have included members of several prominent Dhegihan families. With their help over the past decade, I have recorded many hours of interviews and numerous narratives. Some of the most important information has been given to me during my various yearly trips to the Osage Reservation, especially to observe the June dances—the Ponca-Kansa peace/war dance (known as the Il-Lon-Shka, literally translated as the "ritual [or 'playground'] of the eldest son"). During these ceremonial dances, I work as a "fireman" for one of the informant families. Many revealing discussions have transpired while I carried out my role as fireman, cooking traditional foods for family and guests.

Among those Osage families who have preserved a great deal of their heritage, the RedCorn family is certainly notable. One of the most important pieces of information shared with me by the Osage is a chart that Jim RedCorn was given, according to his brother Andrew E. "Bud" RedCorn, most likely by their uncle Wakon Iron. The chart is an annotated transcription of a Tsi-Zhu tattoo (Fig. 2.1a). Tsi-Zhu is the name of the Dhegihan moiety called "Sky" or the sky people (Bailey 1995:41). Bud RedCorn has said that the chart may have been copied from an ancient drawing in a cave. It is my belief that this historic Osage document should be considered in relation to the numerous Mississippian mound sites that exist at the confluence of the Missouri and Mississippi Rivers, because it may provide insight into the cosmology of the builders of these settlements.

Historical Background

In the early 1950s Fred R. Eggan and James B. Griffin attributed the western Mississippian "complexes" along the Mississippi River—from its confluence with the Missouri River to the mouth of the Arkansas River—to the southern Siouan or Dhegihan speakers (Eggan 1952:40–42; Howard 1968:4). Since

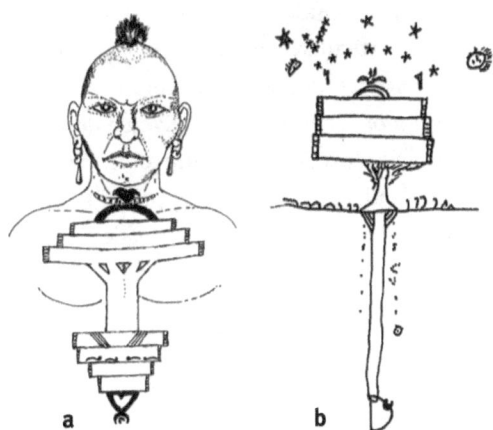

FIGURE 2.1. (a) Tsi-Zhu tattoo on "Man of Mystery" clan male; (b) J. Owen Dorsey's cosmic chart, 1883.

the early 1990s an expanding corpus of ethnographic and archaeological data has presented compelling evidence that the ancestors of the Dhegihans lived in this confluence region (Diaz-Granados 1993:334–42; Diaz-Granados and Duncan 2000:21, 46, 51, 233; Duncan and Diaz-Granados 2004:212–213) and that the Dhegihan Sioux were the linguistic group responsible for Cahokia and these western Mississippian complexes (Brown 2007b:57; Hall 2004:100–102). I believe it can be demonstrated that the historic Osage iconographic representations of the cosmos—where north is "above" and south is "below," west is female/night and east is male/day—are mirrored by the orientation of the mound sites at the confluence (Hall 1997:107–108).

The "serendipitous" period of expansion after AD 1200 is mentioned in the oral traditions regarding the movements of the five cognate tribes: Omaha, Osage, Kansa, Ponca, and Quapaw/Arkansas (Fletcher and La Flesche 1992:35, 37–41; Hall 2004:101–102). George Catlin also affirmed that the Kansa were still part of the Osage in the mid-1830s. In addition, the historic-period Osage are also known to have shared several traits with the Cahokia-centered Mississippian populations, such as shell-tempered pottery (in shapes identical to Cahokia's later Mississippian forms), triangular arrow points, large elliptical knives, disk pipes, and hardstone discoidals (Berres 2001:14–15; Duncan 1981:96–97; Henning 2005:170–171; Yelton 1998:272–274).

These five cognate tribes, the Dhegihans, were inclusive, adopting and absorbing populations. Their affinity for war is a dominant theme of their oral tradition (Tixier 1940:223–224), and their captives would (or could) be adopted into the tribe, particularly among the Osage. As part of the Osage adoption ritual, the Osage creation epic was told to the adoptees, who were seated at the place of honor. They were also given a description of the Osage cosmos, which was a symmetrical, layered universe, held together by a great red oak tree, its axis mundi. The underlying principle of their cosmos was balance among all the forces of the universe (called *wa-kan*) (Duncan and Diaz-Granados 2004:191; La Flesche 1975:193–194). Ethnographic research illustrates that this model held constant across all Dhegihan groups (Dorsey 1885:377–379; Fletcher and La Flesche 1992:70–73).

Diagram of the Osage Cosmos

A visual diagram of the universe is basic to the Dhegihan ideology. During an intensive period of collecting oral traditions by the Bureau of Ethnology between 1876 and 1913, J. Owen Dorsey was given a unique cosmological chart by William Matthews (Dorsey 1885:377–378). This document (Fig. 2.1b), presented to Dorsey in January 1883 and known only from its publication by Dorsey (1885), rewards comparison with the closely related diagram of the Osage cosmos mentioned above that was first shown to me in 1998 by Bud RedCorn. While it is important to remember that these complex charts are separated by more than 125 years, their similarities establish a remarkable continuum across the past five generations of Osage elders and provide valuable insights into Osage beliefs.

The skillfully drawn and now annotated diagram in Bud RedCorn's possession is strikingly similar to the "symbolic chart" given to Dorsey by Matthews.[1] The more recent drawing is in black ink on a sheet of drawing paper. The iconography in the drawing made by Jim RedCorn was annotated in English (Fig. 2.2). I have added further annotations to it based upon my gathering of oral narratives. The Dorsey chart includes the figure of a red cedar, one of the four trees that the Dhegihans associated with the forces of life (Bailey

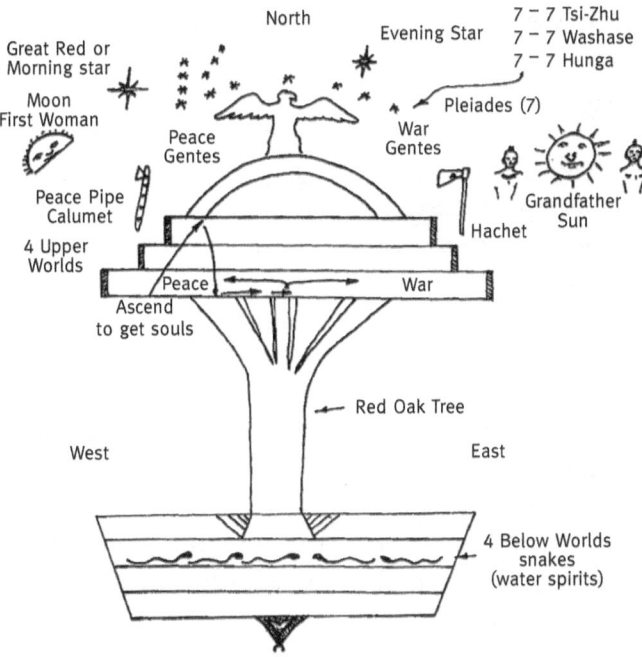

FIGURE 2.2. Andrew "Bud" RedCorn and Jimmy RedCorn chart, 1998.

1995:234–235; Louis Burns, personal communication, 2007). This cedar tree also represents a branched stream signifying the "journey through seven bends of the stream or path of life" (Bailey 1995:234; Burns 2005:157–158) and is thus connected to the general Osage wish to live a long life.

Below the diagram of the red cedar is another representation of the Dhegihan cosmic map of the cosmos. The map depicts the four levels of the Upper World surmounted by an avian figure, identified as Wah'-Kon-Tah E-Shinkah or E-Shinka-Wakon. His name has also been recorded as Ho^n-ga A-hui-to^n, an epithet that Francis La Flesche records as meaning "the Little Holy One" (La Flesche 1975:65; Mathews 1961:746). This figure, whom I shall refer to as Ho^n-ga A-hui-to^n and whom La Flesche defined as synonymous with "Morning Star,"[2] is perched on the arch of the heavens, the rainbow serpent of the day sky.[3] Supporting the four levels of the Upper World and the rainbow is a red oak tree, the tree of life. On the RedCorn diagram, below the roots of the red oak are the four levels of the Beneath World, with water spirits or "snakes" between the second and third levels. The Beneath World is not apparent on the Dorsey chart. Above the rainbow are the moon (Wa-ko^n-da ho^n-do^n), the large red or morning star (Mi-ka'-k'e ho^n-ba-do^n thi^n-kshe), and a group of six stars sometimes known as the "large foot of the goose" (Ta-tha-bthi^n). Next is the evening star (Mi-ka'-k'e ho^n-do^n thi^n-kshe) and a small star (Mi-ka'-ke zhi^n-ga). Under these are the seven stars of the Pleiades (known as Ta-pá), an important constellation because it is the place of origin of the Osage. Finally, on the far right, is the sun (Wa-ko^n-da Ho^n-ba-do^n).

On the very top of the cosmos is the primal spirit or first being (Ho^n-ga A-hui-to^n), who is also known as the "young mottled eagle" (Burns 2005:20–21). This raptor represents the risen sun, and its red color is an allusion to the rays reflecting from the mottled eagle's body (Burns 2005:199). The Matthews drawing of this bird actually depicts it with two heads, as it should be shown, because the two heads are intended to illustrate its dual female/male nature, the all-powerful spirit dwelling in its body. Similar two-headed raptor depictions occur in the seminal pictographic art at Picture Cave in eastern Missouri. Generally regarded as the most important Early Mississippian rock-art site, Picture Cave contains over three hundred carefully drawn and painted images (reflecting many of the characters discussed in this chapter), all brilliantly preserved. Accelerator mass spectrometry dates from pigments extracted from a selection of drawings at this site cluster around AD 1025. The cave is on the lower Missouri River about 100 kilometers west of Cahokia.

Janus-headed raptors have also been found depicted in the cache of copper plates found in Dunklin County, Missouri. These Braden-style repoussé plates probably date between AD 1230 and 1320.

In his essay on the Dhegihan cosmos, Dorsey (1885) refers to the raptor as the red bird. We know from Osage informants that the red bird, the mottled eagle, is "the bird without stain." It is this powerful supernatural being who gives the forms of birds to the soulless spirit beings migrating up from the lowest level of the Upper World on the left (west). As they ascend from the lowest to the highest level of the Upper World, they move across from left to right. There they obtain human souls in the bodies of birds from the female mottled eagle (Dorsey 1885:378–379). The male then gives them human bodies, and they descend to the first level of the Upper World. From there they will descend to the newly created Middle World.

Since I was first presented with this diagram by Bud RedCorn in 1998, I have pursued Osage contacts so that I might be able to add more annotations to Jim RedCorn's cosmological model. The scheme presented in Figure 2.3 is a synthesis of that information. According to Dorsey, William Matthews told him that a part of his chart was tattooed on the throat and chest of members of a secret order (Dorsey 1885:337).[4] As I have suggested above, among the Omaha, Quapaw, and Osage one of the two great divisions is the sky people, identified as Tsi-Zhu. It is the unanimous consensus of the informants who have assisted me that members of this division are always involved in important rituals and are shown deference by the remaining divisions (Fletcher and La Flesche 1992:61).

Characters in the Chart

In the chart that Dorsey was given by Matthews, the lower worlds to the south are represented by a vertical tunnel-like structure. At the very bottom, the arch of the night sky is drawn. Its tiny size belies its importance, for this small component actually depicts the Milky Way (Wa-cí-da u-zho^n-ge) and the goddess of the night, the Moon (Wa-ko^n-da ho^n-do^n). William Matthews explained to Dorsey how the spirit people traveled about the levels of the Upper World in the north and were given souls and human forms by powerful spirits inhabiting the Upper Worlds. He was relating not only the initial creation of humanity but also the "path of awakening" or way of reincarnation (La Flesche 1975:294–295). While recording Matthews's story of

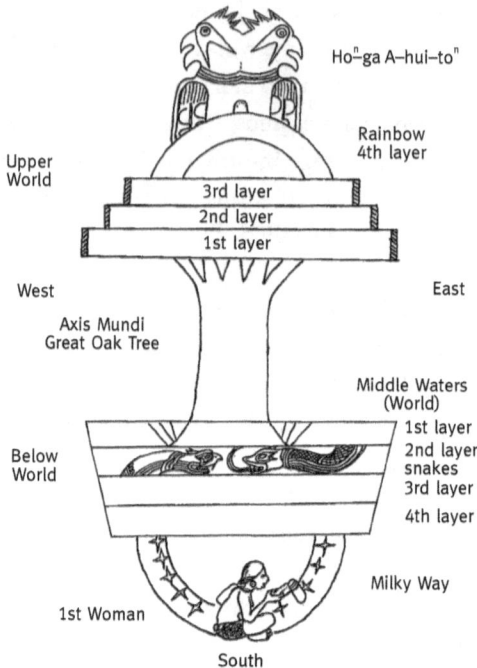

FIGURE 2.3. Synthesis of the 1883 Dorsey and 1998 RedCorn charts.

the creation that accompanied his drawing of the cosmos, Dorsey made some additions to the drawing. Matthews, or perhaps Dorsey, added "squiggle" lines to the broad horizontal of the Middle World to represent the movement of the newly created Dhegihans. In the short time he was with the Osage (forty-two days in January and February 1883), Dorsey was able to corroborate Matthews's information through discussions with other Osage elders (Dorsey 1885:377). For the purposes of this chapter, I have drawn information from Matthews's 1883 drawing and from the James RedCorn drawing that I received from his younger brother Bud. By combining the essential elements from both sources, I could produce a complete cosmic diagram with annotations (Fig. 2.3).

The ancient Dhegihans were discerning enough in their study of astronomy to grasp the role of Venus as both the Morning Star—the male harbinger of the sun—and the Evening Star—the female principle that appears just as the sun enters the earth in the west (Tixier 1940:148). The sun then begins its journey in the Beneath World, which is a female body (Dhegihans consider both the male and female natures to be one spirit being) (La Flesche 1975:361–362). The raptor referred to as the mottled eagle—the primal spirit or first being, known by the name Ho^n-ga A-hui-to^n—also has its counterpart in the Hidatsa/Mandan cosmos. The Mandan call this spirit Hoita, the great power that dwells at the center of the universe, and the Hidatsa call it "Charred Body." It is this character who leads the first people to earth (Bowers 1950:120, 1992:304–305). The Osage early morning song greets the rising sun as the principal abode of Wa-ko^n-da, the great mysterious power that created all things, visible and invisible (Burns 2005:49). These traditions are of great antiquity, and their complex, encoded, and layered structures have endured over time. While minor discrepancies are to be expected, the dominant cosmological principles do form a rational whole (Brown 1997:468–469).

According to Matthews (confirmed by Fletcher and La Flesche), the moon in the Osage cosmos is feminine. In confirmation of a direct extension of that principle, Paul M. Ponziglione, one of the Jesuit priests in charge of St. Paul's Catholic Mission for the Osage in southeastern Kansas from 1852 to 1889, recorded from Osage informants that the First Woman came from the moon (Ponziglione 1897: vol. 1, 11–12). These celestial parents—sky and earth, sun and moon—are the parents of the stars, and the stars are the Dhegihan ancestors (Duncan and Diaz-Granados 2004:204; Fletcher and La Flesche 1992:63–64).

Beneath the path of life, with its attendant cedar tree in Matthews's chart, is a diagram of the universe after the Middle World has been created and peopled by the Dhegihans—those who came from the stars (Fletcher and La Flesche 1992:63–64; Mathews 1961:8–9). These star people received their final human form by traveling through the four levels of the Upper World and are now spreading out to populate a newly created Middle World.

The four Upper Worlds have been separated by the red oak tree, the axis of the universe. This axis mundi is a widespread tradition in the Plains prairie region and is incorporated as a central pole in sun dances and in mourning rituals (Hall 2004:98–100). The Dhegihan examples that express the same value are the two sacred poles of the Omaha. The cottonwood pole—called the "Venerable Man" among the Omaha (with sun symbols painted on the tent in which the pole is kept)—represents the spirit being depicted in both

Matthews's and RedCorn's drawings. The "cedar pole" is its ancient prototype (Fletcher and La Flesche 1992:229).

This ancient "Venerable Man" cottonwood pole represents the resurrected Ho^n-ga A-hui-to^n, who, being the eldest son of the Sun, the one called Morning Star, is an important figure in Dhegihan tradition and has the same powers as his father. Before the creation of the Middle World, Ho^n-ga A-hui-to^n loses his life and his head in a great cosmic ball game (Brown 2007b:93–95). His head is carried to the village of the victors, along with those of his celestial companions. Of course, all levels of the Upper World are plunged into darkness when Ho^n-ga A-hui-to^n's gloriously shining head disappears from its accustomed place, for his head is Morning Star, the harbinger of the sun. His head is recovered when two of his relatives (variously identified as his sons or nephews) magically kill the victorious ball players with special arrows and return the heads of Ho^n-ga A-hui-to^n and his slain companions. Ho^n-ga A-hui-to^n is thus awakened as the axis of the universe along with the shining abode of the sun in the daytime sky (Diaz-Granados and Duncan 2004:207–211; La Flesche 1975:91).

The saviors of Ho^n-ga A-hui-to^n are commonly called the "Hero Twins." These holy "Star" men, the progeny of Sun and Evening Star, represent the two great divisions: the sky and the earth. Two leaders were chosen to help govern the people: one from the Tsi-Zhu "gentle sky" clan of the sky division and one from the "gentle Ponca" clan of the earth division. Thus the sky and earth divisions reflect the dual nature of the universe. This structure also reinforces the role of the cosmic "Twins" and their inherent duality.

Four of the five cognate tribes—the Kansa, Omaha, Ponca, and Osage—preserved bundles (portable shrines) that include hawk imagery in the form of dried and painted hawk skins. Such bundles were clan property among the Osage, and all clans had them (Bailey 1995:50–53). The clans tended to be interdependent; when all Osage clans assembled in the house of mystery, all of the gathered hawk shrines represented the cosmos (Bailey 1995:77). The shrines could only be reconsecrated by the "Men of Mystery," clan priests of the Tsi-Zhu division who are associated with thunder. This represents the singular moment when, as the Middle World is being created, Ho^n-ga A-hui-to^n himself becomes imbued with the transforming power of the sun and becomes the sun. In a parallel change at this same time Hawk (the elder brother of the "Hero Twins"), through the self-sacrifice of his twin brother, Thunder, becomes the new Morning Star (Duncan and Diaz-Granados 2000:10; Lankford 1987:168).

While little mention of this epic ball game story remains in Dhegihan traditions, a peripheral survival of this epic was collected from among the Ioway and Winnebago (Ho-Chunk) people during the early twentieth century. The Dhegihans, however, preserve the poles and staffs and other imagery associated with the story, along with the ball game (Fletcher and La Flesche 1992:196–197). Interwoven in the traditions of the Dhegihans are the symbolic representations of the axis of the universe, the north-pointing tree of life. The Osage Tribal Museum preserves the image of the reincarnated First Man becoming the axis of the universe, in the No^n-pe-wa-the blanket imagery (Bailey and Swan 2004:48).

As previously stated, the Omaha preserved two poles: the "Venerable Man" or "sacred pole" and the ancient cedar pole. The tradition is that the sacred pole is linked to the star that is motionless: Polaris, the North Star (Fletcher and La Flesche 1992:217–218, 229). The sacred pole is secured to an ash-wood foot, which is driven into the ground so that the sacred pole does not have contact with the earth. An attached support (*zhi-be*) keeps the pole—in its tent—pointing to the North Star. This represents the First Man as the axis or center of the universe (Fletcher and La Flesche 1992:221–225).

The Classic Braden art of Cahokia often depicts the spirit beings and ancestors Ho^n-ga A-hui-to^n (Hawk) and his two nephews/sons, the Hero Twins. These three powerful beings create, regulate, cleanse, and resurrect their stellar progeny and are first depicted in paintings and drawings in sacred places (such as Picture Cave in Missouri) just before the Cahokia florescence. They later appear in Dhegihan art as red claystone sculptures (Emerson et al. 2003), engraved figures on marine shell cups (Phillips and Brown 1978:Pls. 1–52), copper repoussé plates (Brown 2007b:78–84), and cedar-wood sculptures covered with thin sheet copper (Hamilton et al. 1974:177).

The ideology embodying a First Man and two male familial helpers, who together constitute a kind of Braden triad, creates a template by which specific images and their accompanying symbolic regalia can be attributed to these supernatural characters (Diaz-Granados 1993; Diaz-Granados and Duncan 2000; Phillips and Brown 1978). Unfortunately, these images are widely scattered in the archaeological record of the Eastern Woodlands of North America. Archaeological investigation at Cahokia's Mound 34 provides strong evidence that the superlative artistic florescence called Classic Braden belonged only to Cahokia (Brown 1989, 2004, 2007c:214).

Even if we are able to connect the Dhegihan cosmos and its star people with the Classic Braden style that emanates from the confluence region in the twelfth and thirteenth centuries, we are still left with much to explain about what happened to the epic portions of their rituals. Paul Radin's collections from the Chewerian-speaking Winnebago (Ho-Chunk) seem to fill some of that void, along with the ethnographic information collected by Alanson Skinner from the Ioway. Additional material was collected by Alfred Bowers from the Mandan and the Hidatsa and by George Dorsey from the Caddo.

We know that the Muskogeans at Etowah had the Rogan Plates by AD 1250–1325, and Swanton collected stories about several of the supernaturals depicted in Classic Braden art (King 2003:89–90; Swanton 1995). The ethnography of the Eastern Woodlands also contains several oral traditions with common ties to Dhegihan sources; among these are the story of Lodge-Boy and Throw-Away Boy from the Creeks and the story of the Owl and the Hawk and the narrative of the Hero Twins from the Alabama. Some basic differences are evident in these tales, however: the Muskogean people place their origin in the Beneath World (Lankford 1987:111). The Seminole, much influenced by European missionaries, believe that they were made of earth by a supernatural creator (Swanton 1995:75). The Iroquoian-speaking Cherokee relate how conflict between two supernatural beings was a part of creation (Gill and Sullivan 1992:55). While the earth-diver set of oral traditions is well expressed among the Central Algonkian peoples, it is only a small part of the Dhegihan creation epic (Burns 1989:58–60; Gill and Sullivan 1992:78). Surprisingly, none of the American Indian groups in the Eastern Woodlands trace their origins to the stars, while all of the Dhegihan groups do (Burns 2005:21; Dorsey 1885:379; Mathews 1961:11). The Osage origin in John Joseph Mathews's account is the sky-lodge of the sun. Only the ruling elite among the Natchez made such a claim.

Moving to the west or feminine side of the cosmos, we encounter a singularly powerful and complex spirit ancestor: Old-Woman-Who-Never-Dies or First Woman.[5] Several of our colleagues have asked me why I have used that name. My answer is always that it is descriptive of her and that, in addition, two of my full-blood friends—one a Hidatsa and the other an Osage—agreed with my use of it and thought that it was appropriate. This female figure never dies; she is the fecund earth; she is the mother of all beings. Her husbands are the "snakes" (Bowers 1992:334), and she is eternally in the embrace of three of them: the Great Serpent, the Missouri River; the Rainbow Serpent in the daytime sky; and the Great Sky Serpent, the Milky Way in the night sky.

In January 2007 I collected a Quapaw creation story from a descendant of Victor Griffin, chief of the Quapaw from 1929 to 1958 (Baird 1980:206). In that story, the Great Sky Serpent fell into the primeval ocean. There he changed into a huge turtle that laid eggs from which the Quapaw hatched. This Quapaw narrative is a revelation: all accounts of the origin of the Dhegihans accept the fact that they came from the heavens. In the Dhegihan narrative, First Woman gives birth to the sun every morning and gives birth to all of her children. Likewise, she embraces all of her children as they come to her body, the grave, at the end of life. In order to receive her children back into her vulva, just as she receives the sun, she turns her body around and upside down just as the sun sets and the night begins. At dawn she returns to her original position in the throes of giving birth to the sun. On a daily basis the earth inverts at dusk and then again at dawn. This action puts the Beneath World on top at night, and the Upper World returns to its familiar position at dawn.

Reflections of First Woman can be seen in the earthly manifestations that exist in a few of the portraits of elite women at the Osage Tribal Museum with stylized spiders tattooed on the backs of their hands. In Dhegihan society, clan "memory keepers" retained the group's complex genealogies in their heads (Baird 1980:206; William Samuel Fletcher, personal communication and DVD tape, 2006). Their knowledge prevented incestuous marriages from taking place, an important concern in a society in which elite Dhegihans arranged marriages to create family alliances and build prestige.

The expensive tattoos related to the spider, who is another manifestation of First Woman, were especially important in Dhegihan Society.[6] My interviews, along with the early nineteenth-century drawings, demonstrate that the feminine spider designs were widely distributed among elite first daughters (Bud RedCorn, personal communication, 1998; Robin Polhamus, personal communication, 2002; Louis Burns, personal communication, 2005; Catlin 1844:Pl. 88). Mathews (1961) gives a thoughtful description of how red-bud charcoal was used to tattoo such spider designs on the backs of the women's hands.

Of all the Dhegihan symbolism, the spider (*tse-zo-be*) has been the most elusive to interpret. The spider asterism is in the constellation Orion (La Flesche 1975:360), and it is the place where "Old Woman Spider" waits to take "First Man" or his successors on a journey into the Beneath World (Lankford 2007c:230). Lankford has shown Orion to be an important portal, so it is here that the spider waits to carry the sun's lineage. It also symbolizes First Woman, as Grandmother Spider, weaving the web or snare of life, the Middle World. The significance of the spider's role in the overall iconography of the Dhegihans can be measured in the appearance of the spider on a separate assemblage of shell gorgets found at Cahokia in western Illinois, at St. Mary's in southeast Missouri, and at other sites (Brain and Phillips 1996:107–108; Mathews 1961:326; Phillips and Brown 1978:179).

Conclusion

The contributions of William Matthews and Jim and Andrew RedCorn provide the essential parts of the Dhegihan cosmic model discussed in this chapter. It is apparent that these men, all from the Tsi-Zhu grand division of the Osage, possessed substantial familiarity with ancient religious concepts. Dorsey's acknowledgment that he had obtained "partial accounts of similar traditions from other Osage" adds weight to the authenticity of his iconographical illustration (Dorsey 1885:378). The rendering technique of Jim RedCorn's twentieth-century ink drawing is more in the style of a tattoo. This stands to reason, since as a young boy he would have been privy to the tattoos worn by older Osage men. Dorsey observed that some of these men had parts of the symbolic chart tattooed on their throats and chests (Dorsey 1885:377). Unfortunately, few photos or paintings of these tattooed men remain.

Arguably, the use of such tattoos would reinforce the accuracy of the cosmic diagram and ensure its survival as a two-dimensional entity. The tragedy of cultural loss is evident in Dorsey's description of the forfeiture of ritual knowledge through disease, the imposition of modern religious education, and the lack of interest among the "younger generations" before it could be passed on (Dorsey 1885:377). Fortunately, a small percentage of Osage—those who escaped the "thorough" assimilation and education in the mission and government schools—were able to carry on the "old ways," if only in memory. And a still smaller percentage continued to tell and hand down the stories, some of which we can still hear today.

Unified dualism is an ever-present theme in Dhegihan cosmology, as represented in the following concepts: sky and earth, male and female, a refreshing rain and a powerful thunderstorm, sun and moon, day and night.

The axis mundi, the great unifier, forms a bridge between the sky with the male sun and Morning Star and the female earth with her attendant Evening Star. Joining First Woman—the earth and the mother of all things—was an unavoidable episode in a Dhegihan's death and awakening. Pottery vessels depicting the First Woman or Old Woman are concentrated in the lower American Bottom, south into northeastern Arkansas and eastward into the Lower Ohio and Cumberland River Valleys (see Chapter 8).

The influence exerted by Cahokia throughout the confluence region is remarkable in its magnitude. I suspect that the movement of Dhegihan ideology, art, and oral traditions impacted an enormous area, as may be judged by the extent of distribution of Classic Braden art objects throughout the Eastern Woodlands (Brown 2004:108). The use of "balanced" composition or structure in shell gorgets and the distinctive court-card design in Classic Braden may both be products of the Dhegihan principle of Wa-Ko^n-da-gi, the sacred balance (La Flesche 1975:194; Phillips and Brown 1978:67). The Children of the Sun epic found among the Alabama and Pigeon Hawk's Gift found among the Koasati, while collected as "tales" among the Southeastern ethnic groups, were part of a complex set of oral traditions in Dhegihan/Chewerian culture. This body of ritual literature was an important part of the essential knowledge in navigating the cosmos after death among the Dhegihans and many of their Siouan neighbors.

The widespread use of pole symbolism—whether a red oak, a cottonwood, or a red cedar—survived not only in archaeological features but also in sixteenth-century European illustrations by Theodor de Bry. While these poles functioned as supports and, more importantly, as pathways, they in turn connect to portals or gateways, enabling supernaturals and mortals to traverse the levels of the cosmos.

The outpouring of art and its accompanying oral traditions occurred over an extended period. Unquestionably, early expressions of the Mississippian Ideological Interaction Sphere or MIIS (Reilly and Garber 2007:3–4) began early within the confluence region. Symbolism involving the long-nosed maskettes, the imagery of Morning Star, is comfortably dated to AD 1025 by a series of AMS dates at Picture Cave (Diaz-Granados et al. 2001). The

Dhegihan cosmos, which I have attempted to "sketch" in this chapter, is a complex, animated, and living entity.

The production of skillfully rendered supernatural beings is unique to the confluence region. Its earliest expression is found in Picture Cave, only a few days' travel up the Missouri River from Cahokia. We can envision how this realistic style, through pictographs, red claystone sculptures, shell engravings, and repoussé sheet copper figures, transmitted the story of the supernatural ancestors for the next two hundred years and allowed them to populate the Middle World. The presence of these supernatural beings reassured the Dhegihans, their children, that they would continue to live and thrive at the center of their universe.

NOTES

AUTHOR'S ACKNOWLEDGMENTS: I am grateful to F. Kent Reilly III for all of his support and for including me in his Iconography Workshop. I thank him and Jim Garber for their editing of this volume, and especially Robert Sharp for his meticulous editing of my chapter. I also thank Carol Diaz-Granados for her work on this chapter. This contribution would not have been possible, however, had it not been for the long friendship and guidance of Andrew Edward "Bud" RedCorn, Osage.

1. J. Owen Dorsey was given the William Matthews chart in January 1883 (Dorsey 1885:377). For the sake of uniformity and clarity, this chart will be referred to as the 1883 chart.

2. E-Ho^n-ga zhi^n-ga is defined as Little Holy One (La Flesche 1975:65), Ho^n-ga-gthe-zhe as "Mottled Eagle": Ho^n-ga and Ho^n-ga A-hui-to^n are used interchangeably. While collecting ethnographic material among the Osage, I encountered the name "E-Shinka-Wakon" in discussions of the rituals of the Osage peyote church. This term is used interchangeably with Jesus Christ, particularly at Easter when the resurrection is described. This title seems to be a modernization of the traditional E-Ho^n-ga zhin-ga as more likely Ho^n-ga-gthe-zhe (the Little Sacred One, the mottled eagle). Ho^n-ga A-hui-to^n combines two ancient ritual terms. Ho^n-ga usually refers to one of the two great tribal divisions and also signifies sacred or holy, an object to be venerated. The child chosen as an emblem of innocence in the peace ceremony is called Ho^n-ga. As a name, Ho^n-ga means "the sacred one" (La Flesche 1975:65). A-hui-to^n is another ritual term, which means "having wings." The name means "the sacred one having wings." Combining Ho^n-ga and A-hui-to^n is the ancient title of the earth-creating aspect of Wa-ko^n-da, the omnipotent and feared creative power of the universe. As Ho^n-ga, "the sacred one," the First Man/First Woman, this

power is drawn in the form of a young mottled eagle with two heads (Dorsey 1885:378) who leads the people to the newly created Earth from the Upper Worlds (La Flesche 1975).

3. To avoid confusion, one title is used to name the characters in the annotated cosmic chart. La Flesche (1975) gives several names or titles for the same supernatural being.

4. James and Andrew RedCorn belong to the Tsi-Zhu moiety and are sons of Harold RedCorn. Since William Matthews was also called "Red Corn," it is probable that these Osage men are all related (Dorsey 1885:377).

5. When Carol Diaz-Granados and I first began our study of Siouan oral traditions, we called her by her Mandan/Hidatsa name, "Old-Woman-Who-Never-Dies" (Bowers 1992:323).

6. The fee for tattooing the spider figure on the hands of a young woman was high. This was only done on the hands of eldest or "first daughters." These tattoos ensured that the recipient would be the subject of a desired match with a young man of an elite family of great wealth (Mathews 1961:325).

REGIONAL STUDIES:
MIDDLE MISSISSIPPI VALLEY

CHAPTER 3
The Regional Culture Signature of the Braden Art Style
James A. Brown

The motifs, imagery, and lexical meanings found among the Osage and cognate tribes of the Dhegiha Sioux have become a productive source of readings for Braden style motifs and compositions (Brown 2004, 2007b; Diaz-Granados 2004; Diaz-Granados and Duncan 2004; Duncan and Diaz-Granados 2000, 2004; Hall 2004; Kehoe 2007; Reilly 2004). Each new identification strengthens the conviction that the culture pattern of the Dhegiha Sioux has a great deal to say about the content of the Braden style. Additional support comes from an analysis of the larger cosmological context of Dhegiha-speaking culture. With these cosmological insights taken into consideration the Braden style emerges more forcefully as bearing the imprint of Dhegiha Sioux and by extension that of neighboring tribes occupying the eastern wooded margins of the Great Plains. Widening of the cultural perspective helps supply an Upper Mississippi Valley origin for the Dhegiha Sioux that archaeological data have yet to support in a conclusive way. One goal of this chapter is to summarize the literature on Braden style readings and cast these into a larger picture. This task allows me to enlarge on a major theme of the Dhegiha and their close cognates—the centrality of death and rebirth as partly embodied in the Earth-Sky duality that is particular to these closely related groups.

The Braden Style

The Braden art style is the name for the form of image-making that has come to be identified quintessentially with the Southeastern Ceremonial Complex, although we now realize that it is only one of several distinct styles composing this complex (Brown 2004, 2007c). The style has been explored in several sets of data: engraved shell cups from Spiro (Phillips and Brown 1978), the Eddyville-style shell gorgets (Muller 1989), and the Cahokia-style carved stone figurines (Emerson 1989, 1997a, 1997b; Emerson et al. 2003). For the present it suffices to emphasize a stock of distinctive matters of content. This includes the personification of different divine powers (that is, embodying spiritual powers in human form), the emphasis on the Birdman in the Morning Star cycle, Earthmother, and a common use of a stock of visual metaphors (Brown 2007c; Phillips and Brown 1978; Reilly 2004). Representations often taken for warriors are more comfortably interpreted as the cosmic combat of the four heroes against the forces of death (Brown 2007b; Brown and Dye 2007).

The style is expressed in both two and three dimensions and on a broad range of media, including painted, engraved, and carved marine shell, freshwater shell, pottery, copper, pipestone, and the rock walls of caves and shelters (Brown 2004; Phillips and Brown 1978). Its homeland was the American Bottom and neighboring lands together with a portion of the Prairie-Woodland borderlands within the Upper Mississippi Valley. A broad distribution is delineated by rock-art identified at Picture Cave in eastern Missouri and at Gottschall Rockshelter in southeastern Wisconsin.

The Braden style has undergone secular changes over a span of 300-plus years. Early expression of this style has been radiocarbon dated at both of these two rock sites within the Emergent Mississippian period (Diaz-Granados et al. 2001; Salzer 2005; Salzer and Rajnovich 2001:4, 40–41). Robert Hall (2004:98) has pointed out that falconoid symbolism in the form of effigy mounds has deep roots extending into the pre–AD 1050 period. The Classic Braden expression of this style appears to have emerged at Cahokia by the Lohmann phase, although it is more commonly found in Moorehead-phase contexts (Brown and Kelly 2000). The final, Late Braden expression is manifest in the following Sand Prairie phase (Brown 2007c; Brown and Kelly 2000). In the Late Braden style such distinctive features of Birdman as the hawk-billed human nose and the circular scalp lock make their appearance (Brown 2007a, 2007c). A recognizable form of this style in the McAdams gorget type continues into the fourteenth century. These shell gorgets provide a logical bridge to the primordial life theme of the spider in postcontact times. In the early twentieth century select, high-status Osage women were tattooed on the wrist with similar spider imagery. Complementary war-related motifs were tattooed on the chests of male warriors (La Flesche 1918).

Although the Braden style was identified mainly through an analysis of the engraved shell record from the Spiro site in eastern Oklahoma, it composes a distinct minority of the site's collection. In some instances Braden material has been reworked locally in the Craig style, but not the other way around. The Craig style qualifies as locally Caddo by numerical superiority and various iconic connections (Brown 1989). From this and other perspectives it is apparent that the Spiro engraved shell collection is composed of a mixture of distinct styles united by a set of common themes. Different strands of archaeological evidence point to a source of production for the Braden style many miles away in the Mississippi River Valley and centered at the great town of Cahokia near St. Louis (Brown and Kelly 2000; Muller 1995, 1999). A very different set of expectations was entertained by workers in the Mid-South region (Howard 1968; Waring 1968b; Williams and Goggin 1956; Willoughby 1932). To them the SECC was a unified complex most fruitfully interpreted in terms of beliefs and practices of Muskogean-speaking peoples in the Mid-South. Alex Krieger's (1945) criticisms of this perspective called attention to regional distinction operating within the SECC corpus. His critique applies equally to those that place the origin of the collections solely at Spiro itself. Only decades later did art styles enter seriously into consideration of the different regional sources of engraved shell as well as other objects (Knight 2006; Muller 1979, 1989, 1995, 1999; Phillips and Brown 1978, 1984). Of those sources the North Caddoan and Upper Mississippian ones dominate; the Mid-South area contributed relatively little.

The Dhegiha Sioux

The Omaha, Osage, Quapaw, Ponca, and Kansa are five "cognate" tribes that speak closely related languages and occupy the eastern margins of the Great Plains. A great similarity of beliefs and practices makes this block of tribes a convenient unit for comparison. At the same time it is important to bear in mind that similarities are shared with neighboring groups in the Prairie-Plains (Hultkrantz 1973). La Flesche (1939) specifically referred to the Otoe and the Pawnee as having religious customs nearly identical with the Osage.

All were composed of exogamous patrilineal clans organized into earth-sky social moieties aligned with a series of oppositions, including the south and north directions. Omaha kinship terminology emphasized the consistent patrilineal bias of these groups. The combination of these two features of social organization clearly separated them from their neighbors (Murdock 1955). This distinctive organization of male descent groups is not found in tribes of the Great Lakes, East, or Southeast (Brown 1991). Each group or clan possessed its own name and a set of personal names, connected either by an identifying symbol or to symbols belonging to the rites they controlled (Barnes 1984; Ensor 2003; Fletcher and La Flesche 1911:38).

The Dhegiha language group includes Omaha-Ponca, Osage, Kansa, and Quapaw (Rankin 1988). Less closely related was the Chiwere language group, including the Otoe, Missouri, and Iowa, with Winnebago as a more remote outlier (Goddard 1996:322). The Dhegiha and the Chiwere are distinctly defined by the adoption in common of the earth-sky moiety organization of their respective societies. The kind of cosmovision implied by this organization is closely linked with cosmogonic myths that have distinctive associated compositions and imagery (Hultkrantz 1973).

The Dhegiha also define themselves in terms of an idealized dispersion within the Mississippi River Valley watershed. The Omaha take a name that means the "against-the-current" or "upstream" people, and the Quapaw correspondingly are the "downstream" or "with-the-current" people, referring to the Mississippi River (Fletcher and La Flesche 1911:35–36). Likewise they have mutually compatible accounts of how the component tribes split apart after once having belonged to a single entity occupying a location at or near the mouth of the Ohio with the Mississippi River in one account (Dorsey 1886; Fletcher and La Flesche 1911:37). These accounts, however, appear to be less about history in the Western sense and more about structural relations among the groups. In this regard they have to be distinguished from cosmological origin accounts that stress upper-world tribal origins (summarized by DeMallie and Parks 2001; see also Hall 1989).

The relevant reference group is one known or strongly implicated in the occupation of the Upper Mississippi River Valley in precontact times. This group consists of Dhegiha-speaking Siouans that have a traditional, near-eponymous connection with this river system. When French explorers encountered these Central Siouans in the seventeenth century, however, they were residing in the Prairie-Plains area and west of the main valley of the Mississippi (Brown and Sasso 2001; Henning 2001, 2007). In the past other groups may have been associated with the Dhegiha; but with the exception of the Skidi Pawnee, we lack clues about such associations.

In his survey of language family movements over time, Michael Foster (1996) accepts the archaeological assessment that the Dhegiha came from the Mississippi Valley (Henning 2007:75). An extensive precedent exists for considering the Mississippian cultures of the Mississippi Valley (particularly near the junction with the Ohio) to be the ancestors of the Siouans—particularly the Dhegiha and Chiwere (including the Ho-Chunk) branches of the Siouan linguistic family (Goddard 1996:322; Myers 1992).

It is not difficult to connect the Dhegiha Sioux to the archaeology of the Prairie Peninsula and to the great townsite of Cahokia. Numerous archaeologists have cited parallels with Dhegiha beliefs and practices to interpret details in architectural and settlement patterning and the conspicuous planting and removal of tall poles (Fowler 1996; Gartner 1996; Hall 2004:100; Holley and Koepke 2003; Kehoe 2007; Kelly 1996, 2003; Kelly et al. 2008).

Objections to the connection between the Dhegiha and Middle Mississippian cultures derive from positions staked out by both culture area classifications and archaeological taxonomies. Neither of these positions is sympathetic to the thesis of this chapter. Ethnologists have been content to regard the Plains tribes as having remote cultural connections to the Mississippi Valley because of their investment in a semimobile way of life with a less complex form of governance than found in the sedentary tribes of the Southeast. The priority placed on the degree of settlement mobility and concomitant cultural practices has erected impediments to connection making. As a consequence scholars have turned to the beliefs and practices of Southeastern cultures when the subject of Cahokia's descendants is considered (Mochon 1972). Archaeologists show complementary preferences. They connect the Omaha to the Upper Mississippian Oneota, a taxon without mounds and widely regarded as having a history that is separate from, albeit parallel with, the complex cultures of Cahokia and Middle Mississippian (Griffin 1952, 1995; Henning 2007). Diaz-Granados and Duncan (Diaz-Granados 2004; Diaz-Granados and Duncan 2004; Duncan and Diaz-Granados 2000, 2004), Hall (2004), and Kehoe (2007) are conspicuous exceptions to this orientation.

Dhegiha Sioux Cosmology

The Dhegiha Sioux have long been recognized as standing apart from other tribal organizations in the roles that their cosmology plays: in rites relating to success in war (framed in terms of defense of tribe members from external threats) and in their emphasis on promoting life-supporting processes—above all in the preservation of the tribe (Hollinger 2005). To these we can add the strong preference for personifying spiritual forces, whether animate or inanimate. Fletcher and La Flesche (1911:68–69) state:

> In the Omaha and the four cognates there appear to be certain stable characteristics which indicate a common ideal of organization, as the two divisions of the tribal circle and the functions pertaining to each; the ceremonies connected with warfare and the awarding of war honors. There seems to be also a common type of religious ceremonial for the recognition of those cosmic forces which were believed to affect directly the life of man, as the rites attending the naming of children and the class of names given, and the customs relating to birth and death.

Like most of their neighbors the Sioux conceive of the universe as tripartite: "Upper World" (placed in the empyrean or highest heaven), this terrestrial world, and "Beneath World" (located beyond underlying waters) (Lankford 2007d). Each was dominated by spirits that could move among the three worlds and could assume the guise of humans on any occasion (Reilly 2004). All spirits could materialize in human form, albeit with telltale features identifying their true identity. The Osage self-depiction of the cosmos is a useful basis for discussion. However, it is uncertain how far the details of this view applied to other Dhegiha Sioux.

Osage cosmology was drafted by a tribesman for J. Owen Dorsey (1885:357) in what has to be a unique diagram. The three parts of the universe are graphically delineated. The empyrean Upper World was occupied by important stars, the sun, and the moon. The Pleiades, the Big Dipper, the Milky Way, and the Morning Star were among the stars. In the lowest register of this Upper World were war clubs flanking a rainbow. A transition to this world was marked by the four world levels that humankind descended to reach the earth. Beneath the lowest level was the red oak tree they landed upon when they fell into "This World." Centered beneath the tree trunk was a shaft that was left unexplained by the draftsperson. It undoubtedly represented the passage to the "Beneath World," usually closed off from access above by water. Commonly, the inhabited middle world was likened to an island surrounded by primordial waters. In the Osage diagram the borders to this world are not indicated one way or another (see Fig. 2.1b).

In keeping with the layered universe the center of the middle world was demarcated on a regular basis by planting a cosmic pole at the center of the camp circle. The He'dewachi ceremony, the Omaha version of the Sun Dance, is a well-described example. According to Fletcher and La Flesche (1911:251–252), this ceremony is an ancient increase rite "related to the cosmic forces as revealed in the succession of night and day and the life and growth of living things." The Osage were reputed to have an analogous ceremony (Fletcher and La Flesche 1911:260).

The procedures used to install the pole bring together a diverse set of cosmological principles. The tree is treated as a human. The woman bearing the "Mark of Honor" "captures" the tree and makes cuts into four sides, one for each of the four directions. As Robin Ridington describes it:

> Two men with hereditary rights painted the pole in bands of black and red to signify night and day, thunder and death, and earth and sky. They dug a hole for the pole at the center of the *hu'thuga* and heaped the dirt from the hole to the east. Between this heap and the pole they cut a figure into the earth. It was a circle open to the east. This figure, known as *uzhin'eti*, was used as an earth altar. (Ridington and Hastings 1997:65)

Another occasion for the construction of such an altar was the sacred ceremony of painting the Sacred Pole (Ridington and Hastings 1997:65).

The obvious parallels to the archaeological Woodhenge at Cahokia reinforce the significance of Dhegiha insights into Mississippian-period architecture and settlement organization. These and other parallels have been described and commented upon from many different perspectives (Fowler 1996; Gartner 1996; Hall 1997, 2004:100; Holley and Koepke 2003; Kehoe 2007; Kelly 1996, 2003; Kelly et al. 2008).

The Camp Circle as a Representation of the Cosmos

Before continuing with the sacred rites that were controlled by individual clans, it is important to learn how the camp circle embodied Dhegiha

FIGURE 3.1. The Sacred Camp (*hu'thuga*) Circle of the Omaha during the He'dewachi (from Ridington and Hastings 1997:Fig. 14). Adapted from Myers, *The Birth and Rebirth of the Omaha* (1992:Fig. 3). Courtesy of the University of Nebraska State Museum.

cosmovision centering around the earth-sky moiety social division. The Omaha camp circle will be used as the primary point of reference because it offers a concise version of these principles (Fig. 3.1). The Osage offer a similar version that is too complex to be dealt with in the present chapter (Bailey 1995). The information that we have for the other three tribes bears out the thesis that each is a variant on the same set of themes, although hardly any clan information has survived about the Quapaw.[1]

During the summer buffalo hunt the entire tribe assembled in a camp circle. It is in this settlement mode that the camp circle becomes an epitome of the cosmological and sociological functions of the dual division. The significance of the summer buffalo hunt was its importance to the supply of food. A great deal of the tribe's food security rested on its success (Fletcher and La Flesche 1911:137).

Among the Omaha the ceremonial form of the camp circle was viewed conceptually simply as a "tribal house" that not only encompassed all the clans but also imposed a strict clan order within the circle (Fletcher and La Flesche 1911:137). Each family's dwelling stood within the circle, where individual clan members would sit within a lodge. The male and female sides of the house replicate the location of the sky and earth moieties. The entrance to the camp circle opened to the east during the summer when tribal ceremonies were being conducted. At other times the opening pointed in the direction of travel. Even then, the order of the tents remained firm regardless of the orientation.

As in so many societies the clans (and to a certain extent the family) were the social unit of primary allegiance. In a way this allegiance was represented by the wealth-creating capabilities of particular descent groups (Ensor 2001, 2003). They were distinguished among tribal lineages as "subclans," which possessed special rites and privileges. These were socially prominent lineages that constituted social houses in the Claude Lévi-Strauss sense (Beck 2007). The tents of prominent men displayed symbols that referred to the rights and obligations of clans or subclans (Dorsey 1894:Fig. 170). The path to chiefship lay in the capacity of the groups to accumulate wealth.

In this light the tribe looks more like a coalition of clans, whose mutual interdependence was structured by important rites parceled out among its participants. Each clan (and subclan) exercised exclusive control over its rites and bundles. The only rites not controlled by individual clans were under the control of sodalities (such as the Shell Society) and were part of the He'dewachi ceremony. Unity was created by interweaving complementary rights and interests. The order of the clan within the circle became a cosmologically ordained way of maintaining collective cohesion in the face of countervailing fissiparous tendencies.

The Earth-Sky Division

The earth-sky dual division was a Dhegiha Sioux means for organizing certain clan functions that were cosmologically grounded (Bailey 1995:33; Fletcher and La Flesche 1911:68–69). At a basic level this organization separated tribal ritual into two mutually supportive groups. Åke Hultkrantz expressed it succinctly:

> [On the south side] the rites and duties of the Earth people concern the physical welfare of the nation, the food supply, the governing power and the maintenance of peace. It is even possible to discern, as Müller [1956:156, as cited by Hultkrantz] suggests, in the arrangement of the Earth clans and their rites, the progression of the summer season: the

first thunder of the spring, the planting of the red maize, the buffalo hunt, the thanksgiving at the sacred pole after the hunt . . . [On the opposite side] The Sky people, on the other hand, took care of those rites by which supernatural aid was sought and secured, rites which were connected with the creation and the spiritual support for man in life and death. In this way the Sky moiety rites also gave a supernatural sanction to the Earth Moiety rites, putting them into effect. The union between the Sky powers and the Earth powers by which all living creatures were once created was thus symbolized and perpetuated in the organization of the tribe, and its meaning was continually present in the minds of the people by the rites and the interrelation of clans and moieties. (Hultkrantz 1973:21)

Tribal functions were divided between the north/sky and south/earth sides in very specific ways. For the Omaha the "northern half" or sky moiety was composed of five member clans; the southern half or earth people likewise had five clans (Fletcher and La Flesche 1911). The placement of each clan tent tended to be dictated by cosmological logic, although it should be stressed that rites and duties controlled by each clan or subclan did not divide ritual responsibilities neatly and without overlap. The specialized knowledge of clans and subclans was created and disappeared as these social units rose and fell in numbers.

Each of the clans on both sides of the camp circle entrance controlled factors in the day-to-day well-being of the tribe. The earth side controlled the Sacred War tepee that once held the most important of the five war bundles. The tepee also housed a sacred cedar pole associated with the war power of the Thunderer as manifested through lightning. This spirit was said to live in a forest of cedars. Bird skins kept within the bundles received their power from the Thunderer (Dorsey 1884:319–320; Fletcher and La Flesche 1911:218–219, 229, 403–416, 452–458).

On the opposite side of the camp entrance stood the clan of the sky moiety, controlling rainfall and moisture-providing nourishment in general. By tapping into the thunder powers of both moieties this arrangement emphasized the impact of both cosmic forces and religious observances. Thunder signals the beginning of the growing season and is thereby a logical prelude to a season with plenty of plant food.

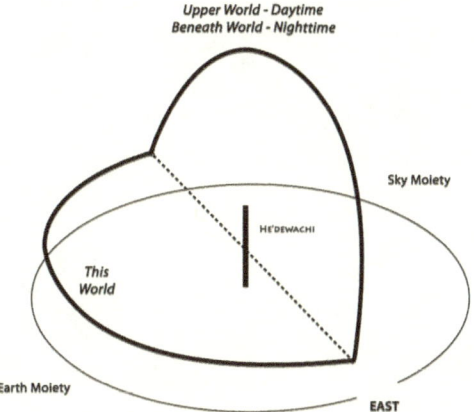

FIGURE 3.2. Reconstructed cosmogram of the Omaha, based on the Sacred Camp (*hu'thuga*) Circle of the Omaha during the He'dewachi.

Viewed from a different perspective the two moieties are not coordinate. The earth-sky moiety organization fits a three-tiered universe. Robert Hall (2004:98–100, 2005) has argued how this could have worked logically. The three cosmic levels have been collapsed onto two dimensions by placing the path of the sun (or the ecliptic) onto the earthen plane (Fig. 3.2). This step locates the male or the sky moiety on the north side of the circle, opposite the female or earth moiety on the south. Hall argues that this leads also to quadrants, presumably representing the seasons, by placing the north at the center of a twofold division of the sky moiety side (Hall 1997, 2004:98–100). These quadrants were invoked explicitly in the Omaha ritual prelude to the intermoiety ball game. In a mythic allusion to the cardinal directions the Omaha referred to the fiery trails of the Thunderbirds that created burnt paths emanating in four directions from the cosmic pole center (Ridington and Hastings 1997:99–104). Omaha and other Dhegiha ritual performances are replete with directional references.

The upper direction is really a conceptualization of both the day and night sky. But it is the path of the sun that provides the rationale for the communitywide ceremonies. The Osage once prayed to the sun two times a day: at midday and sunset. The Omaha provide even greater support. High-status women are tattooed with the Mark of Honor on their forehead and throat in a ceremony that reaches its culmination at high noon, when the impregnating

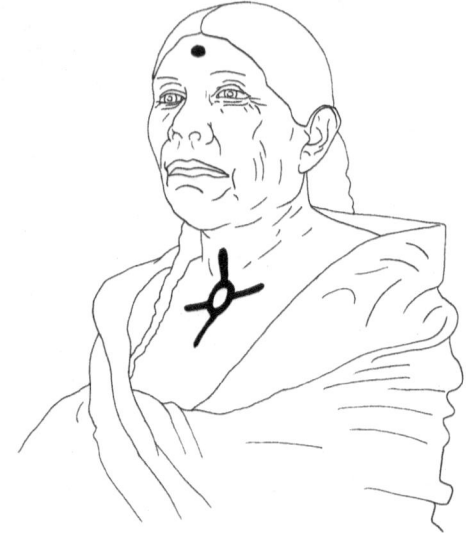

FIGURE 3.3. The "mark of honor," redrawn from photograph (Ridington and Hastings 1997:Fig. 19).

power of the sun reaches its culmination (Fig. 3.3) (Ridington and Hastings 1997:159–165). While the tattooing ceremony was underway, women lay on their back aligned with the path of the sun and with their head to the west.

The question immediately arises: what has happened to the Beneath World? Its absence from the camp circle might seem to be a fatal weakness to the model considered here. But if the Beneath World was rotated into the night sky when the sun had set, the contradiction can be resolved. Just such a rotation is implied by Fletcher and La Flesche (1911:507) when they state: "By the union of Day, the above, and Night, the below, came the human race and by them the race is maintained. The Tattooing . . . [is] an appeal for the perpetuation of all life and of human life in particular." This is precisely represented by the incorporation of both the nighttime and daytime skies into the Sky side of the circle (see Hall 1997:107–108).

This uppermost direction is expressed within the two-dimensional camp circle by placing the zenith position at the north end of the east-pointing camp circle. For the Omaha the sun exerts its maximal strength at its zenith and by extension its virility as well. The star powers are located at precisely this point in the circle. The deer clan (Tapa', a name for the constellation Pleiades) occupied the north or sky side (Ridington and Hastings 1997:120–121). The Deer clan members were custodians of the thunder and the star rites, both male sources of procreation. This clan's control of ceremonies related to the powers of the stars underscores the connection (Ridington 1987). Lankford (2007c:259) elaborated upon the significance of this constellation in the Southeast: "Its easy recognition in the sky, coupled with its ability to mark various important points in the agricultural growing season, should produce an almost universal representation among tribal peoples." Morning Star is just that mythic source for the Osage. In contrast, however, the Omaha had preserved little of the lore of this star when Dorsey and Fletcher and La Flesche undertook their interviews.

At the south point in the camp circle stood a clan with other kinds of bundle power. This is where the sacred pole tent stood that housed "Venerable Man." Next to it was the tent of the sacred white buffalo hide (Tethon'ha). Both stood in front of the lodges of the subclans that controlled the rites of each. The pole of Venerable Man was propped at a 40-degree angle, pointing toward the Pole Star. The song that accompanied its rites evoked the sun while representing the Thunderbird. It also stood for chiefly authority (Fletcher and La Flesche 1911:102). Ridington (1987:156) interpreted this union of opposite sources of fertility as constituting a cosmic complement. Hall (2005) has argued that Venerable Man was propped at an angle close to the 42-degree angle observed on 15 August, the very date on which the Omaha closed the camp circle and moved into their fall villages to harvest their mature crop of maize.[2] The rites of the sacred white buffalo hide ensured the perpetuation of the buffalo herds (Fletcher and La Flesche 1911:284–309; Hall 1997:77–85; Liberty et al. 2001:409).

The male and female principles of procreation are expressed in terms of the duality of male and female, father and mother, the sun and the moon, the Morning Star and the Evening Star, and the sky and the earth moieties. Anomalous as it might appear, these opposing principles do make their home jointly in the sky. If the sky is the home of the Upper World by day and the home of the Beneath World at night, the sky can be visualized as being jointly occupied by these principles (Duncan, personal communication). A shared space can be seen in Omaha ideology, wherein the sun, particularly at high noon, lies at a location that is conceptually analogous to that of the giant sun bier—their term (Osage as well) for the Big Dipper constellation visible at night. Lankford (2007c:152–159) observes that among many of the agricultural Plains groups the Big Dipper was equated to a giant bier carried across the sky. A quotation from Ridington expresses the cultural significance of the camp circle configuration:

The *hu'thuga* reveals the entire circle of creation, the continuous motion of an ongoing creative process. It expresses the thought that lies behind all outward appearance. It gives voice to the mythic idea that human beings were born of a union between the Sky people and the Earth people. This mythic union is not something that happened long ago and far away from everyday experience. Rather it is enacted over and over again in the ceremonies through which the tribe renews its own existence, renews its form of government, and renews its relationship to the buffalo, to the maize, to the seasons, and to the forces of day and night. (Ridington and Hastings 1997:110)

Not surprisingly, symbolic rebirth was conceptualized even more actively. The calumet ceremony, which in the eighteenth century became a widespread ceremony of ritual adoption, was more than a tool for easing the reception of guests (Hall 1989, 1997). At its historic core it was about conferring symbolic rebirth on a particular individual. It used two calumet stems, each with duckbills and other animal parts incorporated into the stem and with feather fans suspended from the shaft. This assembly amounted to the distillation of power made possible by the ritual contributions of specific clans (Fletcher and La Flesche 1911:376–401; La Flesche 1939). The owl tufts contributed by the deer clan were the finishing touch.

Dhegiha Symbolism

The recognition of Dhegiha Sioux myths and religious symbolism in specific images is already well advanced. Rock-art has provided images of the Dhegiha Birdman and Earthmother (Diaz-Granados 2004; Diaz-Granados and Duncan 2000, 2004; Duncan and Diaz-Granados 2000, 2004). Duane Esarey (1987, 1990) argued that engravings on shell gorgets of the Braden/Eddyville style or the McAdams type that bear spiders fit the beliefs and practices of the Osage far better than those of the distant Cherokee. He anticipated the regional contextual approach advocated in this chapter.

In a pathbreaking paper Guy Prentice (1986) contended that the Birger Figurine represented "Mother Corn" or "Our Grandmother." Diaz-Granados (1993:341, 343–345, 354; Diaz-Granados and Duncan 2000:217, 219–220, 236–237) argued for the "Old-Woman-Who-Never-Dies" as a Siouan deity.

This particular divinity—called Earthmother here—can be identified among a broad range of tribes in the Northern Plains and Eastern Woodlands, including the Dhegiha Sioux. Emerson (1989, 1997a, 1997b) contributed an expansion on this identification. Of particular significance for these identifications is the graphic concordance between the details incorporated into these figurines and the story lines in the oral traditions of the Eastern Plains. Earthmother hoeing the back of the puma-serpent recalls her gift of agricultural plants to humankind. The squash growing from the monstrous serpent is a visual realization of that gift. Her backpack reminds us that in some myths she brought seeds to humankind in a bag (Prentice 1986).

The lineup of deities extends well beyond what has been identified to date (Reilly 2004). We have to recognize that the red fireclay figurines associated with Cahokia depict numerous different deities. Some remain to be identified. For example, the "Crouching Warrior" pipe figure from Shiloh appears to represent a deity in the precultural or "wild" period of his career (Reilly 2004:133, Fig. 15). Others are likely to be added to the list. Figural identities are easily distinguished among the diverse activities and costumes depicted in Braden art. The connections to Dhegihan cosmology are facilitated by the emphasis on representation of spirits through human form. The transformation to and from an animal or cultural object and a human form is recounted many times in Dhegiha and Chiwere mythology. In this respect we have to include the neighboring Pawnee as well. This leads to a distinction articulated in Ho-Chunk/Winnebago myths between the human form of a spirit and its "natural" form (Radin 1948). In the instance of the Omaha the "natural form" extends from animals to inanimate objects. In myths such as "How Big Turtle Went on the Warpath" the companions of the mythic warrior turtle turn into a "comb," an "awl," a "pestle," a "firebrand," and a "buffalo bladder" (Welsch 1981:203–216). In commenting on the frog effigy pipe Reilly (2004:135) argued that it "perfectly illustrates the episode in which the companions of Morning Star return, resume their animal forms, and visually manifest the animal powers."

What appear to be set scenes representing episodes from a myth can be found in some sculpture, rock-art, and shell engraving (Brown 2007b). Reilly (2004) has identified at least three myth cycles among the many combinations in human costumery. Two of the three mythic cycles identified, the Morning Star Cycle and the Earth and Fertility Cycle, are depicted prominently in the Braden style; the third cycle, the Path of the Souls, is present, albeit weakly (Emerson 1982, 1989; Knight et al. 2001; Lankford 2007a, 2007b). The importance of these cycles rests on the specific powers that the myths charter. These powers are sustained as long as the capacity to exercise them remains in place (Brown 2007b). Some of the key human/animal spirits are singled out for extended discussion below in order to highlight two kinds of cultural connection: the prominence of earth-sky duality and the employment of a distinctly Dhegihan code for identity.

Dhegiha Cosmograms in Imagery
MORNING STAR AND HUMAN FERTILITY

The Morning Star Cycle is built around the predawn appearance of a bright asterism in advance of the rising sun. The star is very prominent between November to February during the season of dormancy, when food is difficult to procure. The end of this season comes as a great relief, and it is understandable that the rejuvenation of plant and animal life is associated with human health and reproduction. Fertility in general is not what the Morning Star cycle is all about; rather it applies specifically to human life in its multiple aspects, including health, safety, and the protection of one's family. This cycle is particularly important because it places death as a preordained end that normally contains the germ for a new birth. The regular appearance of this bright star in the predawn sky, interrupted by its disappearance, likewise has given rise to narratives of life and death among the deities, phrased in distinctive Amerindian manner as high-stakes gaming (Brown 2007c; Hall 1997; Radin 1948).

The hawk is the principal animal form of Morning Star. Other icons are the forked eye surround, the Long-Nosed God maskette, the chunkey stone, the chunkey pole, and the calumet staff. The images created in Classic Braden style clearly reference a hawk. In certain instances, a true falcon is portrayed by the diagnostic presence of a notch located midway in the upper bill. Birdman is found on sculpture, rock-art, and shell engraving (Brown 1996: vol. 2, 523; Diaz-Granados 2004:143) (Fig. 3.4d).

An important bridge to the past exists in the elbow catlinite pipe belonging to the Omaha pole bundle that has a stylized eye incised deeply into the side of the stone pipe stem (Ridington and Hastings 1997:Fig. 21a, b). Four of these lines stream back from the forward-placed eye. They could represent

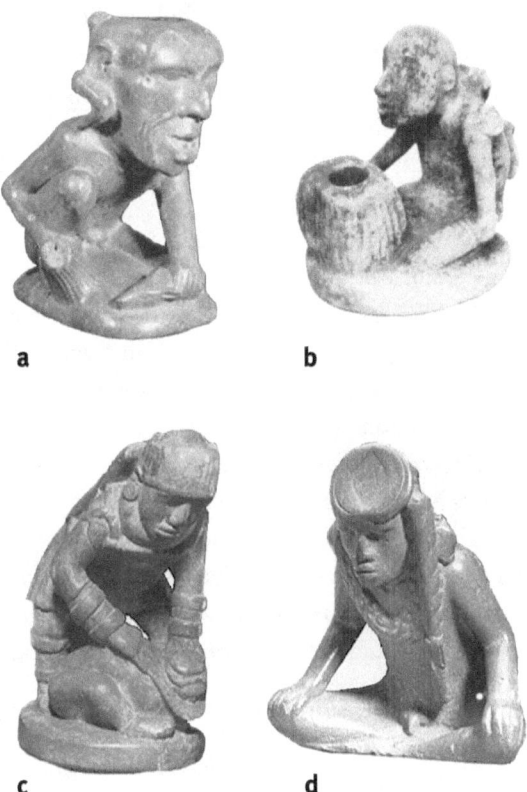

FIGURE 3.4. Braden-style divinities in sculpture (scale varies). (a) Grizzlyman, red claystone, height 23.4 cm, Sam Noble Natural History Museum, LfCrl B99-3. Identifying iconic elements are the hunched back, double hair-knots, bossed forehead, snarling mouth, and deer head in the left hand. Reproduced courtesy of the Sam Noble Museum of Natural History, Norman, Oklahoma. (b) Earthmother, limestone (?), height 25 cm, Smithsonian Institution, National Museum of the American Indian 18/9112. Identifying iconic elements are the sacred bundle basket, basket in the right hand (behind basket), ear of corn in the left hand, and burden basket on her back. Reproduced courtesy of the Smithsonian Institution, National Museum of the American Indian. (c) Turtleman, red claystone, height 24.8 cm, Smithsonian Institution, National Museum of the American Indian 21/4088. Identifying iconic elements are the armor plates on the dorsal and ventral torso, helmet, and mace-shaped weapon cleaving the face of a smaller victim grasped at the foot. Reproduced courtesy of the Smithsonian Institution, National Museum of the American Indian. Photograph reproduced with permission of John Bigelow Taylor. (d) Birdman, red claystone, height 22.5 cm, University of Arkansas Museum UAM 47-2-1. Identifying iconic elements are the sacred bundle worn on the head with the plate inside uncovered, a single long hair braid, the necklace rope of shell beads, long-nosed ear maskettes, and a cape covered in feathers or scalps. Reproduced courtesy of the University of Arkansas Collection, Fayetteville. Photograph reproduced with permission of John Bigelow Taylor.

an unusual four-pronged "weeping eye" or could conform to the typical two-pronged form if the four lines are regarded as outlining the edges of each prong (Fig. 3.5a). The red color of the pipestone is deemed to be appropriate for honoring life (Ridington and Hastings 1997:152). Charcoal in the incisions provides a contrast with the red color of the catlinite (Ridington and Hastings 1997:144).

A related symbol of human fertility is the Long-Nosed God depicted as maskettes in the ears of Birdman/Morning Star (Hall 1997:145–154). Mythically the masks had the capacity to make faces on demand. This animate property suggests that they were minor spirits in their own right. Duncan and Diaz-Granados (2000, 2004:201) have advanced the thesis that they stand for the twin "Children of the Sun."

An important life symbol present is the bilobed arrow emblem. Hall (1989) has elaborated on the history of the bilobed arrow, which has the calumet as its postcontact elaboration (Hall 1989, 1997:48–58). The feature that signifies continuity is the "arrow" in name and imagery. The name makes sense in terms of its reconstructed history (Brown 2007a; Hall 1989). The arrow shaft in pre-Columbian images is fitted into a drawn bow. The ends of the bow are

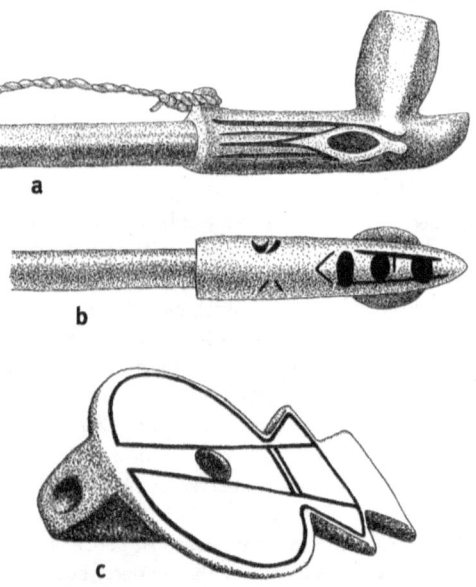

FIGURE 3.5.(a) Pipe of the Sacred Pole, side view; (b) Pipe of the Sacred Pole, bottom view; (c) Pipe of the White Buffalo. All redrawn from Ridington and Hastings 1997:Fig. 21a, b.

decorated with tufts of feathers (Phillips and Brown 1978:86). In later images the tufts are transformed into feather fans in the context of the arrow shaft separation into two calumet-style staffs.

While the sacred hawk/falcon has a central place in Osage cosmology, this bird has been marginalized in Omaha belief. As observed above, it has not been eliminated either in myth or in symbol.

EARTHMOTHER AND VEGETATIVE FERTILITY

Long-competing symbols of vegetative fertility are the puma and the serpent. The human counterpart of these two animals, and perhaps their controlling deity, is Corn Mother or Earthmother (Fig. 3.4b). They appear to have divided powers of fertility. In the Pawnee legend of Owl Medicine, the power of the puma and serpent is represented by their avatar the owl (Dorsey 1906:206–207). Their opposite was Morning Star, as represented by the Sacred Hawk in the Osage legend of the Patient Warrior (La Flesche 1939:9–11). The vulvar motif has been shown to be a recurrent symbolic representation of this female deity (Diaz-Granados 1993, 2004; Diaz-Granados and Duncan 2000). Another associated object is the lidded chest that probably depicts a deep floatweave sacred bundle. The Siouan "Old-Woman-Who-Never-Dies" is the mother of all things in the heavens and the Middle World, also known as the Corn Mother or Earthmother, depending on the group, location, and associated oral tradition (Diaz-Granados and Duncan 2004:143; Townsend and Sharp 2004:30).

In the White Buffalo Hide ritual equipment of the Omaha is a stone pipe bowl of the disk form that reveals the connection of the "keyhole" motif with female fertility (Ridington and Hastings 1997). It contrasts with the prow shape of the elbow pipe accompanying the pole bundle described above in connection with Morning Star. The flat circular disk has a forward projection that makes its outline resemble a keyhole (Fig. 3.5c). The outline duplicates the shape of the small sacred circle surrounding the cosmic pole in the camp circle center and the altar created to the immediate east from the dirt taken from the hole. The pipe bowl hole mimics the architecture of hole for the pole and the earthen altar. These correspondences between the sacred circle and the disk-bowl pipe provide a basic continuity in ritual female earth symbolism between the Omaha of today and the precontact past.

Earthmother holds power over fertility of the vegetative kind. One can posit two aspects to Old Woman: as the bearer of a backpack containing agricultural seeds and as the guardian of a major sacred bundle represented by a large lidded box she protects either by sitting next to it or by laying her hands on it. The Birger Figurine and Schild Pipe are outstanding examples of the former (Emerson 1997a:205–206; Reilly 2004:133, Fig. 17a, b). The Westbrook, the Keller, and the West Figurines (based on the artistic restoration in Duncan and Diaz-Granados 2004:Figs. 12–14) and the so-called Mortar Figure pipe are examples of the latter (Burnett 1945:12–13; Emerson 1989:55; Reilly 2004:Figs. 1, 16). In the Westbrook Figurine we have "Corn Mother" as the provider of domestic plants (Reilly 2004:133, Fig. 1). To gain an appreciation of the potential interconnection of these images with other cycles, Reilly (2004:134, Fig. 17a, b) has placed them into the Morning Star myth cycle.

TURTLEMAN AND WARFARE

While the Morning Star spirit constitutes a certain vision of battle tied to human regeneration, Turtleman embodies outright prowess (Brown 2007b; Brown and Dye 2007). Turtle is a warrior figure embodied in red stone statuary (Brown 1996; Radin 1948). The figures sculpted in stone depict the defeat of a captive (Fig. 3.4c). They bear their turtle identity in the warrior's distinct carapacelike body armor protecting the front and back of his torso. The rounded helmet recalls the shape of a turtle's head. The "Conquering Warrior" pipe figure represents a warrior hero (Dye 2004:198–199, Fig. 16a–b; Reilly 2004:133). I interpret the two Crouching Warrior effigy pipes found at Spiro as representing the hero Turtle. This great mythic war captain among the Omaha, Osage, and Ho-Chunk figures in at least two separate myth cycles. The figures sculpted in stone depict the defeat of a captive.

Fletcher and La Flesche (1911:38) point out that a turtle group is present in each tribe (Omaha, Osage, Kansa, and Quapaw) as a "subclan," charged as "the keepers of the turtle rites of the tribe" (Fletcher and La Flesche 1911:38). The myth "How Big Turtle Went on the Warpath" was collected from the Omaha (Welsch 1981:203–216). Big Turtle is a great warrior who led a team of warrior spirits to battle. They overcame their adversaries by changing into their innate form as an animal, an object, or a force of nature. Armed with the power of fire or a rock or a turtle, they could outperform any of their human adversaries. Fletcher and La Flesche (1911:332) add other survival-conferring details to turtle's power. Swallowing a turtle's heart will make one's heart strong. "The turtle is hard to kill; even when the heart is cut out it will still quiver and the turtle's head will be able to bite after it is severed from the body" (Fletcher and La Flesche 1911:332).

Osage warriors paid dearly for the privilege of being tattooed. The patterns created were declared to be aspects of warfare. Louis Burns (1985:133) lists the sacred ceremonial knife, the sacred pipe, and the thirteen sunrays. The sacred knife tattoo ran vertically down the chest. The sacred pipes slanted upward away from the knife over shoulders. The thirteen sunrays ran parallel with the pipes from the chest and over the shoulders.

GRIZZLYMAN

Yet to be placed into a particular cycle is the power that I have called "Grizzlyman" (Brown 2004:122). The sole exemplar of this deity is a figurine of red claystone from Spiro converted into a pipe (Brown 1996; Emerson et al. 2003) (Fig. 3.4a). The Braden style is unmistakable. This figurine combines features of dwarfism (the hunched back and enlarged head with prominent bossing on the sides of the forehead) with an open, gap-toothed, snarling mouth and a pair of hair-knots that Richard Zurel (2002) has shown to be signature markers of the grizzly bear in frontal view. What is relevant here is the presence of a naming symbol in the figurine composition: the deer head is clasped in its left hand. This kenning for "deer head" or *tapa'* is the name for the constellation Pleiades (La Flesche 1932). Here we have a deity that resides in or more plausibly embodies the constellation itself. The combination of body features and deer head suggests some sort of arch-shaman. Reilly (2004:133, Fig. 18), however, has identified this "Grizzly Man" with the leader of the Giants. How Grizzlyman and the Giants are related remains to be studied.

SPIDER AND PRIMORDIAL LIFE

The spider and its web are an icon for life as a primordial principle. Both are sometimes associated with Earthmother (Fig. 3.6) (La Flesche 1918). The spider motif on gorgets can be related to the spiderweb spun by Earthmother (Diaz-Granados 2004; Diaz-Granados and Duncan 2004; Duncan and Diaz-Granados 2000, 2004). Osage believe the spiderweb is a snare, *ho e ka* (Fig. 3.7). According to La Flesche (1932:63), it is "a term for an enclosure in which all life takes on bodily form, never to depart therefrom except by death. It stands for the earth which the mythical elk made to be habitable by separating it from the water." In other words, it "refers to the ancient conception of life as proceeding from the combined influences of the cosmic forces." Among the Pawnee, Spider Woman is equated with the lunar deity and with the cultivation of squash (Prentice 1986:258, citing Dorsey 1906:211–213). Prentice (1986:251–254) has covered the wide-ranging variations of this deity in the Eastern Woodlands.

Louis Burns (1985:133) described an elaborate tattoo on a high-status woman's chest, back, and arms. She "had two small circles tattooed, one over the other, centered between the eyebrows. Her chest, back arms, hands, and lower legs were tattooed with geometric designs. These were stylizations of the sun, moon, stars, and the earth from which all life originated. Running from her shoulder and down her arm to the wrist were symbols representing life in all forms descending to earth." The possibility that late nineteenth-century Omaha and Osage uses of the tattoo (Fletcher and La Flesche 1911:397; La Flesche 1925:Pls. 15, 16, 17) are a continuation of Late Braden images needs to be pursued (Phillips and Brown 1978:Pl. 55).

THE SERPENT AND THE AFTERWORLD

The serpent and the puma stand as different forms of the life-taking spirit/deity (Brown 1997). Lankford (2007d) has argued that universally the "Great Serpent" is made to represent the Beneath World. When it is displayed as winged, he contends, the reference is not to the serpent's appearance but

FIGURE 3.6. Spider imagery through the ages: (a) a conventional image of the spider tattooed on the backs of both hands of Osage women of honor (La Flesche 1921:106); (b) McAdams-type shell gorget (Holmes 1883).

THE CULTURE SIGNATURE OF THE BRADEN ART STYLE

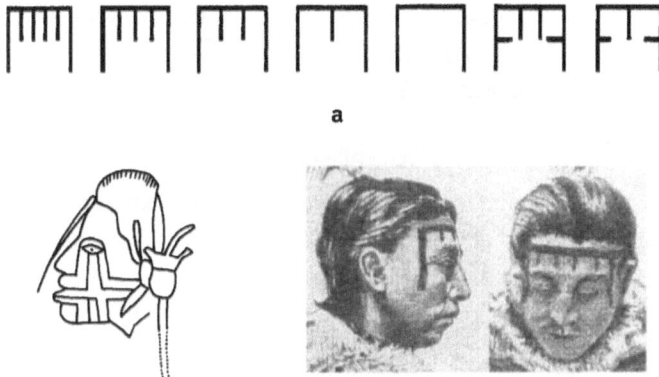

FIGURE 3.7. *Ho e ka* in early usage and in the Late Braden style: (a) *ho e ka* variation according to Burns (1985:Fig. 12); (b) *ho e ka* image from a Late Braden engraved shell cup surface (Phillips and Brown 1978:Pl. 55); (c) *ho e ka* painted on the face of the Xo' ka in the Osage Rite of Vigil (La Flesche 1925:Pls. 16, 17).

to the snake flying in the night sky (Lankford 2007d). This identification of the wing as a locative makes the wingless image conform more closely to the Beneath World serpent known from Southeastern myth and dovetails nicely with Reilly's argument (2004, 2007c) that certain other images from Spiro are also locative signs for depicting the Beneath World spirits in the night sky. Lankford (2007a) has elaborated on the winged serpent and Piasa as such a night sky deity. The winged serpent is emblematic of Lankford's (2007a, 2007b) cult of the Path of the Souls. This cycle is present as a distinct iconic system in the Hemphill and Craig styles sometime around AD 1275, about the same time the oblong-shaped scalp emblem emerges (Brown 2007a). The feature that helps isolate this particular image from serpents in general is the "lazy J" or "rocker-rail" curve to its lower edge. Lankford (2007d:206) has argued that this distinctive bow-shaped curvature to the snake "belly" mimics one way of connecting the stars in the constellation of Scorpio. This constellation rises only just above the horizon during the summer months. The deities connected with night and death have sky identities even though they may be thought of primarily as Beneath World powers. A well-known representation combined the puma and serpent with wings to become the Piasa of postcontact times in the Upper Mississippi Valley (Brown 1997; Phillips and Brown 1978). As a life-taking monster this spirit was widely feared. This cycle is presumably connected with the motifs of skulls and long bones. It is contemporary with the appearance of the winged Piasa, the terrace rainbow motif, and the circular scalp lock (Brown 2007a).

COMPLEXITIES

Not everything is straightforward. Indeed, many perplexities remain. On the cultural side there is the fact that spirits/deities have what could be considered overlapping domains. For instance, life, birth, and fertility are shared in certain ways among the spider, Birdman, Earthmother, and even the serpent. Conversely, many different narrative cycles involve the same key spirit of Earthmother (Prentice 1986; Reilly 2004). This multiple involvement is likely to be more pervasive than we can document today. All of this is complicated by shifts that have taken place through time in the meaning and context of specific icons among different compositions (Brown 2005).

On the symbol side complexity is manifest in the blurred distinctions in images that appear to have very different histories or origins. An outstanding case is the seemingly vague distinction between the Sacred Hawk and the Thunderbird. Whereas the Sacred Hawk is derivative of the twelfth-century falcon, the Thunderbird of postcontact times is associated with the powers of thunder and lightning. As an all-encompassing conflation of birds it has dominated the discussion of bird symbolism in precontact times. Indeed, given the level of discussion to date, one might even assert that they are simply two faces to the same entity.

Such a stance ignores the fact that the Omaha, the Osage, and the Ho-Chunk never confuse the two major avian spirits. Among them the Great Thunderbird is the swallow-tailed kite (*Elanoides forficatus*) or "blackhawk." Blackhawk also figures prominently in Osage rites, along with four other kinds of hawk. The skins in the Omaha Sacred War Pack include this bird (Fletcher and La Flesche 1911:412–413). This leaves the Sacred Hawk to be assigned to another species.

One solution to the problem of discrimination is to decide on the basis of ideologically sensitive attributes. The Thunderbird figures as a cosmic instrument in the perpetual battle between the forces of the sky (and life) and earth (and death). If this is held to be a primary role for the Thunderbird, then the behavior of the swallow-tailed kite fits the bill. This bird preys upon snakes and is frequently sighted in wetland areas seeking out these reptiles. I might add that the bald eagle feeds on fish and can be viewed as another instrument of Above World forces arrayed against those of the Beneath World. With these behavioral attributes in mind the courageous combat of the Sacred Hawk as it is celebrated in legendary combat with the night owl fits an entirely different bird (Brown 2007b; La Flesche 1939:9–11). This legend is recorded for both the Osage and Omaha (Welsch 1981:234–237). Of the power-diving hawks, the peregrine falcon holds top marks, although some of the other species of true falcons (American kestrel, prairie falcon, merlin) could also perform this hunting behavior. Thus, conceptually at least, the hunting behaviors of the various bird species help sort out their potential attachment to distinct powers.

Robert Warren's (2007) compilation of Thunderbird images did not recognize the forked tail as a distinctive marker. Instead, he illustrates the fantail of the hawk, which is particularly prominent when breaking flight. These shell effigies are more likely to be Birdmen than Thunderbirds in the strict sense of the term, particularly when they bear spots on the breast and even collar markings. Their dated age is likewise contemporary with Birdman imagery to the Woodland East. Warren found that these carved shell images were distributed among the Missouri River agricultural sites as early as the Initial Middle Missouri Variant (AD 1000–1200) and were more common throughout the Extended Middle Missouri Variant (AD 1200–1400). Even more than the engraved shell and copper repoussé images of hawks these relatively small but ubiquitous shell images have a distribution that is very telling about the significance of hawk (or falcon) symbolism throughout the Eastern Plains and the Middle Missouri Valley. They make their presence at precisely the time when the more exclusive images were being created in the Mississippi Valley.

One observation will be offered on the appearance of the same icon or spirit in more than one thematic cycle. Earthmother and Birdman are implicated in this example. A prominent icon shown with Earthmother is the deep-set chest/bundle she appears to guard. Is there something significant contained within such a large bundle? A plausible answer to the question comes from the depiction of Birdman with Phillips's "flounce" worn around his midriff (Phillips and Brown 1978:Fig. 268). This article looks suspiciously like a basket burst through the top and bottom, with the warps and wefts carefully delineated. James Duncan (personal communication) has pointed out that Birdman could be depicted in the process of emerging from the basket—perhaps coming to full size in the process. Note that Kent Reilly (2007a, personal communication) has identified as a bundle the small, thin flat-tablet worn on Birdman's forehead. If this narrative line has merit, it would be a case for a linkage between the Earthmother and the Birdman mythic cycles. It is not irrelevant that in Duncan's reconstruction of the Osage pantheon Earthmother stands in the parental role with respect to Morning Star and other deities, whose common characteristic is that they rise and fall in the heavens in a way that fosters their birth and death as a trope (Duncan and Diaz-Granados 2000).

Conclusion

Cosmovision is such a strong manifestation of cultural ideology that arguably it is highly resistant to changes induced by European colonization. Consequently, associated imagery is presumed to be likely to carry across that event and well into the present (Brown 2007b). In the Dhegiha Siouan case cosmovision provides a bridge from the nineteenth-century present to the Braden art style past in the absence of an archaeologically demonstrated bridge. Finding ancient material traces of beliefs for which we have no intelligible texts depends greatly on an adequate characterization of Dhegihan cosmogony. Not only do belief and practice have to transfer to material culture, but a control of the relevant iconography is required as well. The Omaha were taken as representative to simplify the argument. A more complete study should make use of additional material and that of the other Dhegiha as well—particularly the Osage.

The regional framework adopted here follows the now-recognized patterning of Mississippian-period art styles. By assuming that these styles are material manifestations of specific languages, meanings can be inferred for particular iconographic contexts and, by projection, the devices of specific languages. This framework also reinforces a model of social geography that reminds us that--given the large spaces involved--there had to be more limited fields of communication than the entire subcontinent (King 2007a, 2007b, 2007c; Knight 2006; Reilly 2007c).

The earth-sky duality is deemed to be critical in Dhegihan cosmology because it underwrites an ideology of warfare as a prelude to human reproduction. The imagery discussed here is not restricted to the Prairie-Forest border and the Upper Mississippi Valley. The essentials of the belief system and cosmology are widely shared throughout the East. However, the principles embodied in the earth-sky dualism have created a specific version of this system that is linked visually to the Braden style. Examples of this style are particularly strong in representing the Sacred Hawk (as Morning Star) and the Earthmother cycles, both of which are strongly related to plant, animal, and human generation. Multiple connections link the two. Both are displayed in bundle rites under the control of clans associated with the Sky moiety, which (as I have explained) see the night sky and daytime as phases of the same principle.

The creating of human figure identity through the deployment of distinctive dress (and undress) and the use of ancillary symbols is a characteristic of the Braden style. To a virtually unparalleled extent, far greater attention is paid to symbols that identify not only a particular deity but also its particular place in mythic time. Dhegiha still honor these spirits, albeit not divorced from a human aspect.

NOTES

AUTHOR'S ACKNOWLEDGMENTS: I am grateful for the critical comments offered by Carol Diaz-Granados, James Duncan, John Kelly, and George Lankford. The insight they provided has improved the chapter.

1. The only other groups that adopted the earth-sky ideology were the Algonkian-speaking tribes of the Illinois, Miami, and Menominee, who plausibly had extended contact with Siouan-speaking peoples before the arrival of the French (Brown 1991:88–89).

2. The date has another potential significance: the Pole Star is angled approximately the same as the ecliptic, thus making Polaris and the sun approximately equidistant from an alignment projecting directly above the He'dewachi post.

CHAPTER 4

Early Manifestations of Mississippian Iconography in Middle Mississippi Valley Rock-Art

Carol Diaz-Granados

Middle Mississippi Valley petroglyphs (rock carvings) and pictographs (rock paintings), with their copious amount and variety of symbolic motifs, provide an unparalleled inventory of Southeastern Ceremonial Complex (SECC)/ Mississippian Ideological Interaction Sphere (MIIS) (Reilly and Garber 2007) iconography. This corpus of motifs radiates out from the Middle Mississippi River Valley into the Lower Missouri and its tributaries, in the Eastern Woodlands and Southeast. The Middle Mississippi River Valley, particularly the confluence region, and its environs contain the largest concentration of rock-art in the Eastern Woodlands (Grant 1981:137). Emma Lila Fundaburk and Mary Fundaburk Foreman recognized this even earlier than Campbell Grant and credited Missouri as "the center of a Middle West petroglyph area" (Fundaburk and Foreman 1957:93). Klaus Wellmann's sweeping overview of North American rock-art names three concentrations in the Eastern Woodlands. Wellmann states that one "zone extends from Missouri into the Tennessee River valley as far east as Georgia and western North Carolina" (Wellmann 1979:149). The Missouri rock-art region referred to in this discussion (with more than 150 sites, including a copious amount of diagnostic motifs) contains iconography that extends minimally to the west (Spiro), east (Cahokia), south (Moundville), and southeast (Etowah).

Although systematic rock-art research is being carried out in a selection of other eastern states (Alabama, Arkansas, Illinois, Kentucky, and Tennessee) and the number of reported sites in those states is steadily increasing, my point of reference will remain Missouri. This is partly because of the availability of motif charts and distribution maps (Diaz-Granados 1993; Diaz-Granados and Duncan 2000) and this area's proximity to the major Mississippian site of Cahokia. Comparisons to Missouri's rock-art sites containing SECC and related regional (MIIS) iconography will continue throughout as a base of reference.

Current research both in rock-art and in comparative iconography has broadened the scope of this SECC/MIIS and encouraged a growing awareness and acceptance of its regional variations. The basis of a previous ongoing "confusion" has stemmed in large part from the reality of finding particular motifs co-occurring with those not present in the fifty-one motifs on Waring and Holder's expanded list (Waring 1968c:91). This means that along with a number of the "traditional" symbols commonly viewed as arising from the SECC (Waring 1968c; Howard 1968; Phillips 1940; Phillips and Brown 1978, 1984), in some localities we find these traditional motifs portrayed along with other, possibly more regionally specific motifs. This co-occurrence of motifs is significant and should eventually lead to a clearer picture of their intended meaning. The absence or presence of key SECC symbols likewise provides insight into the regionalism factor and may serve as a key to a selection of American Indian oral traditions and belief systems, along with the movement and dispersal of populations.

Although it is difficult to pinpoint the exact groups responsible for producing the rock-art, we can gain insight into what was important to those people through their repeated use of specific motifs. More importantly, this rock-art is found in situ, which offers the potential of providing a map of the extent of usage or influence of the iconography. That is, the location of a rock-art site is where it was originally created—the rock-art is rarely if ever moved, and thus each example of the iconography can be considered site specific. This differs from traditional cultural materials such as clay pottery, copper, and shell items. So with petroglyphs and pictographs we have not only a specific location but an art form with imagery that has an unquestionable association with its creator's oral traditions, lifeways, and/or cosmology. In addition, we can see at least some of the motifs continuing to serve as icons for later American Indian groups, attesting to the longevity of associated oral traditions and beliefs. At the same time, we can begin to comprehend how these regionally important icons fit together to form meaning through their presence, absence, and co-occurrences. Determining the significance of co-occurrences is a tougher task, but one that I believe is ultimately attainable. This emerging awareness of the factor of regionalism in regard to the iconography and the analysis of rock-art motif distribution in the Middle Mississippi Valley in relation to that regionalism are the main foci of this chapter.

Mound Sites and Petroglyph Sites

Scholars often refer to the Classic Braden style Rogan Plates (Fig. 4.1a and b) from Mound C at the great ceremonial center in Etowah, Georgia, as defining (diagnostic) artifacts. Etowah Mounds is one of the four major mound sites in the eastern United States, the others being Moundville, Cahokia, and Spiro (see Map 1 in the Introduction). Although Spiro is more "Plains/Midwest," it is too connected to the material being discussed here to omit it. Both Rogan figures represent a "Birdman" supernatural or better a triumphant "Hawk Being." Brown and Kelly (2000:471) refer to the "Birdman" theme, stemming from the Rogan Plates, "as the 'mother' source for the SECC as an archaeological construct." The Rogan Plates bring many of the SECC symbols together into these two hammered copper repoussé figures. Fourteen of Waring and Holder's seventeen original traits are taken from the iconography on

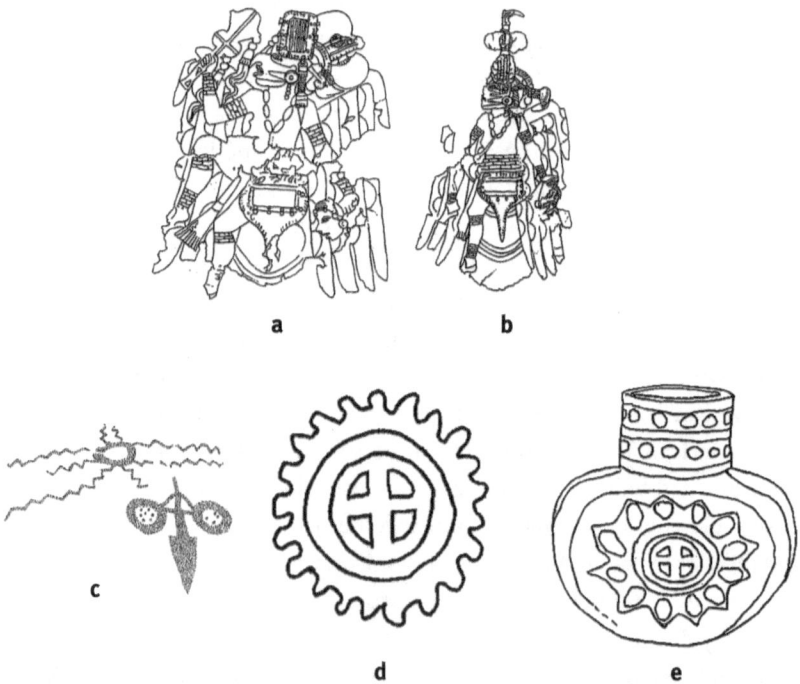

FIGURE 4.1. (a, b) Rogan Plates from Etowah, Georgia; (c) bilobed arrow in red pigment at Lost Creek site, Washington Co., Missouri; (d) petaloid cross-in-circle at Maddin Creek Site, Washington Co., Missouri; (e) pot with petaloid cross-in-circle from Etowah, Georgia.

the Rogan Plates clothing along with several of the ritual objects. These Hawk Beings no doubt represent the encoding of a complex, canonical personality who satisfied a political/societal requirement to achieve origin/renewal ritual in an attempt to keep balance within the cosmos.

This "Hawk Being" is absent in the cultural material at Moundville, Alabama. In fact, anthropomorphic iconography (other than body parts such as hands) is largely absent at Moundville, where serpents, supernatural underwater creatures, and various other Lower World motifs predominate in the arts (Steponaitis 1983; Steponaitis and Knight 2004; and others). Etowah, on the other hand, exhibits both naturalistic (including anthropomorphs) and representational-symbolic iconography (King 2004; Larson 1959; and others). Shell cups from Spiro depict anthropomorphic figures, including the Hawk Being or "Birdman." Much of Missouri's rock-art contains anthropomorphic imagery, hawks, and several "Birdmen" or Hawk Beings. Finely crafted details like the ones seen on the Rogan Plates or Spiro shell cups are lacking in Missouri's stone depictions, however, so it is the general form and silhouette that offer clues to the character being portrayed.

Examining the iconography at five major mound centers, we see what can be interpreted as an artistic and ideological sphere with major ceremonial centers/points north (Cahokia), south (Moundville), east (Etowah and Castalian Springs), and west (Spiro). Much ritual activity occurred within this region encompassing the Mississippi, Missouri, and Ohio River Valleys, and a profusion of ceremonial art was produced here between the Middle or Late Woodland and late prehistoric times. This is not to ignore related sites, because many occur within this same general region (Citico, Lake Jackson, Towasaghy, and Wickliffe, to name a few). There are relations with other sites in general, including Peter Bess Fort, Commerce Eagle petroglyph, St. Mary Common Field, and Bushnell Ceremonial Cave. All of these sites are related through their particular use of SECC/MIIS motifs.

Missouri's "Big Five" petroglyph group (Washington State Park A and B, Maddin Creek, Three Hills Creek, and Wallen Creek) contains a profusion of SECC and related icons that can be compared to the iconography found in materials at the major (and minor) mound sites. These motifs include the mace, bilobed arrow, foot, hand, ogee, hafted celt or monolithic axe, cross-in-circle or sun circle, spinning cross, and spinning cross-in-circle or in two concentric circles. On the other hand, the selection of SECC motifs at Picture Cave (such as the mace, occipital hair-bun, concentric circles as shoulder tattoos, and falconid eye surround) includes neither the bilobed arrow nor the cross-in-circle, seen in abundance in eastern Missouri rock-art. These sites reflect just one example of the selective use of motifs attributable to a general period. The bilobed arrow, found archaeologically in hammered copper and portrayed as headdresses adorning the heads of figures on shell cups from Spiro, Oklahoma, on the Rogan Plates from Etowah, Georgia, and on the stone Willoughby Disk from Moundville, Alabama, is common in eastern Missouri rock-art. Depictions include the only known bilobed arrow pictograph in Missouri (Fig. 4.1c) created in red pigment, although several other versions occur in petroglyph form (discussed later in this chapter).

Other associations with traditional SECC icons are found in the Big Five group in eastern Missouri. All five sites are roughly 50–70 miles southwest of Cahokia Mounds. They were much closer to the St. Louis Mound Group on the St. Louis Riverfront (Big Mound and its associated mounds). Those mounds were leveled, starting in 1812 and culminating with the demise of Big Mound in 1869 (Williams and Goggin 1956). The petaloid cross-in-circle at Maddin Creek (Fig. 4.1d) is comparable to the one on a negative-painted bottle from Burial 81 in Mound C at Etowah (Fig. 4.1e). Similar motifs appear on shell gorgets from the Southeast, including the Cox Mound–style shell gorget from Castalian Springs, Tennessee, and another version is evident in the shell gorget from the Stallings Island Mound in Columbia County, Georgia. This motif is also seen on shell cups from Spiro. A related motif found in eastern Missouri rock-art is the cross-in-circle (or within two concentric circles). Other typical and related motifs include the dot-in-circle, the hand/arm, the falconid or forked eye, and the mace.

The Advantage of Rock-Art: Contextual Aspects

When studying and mapping the spatial distribution of any rock-art, a likely place to begin is with the consideration of context. Context means the location and setting in which the petroglyphs or pictographs were manufactured and the "canvas" on which they were placed. To repeat an important point, rock-art is essentially an in situ phenomenon, found at the very location in which it was created. As an important part of the archaeological record, this gives rock-art an advantage over portable artifacts, such as lithic objects, pottery, copper, and shell, that can travel hundreds of miles through various mechanisms, including intermarriage, war, trade, and other catalysts of economic exchange. Therefore, if we look at the context in which any rock-art (from single motifs to complex panels) was placed, we can begin to understand the probable ritual locations and sacred landscapes that were important for this activity and track the use of icons at specific locations as well as over many regions.

Contexts for rock-art in the Eastern Woodlands include placement on free-standing boulders in open fields, on bluff-tops, or along riverbanks (periodically leaving the rock-art submerged). Rock-art also occurs on bluff facades, on low-lying rock outcrops in cedar glades, in caves, at cave entrances, and in rock shelters on walls or breakdown boulders. This placement choice was no doubt intentional rather than random. The reason for the choice may have been the purpose that the rock-art and its encoded information were intended to serve: to mark identity, ownership, or a sacred location, to express a warning, as a teaching tool or mnemonic device for rituals, for storytelling, or to sanctify a place or event (Diaz-Granados 1993; Diaz-Granados and Duncan 2000).

Advantages of Rock-Art: Temporal Aspects

Rock-art also has the potential to date a site. Certain motifs, and even large complex panels, can sometimes be relatively dated if diagnostic artifacts are depicted—that is, by comparison to items from the archaeological record that have been dated by radiometry or other absolute methods. The depiction of diagnostic artifacts gives the researcher an advantage when working with rock-art, which is usually unstratified and difficult to date. Such items include the bow and arrow, the bilobed arrow, and the mace. These motifs do not appear in all rock-art but are present at a selection of sites in Missouri as well as in Illinois, Arkansas, Kentucky, Tennessee, Alabama, Georgia, and other surrounding states.

The presence of these recognized SECC/Mississippian motifs is useful in the relative dating of rock-art in the Eastern Woodlands, where chances are slim to zero for the employment of anything similar to cation-ration dating of the rock patina. This handicap is attributable to the variable climatic conditions and rapid, albeit irregular, weathering patterns in eastern North America. We know that most Missouri rock-art is attributed to the late prehistoric, although recent pigment dating of pictographs has moved the dates somewhat earlier (Diaz-Granados et al. 2001). Wellmann recognized the early iconography in some of the rock-art three decades ago when he cited Alex Krieger (1945) and William S. Webb and Raymond S. Baby (1957:102–108), noting that "many of the techniques, artistic concepts, and ritualistic associations which underlie this 'Southeastern Ceremonial Complex' were already well developed in Hopewellian and Adena times, i.e., before A.D. 700" (Wellmann 1979:156).

One facet of the temporal aspect is the dating of pigments extracted from pictograph panels. Work in this field has been done in Missouri (Diaz-Granados et al. 2001), in Wisconsin (Steelman et al. 2001), and in Arkansas (Sabo and Sabo 2005). The process involves removing from a pictograph the smallest amount of pigment that can be dated. During the initial dating project that took place at Picture Cave in 1996 and a subsequent sampling in 2003, pigment samples were taken and processed through the plasma chemical extraction technique at Texas A&M Analytical Chemistry Department by Marvin Rowe and his colleagues. The samples were then sent to the Lawrence Livermore Lab to be dated by accelerator mass spectrometry (AMS). The resulting assays give a date range that can be paired with the iconography in the pictographs, assuming that the wood was charred and used within a reasonable length of time—that is, shortly after the tree was "cut" (or died) and burned (Diaz-Granados et al. 2001).

A Caveat

It is important to pay attention to the manner in which ancient artisans treated a single motif or symbol, depending on the media or material used and its variations. These variations can be the result of stylistic preferences or a factor of media confines. Also, the more complex a motif is (the more elements it contains), the stronger the argument for its association with like motifs. The Underwater Spirit (see Diaz-Granados and Duncan 2000:Pl. 15) on the wall at Picture Cave (dated to 950 +/- 100 BP) is an obvious example. It contains a number of elements: the fanged mouth, ear spools, antlers, and serpentine body. About 120 miles south—translated into three-dimensional artifacts—we see the Underwater Spirit (aka Cat Monster) pots from southeastern Missouri and northern Arkansas. Again, these figures include a number of similar elements and represent the same character (or group of characters). In petroglyphs they can take the form of a simple long-tailed quadruped or horned serpent. The "Old Woman" pots (obviously old women forms and most assuredly representations of the female supernatural with which so many of the oral traditions are concerned) when translated into two-dimensional rock-art become the vulva motif. Eastern Missouri has several examples—a likely case of a ritual "shorthand" symbolic communication system.

Sometimes these motifs have a way of escaping comparison because of the change in media. Another example is the fenestrated shell gorget found at Cahokia in the Ramey field between Mound 34 and Monks Mound and a pictograph on the ceiling at the Willenberg Shelter. Initially, they may look different, but the gorget would fall apart without the cross pieces. So the shell artisan cleverly left in the "rays" to hold the gorget together and placed the cross motif in the very center. Nevertheless, they can still be considered the same motif—basically a cross in a circle surrounded by multiple concentric rings. This is an excellent example of media controlling form, but more than likely delivering the same message. For this reason, we should pay close attention to these motif correlations, when the medium changes or obscures the similarity between icons.

Regionalism Factor and Co-occurrences

Possibly the most fruitful and yet to be fully explored avenue of rock-art analysis in eastern North America is the mapping of the distribution and frequency of motifs and their co-occurrences. Granted, it will be a major task, but this will make it possible to determine the significance of a particular motif, the distribution of its use across the landscape, and possible movement of like styles and dispersal of populations, groups, and even individual artisans. Information is available from the major SECC/MIIS centers of Cahokia, Spiro, Etowah, Moundville, and some smaller peripheral mound sites. Unfortunately, most of the surviving material from Missouri's major mound center on the St. Louis Riverfront was lost in a fire. In any case, studying the distribution and co-occurrences of motifs and styles—meshed with the known iconographic data from the SECC/MIIS—affords a means to trace the movement of this imagery and the early people and ideologies they represent.

In examining the rock-art associated with the SECC/MIIS, I am looking at a selection of significant and widespread motifs that figure strongly within this sphere and tracking their dispersal and co-occurrences (see the motif distribution maps for Missouri rock-art in Diaz-Granados 1993 and Diaz-Granados and Duncan 2000; see also Brain and Phillips 1996 for southeastern shell gorgets). For example, fifty-one motifs, including a selection of the SECC symbols, along with some of their co-occurrences were plotted in a search for evidence of any groupings (Diaz-Granados 1993; Diaz-Granados and Duncan 2000). Among the SECC's defining motifs, the bilobed arrow, mace, cross-in-circle, and petaloid cross-in-circle are all portrayed in the rock-art of Missouri and some contiguous states. The forehead plaque, ogee, falconid eye-surround, and Underwater Spirit are all present in Missouri. I am speaking here of a similarity in iconography occurring between Etowah and eastern Missouri—a distance of just under 500 miles. Other symbols portrayed in the Rogan Plates include the striped scalp (apron), columella shell necklace, shell bead ornamentation, and others currently absent in Missouri rock-art. With regard to body adornment and paraphernalia, it should be noted that it would be difficult to execute such minutiae in friable stone as well as for those details to survive the centuries in the midwestern climate.

Connecting the Iconography to the Oral Traditions

The connection between prehistoric motifs and oral traditions gathered by early ethnographers has its naysayers. However, the longevity of both the oral traditions and the basic supernatural characters discussed in these stories supports an association with the frequently depicted motifs. Repeated portrayals of characters with the same specific attributes must bear consideration. The portraiture of Morning Star/Hawk and members of his family occurs on a sandstone wall in the dark zone of a Missouri cave. Hawk, with his father's head/upper torso in his right hand and a bow and arrow in his left hand (Fig. 4.2f; see Diaz-Granados and Duncan 2000:Pl. 17), is believed to be among the oldest images in this cave.

The most distinctive feature is Hawk's ear ornament—a white, long-nosed shell maskette. Diaz-Granados and Duncan (2000) believe that this panel, although not directly dated, is pre–AD 1000. Two salient features set it apart from the later, dated images at the cave. What appears to be white pigment in its composition is actually an effect produced by the careful removal of the patinated and slightly darker sandstone surface, revealing the much lighter matrix. Also, the ancient rendering technique uses a type of engraving—a technique and style found in no other pictographic examples currently

EARLY MANIFESTATIONS IN ROCK-ART 73

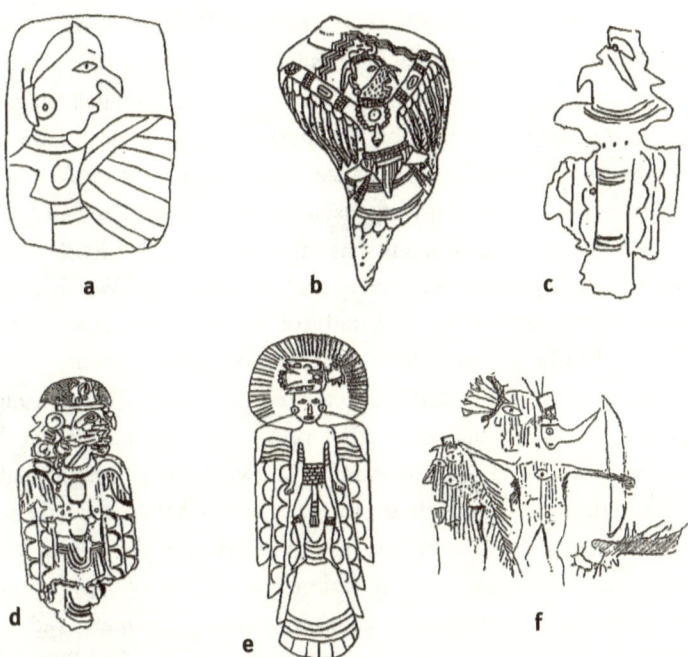

FIGURE 4.2. (a) Cahokia Birdman/Hawk Being, western Illinois; (b) Hawk Being on Spiro shell cup, Spiro, eastern Oklahoma; (c) Peter Bess Fort Hawk plaque, Scott Co., southeastern Missouri; (d) Wulfing Plate (Cat. #112), Dunklin Co., southeastern Missouri; (e) forehead plaque (Hamilton et al. 1974:156), Etowah, Georgia; (f) Morning/Evening Star (Hawk, Red/Blue Horn) at Picture Cave, eastern Missouri.

known in Missouri rock-art. While this image is related in basic style to a figure at the Gottschall Rockshelter site in Wisconsin, the Missouri example is clearly more complex and distinct (Salzer 1987).

After obtaining the AMS dates on the pictographs associated with the mace, falconid eye surround, hair-knot, underwater spirit, "man of mystery" hat, concentric circles, nested semicircles, cruciform arrow, and forehead plaque, we pointed out that the SECC motifs have a much longer history than scholars first believed (Diaz-Granados et al. 2001). The weighted average of these AMS dates is AD 1025. We also believe that the Hawk or Morning Star figure depicted at Picture Cave may contain some of the most (if not the most) information-laden imagery in the Mississippi and Missouri River Valleys. This Hawk/Star figure can be compared to the "Resting Warrior" pipe from

Spiro, Oklahoma, and to the Rogan Plates from Etowah, Georgia, through various elements. In addition, the figure's facial and torso stripes, long-nosed maskette ear ornament, multiple eyes on the chest, forehead plaque, and arrows in the plaque all have their counterpart explanations in the ethnographic literature. Furthermore, because thirty long-nosed maskettes (often in pairs) have been found in an expanse of eleven states (Duncan and Diaz-Granados 2000:2–3), we can safely make the statement that long-nosed maskettes were both important and widespread in the Eastern Woodlands. Then consider that many stories and oral traditions gathered in the ethnographies refer to twins, brothers, heroic duos, *and* the "long-nosed" brother. These stories and allusions to long-nosed characters continue into historic times. We can only proceed on the supposition that a connection exists and that the iconography, so widespread, was not random drawing but an intentional mnemonic device to recall (retell) these stories or perform their related rituals.

Charcoal pigment later removed from a drawing of the "Black Warrior" in Picture Cave yielded an AMS radiocarbon date of 965 +/- 35 years BP. This age agrees with the four previous accelerator mass spectrometry radiocarbon measurements on the three other images that were dated in Picture Cave. There is no statistical difference in any of the resulting dates. From these data we conclude that a flurry of painting and activity occurred at this site, probably between AD 950 and AD 1050.

This information hints at the possibility that the genesis of the SECC/MIIS may even precede the construction of Cahokia. Late Woodland images from Illinois (see Brown 1989) and Picture Cave on the Lower Missouri River support the hypothesis that the symbolism is quite ancient. It could be that the oral traditions and rituals that most likely accompanied at least some of the pictograph production helped serve to formulate a "congress" of Late Woodland people whose cooperative efforts resulted in the development of the western Mississippian centers at the confluence of the Mississippi, Missouri, and Ohio Rivers—that is, the St. Louis Mounds, East St. Louis Mounds, and Cahokia Mounds and the major sites in Mississippi and New Madrid Counties, Missouri.

Motif Comparisons between Sites

I have developed a "short list" of SECC motifs or motif categories for discussion in this essay and will use the most prominent ones found in Missouri rock-art. This obviously lends a regional aspect to this study, but I feel justified in doing so because of the ample amount of SECC motifs present in Missouri rock-art and their association with other major Midwest and southeastern sites. These can serve as singular motifs or in conjunction with other SECC (or suspected regional SECC) symbols. Of the many motifs and motif categories, I have limited the discussion here to ten.

1. Bird, Birdman, Falconid Eye-Surround
2. Serpent
3. Quadrupeds
4. Anthropomorphic: Hand/Arm, Foot, Pit and Groove, Vulva forms
5. Concentric Circles, Dot-in-Circle
6. Cross-in-Circle, Spinning Cross-in-Circle
7. Mace
8. Bilobed Arrow
9. Ogee
10. Underwater Serpent/Spirit

Bird. The bird is the most frequently portrayed motif in Missouri rock-art and is depicted in a variety of styles and forms. It is found alone, in multiples, co-occurring with other motifs, and at times transformed into a therianthropic figure: part avian, part anthropomorph. The "Birdman" portrayed on the Cahokia Birdman tablet (Fig. 4.2a), the Spiro shell cups, such as the Craig B–style engraved-whelk shell cup (Fig. 4.2b), the Peter Bess Fort Hawk plaque from Scott County, Missouri (Fig. 4.2c), the Wulfing Plates from Dunklin County in southeastern Missouri (Fig. 4.2d), and the Rogan Plates from Etowah, Georgia (Fig. 4.1a and b), all appear to represent the same celestial being or similar character in the oral traditions.

The Peter Bess Fort Hawk copper plaque has an important role to play in linking habitation and ritual sites with rock-art. This applies particularly to the similarity between the copper hawk plates—a part of the Missouri-Etowah connection. In the early 1960s Floyd Vavak, an employee of the Army Corps of Engineers, excavated a mature female burial with a Hawk plaque on the forehead (Hamilton et al. 1974:161–162). This site is not far from the southeasternmost petroglyph known in Missouri—the Commerce Eagle site. That copper hawk plaque is clearly related to the Wulfing Plates from Missouri as well as to the plates from Fulton County, Illinois, Etowah, and Spiro.

This plaque is shown being worn on the forehead of a full-face anthropomorphic Hawk figure from Etowah (Hamilton et al. 1974:156) (Fig. 4.2e). The conspicuous absence of Caddoan pottery from sites to the south and west or contemporary pottery from Etowah and points in between indicates a unilateral movement of Classic Braden–style hawk material from southeast Missouri, if indeed that was a possible production site of Classic Braden materials. Many eastern Missouri rock-art sites depict examples of the hawk. Although they are carved in stone without the details seen on copper and shell, the hawk silhouette is still obvious: a few are apparent "Hawk Beings," while those with simple bifurcated tails may also represent therianthropes.

The falconid eye-surround is considered a signifier of a cosmic level: Upper World portrayed by two extensions and Lower World by three (Kent Reilly, personal communication, 2004). This motif (with two extensions) is found at Picture Cave on the Black Warrior, the red-sash figures, and the Giant and may be its earliest manifestation in the region. The front-facing Underwater Spirit portrayed at Picture Cave does not have the eye-surrounds but does have the dot-in-circle eyes that mimic those of the long-nosed maskette seen in a panel on an opposing wall in the cave. This "dot-in-circle" eye or "fish eye" is common to both the long-nosed maskette and the Underwater Spirit at Picture Cave. The long-nosed maskette represents the "wild brother" who was raised by a water spirit in the Children of the Sun or Twins Cycle. The "dot-in-circle" eye denotes "wildness" and the ability to "resurrect," as told in the oral traditions. It is also water related. In the Mandan oral traditions the "Wild Brother" represents the wild, unbridled prairie storms that rejuvenate and replenish the earth in the spring (Bowers 1965; Duncan and Diaz-Granados 2000). The earliest-dated SECC motifs (falconid eye-surrounds, maces, hawk feather–design or scaled garments, singular upright feather, hat similar to the classic Braden turbans, and dot-in-circle eyes) are all present at Picture Cave and date to a weighted average of AD 1025, as noted (see Diaz-Granados et al. 2001).

Serpent. The serpent motif appears alone and in conjunction with other motifs and is abundant in the art of the SECC/MIIS. It is one of the most prolific motifs in Missouri rock-art. At the Rattlesnake Bluff site, near the Bourbouse River, a serpent executed in black pigment that appears to represent a timber rattlesnake (Fig. 4.3a) is depicted on a bluff near the Dancing Warrior painted in red pigment and in Classic Braden stance and profile. At the

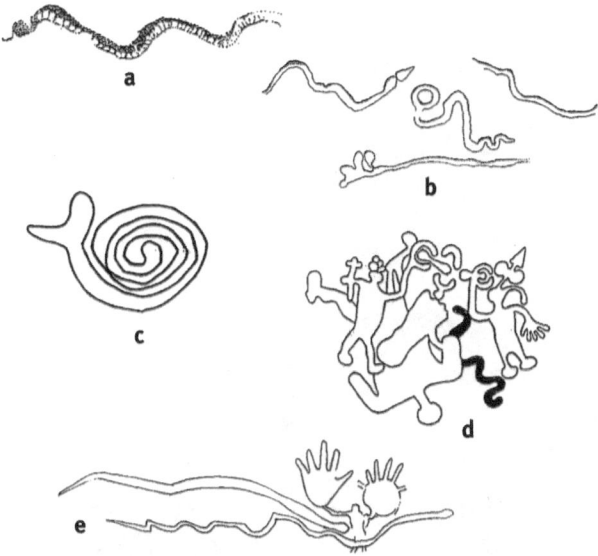

FIGURE 4.3. Serpent motif: (a) Rattlesnake Bluff site, Franklin Co., Missouri; (b) Plattin Creek site, Jefferson Co., Missouri; (c) Washington State Park A; (d) Maddin Creek site (with serpent darkened), Washington Co., Missouri; (e) Rocky Hollow site, Monroe Co., Missouri.

Plattin Creek site the serpent is carved in multiples around a concentric circle (Fig. 4.3b). At Washington State Park there are a number of undulating serpents as well as a coiled representation (Fig. 4.3c). A serpent is present in the complex panel at Maddin Creek (Fig. 4.3d), appearing with the bilobed arrow, foot, hafted axe, and a vulva form. Other serpents travel through the linear complex panel at the Rocky Hollow site (Fig. 4.3e). According to oral traditions, serpents are interchangeable with lightning or arrows. These are all metaphors for one another, depending on the intent of the oral tradition being told. Rock-art serpents often appear undulating, with an arrow-like head. This could possibly refer to the belief that serpents can turn into arrows—as in the Winnebago story in which the arrows of Red Horn (or Blue Horn) immediately turn into serpents when he sets his quiver on the ground (Radin 1948). Serpents and serpentine figures are common in the mortuary art at Moundville and are included in the art from Spiro. Serpents are also referred to in oral tradition as "the husbands of the Old-Woman-Who-Never-Dies" (Bowers 1965:334), so it is no surprise to find vulva motifs depicted in conjunction with serpents.

FIGURE 4.4. Deer: (a) Deer #1, Thousand Hills State Park petroglyphs, Adair Co., Missouri; (b) Deer #2, Thousand Hills State Park petroglyphs, Adair Co., Missouri; (c) Paydown Deer site, Maries Co., Missouri; (d) Picture Cave, eastern Missouri.

Quadrupeds. Quadrupeds are relatively common in Missouri rock-art and in at least some instances may portray a supernatural figure rather than an actual deer or wapiti. Their frequent presence in the rock-art warrants their inclusion in a regional variant of the SECC. Although they are not considered a major SECC motif, Howard (1968:10) wrote that "perhaps deer should be included." Two prominent deer portrayals occur at Thousand Hills State Park (Fig. 4.4a, b). This motif is also seen at the Paydown Deer site (Fig. 4.4c), at Picture Cave (Fig. 4.4d), and at several other sites.

A deer image, when illustrated with arrows in its back, probably refers to a hunt, but other references may be present in other deer images. Although deer portrayals are not so common in the iconography of the SECC, deer antlers are used to depict headdresses or signifiers of particular characters, asterisms, or cosmic levels on shell gorget figures and underwater spirits. Other obvious quadrupeds in rock-art do not have sufficient details for even preliminary identification. The Thousand Hills, Washington State Park, and Deer Run Shelter sites include quadrupeds that depict "longtails"—possible variations of the Underwater Spirit. In some cases deer may represent an aspect of the Old-Woman-Who-Never-Dies and, according to modern Dhegihan oral traditions, the sinister character "Deer Woman" (discussed below).

Anthropomorphs. At some sites anthropomorphs are seen in active postures, as though they are playing a game. At Washington State Park B is a petroglyph portraying an anthropomorph with a stick and circle/ball or chunkey stone (Fig. 4.5a). Another figure shown with "a stick" and circle is found at the Mitchell Site (Fig. 4.5b). Other anthropomorphs appear in Missouri petroglyphs pictured in conjunction with a large avian accompanied by a stick and one or more circular depressions (at Maddin Creek) (Fig. 4.5c). This could allude to a giant bird, "Storms-as-He-Walks," who plays a stickball game with "Morning Star" (Hawk or Red Horn/Blue Horn). At least four possible portrayals point to this oral tradition in Missouri rock-art. This is a major theme of Jasper Blowsnake's Red Horn Cycle (see Radin 1948) or at least a variant of

FIGURE 4.5. Stickball player: (a) Washington State Park B, Washington Co., Missouri; (b) Mitchell site, Randolph Co., Missouri; (c) Maddin Creek boulder, Washington Co., Missouri.

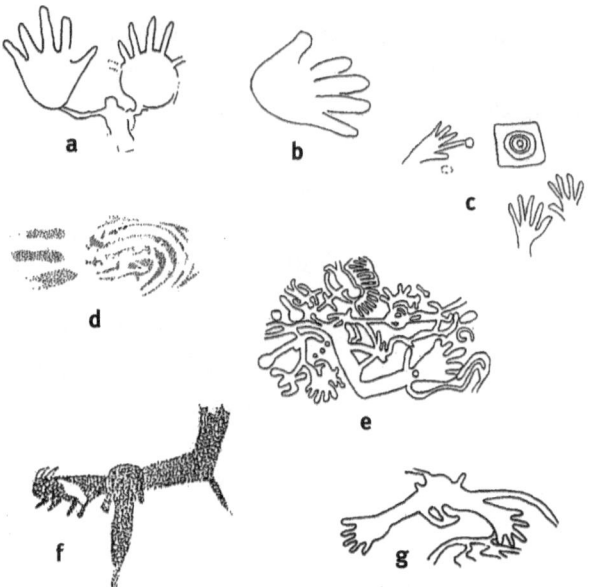

FIGURE 4.6. Hands: (a) Rocky Hollow site, Monroe Co., Missouri; (b) Three Hills Creek, St. Francois/Washington Co., Missouri; (c) Schneider site, Gasconade Co., Missouri; (d) Deer Run Shelter site, St. Francois, Co., Missouri; (e) Maddin Creek site, Washington Co., Missouri; (f) Picture Cave, eastern Missouri; (g) Peene-Murat site, Gasconade Co., Missouri.

that oral tradition. The antiquity of the petroglyphs is known, and their occasional connection to the stickball and chunkey game is unquestionable.

Hand/Arm. Hands are on the list (Waring 1968c:91). They are a prominent icon on gorgets and pottery from Moundville and on gorgets from Spiro, with and without the central eye. Enlarged hands are present on the "shaman" figure at the Rocky Hollow site in northeast Missouri (Fig. 4.6a), along with serpents, quadrupeds, and a turtle but no obvious SECC motifs. Only a few examples of hand-only motifs are known in Missouri: a single hand on a small boulder at Three Hills Creek (Fig. 4.6b), multiple hands at the Schneider site (Fig. 4.6c) in conjunction with concentric circles within a square outline, and at the Deer Run Shelter site (Fig. 4.6d). The forearm is present at a minimum of three sites bearing SECC motifs: Maddin Creek (Fig. 4.6e), Picture Cave (Fig. 4.6f; see Diaz-Granados and Duncan 2000:Pl. 16), and Peene-Murat (Fig. 4.6g). A fourth site depicting an arm at White Rock Bluff may be earlier, as there are no SECC symbols present. Two pigment samples were taken from the Picture Cave forearm and dated to AD 950 and AD 860 uncalibrated. The 14C dates, in years BP, are 1000 +/-70 and 1090 +/-90 (Diaz-Granados et al. 2001).

Foot. The foot motif is particularly interesting because it is often portrayed in eastern Missouri in conjunction with SECC motifs. However, it is conspicuously absent in the Waring and Holder listing (Waring 1968c:91). Although the foot (feet) obviously played an important role in the oral traditions and belief systems of prehistoric American Indians and appears frequently in Mississippi Valley rock-art, it was not considered part of the SECC iconography. This leads me to believe that it is a regional variant; but, again, the SECC listing was based completely on portable artifacts, without any consideration of the emerging rock-art record. The foot has been referred to in the ethnographic literature as representing brave warrior deeds (Bailey 1995:187; Fletcher and La Flesche 1992:434). Elsewhere it is said to represent "prayers" (Revard 1987:460). The foot motif co-occurs in the midst of the complex

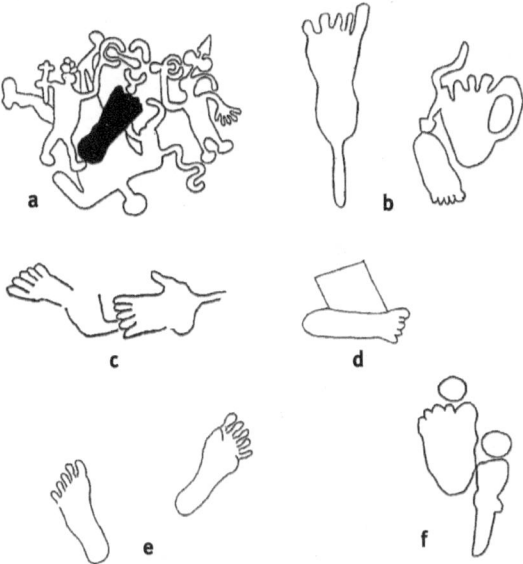

FIGURE 4.7. Feet: (a) complex panel at Maddin Creek site (with foot darkened), Washington Co., Missouri; (b) foot/mace and two feet at Washington State Park B, Washington Co., Missouri; (c) two feet at Anheuser site, Jefferson Co., Missouri; (d) foot and square at the Riviera site, Jefferson Co., Missouri; (e) St. Louis Riverfront footprints, St. Louis, Missouri; (f) foot with mace and two circular depressions, Donnell site, Jefferson County, Missouri.

panel at Maddin Creek that portrays the "twins" or "brothers" and an upside down (dead?) larger figure (giant?) (Fig. 4.7a). The bilobed arrow, a hafted celt, a serpent, and a vulva motif all co-occur within this panel. A major Missouri petroglyph site, Washington State Park B, includes a foot with a "handle" (foot-mace?) and several other foot petroglyphs (Fig. 4.7b). On the bluffs of the Mississippi River are two unusual footlike carvings: one foot at the Anheuser site showing another possible "handle" (Fig. 4.7c) and a crude foot in conjunction with a square at the Riviera site (Fig. 4.7d). The St. Louis Riverfront footprints (Fig. 4.7e) and the Donnell site foot and mace (Fig. 4.7f) are just two of many examples.

Pit and Groove. The pit and groove motif is so widely found in the rock-art record that it cannot be considered unique to Missouri or to the SECC. Nevertheless, it is mentioned here because it frequently appears along with SECC iconography in Missouri (e.g., Figs. 4.8a and b, Three Hills Creek and Bushnell Ceremonial Cave). As a widespread motif (or element) it has been

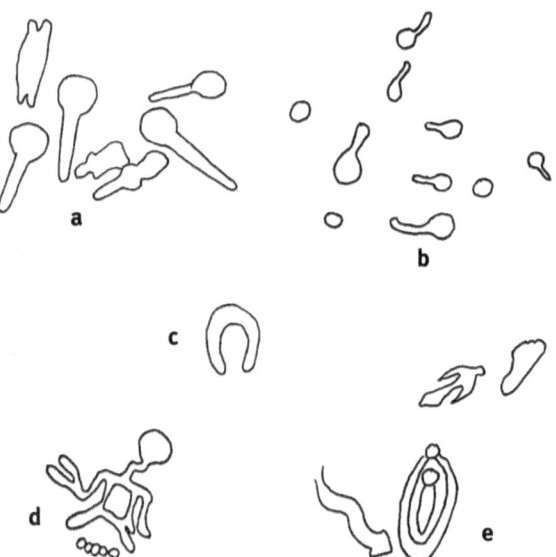

FIGURE 4.8. Pit and groove: (a) Three Hills Creek site, St. Francois/Washington Co., Missouri; (b) Bushnell Ceremonial Cave site, Ste. Genevieve Co., Missouri; (c) typical vulva form found in Missouri rock carvings; (d) possible Deer Woman figure at Maddin Creek site, Washington Co., Missouri; (e) serpent, vulva, bird at Washington State Park A, Washington Co., Missouri.

interpreted as either a phallic or vulva form and alternately as a possible celestial image.

Vulva Form. The other anthropomorphic signifier is the vulva, another motif that was not considered part of the 1945 list of fifty-one SECC traits. Again, this motif may be a regional variation in the SECC but is evident mainly at sites on the west side of the Mississippi River. This may signify the western/sunset/death connection to the "Old Woman" deity. Missouri's rock-art includes a variety of vulva forms, but the most prevalent is the "U-shaped" or "horseshoe-shaped" motif (Fig. 4.8c). Its frequent use indicates its significance. One of the most interesting usages occurs at the Maddin Creek site. This depiction shows a figure with an obvious "deer hoof" for a hand—the deer hoof, which is also "U-shaped," is a version of the vulva form. This could very well be a signifier to indicate Deer Woman or the Old-Woman-Who-Never-Dies undergoing a transformation into Deer Woman (Fig. 4.8d) and birthing her progeny in the form of several small ovals.

At times the vulva is portrayed in conjunction with a bird or a foot or with serpents and at some sites bears "traditional" SECC iconography (e.g., the Maddin Creek and Washington State Park petroglyphs). What could be considered a "shorthand" grouping in Missouri rock-art is the juxtaposition of vulva, serpent, and bird (Fig. 4.8e). These figures may represent the Old Woman/Earth; her husband, the Great Serpent or "Grandfather Snake"; and her firstborn son, "Hawk" (or Birdman). The iconography of this grouping combines the earth/Middle World/Lower World with the Upper World powers, a potentially potent tool in uniting clans of diverse origins.

Circles/Concentric Circles. The circle, alone or with other motifs, is the most frequently portrayed geometric form in Missouri rock-art. It is represented as concentric circles, the cross-in-circle, the petaloid (or rayed) cross-in-concentric circles, the dot-in-circle, and circle chains. The Frumet site, on a river bluff, has two of the most impressive circle motifs: a dot-in-circle and two concentric circles, both in red pigment (Fig. 4.9a). A large and impressive dot-in-circle rendered in red pigment is depicted at Picture Cave (Fig. 4.9b). A small dot-in-circle petroglyph is still evident at the Bushberg-Meissner site on the Mississippi riverbank (Fig. 4.9c) and concentric circles along with the cross-in-circle motifs are found at Bushnell Ceremonial Cave (Fig. 4.9d), both in southeastern Missouri. Burns refers to the dot-in-circle motif as the

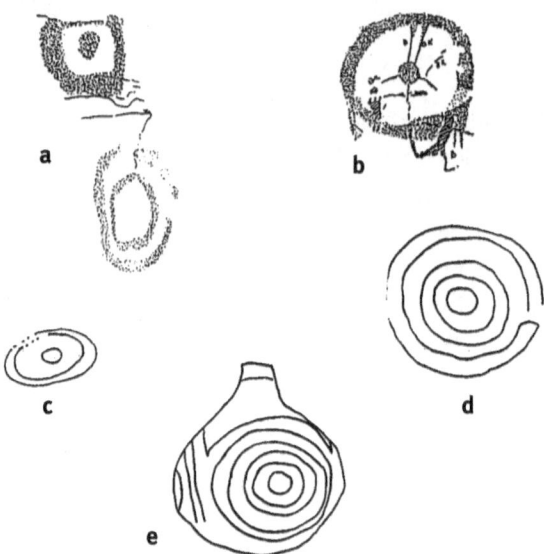

FIGURE 4.9. Dot-in-circle: (a) Frumet site, Jefferson Co., Missouri; (b) Picture Cave, eastern Missouri; (c) Bushberg-Meissner site, Jefferson County, Missouri; (d) Bushnell Ceremonial Cave, Ste. Genevieve Co., Missouri; (e) vessel, Perry Co., Arkansas.

Isolated or Sacred Earth (Burns 1994:13–14, 18). This motif was used by the Osage into the late nineteenth and early twentieth centuries as a symbol for the Isolated or Sacred Earth Clans. Other examples are found on pottery vessels (e.g., Fig. 4.9e, from Perry Co., Arkansas).

Cross-in-Circle and Spinning Cross-in-Circle. The cross-in-circle is present in materials from Cahokia, Spiro, Etowah, and Moundville, although not so common at the latter location. A petaloid cross-in-circle is carved into a boulder at Maddin Creek and appears in conjunction with a variety of bilobed arrows, feet, an ogee, vulva forms, a hafted celt, and cupules (Fig. 4.10). (This boulder is discussed throughout this chapter because of its major iconographic and diagnostic motifs. For a discussion of the petaloid motif, see Reilly 2007c.) Although the basic cross-in-circle appears to cover a long time-span, it is definitely viewed as part of SECC iconography and is depicted frequently in Missouri rock-art. The most typical form is the cross-in-circle and the cross in two concentric circles (Fig. 4.11a), two motifs prevalent on Spiro shell cups from Oklahoma, spider gorgets from southeast Missouri, and

EARLY MANIFESTATIONS IN ROCK-ART

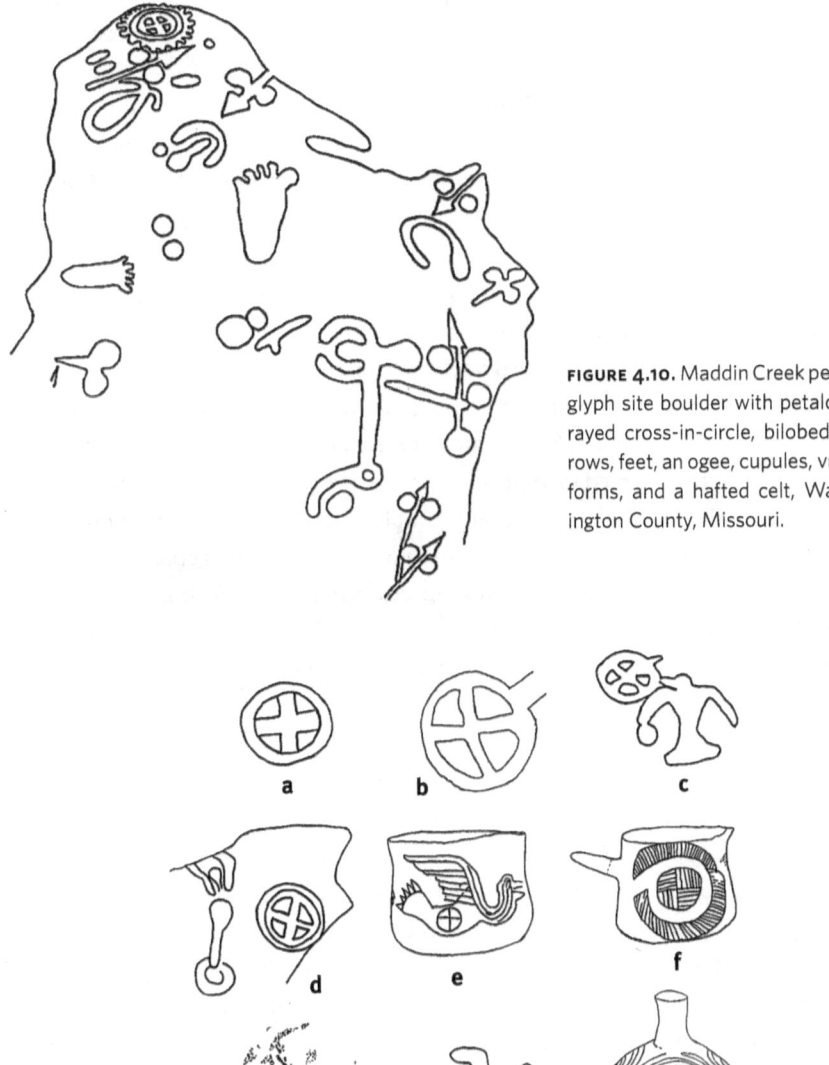

FIGURE 4.10. Maddin Creek petroglyph site boulder with petaloid/rayed cross-in-circle, bilobed arrows, feet, an ogee, cupules, vulva forms, and a hafted celt, Washington County, Missouri.

FIGURE 4.11. Cross-in-circle: (a) typical form seen on Spiro shell cups, Missouri spider gorgets, and gorgets from Georgia, Tennessee, and other areas; (b) Bushnell Ceremonial Cave site, Ste. Genevieve Co., southeast Missouri; (c, d) Three Hills Creek site, St. Francois/Washington Co., Missouri; (e) pottery vessel, Fulton Co., Illinois; (f) Cahokia beaker, western Illinois; (g) Lost Creek site, Washington Co., Missouri; (h) Bushberg-Meissner site, Jefferson Co., Missouri; (i) pottery vessel, Lee Co., Arkansas.

gorgets from Georgia, Tennessee, and other regions. Examples can be seen at Bushnell Ceremonial Cave (Fig. 4.11b) and at several other Missouri rock-art sites.

The frequent appearance of the cross-in-circle motif within the assemblage of SECC icons makes it important when searching for comparisons. The motif is not always a simple cross or a single circle but often a cross within a double concentric circle, rendering it more compelling and complex. That is, it contains a number of elements: vertical line, horizontal line, inner circle, and outer circle. One of the most prominent panels at the Three Hills Creek site in Missouri portrays a bird with a cross-in-circle in or at its beak (Fig. 4.11c). The cross-in-circle coupled with an Upper World figure (in this case a bird) strengthens the statement being made that relates these locatives to upper levels of the cosmos. This example appears to encode a reference to the "son of the Sun"—the avian representing the Hawk/son and the sun circle representing the Sun/father. Another example at this site (Fig. 4.11d) couples the motif with the vulva form and pit and groove, bringing together the Sun/father and the Earth/mother. The cross-in-circle in both forms is seen on pottery vessels (e.g., Fig. 4.11e, from Fulton County, Illinois). One of the variations on this basic motif is portrayed on the clay beaker found at Cahokia (Fig. 4.11f).

This motif in its "spinning" form within a circle or two concentric circles figures prominently at Moundville in the Carthage-style copper pendants and gorgets as well as on the Hemphill pottery. In Missouri it is depicted in red pigment on the outer ceiling at the Lost Creek Shelter (Fig. 4.11g). This is the only known "spinning cross-in-circle" currently known in Missouri rock-art, although a simple spinning cross sans circle ("swastika") motif (Fig. 4.11h) is found at the Bushberg-Meissner site. This same "spinning cross" is portrayed on pottery (Fig. 4.11i) in its various forms as well as on shellwork at Spiro (Phillips and Brown 1978). A spinning cross sans circle is seen on the back of the neck of a "Cat Monster" pottery vessel from Crittenden County, Arkansas.

In the extreme southeastern corner of the Missouri boot-heel are a cluster of Nodena-like Late Mississippian sites that date from AD 1400–1700 (Morse and Morse 1983; Morse 1990). Earlier work by Williams (1980) had assigned the designation "Armorel Phase" to three of these sites. Williams also used "Markala Horizon" to indicate that these sites were the latest Mississippian occupations and that they extended into the historic period, as early trade objects of European origin and were found in situ with Late Mississippian burial goods of Native manufacture. Many of these items display the spinning-cross motif.

The ubiquitous engraved Bell Plain ware with Water Spirit imagery and elaborate spinning or swirling cross motifs bears a striking similarity to late Moundville (O'Brien 1994). The catalogue of the Leo Anderson collection, primarily pieces from Pemiscot County in southeast Missouri (Price and Price 1979), records evidence of fragments of Moundville disk palettes with notched rims, at least one of which is engraved. The presence of palettes (disks) along with "Path of Souls" imagery engraved on Bell Plain bottles with flattened spherical bodies and flaring necks with beveled inner rims is a signature of these sites. One incised short-necked bottle from southeast Missouri in the Harold Mohrman collection has the double or court-card avian motif incised on the body (Howard 1968:46).

A survey of several excavated collections from the Berry, Campbell, and Kersey sites in Pemiscot County indicates that flattened drilled spatulate objects and plentiful amounts of marine shell ornaments similar to Moundville and shell "mask" gorgets are present during the Late Mississippian period in the Pemiscot Bayou area. Furthermore, the presence of Walls Engraved vessels with spinning crosses, Piasas (water spirits), and avian "bead spitters" in court-card symmetry indicates that the Armorel Phase sites in Pemiscot County, Missouri, share significant similarities with the Moundville iconography.

Mace. The mace is represented in cultural items at Spiro, Etowah, and Moundville and in Missouri rock-art. Cahokia has not been excavated in enough strategic localities to produce sufficient material along this line. The mace is common in eastern Missouri rock-art. A classic mace is present in the Washington State Park petroglyphs (Fig. 4.12a). The mace also occurs in the raised hand of the Dancing Warrior at Rattlesnake Bluff (Fig. 4.12b). In one of the earliest dated depictions (Picture Cave, AD 1025) a mace is carried by two different celestial beings. The maces of the Black Warrior and the "Giant" (Fig. 4.12c) are both remarkably similar to examples from Spiro (Hamilton 1952:Pls. 35–39, 41) (Fig. 4.12d). Another can be seen at the Willenberg Shelter (Fig. 4.12e). Similar mace forms are found on the Douglass Gorget (Fig. 4.12f) from New Madrid County, Missouri, on a gorget from Castalian Springs, Tennessee (Fig. 4.12g), and on one of the Rogan Plates (Fig. 4.12h). Whether they are cosmological signifiers (Douglass Gorget) or imperative

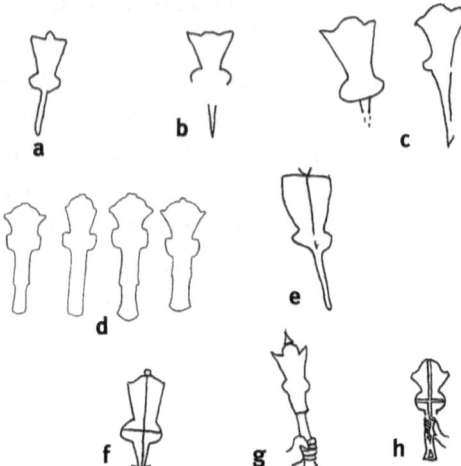

FIGURE 4.12. Mace: (a) Washington State Park B, Washington Co., Missouri; (b) Rattlesnake Bluff site, Franklin Co., Missouri; (c) Picture Cave, eastern Missouri; (d) Spiro (Hamilton 1952:Pls. 36–39, 41); (e) Willenburg Shelter, Franklin Co., Missouri; (f) Douglass Gorget (detail), New Madrid Co., southeastern Missouri; (g) gorget (detail) from Castalian Springs, Tennessee; (h) Rogan Plate (detail), Etowah, Georgia.

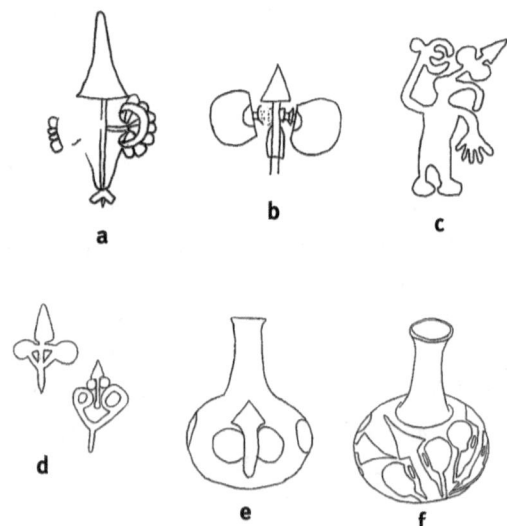

FIGURE 4.13. Bilobed arrow: (a) Willoughby Disk, Moundville, Alabama; (b) shell cup from Spiro, eastern Oklahoma; (c) Maddin Creek site, Washington Co., Missouri; (d) on boulder, Maddin Creek site, Washington Co., Missouri; (e) pottery vessel, Lee Co., Arkansas; (f) pottery vessel, Tunica, Mississippi (see also Fig. 4.1c).

to a triumphant warrior's stance (Rogan Plate, Dancing Warrior, Black Warrior), they are remarkably uniform in appearance from eastern Missouri into northwestern Georgia (Etowah).

Bilobed Arrow. The bilobed arrow is present on the Willoughby Disk from Moundville (Fig. 4.13a), on shell cups from Spiro (e.g., Fig. 4.13b), and at Etowah on both of the Rogan Plates (Fig. 4.1a and b). At Maddin Creek the complex panel with the "Twins" and Giant portrays one of the twins with the bilobed arrow in his hair (Fig. 4.13c). The figure also sports a "ponytail" that could represent his red or blue "horn" or braid. This braid is comparable to the "red horn/braid" on the "Resting Warrior" figure (pipe) from the Craig Mound at the Spiro site in Oklahoma as well as the braid on each of the Rogan Plates. Curiously, the bilobed arrow on one of the Rogan Plates from Etowah is topped with a plume or tassel, as are some of the bilobed arrows on the shell cups from Spiro—a distance of roughly 700 miles. Phillips and Brown (1978) recognized several similarities between the two sites.

The only known pictograph in Missouri of a bilobed arrow rendered in red pigment is at the Lost Creek site (Fig. 4.1c). A Maddin Creek boulder depicts two additional bilobed arrows (Fig. 4.13d) similar to those on the Spiro shell cups, while one of the Maddin Creek boulders previously discussed displays a number of bilobed arrows of a different style (see Fig. 4.10) in conjunction with the petaloid cross-in-circle, an ogee, two feet, and a hafted celt. An obviously significant motif, bilobed arrows are also depicted on pottery vessels (Fig. 4.13e and f), in copper repoussé cutouts, and on portable stone items.

Ogee. The ogee has a wide distribution in the Eastern Woodlands (Phillips and Brown 1978:153–154). The ogee can be one sided but is most typically two sided (Fig. 4.14a, b, d, g, h). The ogee is present in the Carthage-style copper pendants from Moundville (Fig. 4.14b) and on a disk from Arkansas County, Arkansas (Fig. 4.14d). A rock-art example is found at the Peene-Murat site (Fig. 4.14c) in Missouri. A looped ogee (Fig. 4.14e) that co-occurs with bilobed arrows, a petaloid cross-in-circle, and feet at the Maddin Creek site (see Fig. 4.10) is similar to the eye surround on the diorite waterfowl/serpent bowl (Fig. 4.14f) from Moundville. In this case the double play of the serpent-bird iconography probably suggests the transmigration between two cosmic levels. On the Maddin Creek boulder, combined with the bilobed arrows (a Morning Star/Hawk motif) and sun circle (Father/First Man

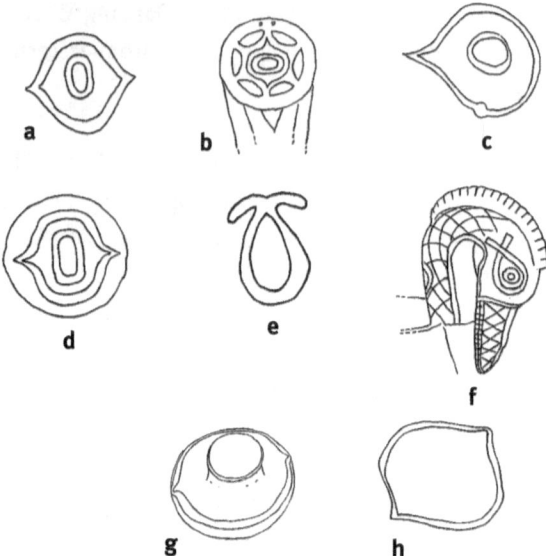

FIGURE 4.14. Ogee: (a) Spiro (Phillips and Brown 1978:154); (b) copper pendant, Moundville, Alabama; (c) Peene-Murat petroglyph site, Gasconade Co, Missouri; (d) disk from Arkansas Co., Arkansas; (e) Maddin Creek site, Washington Co., Missouri; (f) diorite bowl from Moundville with looped hawk eye-surround/ogee; (g, h) vessels, Pemiscot County, southeastern Missouri.

motif), it appears as a cryptic encoded message denoting father/son, Upper World, or other chiefly matters.

In some examples, depictions of the ogee bring to mind a version of the vulva form and might serve as a metaphor for a portal. The ogee becomes a prevalent feature in Late Mississippian ceramics in the Pemiscot County area in southeast Missouri. The ogee is modeled on the shoulder of short-necked Bell Plain jars with flattened globular bodies and on other clay vessels from southeast Missouri. The circular opening serves as the "pupil" of the eye (Fig. 4.14g). The ogee appears on Classic Braden shell work and may be represented on the "Resting Warrior" forehead plaque.

Underwater Spirit. Various Moundville pieces represent the Underwater Spirit (aka Cat Monster) in its many forms. One example is the winged, horned serpent with the triple eye-surround that is seen on Hemphill-style pottery in Alabama. This supernatural being is represented in pottery in southeast Missouri (Fig. 4.15a) and northern Arkansas, both on the surface and molded into the rim (Fig. 4.15b), and in Mississippi (Fig. 4.15c) in an artistically different style. In the Missouri boot-heel, Water Spirit imagery occurs on gourdlike hooded bottles. The most spectacular examples are the Sikeston variety of negative-painted quadruped bottles, long thought to be "dogs" but now recognized as Underwater Spirits. Another version of the Underwater Spirit is seen in the fire-clay Birger Figurine from Illinois (Fig. 4.15d with face detail) and on shell cups from Spiro, Oklahoma. A classic rendering at Picture Cave (Fig. 4.15e) shows a stylistic (possibly temporal) difference from the Hemphill "winged-toothed-antlered" serpent (Fig. 4.15f). A number of Missouri sites have less elaborate versions of this long-tailed being, either carved (Fig. 4.15g) or painted (Fig. 4.15h).

FIGURE 4.15. (a) Underwater Spirit/Cat Monster pottery vessel, Pemiscot Co., southeastern Missouri; (b) pottery vessel, Blytheville, Arkansas; (c) pottery vessel, Coahoma County, Mississippi; (d) Underwater Spirit on Birger Figurine (and serpent face detail), Illinois; (e) Underwater Spirit at Picture Cave, eastern Missouri; (f) Underwater Spirit as the "winged-toothed-antlered serpent" on Hemphill-style pottery, Moundville, Alabama; (g) Long-tail at Thousand Hills State Park site, Adair Co., Missouri; (h) Long-tail at Deer Run Shelter, St. Francis Co., southeastern Missouri.

Summary and Discussion

If we compare some of the outstanding SECC/MIIS iconography-laden examples from the major mound sites, such as those found on the Rogan Plates (Fig. 4.1a and b), the Moundville copper pendants, and the Spiro shell cups with the motif co-occurrences in Missouri rock-art, we can discern how they work together—or at least see that they do work together. That is, they were purposely juxtaposed. It is obvious that two or more of these interacting motifs are used as a symbolic "shorthand" within the rock-art to imply a greater meaning than just the parts portrayed. The most notable examples (as previously discussed) are the two groupings at Maddin Creek (the Twins and Giant in Fig. 4.7a and the petaloid sun circle and bilobed arrows in Fig. 4.10). Other examples include the mace and foot, bird and vulva form, foot and bilobed arrow, and bird and cross-in-circle.

These repeated motif combinations unquestionably had symbolic significance during the Mississippian period and perhaps also earlier in the Woodland period. The bilobed arrow and mace, being two of the major attributes of the Hawk Being (or "Birdman"), belong primarily to the Upper World realm of the cosmos. When these two motifs are combined with the ogee, they may signify a celestial journey, the eye and eye-in-hand being associated with the portal to another level of the cosmos or "Path of Souls" (Lankford 2004:212–213). The hafted celt is connected to warfare and the feet to the brave warrior (Hawk Being) deeds referenced in the ethnographies. Although the precise meaning or intent may be unknown, we can be fairly certain of the significance of the component parts repeated in the rock-art multiple times across a broad territory and can certainly fathom their probable meanings (as discussed earlier) from the available ethnographic literature.

By analyzing the co-occurrences and variations found in the rock-art motifs, we can infer the meanings encoded in these symbols. It appears to be a mixing of Late Woodland, Middle Mississippian, and Oneota iconography in the Middle Mississippi Valley region. This does not come as a surprise, because this riparian landscape was surely marked by a trafficking of exotic goods, information, technologies, and oral traditions from many points north, south, east, and west over an extended period. In addition, I believe that the material under examination has its origins in early Dhegihan culture, on the basis of content. The Dhegihan Sioux language was spoken by the cognate tribes of the Osage, Omaha, Ponca, Kansa (Kaw), and Quapaw.

The Osage and Quapaw/Arkansas were the first tribes of this major linguistic group known to be encountered in this region. At that time the Osage were in control of the better part of four contiguous states and were assuredly not newcomers to the region. They were most likely descendants of the proto-Dhegihan groups that constructed, thrived at, and eventually abandoned nearby Cahokia (Diaz-Granados 1993; Duncan and Diaz-Granados 2000; Diaz-Granados and Duncan 2004).

There is a movement of SECC symbols (e.g., Birdman/Hawk Being, Piasas/Underwater Spirit, bilobed arrows, feet) from north to south and from east to west and west to east. The corpus of significant artifacts bearing the elite symbolism characteristic of the Cahokia subarea at the confluence seems to begin a southward migration just before AD 1200. We see a burst of rock-art along the eastern Ozark highlands and a dramatic increase in SECC/MIIS symbols. During this florescence and complexity in the rock-art, many of the adjacent mound sites were increasing in size. Sacred objects such as marine shell gorgets and copper plates in the Braden style appear in the grave goods at Mississippian centers south of Cahokia in the southeast quadrant of Missouri, the same area in which the bulk of the rock-art sites occur. Several sites west of Sikeston Ridge (e.g., the Powers site) show abandonment and burning, and the inhabitants exhibiting a Caddoan ceramic tradition also appear to have been pushed westward.

In spite of the regional variation, the predominant motifs and their associated oral traditions have apparently persisted through centuries in their various forms. It stands to reason that motifs serving as mnemonic devices for oral traditions (which is the case in at least some rock-art panels) were handed down for numerous generations. The symbols delineate specific characters who appear in widespread oral traditions of epic proportion. This is evident in much of the ethnographic material from the Southeast, Midwest, and Eastern Plains. Several common themes appear to link the icons with the oral traditions in this great expanse, once again with regional variations, as would be expected. An example of the lasting importance and strength of this system is the western Mississippian or proto-Dhegihan peoples, who are on record as still using some of these symbols (such as the long-nose, mace, eye, woodpecker, hand, and serpent) well into the late nineteenth and early twentieth centuries.

As the possible epicenter of this collection of narratives and its accompanying iconography and artifact assemblages, I would single out the region surrounding the confluence of the Missouri and Mississippi Rivers, surely the most important prehistoric crossroads in North America. The concentration of rock-art, evidence of in situ ritual activity, and employment of powerful and/or sacred motifs support this assertion.

According to Jeffrey Brain and Philip Phillips (1996:339), "evidence of direct Etowah-Moundville contact is notably sparse." While this may be true on the surface, this seeming disparity may be a matter of different industries, intent, or purpose—with Moundville's concentration on Lower World matters and Etowah's on the Upper World—and not necessarily evidence of lack of contact or intercourse. The relative abundance of SECC motifs at Picture Cave (such as maces in conjunction with turbans and trailers, red sashes, falconid eye-markings, figures with occipital hair-knots, and a large single upright feather, all within an interval dating from AD 940 +/-80 to 1090 +/-90; see Diaz-Granados et al. 2001) is notable and connects this site on various levels with the outlying mound centers. In addition, it connects these SECC/MIIS icons with the earliest known dates for these objects in the eastern United States. This information should be included in any search for the origins of the SECC/MIIS, although two obvious motifs are absent at Picture Cave: the bilobed arrow and the cross-in-circle. This in itself has special meaning. This rock-art imagery is relatively new information that was unavailable to Waring and Holder, Howard, Brain and Phillips, and others. In addition, the congruency of the early five-date cluster for the Picture Cave panels strengthens the argument for a Middle Mississippi Valley genesis of the iconography and its associated ceremonialism.

In conclusion, this body of SECC/MIIS icons does not appear to be spatially static or confined to a particularly limited time frame; it was part of a strong but understandably evolving system of symbols used for message transfer and social and economic control by the ruling factions. This social and economic system was obviously expanding, along with accompanying rites and rituals needed to establish kinship and economic ties with neighboring groups (for example, see Duncan and Diaz-Granados 2000). Aside from regional stylistic variations within the iconography, many of these motifs that no doubt accompanied the oral traditions had great longevity. These symbols are repeated in numerous artifacts over a wide expanse and support the manifestation of a pantheon of characters with a rich and lasting set of oral traditions—major narratives. Several common themes link the icons with the oral traditions in this large interaction sphere (again with obvious regional variations, as reflected in the diversity of motifs and co-occurrences). Although the grouping of icons at rock-art sites may not be considered a "writing system," it was unquestionably a shorthand system of communication for another time. It is our job to continue to recognize and identify the regional variations, determine how and why icons are grouped, and explore their connection to the ethnographic literature.

AUTHOR'S ACKNOWLEDGMENTS: I would like to acknowledge Professor F. Kent Reilly III, for his acute awareness of the importance of the iconography found in rock-art and its relation to the iconography in all other types of cultural materials. I am grateful to Dr. Reilly for his ongoing leadership and pioneering efforts in the elucidation of American Indian iconography as well as his support of my ongoing research. I would also like to thank Jim Duncan for reading this manuscript and for his valuable input, George Lankford for the initial editing of this manuscript, and Jim Garber and F. Kent Reilly for their editing and comments on various drafts.

REGIONAL STUDIES:
LOWER MISSISSIPPI VALLEY

CHAPTER 5
Mississippian Ceramic Art in the Lower Mississippi Valley
A Thematic Overview
David H. Dye

The potters, as Griffin is fond of saying, unaware that archaeologists were going to feel strongly about the individuality of these designs, mixed them up in all possible combinations.
PHILIP PHILLIPS, *Archaeological Survey in the Lower Yazoo Basin, Mississippi, 1949–1955* (1970: 44)

Over the years discussions of Mississippian iconographic art have focused on figural images portrayed in marine shell and copper. Since the earliest discussions of late prehistoric art, the Lower Mississippi Valley has been largely excluded from these dialogues despite the great wealth of ceramic art. Waring and Holder (1945), for example, dismissed the Lower Mississippi Valley from their considerations of Mississippian ceremonialism because ceramics were not considered a meaningful component of cultic sacra.

The Mississippi Valley has been neglected in these discussions for two primary reasons. First, representational art forms such as engraved shell gorgets and cups, symbolic weaponry, and repoussé copper are only sporadically present in comparison to the great artistic centers such as Etowah, Moundville, and Spiro, which have produced impressive works of art. The impetus for the emergence of regional art styles is now thought to have had its origins in the Classic Braden world, a canonical art style with an ancient tradition in the Midwest (Brown 2004). The Mississippi Valley is believed to have been out of the loop in the great exchange systems.

Second, the Lower Mississippi Valley's surviving artwork is limited almost wholly to ceramic art forms, rather than the figural works in copper, flint, and marine shell. Archaeologists generally regard ceramics as culinary ware rather than as utilitarian ritual pottery. Recently researchers have emphasized ceramic vessels in terms of their political and ideological roles and not their economic uses (Blitz 1993; Pauketat and Emerson 1991; Rees 1997). But the fact remains that pottery is perceived by most researchers as easily reproduced and unrestricted. As a prominent Mississippi Valley archaeologist said several years ago, the Lower Mississippi Valley was a watered-down version of the classic Mississippian art centers of Etowah, Moundville, and Spiro.

A regional approach reveals that the Lower Mississippi Valley is not lacking in Mississippian art of its own but was connected to the Classic Braden world for at least five hundred years. Motifs and themes of ceramic art in the Lower Mississippi Valley reflect a basic and profound articulation with other regions. Many of the most basic Mississippian religious motifs are emphasized repeatedly on ceramics, underscoring the use of pottery in rituals of life, death, and world renewal.

A veritable explosion of ceramic art took place in the Eastern Woodlands in general, and the northern portion of the Lower Mississippi Valley (LMV) in particular, at the beginning of the thirteenth century AD. Ceramic crafting achieved new and innovative dimensions in the Crowley's Ridge Lowlands of northeastern Arkansas, southeastern Missouri, and the adjacent Mississippi alluvial valley of northwestern Mississippi, western Tennessee, and western Kentucky. Mississippian ceramics evolved over some six hundred years; unlike other Mississippian areas, LMV potters maintained a high level of crafting from initial beginnings well into the seventeenth century. The various ceramic forms include a number of decorative motifs and vessel shapes that changed over time, providing significant temporal markers and evidence of great artistic innovations and traditions. Yet a general conservatism existed in the basic artistic themes, furthering a long tradition in the use of ritually significant motifs in ceramic art.

The guiding premise of this chapter is that much of the Mississippian ceramic art in the LMV is an assemblage of forms and motifs created for and used by ritual practitioners. This "utilitarian ritual ware" (Emerson 1989:65) appears to have been restricted to a set of privileged or perhaps elite individuals with varying degrees of elevated rank and status over their neighbors. Several lines of evidence support this contention. First is the pervasive evidence for the use of many of the fineware vessel forms, especially modeled (i.e., effigies), painted, engraved, incised, and appliquéd bottles and bowls. Basal abrasion, lip chipping, rim damage, general body wear and breakage, and interior encrustation all point to extensive and intensive vessel use. Jars, on the other hand, do appear to have been used for mundane cooking, but their use for ritual preparations is not obviated by their otherwise domestic tasks. Second, the surface treatment of the vessels goes far beyond mere decoration: their embellishment includes highly charged symbolic and metaphoric images, motifs, and themes that reference Other World conceptions. That is, many vessels have been modeled, painted, incised, engraved, or appliquéd for purposes that far exceed any economic or dietary functions. Third, the skill level in crafting suggests that the manufacture of fineware or at least the application of the symbolic imagery was limited to persons who possessed the requisite skills and perhaps "owned" the motifs. Fourth, the context of the vessels underscores the restricted use of fineware. Where scientific excavations have taken place, the spatially demarcated nature of the ceramics is evident. For example, C. Andrew Buchner (2003:100) notes: "During the 3MS599 Middle Mississippian occupation, the use of these rare ceramic types is fairly restricted and we propose that these decorated vessels were the possessions of a local elite family that lived in the walled Structure 1 compound and performed communal rites and ceremonies with other households nearby (but outside their compound)."

Fineware vessels would have been interred with the ritual practitioners upon their death. Such an individual would be a member of a small privileged or elite family/lineage segment or sodality of a village or town. At any one time in a village, ritual vessels would be limited in number and restricted to elite compounds and charnel house or ancestor shrine contexts. Thus fineware served the purposes demanded by ritual concerns rather than displaying "decoration" for aesthetic interests. In fact, rather than being merely "decorated," fineware ceramics represent a microcosm of the Mississippian world.

The northern portion of the Lower Mississippi Valley was one of the most densely occupied regions of the Eastern Woodlands during the Mississippian period. Bounded on the west by the Ozark Plateau and on the east by the loess bluffs, the villages and towns of the LMV were primarily confined to natural levees along meander lakes, although some sites were located on the lower slopes of Crowley's Ridge and along the bluff tops at the margins of the great alluvial valley.

Perhaps the earliest attempt to categorize ceramics in the Mississippi Valley was by William Henry Holmes (1885, 1886b, 1903), whose outstanding classification of late prehistoric pottery from the LMV set the tone for much future research. Holmes worked for the Smithsonian Institution and classified large public holdings of whole Mississippian ceramic vessels from the Eastern Woodlands into five spatially discrete units (Holmes 1903). His classificatory work helped set the stage for typological developments for future researchers and was a major substantive contribution, because it laid the groundwork of archaeological knowledge for ceramics for a large part of eastern North America (Willey and Sabloff 1993:87). Holmes was as much a master draftsman and artist as he was an archaeologist and illustrated as well as classified the large quantity of vessels. He observed that certain pottery types had specific geographical and distributional correlates, which allowed him to group them into spatially discrete entities. The ability to place ceramic vessels into meaningful blocks of time was still in the future.

Holmes worked primarily with a large ceramic collection housed at the Davenport Museum which had been collected earlier in the nineteenth century by Wilfred P. Hall, who had excavated large numbers of vessels from the LMV (Griffin 1981). Holmes defined several pottery regions within eastern North America and in so doing went beyond previous studies by discerning stylistic differences in ceramic designs and forms to create spatial units for whole vessels. His Middle Mississippian region therefore was based on a distinctive set of attributes. He delineated geographical-cultural variation, based on the classification of ceramics, into a systematic comparative perspective. His work was instrumental in the "culture area" formulations of other anthropologists (Willey and Sabloff 1993:87).

Based in part on the earlier work by Holmes and contemporary studies in ceramic classification, Philip Phillips organized large assemblages of whole ceramic vessels. Building on the work of Holmes, Phillips (1939) too had assembled a large corpus of ceramic vessels from the Lower Mississippi Valley, primarily through his photography of public and private holdings.

Phillips's ceramic analysis culminated in the landmark development of a series of types and varieties based in part on whole vessels whenever possible (Phillips 1970). The type Carson Red on Buff, for example, was based mainly on whole vessels (Phillips 1970:62). Phillips wished to develop a methodology that would create a classification system in which "types, varieties, and modes are vehicles for the expression of cultural and historical relationships" (Phillips 1970:23).

As was the case with archaeology in general in the mid-twentieth century, Phillips believed potsherds were not going "to tell us very much about cultural and social behavior" (Phillips 1970:23), but his classification system provided future researchers with the organizational framework which allowed them to compare varying ceramic sets through time and space over a wide geographic region in the Lower Mississippi Valley. His main purpose was "to enable comparisons to be made with other complexes" (Phillips 1970:36). Phillips cautioned future archaeologists: "Whether we can go so far as to predict that ultimately, having performed their function in analysis, types and varieties will wither away, is another question. It is at least a possibility, and perhaps a further reason for not taking them too seriously" (Phillips 1970:36).

In following Phillips's advice and in an attempt to move away from the type-variety concept, recent researchers in the LMV have sought an attribute-based approach to ceramics in order to record and compare stylistic variation of whole ceramic vessels (Brown 2005; Mainfort 1999; Tavaszi 2004). Such studies attempt to go beyond the traditional type-variety method proposed by Phillips in order to allow a more detailed intra-assemblage and inter-assemblage analysis than typological approaches provide. Their approach is more in line with Holmes's earlier methodology of using specific attributes to identify ceramic assemblages and their spatial extent. The attribute methodology is more sophisticated and nuanced in methods and analytical techniques and operates at the assemblage level.

Maria Tavaszi outlines the shortcomings of the type variety system: one jar, if broken, "would produce sherds that could be called Mississippi Plain, Kent Incised, Barton Incised, and Ranch Incised." She notes that the "attribute approach used here reveals that an additional 65% (n = 128) of the vessels that would normally be classified as plainwares . . . have additional stylistic elements that are anything but plain" (Tavaszi 2004:90). "Whole vessel analysis offers superior data with which to examine temporal and spatial variation" (Tavaszi 2004:3). It should be noted that both Holmes (1885, 1886b, 1903) and Phillips (1939, 1970) embraced the concept of basing their analyses on the study of whole vessels. Phillips in particular was well aware of the shortcomings of types and varieties, including multiple types being found in one vessel.

Lankford has recently pointed out that ceramic complexes in the LMV do not belong to a single ceramic complex but rather represent a concentration of art forms which do not observe boundaries. The concentration of art forms in the LMV "appears to be a center of a distribution pattern that ranges far beyond the valley itself" (Lankford 2006:1). He notes: "Southwestern contacts in the Southeast happened several times over the course of several centuries, which argues for some long-term functioning of a trade network from the Southwest at least as far as the Mississippi Valley" (Lankford 2006:19).

In this chapter I provide a brief thematic overview of ceramic art in the northern portion of the Lower Mississippi Valley in order to examine various art forms through time. After I studied Mississippian ceramics for two decades, visited museum collections, photographed ceramics from numerous sites, and worked with archaeologists, several themes began to emerge. One of the keys to understanding thematic issues rests on looking at overall trends. Such an emphasis on ceramic traditions differs from a perspective that looks at ceramic change over a relatively short time-span. For example, Morse and Morse (1990) identify three ceramic horizons in the LMV (Varney, Beaker, and Matthews), which emphasizes the limited life span or duration of specific ceramic types. Use of the type variety system contributes to the sense of short ceramic life spans, as one type comes into being while a related or similar type declines. Archaeologists of necessity must break up blocks of time in order to gain control over finer temporal increments for assessing culture change. Yet the emphasis on finer and finer temporal divisions leads to difficulty in defining themes in ceramic art which exist over relatively long periods. While types and varieties are based on stylistic elements and motifs to some extent, the methodology prevents analysis on the scale of motifs and themes in ceramic art.

In order to stress the decorative elements and emphasize broad spatial patterns, I have avoided using type and phase names. In presenting such a brief and generalized view of the LMV ceramic complexes, a certain amount of specificity and accuracy will undoubtedly be sacrificed. My emphasis is on the major ceramic motifs and themes revealed by an examination of large blocks of time.

Ceramic Art in the LMV

From AD 400 to 700, prior to the emergence of Mississippian culture, LMV potters made large grog-tempered or sand-tempered jars with round bases for domestic purposes. Surface finishes were plain, red slipped, or impressed by paddles wrapped with cordage, nets, or fabrics. In general, fabric-marking predominated to the south, while cord-marked pottery was localized to the northern area (Morse and Morse 1996b).

Substantial social, political, and technological changes took place in the LMV around AD 800 to 850, with the emergence of Mississippian culture in northeast Arkansas and southeast Missouri (Morse and Morse 1989, 1996a,

1996b, 2000). No developmental phase is evident in northeast Arkansas, prompting Morse and Morse to suggest that the inhabitants of the Zebree site, for example, may have emigrated from elsewhere, such as the Portage Open Bay area of southeast Missouri, which has a Mississippian developmental sequence (Morse and Morse 2000:351). The Zebree inhabitants appear to have brought with them ideas about maize-based horticulture and a variety of other innovations, which may have had their ultimate source in the Cahokia area via southeast Missouri (Kelly 1991). Rituals associated with corn agriculture and new social arrangements also may have been introduced, which required specific ceramic assemblages that emphasized a transformed cosmological order.

Shell-tempered pottery became widespread by AD 800, originating in the LMV. By AD 800–900 major changes in pottery technology took place in connection with other technological and social changes of the ninth and tenth centuries (Morse and Morse 1996a:11). Stronger and lighter vessels could be constructed with the new tempering agent and ceramic vessels could easily be modified into a variety of forms, including effigies. Shell-tempered pottery was a true technological breakthrough in ceramic production and would give rise to a series of innovative and distinctive pottery horizons and traditions.

The proximity of Cahokia may have been a significant and widespread influence on LMV populations. In comparing Cahokia and northeast Arkansas, Morse and Morse (2000:353) note: "Mutual trade and knowledge between these two districts or regions manifest themselves in the ideas, artifacts, and raw material shared by both." These shared traits include the "bow and arrow, house type, discoidal, hooded bottle shape, bone harpoon, microlithic industry, pottery disc, and elbow pipe form" in addition to the use of imported cherts (including hoes and other bifaces) and the exchange of conch shell from sites in the American Bottom, perhaps Cahokia itself (Morse and Morse 2000:353).

Mississippian culture in the LMV developed earliest in the Cairo Lowland of southeast Missouri, perhaps stimulated by its close proximity to Cahokia, located in the American Bottom across the Mississippi River from modern-day St. Louis. The American Bottom and the Cairo Lowland are connected by a 275-km narrow riverine corridor of the Mississippi River. Morse and Morse (1983:216) note early cultural connections between the Cairo Lowland and Cahokia. Triangular projectile point forms and several pottery varieties, especially red filming and incising on non-shell-tempered pastes, are a few of the shared characteristics. In addition, Burlington and Crescent Quarries cherts appear on these early Mississippian sites, along with copper.

To the south of southeastern Missouri at the northeastern Arkansas Zebree site, Morse and Morse (1983) found several connections with Cahokia. Perhaps the most significant association is the shell bead industry and associated tool assemblage. Conch shell beads were manufactured in local households by drilling imported conch shells with microlithic tools similar to those at Cahokia. Cherts used in bead drilling came from the Crescent Quarries located 35 km southwest of the Cahokia area. Presumably a long-standing trade existed in conch shells and drilling and grinding tools. Morse and Morse note:

> There are artifact similarities to Cahokia in the Central Valley, but to date only a few artifacts possibly manufactured at Cahokia have been recovered. Yet contact with, knowledge of, and trade with the Central Valley was certainly involved. In addition, there probably was a basic linguistic relationship. (Morse and Morse 1983:238)

The close ceramic associations with Cahokia are seen at the Zebree site, with its burnished, red-slipped vessels, including everted-rim, flat-based, globular jars without handles, large shallow salt pans, hooded bottles, juice presses, and simple bowls. Although ceramic assemblages in the LMV are variable, plain and red filmed pottery dominated many of the ceramic assemblages, with red-filmed ceramics constituting the major diagnostic horizon marker for the ninth and tenth centuries. Morse and Morse (1990:156–157, 2000) term the widespread use of red filming the Varney Horizon. Salt pans and large jars, in addition to smaller vessels, have unpolished interior red-filmed surfaces, while small vessels with constricted orifices have unpolished exterior red-filmed surfaces. The paint for red filming was derived from red ocher obtained from the Ozark Highlands sources of ironstone concretions and hematite. Red ocher may have been a major trade item for the LMV (Morse and Morse 2000:351).

Vessels had little variation in shape but did vary in size; jars, bowls, pans, hooded bottles, and funnels were not embellished apart from red filming. Effigy forms were apparently not made. Salt pans and pottery funnels were used in salt manufacture by soaking American lotus (*Nelumbo lutea*) and then evaporating the water in order to retrieve the salt residue.

By approximately AD 1000 small clusters of Mississippian settlements were spread throughout the Mississippi Valley from about modern-day Memphis to St. Louis. A great deal of ceramic innovation occurred in a relatively short time, based on changes in pottery assemblages. Red filming begins to decrease quickly as a new ceramic assemblage appears: small burnished jars with loop or riveted jar handles, long-straight-necked bottles with flat bases, beakers, and beaker-shaped bowls with rim effigies. The new suite of ceramic fineware may represent a reorientation in ritual that emphasizes mortuary ceremonialism. Morse and Morse (1983:246) note: "Death is apparently this society's major excuse for ceremonial gathering."

Morse and Morse (1990:157–158) term this spatially widespread set of ceramics the Beaker Horizon and place it between AD 1000/1050 and 1150. Bottles, beakers, and bowls may be polished, painted, or incised. Polished, narrow-rim plates were incised with line-filled alternating triangles on the rims. Rim effigies of bowls often include birds or human heads, and handles sometimes are shaped as frogs and bird talons. Jars have high prominent shoulders with continuous undulating lines running around the shoulder of the vessel. Long-necked bottles often have dimple bases and angular shoulders. In addition to ceramic vessels, painted conch shells, used as cups, have been reported.

Sherds representing vessels exchanged from distant areas have been found in twelfth-century contexts, underscoring the matrix of exchange networks. For example, in the John's Lake area trade vessels from the Lower St. Francis Basin to the south and Cahokia to the north have been found. The Cahokia Ramey Incised jar and a local copy had forked eye motifs running along the rim. As Buchner (2003:174) notes, "The presence of a SECC item in a discrete nonhabitation mortuary area is indicative of increasing complexity with the local community, and participation in the regional ideological system."

These Ramey Incised jars were traded widely as an exchange item and subsequently imitated in local contexts. Timothy Pauketat and Thomas Emerson (1991:924) write: "The dispersal of these American Bottom vessels ... or simply the spread of the vessel style itself no doubt was related to Mississippian political centralization and the enlarged exchange networks of the Mississippian elite."

Morse and Morse (1983:241) believe these innovations were "restricted primarily to the development of a ceremonial ware." Similar beakers were crafted at Cahokia as early as AD 1000, but it must have been the rituals and ideas which diffused into the LMV, as the LMV beakers are of local manufacture; few trade beakers have been found. The beaker appears to have functioned as a ceremonial drinking vessel (Morse and Morse 1996a:15, 2000:354), and the ceramic assemblage in general appears to have been used for mortuary libation ceremonies (Morse and Morse 1983:246). A similar beaker from the Crable site in Illinois illustrates a crested bird that has a cross-and-circle associated with it, perhaps denoting an early form of figural art which emphasizes the Above World (Hathcock 1988:53).

In one example, a beaker capping a bottle suggests that the two vessels were used together, the beaker being used to consume the contents of the bottle (Morse and Morse 1983:Fig. 4f). Burial associations further indicate that beakers were special vessels used for rituals in which libation was critical. Beakers consistently occur with bottles, bowls, and small jars as burial associations. The burials are normally sets of bundled, disarticulated bones rather than articulated skeletons, suggesting that they were curated until the proper time for burial had arrived. Such rites of intensification "are calendrically based, community-focused rites that play a critical role in the resolution of cosmological discontinuities in the annual ritual sequence" (Pauketat and Emerson 1991:919).

Perhaps the libation was cooked in jars, poured into bottles, and in turn poured into the bowls or beakers from which it was consumed, a pattern of ritual medicine preparation and consumption with a long tradition in the Eastern Woodlands. I have suggested elsewhere that bottles may have been used in the preparation of ritual medicines and served to transform the cooked "medicines" into a sacred drink; thus the motifs which embellished the bottles were important ritual transformational elements (Dye 2007).

Many of these eleventh- and twelfth-century sites were burial mound clusters with little if any resident population. The vacant ritual center often included mounds in varying states of use, including a council house, a bundle burial storage/charnel house, and a mound burial chamber (Morse and Morse 1996a:15). The settlement pattern was a set of dispersed farmsteads and small villages ritually connected to the vacant mortuary centers.

Ceremonial centers postdating AD 1150 reveal evidence of residential debris, suggesting that dispersed populations were beginning to move into the mound precincts and transforming them into central places which then had to be protected through fortification. These fortified ritual villages continued to be surrounded by hamlets and farmsteads (Morse and Morse 1989, 1996a:18, 2000:355). Apparently, the contents of the ritual centers were the items to be protected and not the social labor of the populations. Whatever was being protected could be taken or destroyed by enemy raiders. Evidence from slightly later suggests that a major object in warfare was the appropriation or destruction of one's enemies sacra and connections with the Other World (Dye and King 2008).

With the transformation of the vacant religious centers into fortified villages with a core resident population, rituals once again began to change, including a concomitant decline in beakers, narrow-rim plates, and jars with loop and riveted handles (Payne 2007). Beakers drop out of the ceramic assemblage altogether, while over time plate rims widen and jars begin to be incised on the shoulders with running arches or chevron motifs. Also present are large, red-slipped jars without appendages and line-filled triangles and rectilinear motifs placed on the upper surface of plate rims. Fine paste ceramics, appearing as Varney red filming declined, were favored for special and more elaborate serving and special-purpose vessels (Buchner 2003).

Morse and Morse (1990:158) have termed the AD 1200–1400 period the Matthews Horizon and note that it was a time of great change. The braided stream surfaces of the western St. Francis Valley were abandoned, and populations increasingly nucleated in the meander belt surfaces of the eastern St. Francis Valley.

During the period AD 1200–1250 incising continues on the rims of plain, red-filmed, negative-painted, and incised plates. Similar plates were being made by potters throughout the Midwest and Mid-South at this time. Earlier plates tend to have narrower rims and later plates have wider rims (Orr 1951). Red-slipped vessels and incised vessels occur in roughly the same proportion (Wesler 1991).

Jars continue into the thirteenth century and exhibit a variety of motifs on the shoulders and rims, including running or continuous incised arches, meanders, and undulating, curvilinear, or rectilinear guilloche lines. In some examples, punctations accompanied the lines on the jar's shoulder (Fig. 5.1). The fourteenth century witnessed the appearance of new rim treatments, including notches and nodes. The standard plate begins to replace the narrow rim plate, but the proportion of incised vessels now exceeds that of red-slipped vessels. The increasing rarity of red-slipped pottery is illustrative of a widely noted regional pattern whereby red slipping gradually drops out of the later Mississippian decorative repertoire (Wesler 1991). After mid-century strap handles dominate jars and are often decorated with double nodes, ridges, or grooves. Beakers and plates are rare but do occur as a minority ware. Plates typically are deep, with wide rims.

Surface treatments and motifs emerge in the fourteenth century that eventually dominate the ceramic assemblages of the following centuries (Buchner 2003; Payne 2007). Although running incised meanders were the primary jar motif, jars with line-filled triangular, crosshatched, and other linear patterns on the rims were also found in small numbers. Likewise, the primary painted bottles were red on buff (Fig. 5.2), while red and white bottles were a minority ware. Engraved bottles begin to appear in small numbers. Vessel shapes include standard jars, narrow rim and standard plates, narrow-necked, carafe-necked, and hooded bottles, bowls, funnels, and pans. Appendages consist of grooved strap handles, bifurcated lugs, and a small number of loop handles.

Centering and alternating of motifs represents an ancient principle in the Southeast, especially in the Coles Creek Culture to the south and southwest of the LMV. Thirteenth- and fourteenth-century motifs include interlocking scrolls, ogees, sunbursts, cross-in-circles, nested triangles and circles, and alternating terraces that are often painted, incised, or engraved. Figural art emphasizes the Great Serpent (Fig. 5.3), while modeled vessels generally depict females seated in highly stylized positions. The female effigies appear to represent residents of the Beneath World, such as Old-Woman-Who-Never-Dies (Fig. 5.4).

Negative painting is almost a horizon marker of the thirteenth and fourteenth centuries. Negative-painted plates throughout much of the Midwest and Mid-South "have a consistent, recurrent design theme; they are representations of the cross-in-circle and sun circle motifs" (Hilgeman 2000:191). The content of the plate rim designs (the cross-in-circles and sun circles) strongly suggests that they are ritually significant motifs. The plate layouts and accompanying motifs link the vessels to the Southeastern "fire-sun-deity complex" (Waring 1968b:33) and, by extension, to the New Fire and Green Corn ceremonies or other similar local rituals. Sherri Hilgeman documents a shift from rayed, sun-circle layouts on narrower rim standard plates to cruciform or cross-in-circle layouts on wider-rimmed deep rim plates (Hilgeman

CERAMIC ART: A THEMATIC OVERVIEW

FIGURE 5.1. Jar with incised arches and punctations, Mississippi Co., Arkansas. Photograph © David H. Dye.

FIGURE 5.2. Red on buff painted bottle, Poinsett Co., Arkansas. Photograph © David H. Dye.

FIGURE 5.3. "Great Serpent" bowl, Mississippi Co., Arkansas. Photograph © David H. Dye.

FIGURE 5.4. "Old-Woman-Who-Never-Dies" bottle, Crittenden Co., Arkansas. Photograph © David H. Dye.

2000:202). She suggests the plates were made and fired by a potter and then painted by a part-time ritual specialist (Hilgeman 2000:202). As grave goods they may have been interred with the specialists as mortuary accompaniments to the Other World.

Around AD 1400 a number of changes once again begin to take place. Jars with continuous or running curvilinear or rectilinear motifs on the shoulders or rims begin to be replaced by jars with bands of repeating line-filled triangles, perhaps a carryover from the plates which had line-filled triangles on the rims. Jar bodies begin to be covered with punctations.

Deep-rim incised plates with wide rims are diagnostic of the period AD 1300–1450, but sometime in the early fifteenth century incised plate forms and funnels disappear from the ceramic assemblages. Red and white painted bottles and bowls replace red on buff bottles in popularity (Fig. 5.5), but red on buff decorations continue into the historic period. Alternating red and white triskeles, swastikas, and multiple line spirals were painted on bowls, bottles, and effigy forms made with a fine shell-tempered paste (Fig. 5.6). In addition to triskele and swastika scrolls, alternating and reversed terraces, alternating vertical panels and stripes, and interlocking meanders are found on bottles, including effigies (Phillips 1970). These motifs are also commonly incised and engraved on a variety of vessel forms as well as being painted.

Open bowls now exhibit rim notching, and fine shell-tempered pottery is found in higher frequencies. Around AD 1450 jars are also incised with interlocking scrolls, which at this point become a major artistic theme running through all vessel forms and surface treatments.

Although effigies have been an important component of the ritual ceramic repertoire, many more forms are added to the inventory beginning in the fourteenth century. They embrace a wide variety of forms, including alligator, anhinga, animal, basket, bat, bear, beaver, bird, buffalo horn, canoe, cat monster, corn, corn god, crawfish, deer, dog, duck, fish, frog, goose, gourd or squash, hawk, human, mace, opossum, otter, owl, rabbit, serpent, shell, shell univalve, turkey, turtle, underwater monster, unidentified animal, unknown, whelk shell, and zoomorph (Brown 2005:Table 7.1; Hathcock 1988; Phillips 1939; Tavaszi 2004). These writers placed some of the names in quotation marks, while others were prefaced by "possible." Anyone who has examined LMV effigies undoubtedly comes to the same conclusion; many if not most of the vessels are impossible to identify in terms of the world as we know it. The reason for the great difficulty in assigning modern scientific biological

FIGURE 5.5. Red and white painted bottle, Cross Co., Arkansas. Photograph © David H. Dye.

FIGURE 5.6. Effigy bowl, Lee Co., Arkansas. Photograph © David H. Dye.

nomenclature to the vast range of effigy forms is that the notions of representation resided in the artists' minds and not in the natural world. The natural world was the template for various effigies in many cases, but in general they represented beings of another world and not this one.

During the period AD 1450–1550 parallel incising on jars becomes the vogue as jars in general incorporate new handle elements: triangular strap and appliqué handles and vertical appliqué handles (Fig. 5.7). Rims of bottles, jars, and bowls exhibit beveled interiors. Gadrooned bottles continue in popularity (Fig. 5.8).

FIGURE 5.7. Jar with vertical appliqué handles, Mississippi Co., Arkansas. Photograph © David H. Dye.

FIGURE 5.8. Gadrooned bottle, Mississippi Co., Arkansas. Photograph © David H. Dye.

In the mid-sixteenth century appliquéd strips are applied to the bodies of standard jars, while the same effect is given to the bodies of bottles through gadrooning. Thin, long clay strips are also applied vertically to the necks of bottles as well as jars and helmet-shaped jars or bowls. Large jars at this time occasionally serve as burial urns, a widespread characteristic of late sixteenth-century cultures, especially in south-central Alabama.

By the mid-seventeenth century a decline takes place in the types of ritual vessels (Mainfort 2001, 2004). Appliqué, with punctations on the clay strips, is placed on the necks and shoulders of helmet-shaped bowls/jars, parallel incisions and nodes are added to standard jars, and engraving represents the last element of the rich ritual ceramic sets in the LMV.

Between approximately 1560 and 1580 a major drought took place (Stahle, Cleveland, and Hehr 1985; Stahle et al. 2000), which "essentially destroyed the existing regional ecosystem" (Mainfort 2004:7). The devastating drought brought about a lack of sustainability for LMV inhabitants (Fisher-Carroll 2001). When French explorers visited the LMV in the late seventeenth century, the valley was virtually depopulated.

Summary

Polities in circumscribed river valleys, such as the Etowah and Black Warrior River Valleys, enabled consolidation of neighboring groups and the appropriation of social labor and surplus food as tribute. For example, Moundville had consolidated its neighbors by AD 1250 for a distance of 40 km along the Black Warrior Valley. In the lower portion of the Northern Mississippi Valley, on the other hand, incorporation of adjoining local groups would have been more difficult, as neighbors had a greater number of allies with which to ally themselves in order to fend off aggressive polities. With the resulting lack of political complexity, highly skilled crafting in workshops would have been limited. Likewise, access to marine shell, symbolic weapons, and copper would have been difficult to obtain through long-distance exchange routes. George Sabo (1993:208) notes that sixteenth-century political organization in the northern portion of the Lower Mississippi Valley was characterized by "independent hereditary lineage societies" in which "competition . . . seems to have been endemic." This type of lineage organization would have lacked the ability for neighboring groups to consolidate effectively. The resulting implication is that utilitarian ritual ware would become the foundation for endless ritual feasting among political groups engaged in endless internecine rivalries and factional competition.

AUTHOR'S ACKNOWLEDGMENTS: I am indebted to George Lankford for his helpful comments on an earlier draft of this chapter. I thank Kent Reilly for his leadership and organization of the Texas State University Iconography Workshop. My ideas on the subjects of Mississippian art have benefited from the enlightening experience of the workshop and from discussions with the workshop members. And to the volume editors, George Lankford, Kent Reilly, and Jim Garber, I offer my appreciation for their invitation to contribute. All errors, of course, are mine alone.

CHAPTER 6

The Great Serpent in the Lower Mississippi Valley

F. Kent Reilly III

In the Late Mississippian period (AD 1400–1541) certain specialized pottery vessels produced in the Lower Mississippi Valley (LMV) were either sculpted or incised with an interesting array of zoomorphic figures. Such zoomorphic imagery is entirely lacking in the abstract designs on Ramey Incised pottery produced at Cahokia during an earlier period. Prominent among these zoomorphic images is a series of winged serpents, although the serpent imagery is not limited to winged creatures. These winged serpents from the LMV are undoubtedly related in some way to the winged serpent imagery found on the somewhat earlier (AD 1300–1450) Moundville Engraved, *var. Hemphill* pottery (Steponaitis and Knight 2004); certainly, even an initial examination offers evidence that these engraved vessels from Moundville are at least stylistically related to winged serpent images from the LMV (Childs and McNutt 2002). A more detailed study, however, reveals many stylistic differences between the genres. Visually, their basic design consists of U-shaped snakelike bodies, equipped with rattlesnake "buttons" on their tails. Although the heads of these winged serpents show some variety, most have snarling visages and sharp fangs. Their heads are usually topped with antlers, with some notable exceptions. The wings of this supernatural creature consist of a wingbar with clothlike feathers attached, again with variation in their construction. These differences in winged serpent renditions are further heightened by the fact that the LMV supernaturals are often shown with groupings of secondary images while Moundville's winged serpent imagery is accompanied by no other symbols or motifs.

Without question, the winged serpents from both Moundville and the LMV represent the same Great Serpent that seems ubiquitous in the Native American ideological systems of eastern North America (Lankford 2004, 2007d; Smith 1995). The focus of this chapter is to demonstrate that—while the Moundville winged serpents inhabit the sky realm exclusively—the LMV winged serpents can be identified by their respective specific secondary symbols as inhabiting the watery Beneath World just as often as they travel in the celestial realm of the Above World.

Cosmology and the Great Serpent

Archaeological, ethnographic, and art-historical studies clearly reveal that the Native Americans of the Eastern Woodlands viewed themselves as inhabiting a multileveled cosmos. Although the number of cosmic levels varied somewhat from group to group, the most common view was that the cosmos consisted of at least three levels: the Above World, the Beneath World, and the Earthly Plane (Lankford 2004, 2007d; Reilly 2004). An axis connected these three realms, often in the form of a prominent feature on the landscape such as a sacred mountain or tree. This axis could also exist as a ritual fire or sacred pole. The cosmos itself was animated and inhabited by groups of beings in each level. Thus many Native Americans viewed their world as a "peopled cosmos," even if some of its inhabitants were "other than human persons" (Smith 1995:43–63). Some groups (such as the Muskhogeans) saw the sky realm as a stony bowl that rose and fell at the horizon. Others (including the Osage, Omaha, and Anishnaabeg/Ojibwa) interpreted the setting sun and the approach of night as the Beneath World rotating up into the night sky (see Chapter 2). George Lankford has convincingly proposed that the location of the Great Serpent within the night sky corresponds to the constellation Scorpio (Lankford 2004, 2007d). Functioning within this nocturnal celestial location, the Great Serpent serves as guardian of the "Path of Souls" or Milky Way (Lankford 2007a). Along this "Road of Light" the souls of the dead journey to the Great Serpent's "Realm of the Dead."

The Great Serpent not only dwelt in the Beneath World as the master of beneath and underwater creatures but reigned as Lord of the Realm of the Dead. This powerful supernatural presence was envisioned as a netherworld being who could assume the form of a Great Panther. With its elongated tail, this Great Panther could roil the waters of lakes, rivers, and ponds into whirlpools and thus caused many deaths among humankind. Nevertheless, this fearsome creature's power could help an individual courageous enough to seek and channel it.

The Archaeology of Symbols

As Mary Nooter Roberts and Allen F. Roberts have discussed in their study of Luba art and iconography (Roberts and Roberts 1996), symbols and their contextual placement on objects can serve as mnemonic devices that cue storytelling memory. Thus such motifs aid the renewal of myth, ritual, and even history in nonliterate societies. Likewise, the placement of Great Serpent imagery on specific vessel forms (often bottles in the LMV) assuredly functioned to manifest a supernatural power that otherwise could not be seen. Imagery could, for example, have identified a vessel as containing special substances, sacred contents, or perhaps ritual "medicine" used in ceremonies in which the Great Serpent acted as the major supernatural. These symbols would then have triggered memory on a cosmic scale, much as on a more pedestrian level the "Rx" symbol and instructions on the label of a prescribed medication alert a patient today to the contents of a small orange plastic bottle. The image of the Great Serpent on a pottery vessel very well may have identified the medicine it contained, while linking it with specific rituals that this supernatural controlled.

In a different interpretation of this imagery, Vernon J. Knight has proposed that such "monstrous" images as the Great Serpent functioned not only as communicative symbols but also as the instruments through which elites enhanced their political power by controlling esoteric knowledge (Knight 1989). He further argues that the encoding of images such as the Great Serpent is just as likely to be an effort to mystify and render hermetic a specific aspect of esoteric knowledge through symbolism obscure to the uninitiated. By manipulating such imagery, the elites ritually institutionalize their control. The deliberate effort to obscure symbolism through the visualization of fearsome monsters heightens the power of the ritual practitioners who can manipulate and control such signs. Perhaps expressions of identification, education, and control of esoterica were not mutually exclusive and were integral to the totality of Great Serpent imagery.

The Great Serpent and Moundville

Located in west-central Alabama on the Black Warrior River, Moundville is the second largest Mississippian site, after Cahokia. Between AD 1250 and

1500 Moundville was a major center of artistic and craft production (Knight and Steponaitis 1998; Steponaitis and Knight 2004). Upon the many stone, copper, and clay items created at Moundville, winged serpent imagery plays a prominent role. Great Serpent or winged serpent symbolism at Moundville first occurs as imagery engraved on Hemphill pottery. Hemphill engraved ceramics are associated closely with a burial cult that manifested itself in the late Moundville II phase, ca. AD 1350–1400. A number of scholars (Gillies 1998; Lacefield 1995; Schatte 1997; Steponaitis 1983; Wimberly 1956) have ascertained that the most common shapes for Hemphill engraved vessels are cylindrical bowls and subglobular bottles.

Thematically, Hemphill engraved pottery bears a range of motifs that include winged serpents with U-shaped bodies (Fig. 6.1c). To date, Kevin Schatte (1997) has conducted the most thorough exploration of Great Serpent or winged serpent imagery at Moundville. He found that all but two of the Hemphill vessels bearing winged serpent imagery were subglobular in form (Schatte 1997:8). In a computer analysis of the styles in which winged serpent imagery manifested itself, Schatte also determined that winged serpents fell into ten separate stylistic groupings, each characterized by differences in body decoration and head and wing formation as well as in eye surrounds and other markings. These ten identifiable style groups may represent different functions within the corpus of winged serpent ideology.

If this analysis ultimately proves true, each of Schatte's groupings may function in a manner comparable to the imagery and ideology of the Virgin Mary within the practice of Roman Catholicism. Different images of Mary carry distinctive motifs or markings. These distinguish the Virgin of Guadalupe from Our Lady of Carmel from Our Lady of the Sacred Heart. Each category of symbolic motifs forms a subset within the iconography of the cult of the Virgin Mary. Although all essentially represent the Virgin Mary, each possesses a slightly different ideological function within the overall cult and logically stimulates the recollection of particular narratives or events. The groupings that Schatte identifies, however, may also suggest the presence of an individual workshop or *taller* at Moundville, wherein a master ceramic artist supervised others who were producing winged serpent imagery. Yet each artist may have incorporated a personal artistic "signature" into the finished images. Many of the subglobular bottles, for example, carry pairs of winged serpents (Fig. 6.1d). Close examination of these engraved supernaturals

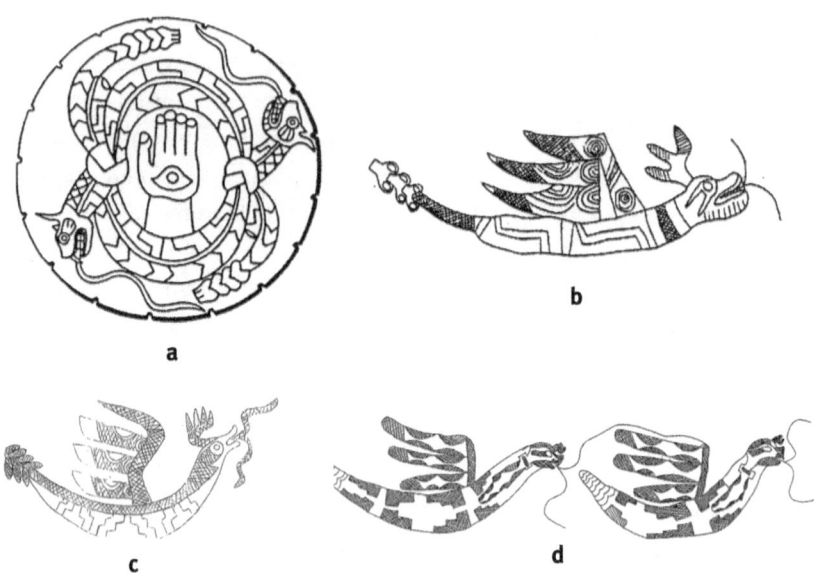

FIGURE 6.1. Rattlesnakes: (a) Rattlesnake Disk, drawn from a rubbing by Barbara Page (Phillips and Brown 1978:Fig. 208); (b) subglobular bottle with engraved Moundville winged serpent, drawing by F. Kent Reilly III; (c) incised U-shaped winged serpent on Bell Polished bowl from the Beck Plantation, drawing by Terry Childs; (d) two winged serpents on subglobular bottle from Beck Plantation, drawing by Marcia Taylor.

reveals that each member in a pair is virtually identical to the other, suggesting the deliberate replication of the same winged serpent on opposite sides of the bottle (Steponaitis, personal communication, 2007).

As mentioned above, Lankford associates the winged serpent and other motifs engraved on Hemphill pottery with the broader theme of the celestial Path of Souls (Lankford 2004, 2007b). The wings in this imagery serve as symbolic locatives, which are elements that identify the location where an episode or event is occurring within the context of a larger work of art. Lankford argues that the function of the wing within the corpus of winged serpent imagery is to signal that this composite being exists as a serpent in the sky realm (Lankford 2007a). Hemphill engraved pottery excavated at Moundville shows signs of use, which strongly suggests that these vessels were not solely intended as grave goods. Perhaps containing sacred medicine, they were used in a variety of rituals that emphasized the ideology of the Path of Souls. Indeed, at Moundville Hemphill pottery with its engraved motifs may have functioned as an analog to the Book of the Dead in other cultures. In this hypothesis, each Hemphill vessel contained powerful medicine that would assist the soul of the deceased on the path to overcome the tribulations that the supernatural entity engraved on the bottle represents.

Within the corpus of Moundville winged serpent imagery on Hemphill engraved pottery, each winged serpent bears no other locative than its own wing. As we will see, this single locative construction contrasts with the Great Serpent imagery, winged or wingless, that the LMV artisans produced during the same period on their engraved pottery.

The LMV in the Middle Mississippian Period

The LMV extends south on both sides of the Mississippi River from southern Illinois and Missouri to the mouth of the Arkansas River (O'Brien and Dunnell 1998). One of the most intensely studied archaeological areas, the LMV contains hundreds of sites that produced both a range of pottery types and an ever-expanding pottery type variations corpus (Childs 1993; Phillips et al. 1951). Artistically, one of the finest types is the Walls Engraved, though many striking unengraved pots, such as the Rhodes and O'Byam types, also are found (Childs 1993; Dye 1998). Archaeological excavations reveal that the LMV possessed one of the highest population densities in the Eastern Woodlands during the Middle and Late Mississippian periods. Population density undoubtedly led to geographically smaller polities than those in other areas. Excavations in some areas around Memphis, Tennessee, reveal that the Mississippian-period population was so dense that it now is difficult to determine where one village left off and another began (Dye, personal communication, 2002). As Chet Walker has described, the LMV area was home to several remarkable traditions of sculpted, painted, and engraved pottery (Walker 2004).

Serpents and the Art of the LMV

Both engraved and incised depictions of serpents, winged or not, figure prominently in the LMV artistic corpus. As Terry Childs (1993) has suggested, this level of variation suggests the presence of individual workshops at LMV sites such as Belle Meade and Beck in Arkansas and Campbell and Berry in the "boot-heel" area of Missouri. One striking pair of wingless serpents is engraved on a beaker from the Kersey site (Pemiscot Co., Missouri) (Fig. 6.2a and b). In this instance, the intertwined bodies of two serpents create an aperture that ordinarily would be vacant space. Here, however, the anticipated vacant space encloses a four-armed swirl motif, a symbol that Lankford has identified as marking the underwater Beneath World (Lankford 2004). Accepting his analysis as correct, I also suggest that in some instances the appearance of this motif signals the watery Beneath World in its aspect as the night sky. Certainly the overall composition of the Kersey beaker is highly reminiscent of that on one of the stone palettes at Moundville, the well-known Rattlesnake Disk (Fig. 6.1a). Both works of art bear the intertwined bodies of two serpents, specifically rattlesnakes, that form negative spaces that may very well designate portals. Given that the Rattlesnake Disk portal encircles the hand-and-eye motif, a known celestial marker (Lankford 2007a), while the Kersey site beaker bears a rattlesnake-framed portal through which the swirl-cross motif emerges, we have a thematically consistent though stylistically different set of objects marking the Beneath World or more generally promising transition from one realm to another.

The Kersey vessel is not the only example of LMV ceramics bearing rattlesnakes in a shape that strongly suggests the ogee. Several other vessels from the Bradley and Rose sites in northeastern Arkansas bear an ogee surrounding the neck of a vessel: when a substance is poured from the vessel's spout, it is also passing through the ogee (Fig. 6.2c). In at least two instances, overlapping rattlesnakes surround the vessel spout as substitutes for the ogee with equivalent symbolic significance. On one of these examples, from Richardson Landing (Tipton Co., Tennessee), the rattlesnakes defining the ogee have, instead of rattles, motifs resembling war clubs or maces (Fig. 6.2d; Dye, personal communication, 2007). Thus, according to the long-established opinion of Roy Hathcock, the origin of the ogee itself is an "objective abstract version of entwined rattlesnakes" (Hathcock 1988:Fig. 160). Recently, however, Robert Sharp has suggested that the snake-ogee connection also derives from a natural prototype: the specific body markings of the copperhead, three species of which cover the entire Southeastern region in which ogees have been found (Sharp 2007).

LMV winged serpent representations do superficially resemble their Moundville counterparts. Two such images incised on two separate vessels from the Beck Plantation (Crittenden Co., Arkansas), for example, recall their Moundville counterparts. The first, executed on a Bell Polished flat-bottomed

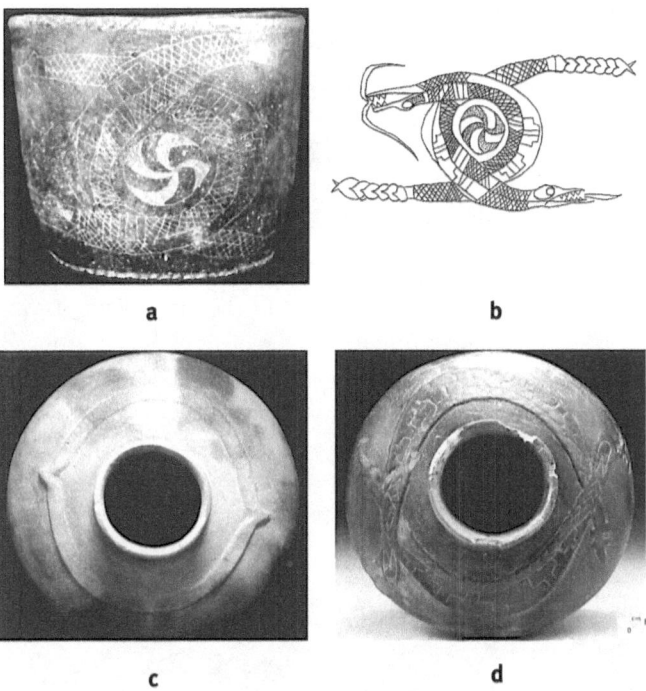

FIGURE 6.2. (a) Incised beaker from the Kersey site (from Hathcock 1988:Pl. 144); (b) incised intertwined serpents from the Kersey site beaker, drawing by F. Kent Reilly III; (c) subglobular vessel with encircling ogee from the Bradley site, photograph by David H. Dye; (d) subglobular vessel with entwined rattlesnake ogee from Richardson Landing, photograph by David H. Dye.

bowl with flaring walls and a rope rim, depicts a U-shaped winged serpent (Fig. 6.1c). This figure has unusually dense cross-hatching, yet its wing construction appears less complex than that of Moundville winged serpents. The second vessel from Beck Plantation, a subglobular bottle not unlike pieces from Moundville, features a pair of identical U-shaped winged serpents (Fig. 6.1d). As often as not, LMV winged serpents are equipped with clawed feet. In contrast to the artisans of the Moundville corpus, LMV potters and artisans produced images of the Great Serpent in its feline aspect. This particular depiction appears incised on beakers as well as on large open-mouthed bowls with three-dimensional images of the Underwater Panther, using his elongated tail to adorn the rim. LMV potters also incised frontal images of the Underwater Panther on long flared-neck vessels. One such bowl from the

Berry site (Pemiscot Co., Missouri) not only bears this frontal image (Fig. 6.3a and b) but also has a raised, low-relief depiction of a serpent—perhaps the Great Serpent variant of the Underwater Panther—that serves as the vessel's base (Fig. 6.3c and d).

Eye Surrounds Functioning as Locatives

Interestingly, the Great Serpent and its Underwater Panther variant are equipped with distinctive eye surrounds. In the symbolism of LMV art, eye surrounds in some instances function as locatives. The two-pronged eye surrounds that have been said to identify supernaturals located in the sky also function that way in the symbolism of the LMV (Brown 2007b:85; Reilly

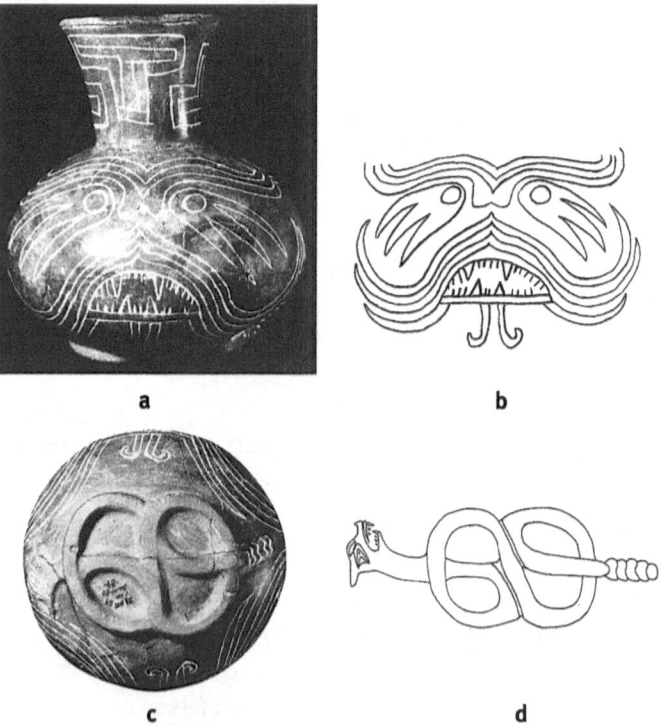

FIGURE 6.3. (a) Incised Underwater Panther on long flared-neck vessel from the Berry site, photograph by David H. Dye; (b) drawing of the Berry site vessel by Terry Childs; (c) bottom of the Berry site vessel, photograph by David H. Dye; (d) drawing of the Berry site vessel by Jack Johnson.

2004:130), while three or four-pronged eye surrounds mark supernaturals located in the watery Beneath World (Reilly 2004:130). This certainly appears to be true of the imagery of the engraved bottle from the Berry site (see Fig. 6.3). The frontal Underwater Panther has a three-pronged eye surround, while the Great Serpent variant uses a double-pronged eye surround, rather than the wing motif, to identify its location in the Above World or celestial realm.

Distinctive LMV Winged Serpent Representations

According to Childs (personal communication, 2009), two of the best-known LMV winged serpent representations come from the Pecan Point area in southeast Mississippi Co., Arkansas (Childs 1993; Perino 1960). The example now in the Hampson Museum is from the Pecan Point site, Arkansas (3MS78). The better-known Pecan Point or Perino vessel (Fig. 6.4a, b) is in the Gilcrease Museum but was recovered from the Friend's Mound (3MS6) in Arkansas (Phillips and Brown 1978:200). Like other renditions of this preternatural image, the Gilcrease Museum example shows two differentiated paired figures. The bodies of these two supernaturals are not U-shaped, however, and their bellies are bowed and equipped with clawed feet. The eye surround closely resembles the eye surround on all of the three winged serpents from the Beck Plantation ceramic corpus. Another distinctive trait of this object is that it depicts the winged serpents in both frontal and profile views. The foot of the vessel on which these images are depicted is incised with what must surely be a symbolic locative: a series of concentric circles divided into eight portions by radiating lines (Fig. 6.4c). In the middle of this construction, which resembles a spiderweb, the potter has placed a swirl-cross motif. On the basis of the evidence presented thus far, the swirl-cross motif is signaling the viewer to understand that this winged serpent lies in the watery underworld, perhaps in its function as the night sky (Reilly 2004; see Chapter 2).

One rather crudely incised vessel from the Parkin site (Cross Co., Arkansas) bears a strikingly clear depiction of a winged serpent in the watery Beneath World (Fig. 6.4d, e). This depicts a wingless, long-snouted, antlered serpent devouring an anthropomorphic figure. Interestingly, the snake's rattles are replaced by the same scepter or war-club motif on the Richardson Landing vessel that was surrounded by the ogee-forming serpents. Around this serpent triangular elements appear. Nearby are two more

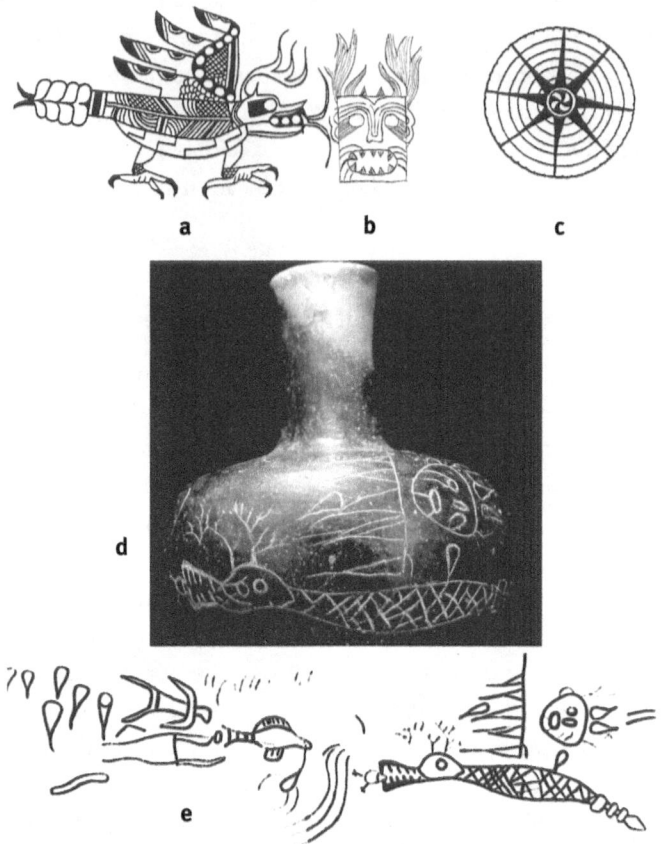

FIGURE 6.4. (a, b, c) Winged serpent representation on vessel from Pecan Point site (Phillips and Brown 1978:Fig. 262); (b) drawing by Terry Childs; (d) incised vessel from the Parkin site, photograph by David H. Dye; (e) Parkin site vessel, drawing by Marcia Taylor.

anthropomorphic figures. The fish positioned directly in front of the long-beaked serpent assures the viewer that the action is located in the watery realm. Thin lines above the serpent delineate an anthropomorphic figure from which triangular featherlike elements hang. This crudely incised figure also seems to be wearing feathers on his head, suggesting a Birdman or Falcon Dancer.

The composition on a flared-rim plate or bowl from the Kent site (Lee Co., Arkansas) also uses a winged serpent as a locative (Fig. 6.5a). This image seems to include traits from its counterpart, the Underwater Panther. The serpent's head appears feline and has pointed catlike ears and a feline snout instead of antlers. A forked tongue emerges from the serpent's mouth, and its eye is equipped with a two-pronged eye surround. The supernatural's body is not U-shaped; instead, it displays the sinuous curves of a serpent in motion. The serpent body is positioned so that it appears to be rearing up on its two back legs. Two fish above and below this sinuous serpent clearly locate the action in the watery Beneath World once again. In addition, the lower fish rests on a skull with a forked tongue. I believe that this skull likewise functions as a locative, reemphasizing that the winged serpent is in the realm of the dead as well as in the Beneath World. On the bottom of this plate a head is incised, with a long nose that mimics the serpent's sinuous curves (Fig. 6.5b). This head also has a cleft tongue and a two-pronged eye surround. I propose that this skull clearly represents a more anthropomorphic version of the shape-shifting Great Serpent.

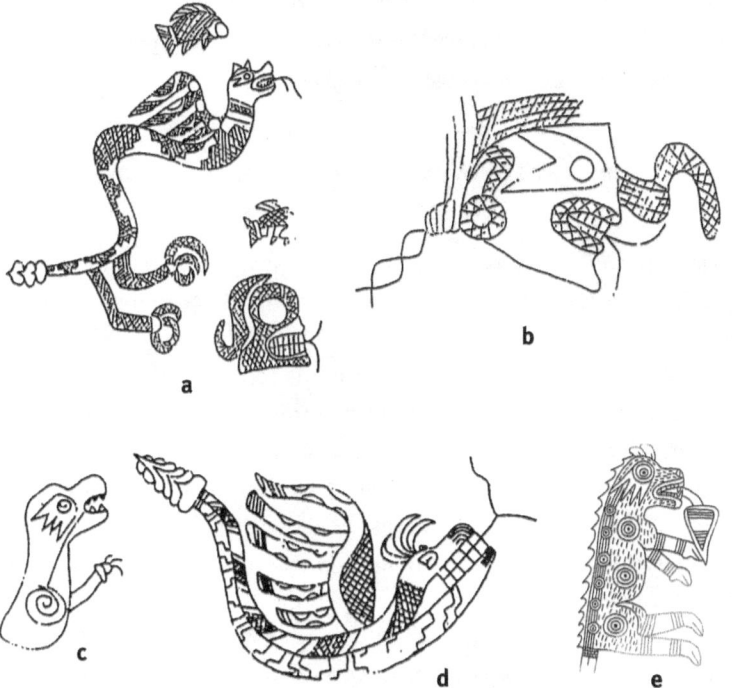

FIGURE 6.5. (a, b) Incised imagery on flared-rim plate from the Kent site, drawing by Terry Childs; (c, d) incised imagery on subglobular vessel from Pecan Point, drawing by Terry Childs; (e) Underwater Panther from Spiro (Phillips and Brown 1984:Pl. 225).

Both the feline and winged serpent aspects of the Great Serpent are clearly engraved on a subglobular vessel or cup from Pecan Point, Poinsett Co., Arkansas (Fig. 6.5c, d). This image is beautiful in both form and execution. The sinuous winged serpent as well as the rattlesnake buttons on the tail are very finely rendered. The serpent's outside head seems feline, while the teeth are those of a human, perhaps indicating the serpent as a transformation figure. A spray of feathers replaces the usual antlers on this winged serpent, which also has a forked tongue. Behind this winged serpent, a feline snarls—surely the Great Serpent performing as Underwater Panther (Fig. 6.5c). A four-forked eye surround frames the feline's eye. In the middle of its body a spiral element connects to the open and snarling mouth. In overall form this Underwater Panther strikingly resembles a feline found on one of the Spiro shell engravings (Fig. 6.5e) (Phillips and Brown 1984:Pl. 225). Thematically, this Pecan Point cup clearly renders at least two aspects of the Great Serpent: the Underwater Panther and the winged serpent. Combining both these images within the same composition is another major stylistic difference, or lack of concordance, between the winged serpent at Moundville and its construction within the art of the LMV.

Images of the Underwater Panther as Sculpted Ceramic Rim Adornments

Undoubtedly the LMV was home to a great sculptural tradition in clay, as Walker has observed (2004:219). Among the finest specimens of this sculptural tradition is a series of Underwater Panther images in which the ceramic vessels themselves form the body of this feline supernatural. Created between AD 1300 and 1500, impressive examples of this three-dimensional Underwater Panther genre have been found at several locations. Among them, two bowls from Arkansas are adorned with this supernatural feline's head and tail (Fig. 6.6). In both representations the feline displays a three-pronged eye surround and an open, snarling mouth. Furthermore, the long sinuous tails of both examples visually echo the serpentine bodies engraved on the pottery discussed above. Note also that the example from the Belle Meade site (Crittenden Co., Arkansas) carries a swirl-cross motif incised on the back of its head, once again a seminal link between the depiction of the Underwater Panther, this locative, and our understanding of the powers that rule the Beneath World (Fig. 6.6, bottom).

FIGURE 6.6. *Top,* bowl depicting sculptural form of the Underwater Panther, photograph by David H. Dye; *bottom,* swirl-cross on the back of the head of a similar vessel, photo by David H. Dye.

Images of the Great or Winged Serpent as Stone Sculpture

The development from sculpture in clay to sculpture in stone may seem to be a simple step, yet to a large extent the LMV artistic corpus conspicuously lacks stone sculpture. Sometime before 1917, however, a group of five smoking pipes was excavated from the top of what is now known as the Emerald Mound (near Natchez, Mississippi). These stone pipes, carved in limestone in what has been called the Bellaire style (Brain and Phillips 1996), now are known collectively as the Perrault pipes. At least one of these pipes has been identified as a winged serpent (Brown 1926:260, Figs. 223–224). Although

132　　　　　　　　　　LOWER MISSISSIPPI VALLEY

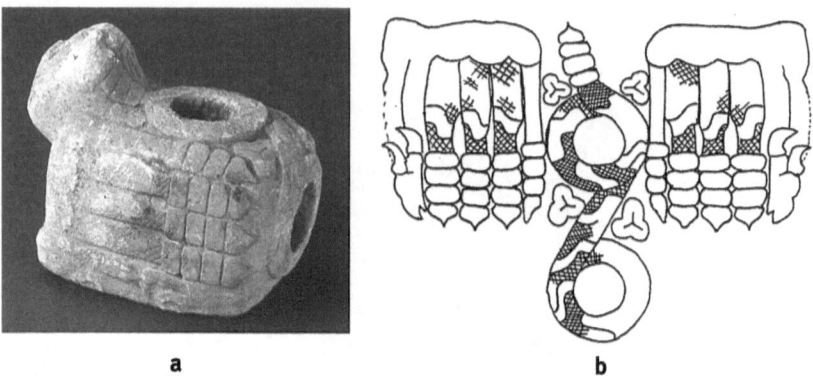

FIGURE 6.7. Perrault winged serpent pipe: (a) photograph by David H. Dye; (b) fold-out drawing by Jack Johnson.

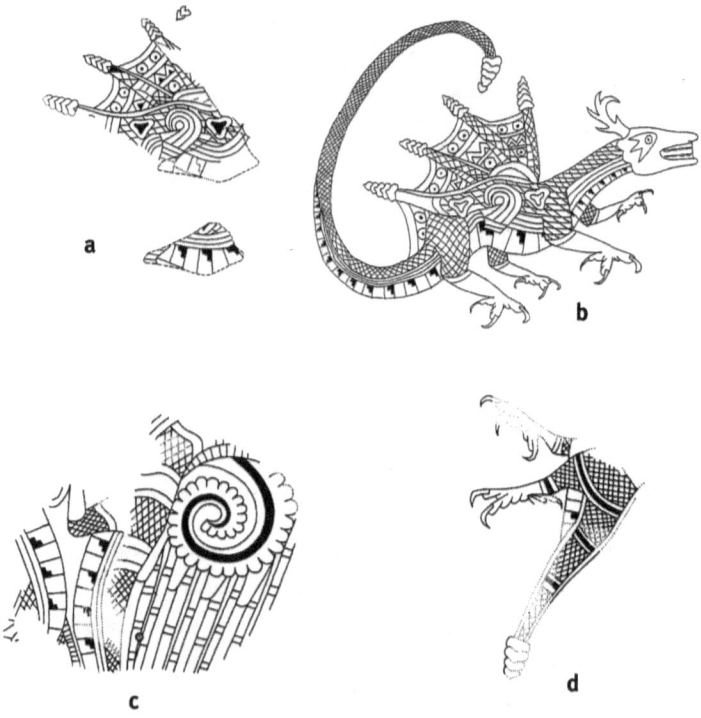

FIGURE 6.8. Serpentlike Underwater Panthers: (a, c, d) shell fragments from the Craig Mound, Spiro, Oklahoma (Phillips and Brown 1978:Pls. 32, 33); (b) reconstruction of a Winged Supernatural, drawing by Jack Johnson.

badly eroded, enough of the figure's head remains to identify its feline ears and open snarling mouth (Fig. 6.7a). The creature formed by this pipe is equipped with clawed feet and a long, sinuous rattle-tipped tail originating at the stem hole then wrapping itself around the smoking bowl. The pipe bowl is bordered by four trilobed elements, a symbol known to be related to serpent imagery. Carved on either side of the figure is a row of four staffs, each one topped by rattlesnake rattles (Fig. 6.7b). An examination of carved shell fragments from Spiro reveals the function of these staffs. They actually are wing-bars supporting a wing detailed with elaborate patterns (Fig. 6.8a) (Phillips and Brown 1978:Pl. 8). Enough shell fragments survive to allow me to posit a reconstruction of this great winged serpent (Fig. 6.8b). Like its Perrault pipe counterpart, this reconstructed supernatural bears trilobed symbols and has an elongated tail ending in rattlesnake rattles (Fig. 6.8b). Two other carved shell fragments from Spiro depict this same great winged serpent with its serpent markings and clawed feet (Fig. 6.8c, d) (Phillips and Brown 1978:Pls. 32 and 33). Unfortunately, in each case the fragments are so incomplete that a reconstruction of the full image (as discussed above) is extremely difficult.

Conclusion

At the conclusion of his article "World on a String," George Lankford suggested that the Moundville polity enjoyed a special relationship with the Beneath World that other areas did not share (Lankford 2004:214–217). An examination of the winged serpent and Underwater Panther imagery in the LMV clearly illustrates that this area also shared Moundville's preoccupation with the Beneath World and the realm of the dead. LMV winged serpent imagery and symbolism, unlike Moundville's, seem greatly concerned with the information that locative placement generated. Certainly the Underwater Panther imagery that was explicit in the art of the LMV was implicit in the art of Moundville. The two iconographic corpora are decidedly similar, but the LMV tradition was not copying the winged imagery from Moundville. For instance, identical paired winged serpents rarely are represented in LMV art, in contrast to their frequent occurrence at Moundville. A more likely scenario is that Moundville and the LMV culture shared a broad ideological system that was reflected in the templates used visually to manifest those things from the watery Beneath World that ordinarily could not be seen. Like the people of Moundville, the inhabitants of the

LMV almost certainly used this highly charged imagery in rituals associated with guiding the dead onto the Path of Souls. Also like their Moundville counterparts, the skilled artisans of the LMV focused much of their creativity on the highly prized, specialized ceramics used in funeral rituals that quickened the release of the soul. Stylistically, however, the artists and artisans of the Lower Mississippi Valley were more interested in representing a broader vision of the Beneath World, encompassing both its inhabitants and the supernatural geography that ultimately became the home to all.

AUTHOR'S ACKNOWLEDGMENTS: This chapter was written with the aid of Terry Childs, Marcia Taylor, and David Dye. I extend my thanks and gratitude to these individuals for their permission to use their photographs and drawings and in particular to Terry Childs for his contribution to the archaeological perspective of the chapter.

REGIONAL STUDIES: CUMBERLAND VALLEY

CHAPTER 7

Iconography of the Thruston Tablet

Vincas P. Steponaitis, Vernon James Knight, Jr., George E. Lankford,
Robert V. Sharp, and David H. Dye

The Thruston Tablet—also known as the Rocky Creek Tablet—is among the most interesting and unusual artifacts ever found in the American South. It consists of an irregular limestone slab 19 inches long, 14 inches high, and 1 inch thick (about the size of a cafeteria tray). One side of the tablet (which we think of today as the obverse or front) is covered with engraved designs, consisting of many human forms arranged in multiple scenes. The tablet also has engraved images on the reverse, but these are faint and less distinct. The tablet is clearly Mississippian in age and probably dates to the late thirteenth or early fourteenth centuries AD.

Here we present our recent studies of the tablet's imagery. We begin by reviewing past research on this object and describing our own recent investigations. We then present our analysis of the tablet's iconography, a possible interpretation of its meaning, and a discussion of the tablet's thematic and stylistic relationships.

Previous Studies

In *The Antiquities of Tennessee and the Adjacent States* (1890) Gates P. Thruston announced the discovery of an intriguing petroglyphic tablet in Sumner County, Tennessee, reportedly found on Rocky Creek, "near the stone graves and mounds of Castalian Springs," and published a rendering (Fig. 7.1). The location he described is actually now in Trousdale County, just across the Sumner County line.[1]

The tablet was even then in the holdings of the Tennessee Historical Society, having been presented "about twelve years ago" (ca. 1878), and it remains today part of the collection of the Tennessee State Museum in Nashville.[2] A prosperous lawyer, Thruston himself had amassed a sizable collection of Native American objects, principally as supervising archaeologist for

FIGURE 7.1. The first published illustration of the Thruston Tablet (Thruston 1890:Pl. 2).

the excavation in the late 1880s of some 4,000 stone-box graves on the Noel Farm site on Brown's Creek just outside Nashville (Fletcher 1891; Kelly 1985). Although the tablet that has come to bear his name was neither his discovery nor even part of his collection, he devoted considerable attention to it in the study of prehistoric artifacts that he prepared at the request of the Historical Society.

Thruston characterized the tablet as "an ideograph of significance, graven with a steady and skillful hand," that "probably records or commemorates some important treaty or public or tribal event." He described in general terms the principal figures and scenes depicted on it: "Indian chiefs, fully equipped with the insignia of office, . . . arrayed in fine apparel." Yet anyone intrigued by this limestone slab must recognize that Thruston's remarks nonetheless reveal a degree of prescience in his attention to particular elements inscribed on the stone surface:

> The dressing of the hair, the remarkable scalloped skirts, the implements used, the waist-bands, the wristlets, the garters, the Indian leggins and moccasins, the necklace and breast-plates, the two banners, the serpent emblem, the tattoo stripes, the ancient pipe—all invest this pictograph with unusual interest. (Thruston 1890:91)

His own interest sufficiently piqued, Thruston applied himself to providing some context for understanding it. For the style of dress, he recalled a reference by A. J. Conant to a vessel from southeast Missouri depicting figures "clad in flowing garments gathered by a belt at the waist and reaching to the knees" (Conant 1879:94, in Thruston 1890:91–92). Thruston regretted the absence of details in the depiction of several of the faces, the hair ornaments, and more, "partly lost by the disintegration of the stone, owing to its great age." Despite its condition, however, he found other points of comparison: the depictions of waist-bands and garters were similar to those on the copper plates from Etowah, and the treatment of hair-knots reminded him not only of the Etowah plates but also of pottery heads and shell gorgets from Tennessee.

The tattoo marks on the faces were also of interest, and Thruston compared them to a head-pot from the St. Francis River area of Arkansas that bears four "strongly marked" lines on its face and to images recorded on other Native American pictographs documented by Garrick Mallery (1886:175). He observed as well that the pipe being smoked in the scene at the bottom of the tablet could be readily compared to one shown in his own book, a stone pipe also from Sumner County (Thruston 1890:208, Fig. 113). Finally, he addressed what he took to be three shields or banners: two on the primary side of the stone, the third on the reverse. What he took to be a "double serpent emblem" on one shield was thought perhaps to be "the badge or totem of the tribe, clan, or family that occupied the extensive earth-works at Castalian Springs . . . near where the stone was found" (Thruston 1890:96). He posited that such an emblem was a favorite of "the Stone Grave race of Tennessee" and a common element on local shell gorgets, just as the "circles or sun symbols" that appear on the figures and at the top of the stone are the most frequent design on gorgets found near Nashville. In summary, although he regretted the partial disintegration of some surface features, he remained impressed by its content: "We doubt whether any inscribed stone of more archaeological value has been discovered among the prehistoric remains of the Mississippi valley" (Thruston 1890:97).

In 1891 William H. Holmes published his own rendering of the Thruston Tablet, which was not based on Thruston's line drawing and differed from it in numerous details of major and minor significance (Fig. 7.2). From the shape of the stone itself to the position of principal figures with respect to each other to the inclusion of elements entirely missing from Thruston's

FIGURE 7.2. William H. Holmes's drawing of the Thruston Tablet (Holmes 1891:Pl. 1).

version, Holmes's treatment was both bolder in its delineation of these principal figures and subtler in the care with which ambiguous or obscure elements were captured. In fact, he presented a richer and more complex object overall. Nonetheless, the stone was not without its flaws:

> The shape is unsymmetric and the outlines uneven, portions having been broken away in recent times. Both sides have been well covered with engravings, but the reverse side has been subjected to more active weathering and retains but imperfect traces of the devices.
> (Holmes 1891:161)

But from his examination of it Holmes brought new information to the fore: "In a few cases parts of the costume were painted red, the color being now barely traceable." He also suggested that part of the complexity of the stone, part of the difficulty of rendering it, resulted from its use as a palimpsest:

> The engraving appears to have been done at somewhat distinct periods, as indicated by differences in the degree of weathering of lines

within the same space. The more recently executed figures have been drawn over the earlier, resulting in places in great confusion. (Holmes 1891:161)

In attending to his basic description of what is visible, Holmes stated that, contrary to Thruston's interpretation of "friendly salutation," the four standing figures may actually have been engaged in a "warlike" encounter or at least a "mock contest" (Holmes 1891:162). Like Thruston, he placed great importance on the figures' costumes and accoutrements, in particular their headdresses of "knotted hair . . . plumes, and . . . lofty crests" and their skirts, "plain, scalloped, or fringed, and . . . decorated . . . with circles or scroll-work" (Holmes 1891:162–163). He noted their wrist-bands, anklets, moccasins, and gorgets as well as their tattoos and the "serrate band" that ornaments the large shield. But "as to the significance of the various devices upon the costumes and weapons, it is perhaps useless to speculate" (Holmes 1891:163).

Holmes took pains to describe some of the ambiguous, obscure, or underlying elements, among them the scene depicted in the upper left corner of the stone (where he detected rows of human heads, "each roundish figure [with] a suggestion of plumes"), the "delineation of the sun," roughly above the third of the four principal standing figures, and, in the lower part of the stone, "traces of at least five figures occupying parts of the space in common" (Holmes 1891:163). He noted the resemblance between the design of the enclosure in which one figure sits and that of the shield held by the figure above. Although somewhat puzzled by what the sixth figure is grasping ("a weapon, perhaps"), he remarked that this personage's headdress was distinctive.

Finally, on this face of the tablet, Holmes described what he believed to be, over to the right among the "confused and partly obliterated figures and parts of figures," a leg, the "most recent" of the images inscribed on the stone in this area. As to the reverse side of the tablet, Holmes described the elements simply: a figure with a bow and arrow and a figure seated within an enclosure holding "a weapon, rattle, or wand in the left hand" (Holmes 1891:164). He remained uncertain whether these figures were meant to be understood together or separately and concluded that "the significance, if there is any significance, of all or of any one must remain obscure." Yet "the differences in costume and markings are pronounced, but not so pronounced that all may not have pertained to one tribe" (Holmes 1891:164). He concluded with the statement that the stone's "authenticity has not been questioned," and, diminishing the merits of his own "rude sketch," he awaited the publication of an "elaborate illustration" of the tablet, forthcoming from Garrick Mallery of the Smithsonian Institution's Bureau of Ethnology.[3]

Mallery's contribution to the study of the Thruston Tablet proved to be minimal, however, except in regard to the quality of the reproduction he provided in the Bureau of American Ethnology's Tenth Annual Report, the first published photograph of the object (Fig. 7.3). This photograph of the primary face of the stone did capture some of the surface blemishes that bothered both Thruston and Holmes, while successfully rendering the major features—as well as extraneous marks of pitting, scratching, and spalling and exfoliation—with great fidelity. He provided no commentary other than an extended quotation of Thruston's earlier description (Mallery 1893:733–734).[4]

A much more extensive analysis of the tablet was undertaken by William Myer (1928), Tennessee's first professional archaeologist. Based on Holmes's drawing, Myer interpreted the tablet as a storyboard: "the record of a war between the prehistoric Indians at Castalian Springs and some other band."

FIGURE 7.3. The first published photograph of the Thruston Tablet (Mallery 1893:Pl. 51).

He discussed the Thruston Tablet alongside the Castalian Springs Tablet, another engraved limestone slab that he had published some years earlier (Myer 1917:100). He also compared its designs to those on pottery and shell artifacts found elsewhere in the Cumberland River basin.[5]

Significantly, Myer offered a more detailed description of the imagery on the reverse face, previously mentioned by Holmes:

> About all that can be made out with any reasonable certainty is the nearly nude figure, with possibly a trace of a breech cloth . . . He holds an undrawn bow and an unplaced arrow in his left hand. A figure can also be seen, seated, either in a building or on a mat . . . He appears to hold something like a string of wampum or a rattle in his left hand. The mat or house has similar decorations to those on the border of the shield and on the house on the opposite side of the tablet. (Myer 1928:104)

He explicitly referred to a figure illustrating this panel, but regrettably this figure was not included in the printed article.

The Thruston Tablet has been reproduced and studied several times since Myer (Parker 1949; Fundaburk and Foreman 1957:Pl. 56; Verrill and Keeler 1961; Keeler and Verrill 1962; Phillips and Brown 1978:181–182, Fig. 253; Drooker 1992:Fig. 18), but, surprisingly, the images upon which some of the later examinations were based were greatly inferior in quality to those of Holmes and Mallery. Moreover, several of these later studies were handicapped by the very lack of visual information provided by Holmes's and Mallery's reproductions.

Malcolm Parker's (1949) study in *Tennessee Archaeologist* is a case in point. Parker, an amateur archaeologist, was aware of Thruston's description of the tablet but not of those by Holmes, Mallery, and Myer. He published photographs of the obverse and—for the first time—the reverse sides (Fig. 7.4). Yet the engraving was so hard to see in these photographs that the journal's editor (T. M. N. Lewis) highlighted the lines on the photographs with white ink. Despite Parker's belief that "accuracy in following the original engravings can be regarded as fairly reliable" (Parker 1949:14), elements are missing from Parker's reproduction that were visible in both Holmes and Mallery and that are still visible on the face of the stone today. In addition, a comparison with Holmes and Mallery shows that many of the inked lines are at best only an approximation of the underlying designs.[6] Parker attempted at the end of his brief study to explain the presence of initials ("H S") that appear at the bottom of the stone, concluding that they were scratched upon the tablet in 1937 by "a careless W.P.A. worker" charged with cleaning and repairing museum objects. In fact, these initials are visible in Mallery's 1893 photograph, so Parker's conclusion was incorrect. Even so, as we shall see presently, the tablet was indeed damaged between Mallery's and Parker's times, albeit in a different way.

Fundaburk and Foreman (1957:Pl. 56) relied upon Parker's illustration of the Thruston Tablet's obverse panel for their catalog, showing it redone as a line drawing. In their brief caption, the authors cited Thruston but none of the other early descriptions. Because their catalog has been so widely used as a reference, we suspect that this omission has contributed to the general loss of memory regarding the work of Holmes, Mallery, and Myer on the tablet.

By far the most unusual treatment of the Thruston Tablet appeared in a pair of articles written by Ruth Verrill and Clyde Keeler (Verrill and Keeler 1961; Keeler and Verrill 1962). Initially unaware of the work of Holmes, Myer, and Parker, these authors produced a drawing of the obverse panel traced from Mallery's photograph. They interpreted the images as portraying a battle fought between local Indians and Vikings. Among the engravings they saw glyphic inscriptions, a Phrygian helmet, and a Viking longboat. By the time of their second article they had found the Holmes and Parker references and had examined the stone firsthand, yet none of this changed their interpretations.[7] They did, however, provide some useful information on the stone's condition, which echoed, in part, Parker's earlier remarks:

> The soft stone had been badly damaged, mainly by W.P.A. workers, detailed to "clean it" in 1937. It appears as though someone had coated this stone with varnish and then, thinking better of it, had tried to scrape or sand off the varnish, thus removing all traces of some of the important lines shown clearly on the Smithsonian photograph published in 1893. A wide arc was gouged across the lower figures on the stone and in this, as well as elsewhere, some of the varnish remains. (Keeler and Verrill 1962:29)

The "wide arc" they described can be seen in Parker's earlier photograph (1949:Fig. 1) and is still visible today.

ICONOGRAPHY OF THE THRUSTON TABLET 145

FIGURE 7.4. The Thruston Tablet as illustrated by Parker (after Parker 1949:Figs. 1-2): (a) obverse face; (b) reverse face. The engraved lines are inked on the photograph.

In their monumental study of shell engravings from Spiro, Philip Phillips and James Brown briefly discussed the Thruston Tablet, making reference to an illustration redrawn from Parker's inked photographs (Phillips and Brown 1978:181–182, Fig. 235). After mentioning the possibility that the tablet had been altered, they expressed doubts about the "stylistic purity" of the incised images—not realizing that much of the problem was due to the poor quality of Parker's depictions. Even so, their overall assessment was prescient:

> Possibly this accounts for the little there is to be said about Spiro connections from the standpoint of style. On the other hand, a glance at these drawings will sufficiently convey the amount of exegesis that would be required for iconographic comparisons with Spiro. A whole chapter could easily be devoted to the subject, but this is not our primary concern. (Phillips and Brown 1978:182)

The tablet's thematic connections with Spiro engravings will indeed be considered in a later section of this chapter.

One additional mention of the Thruston Tablet worth noting was in a study of Mississippian textiles from Wickliffe by Penelope Drooker (1992:77, Fig. 18). Relying on Holmes's early drawing, she describes the garments worn by the principal figures and concludes that three of these garments with jagged fringes were "more likely to have been made from skins than from cloth."

Recent Investigations

Our own work with this tablet began in June 2005, at the Mississippian Iconography Workshop sponsored by Texas State University's Center for the Study of the Arts and Symbolism of Ancient America. Our baseline for this initial work was the drawing of the tablet that Holmes published in 1891. We agreed with Holmes's assessment that the tablet was a palimpsest, so our first task was to separate this palimpsest into its constituent elements. We accomplished this task by manipulating Holmes's drawing with Adobe Photoshop, pulling apart the drawing, line by line, into what became three distinct layers. While this operation was helpful, it also left us with an awareness that certain issues could not be resolved by working with the drawing alone. Hence we made plans to examine the tablet firsthand.

In August 2005 we spent two days at the Tennessee State Museum in

Nashville doing just that. We examined the tablet under raking light, sometimes assisted by a hand lens. In order to record the fine incisions of the Thruston Tablet, we tried several approaches. First, a laser scanner was used, but the image obtained was not sufficiently clear. Next we attempted to produce a "rubbing" of the tablet, but many of the lines were too faint and indistinct to leave a trace on the paper. Finally, we tried old-fashioned photography. We shot the tablet with a medium-format camera (Hasselblad 553ELX) mounted with a Zeiss macro-planar 120 mm lens. A fine-grained film (Kodak Ektachrome ASA 64) was used to record as much detail as possible. With raking light from an overhead soft box we moved the tablet into position in order to record the various undulations in their best possible light. Once the numerous exposures were taken and the film was developed, the transparencies were then scanned with a Nikon Super CoolScan 9000 ED film scanner, which produced digital images with great clarity. We also took numerous photographs with a Nikon D-70 digital camera. The resulting images allowed us to examine the tablet with a high degree of detail. This examination, together with the extensive published record of this artifact, led us to the following conclusions.

1. The tablet has sustained considerable damage since the 1890s. For one thing, the surface has been eroded, especially on high spots on the stone, so that many of the details depicted in Holmes's drawing and clearly visible in the Mallery photograph are now no longer visible. The obverse face has suffered a number of gouges or cuts, including a large arc at the bottom of the obverse face, which were later painted over to make them less visible. Moreover, the lines engraved on both sides of the stone have been highlighted on at least two occasions, when it appears that ink—visible as two distinct colors—was used to fill the fine channels of incising. The ink lies *within* the incised lines; it has not been used to draw images *upon* the tablet. Exactly when this damage and highlighting took place is unknown. Parker's photograph indicates that the gouges and repairs had taken place by 1949, photographs in the museum files show that the inking had occurred by the 1950s, and Keeler and Verrill's account places the surface erosion prior to 1962. Perhaps, as the published accounts suggest, a careless Works Progress Administration worker was at fault, but we found no independent confirmation of this story in the museum's records. Nor did we see any evidence of varnishing and sanding or of fresh incising that might have been done to "improve" the figures after the tablet's discovery (cf. Keeler and Verrill 1962; Phillips

and Brown 1978:182). The damage we saw may well have occurred as a result of either surface exfoliation or careless handling over time. The "varnish" described by Keeler and Verrill appears to be a brownish paint that was selectively applied (sometime prior to 1949) over nicks and gouges on the surface in order to make them less visible.

2. Holmes's drawing (1891) and Mallery's photograph (1893) are currently the best depictions of the tablet in print. Parker's inked photographs (1949) and all subsequent derivative illustrations are far less faithful to the original. Because of the erosion and highlighting just described, it would be impossible to make a fresh drawing from the original that captures all the details visible in those two early illustrations.

3. Despite the quality of the Holmes and Mallery images and the subsequent damage, our recent examination revealed a few details that Holmes missed. The most important of these is the head of a fish on the obverse side. The body and tail of this fish had been drawn by Holmes, but their meaning was enigmatic until we found the missing head. This element is so faint that it is not surprising Holmes missed it. It can only be seen when raking light is applied to the surface at just the right angle (Fig. 7.5). Our examination of the reverse face also revealed many details that were not picked up in Parker's published photograph.

As a result of these observations, we decided to use a slightly modified version of Holmes's drawing for our iconographic study of the obverse panel (Fig. 7.6). We recognize that Holmes's drawing is not perfect. A comparison with Mallery's photograph clearly indicates that the outline of the stone is not exactly rendered and that the "aspect ratio" of the drawing is slightly compressed vertically. Nevertheless, Holmes was a trained artist and careful observer, and he captured most essential features of the composition with great fidelity. The only things he missed were the head of the fish and a few insignificant lines. He also deliberately omitted some recent additions to the tablet which are irrelevant to our study. Hence, by simply adding the head of the fish, we produced a line drawing that served us well for present purposes. Informed by our observations and taking into account this modification, we then refined our initial separation into layers, using the same image-editing software as before.

The reverse panel was a different story. The only published drawings were based on Parker's inked photograph, which was a very poor depiction of images on the stone. So we created an entirely new drawing of the reverse

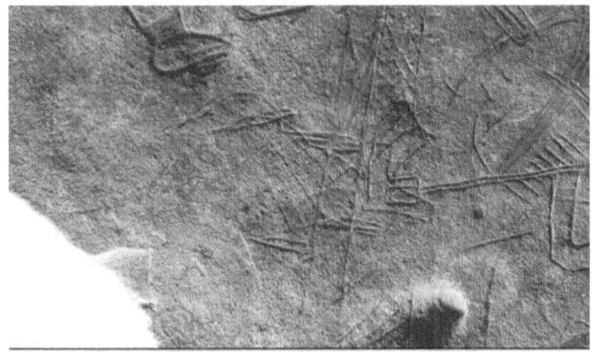

FIGURE 7.5. The head of a fish on the obverse face, made visible by raking light: *top*, photograph taken in 2005; *bottom*, line drawing of the fish, framed as in the photograph. This element was missed by Holmes (1891) but discovered in our recent investigation.

panel, based on the photographs and notes we made during our visit to the museum (see Fig. 7.17). This new drawing is far more accurate than anything previously published.

Using these drawings as a baseline, let us now turn to a description and analysis of the tablet's imagery.

The Obverse Panel

To call one face the "obverse" presupposes information about the original artist's (or artists') intent that we simply do not possess. Thus we have arbitrarily assigned this designation to the side that, by virtue of the boldness and clarity of its designs, has historically attracted the most attention. Alternative interpretations are certainly possible. Myer, for one, assumed exactly the opposite. He called the other face the "top side" because it was more eroded and therefore must have been facing upward in its original context (Myer 1928:104).

FIGURE 7.6. The obverse panel, based on Holmes (1891) with minor additions.

FIGURE 7.7. The Foreground layer on the obverse panel. Numbers along the tablet's margin identify the three Foreground groups.

As mentioned previously, our analysis starts from the premise, first articulated by Holmes (1891:161), that the tablet's obverse panel is a palimpsest—a drawing that consists of distinct superimposed layers. Understanding the tablet's iconography requires that we "unpack" the layers and study each one separately.

For present purposes we recognize at least three layers on the tablet's front. There may be more, as some layers show a clear internal consistency, while others may be palimpsests in their own right. But three is the minimum number that we can confidently recognize based on superposition, execution, and thematic coherence. These serve as the starting point for our description. For convenience, we call these layers the *Foreground*, the *Background*, and the *Leg*.

THE FOREGROUND

Of all our layers, this one is visually the most prominent and stylistically the most coherent (Fig. 7.7). The boldness of the lines in the Foreground layer, particularly in comparison to the Background, suggests that the former was applied on top of the latter, as if the artist was making sure that the designs were visible against the "noise" of the lines already there. In every instance of overlap between these layers, we carefully examined the lines with a hand lens, looking for direct evidence of superposition. Suffice it to say that the evidence was never definitive, but in a number of cases it suggested that our stratigraphic hypothesis was correct. Needless to say, the erosion of the surface and the inking of the lines made resolving this question much more difficult than it would have been in Holmes's time.

The details of form and execution argue strongly that all the figures comprising this layer were engraved by a single artist. The heads are bulbous, balanced on skinny necks, and have a pronounced occipital bulge. The bridge of the nose connects to a high forehead in a peculiar way. The eyes are almond-shaped, without pupils, and are placed too far to the rear. The artist seems to have an aversion to ears, and there are none of the ear spools so characteristic of Mississippian figural art. The arms are skinny, almost rubbery at the elbows, with little attempt to portray hands. The feet are clumsy lumps.

The Foreground consists of three distinct scenes, each involving two different characters. In fact, the characters in each scene may be the same, but appearing in different guises.

FIGURE 7.8. Three depictions of "Line Face" in the Foreground layer.

One character we call *Line Face*, because of the multiple lines that run from the nose to the back of the jaw, presumably either a tattoo or face paint (Fig. 7.8). Line Face always wears shoes without any fill or color. His garment is fringed, with an irregular hemline that suggests it is made of hide (Myer 1928:103; Drooker 1992:77). In one case a texture (perhaps fur) is indicated by hachures. His garment also bears round figures in all three cases. He wears a collar or necklace in all three images and has concentric circles on his chest or stomach. In two cases his garment bears an unusual device shaped roughly like an asterisk. This character thus has six diagnostic traits: horizontal facial marking, light moccasins, a fringed garment with irregular hemline, a necklace, concentric circles on the torso, and an asterisk motif.

The second character we call *Star Eye* (Fig. 7.9). He usually has a rayed eye-surround, although in one case this device seems to be replaced by a rayed gorget worn on the chest. When shoes are visible, they are darkened with hachure and in one case with red pigment, which was first noted by Holmes (1891:163) and traces of which are still present. In each of the scenes on the obverse panel Star Eye is associated with a distinctive border of roundels and lines, albeit in different locations. In one case the border appears on a shield; in another it is found on the garment; and in a third it occurs as the border of an enclosure in which Star Eye sits. These three motifs—rayed eye, dark shoes, and roundel border—appear to be the diagnostic traits identifying this character.

We recognize the possibility that the figure with the gorget instead of the eye surround may be yet a third character (Fig. 7.9, middle). Indeed, most

ICONOGRAPHY OF THE THRUSTON TABLET 153

FIGURE 7.9. Three depictions of "Star Eye" in the Foreground layer.

previous commentators have assumed that this figure is female, presumably because of the "skirt" (Thruston 1890:91; Myer 1928:101; Parker 1949:16; Verrill and Keeler 1961; Drooker 1992:77). As Phillips and Brown (1978:95) have noted, however, "the presence or absence of skirts has nothing to do with male and female" in Mississippian art. There are many examples of apparently male figures wearing such kilts in the shell engravings from Spiro (see Phillips and Brown 1978:95–97). Given the absence of definitive female characteristics and the similarities to the other figures (including shell beads at the knees and ankles), we lean toward seeing this figure as being male and another manifestation of Star Eye.

The other motifs present with the two characters are not consistent, and their variability suggests that they are thus part of the story rather than identifiers of the individuals. Some appear only with Star Eye: a shield, a spear, and a sash or belt (held in the hand). Line Face, on the other hand, bears a woodpecker axe, a serpent staff with tassels, and a fan-shaped bustle. Every figure wears a headdress of some kind. Each of the two characters appears once with a feather headdress and once with a raccoon binding. Star Eye wears a bilobed arrow in his hair once, and Line Face appears in a bulbous headdress once. Such variability suggests that the headdresses indicate social roles rather than identity, and they are thus probably part of the story.

For convenience we refer to the three scenes as Foreground Groups 1–3, numbered clockwise from the upper left.

Foreground Group 1. The left figure, Line Face, is turned in profile to Star Eye (Fig. 7.10a). His left hand reaches behind the shield edge, and his right

FIGURE 7.10. Scenes in the Foreground layer: (a) Foreground Group 1; (b) Foreground Group 2; (c) Foreground Group 3.

holds a woodpecker axe. Star Eye, mostly hidden behind the shield, holds a spear in his right hand.

Foreground Group 2. Star Eye is on the left with a sash or belt in his right hand (Fig. 7.10b). He faces Line Face in profile. Line Face's left arm is difficult to characterize, but he may be holding a bustle or rattle in his hand, which is on his side. The two of them appear to be greeting each other, because Star Eye's left hand is raised in a "high-five" with Line Face's right hand, and each figure has an extra arm in a different position: Star Eye's second left hand is at Line Face's side and Line Face's second right hand is on Star Eye's shoulder. The double arms suggest an indication of motion or multiple locations, a hint of an artistic convention illustrating action.

Foreground Group 3. On the left side Star Eye sits facing left in a square enclosure defined by a roundel border, smoking a long pipe held in his right hand (Fig. 7.10c). He wears a bilobed arrow in his hair, a necklace, and a robe gathered around him. Separating him from the figure of Line Face on the right is a petaloid staff with a bow and arrow across it. The figure of Line Face wears a large bulbous headdress and bears a broken staff or spear with dangling objects (which may also be present in Foreground Group 1). He is turned almost on his back away from the staff and Star Eye. That position is unique in the storyboard, and it may have more to do with the remaining amount of space for the design than with any special meaning.

THE BACKGROUND

The Background layer shows much less thematic consistency than the Foreground (Fig. 7.11). To some extent it was defined by process of elimination: once the Foreground and the Leg were removed, this is what was left. So we cannot be certain the scenes comprising the background were drawn at the

FIGURE 7.11. The Background layer on the obverse panel. Numbers along the tablet's margin identify the three Background groups.

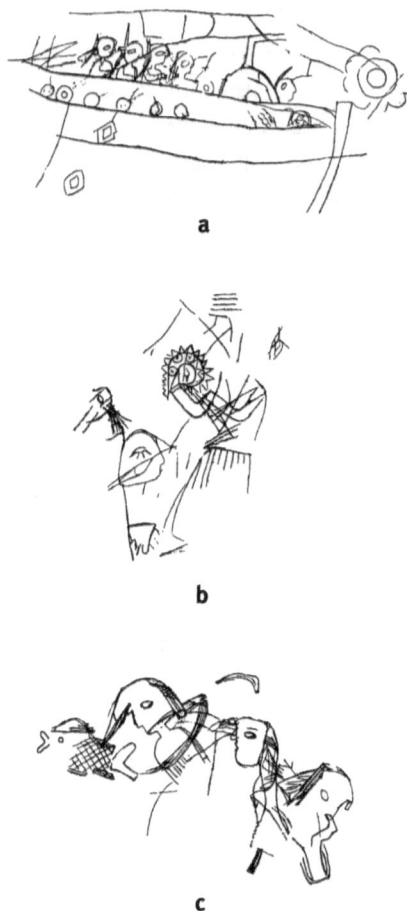

FIGURE 7.12. Scenes in the Background layer: (a) Background Group 1, the "Gallery"; (b) Background Group 2; (c) Background Group 3.

same time or that they are thematically related. They do, however, share a certain crudeness in execution (as compared to the Foreground) and are done in a shallower incision (whether by intent or due to erosion is not clear). Moreover, the three scenes do not overlap in a way that would suggest temporal discontinuity. So for now we will treat them as a set, while readily admitting the possibility that they might not be.

The fact that the middle area of the tablet is blank in regard to background images calls for interpretation, but little can be said. The empty middle may have been intended as a working area for some ritual activity, such as mixing sacred substances. It may have resulted from the erosion of an earlier engraving, as the stone does show evidence of wear, particularly on the high spots. Yet even if some erosion took place, it seems unlikely to have obliterated all traces of an earlier composition. Thus we are inclined to believe that the blank area was intentional.

As before, we refer to the three clusters of images as Background Groups 1–3, numbered clockwise from the upper left.

Background Group 1. This is the scene we call the "Gallery" (Fig. 7.12a). It depicts a row of people, viewed from the side, with only their upper bodies and heads visible. Their lower bodies are obscured by a horizontal device drawn with parallel lines. Interspersed among the figures is a semicircular object, and above them are two more parallel lines and a petaloid motif.

This scene has previously been interpreted as a Viking longboat (Verrill and Keeler 1961; Keeler and Verrill 1962), an idea that we may safely set aside as being historically implausible. One might also interpret it as a canoe, yet it bears little resemblance to the one definite canoe image we have from Mississippian times (Phillips and Brown 1978:Pl. 160). Moreover, a canoe fails to

FIGURE 7.13. An Ojibwa Midé lodge meeting (after Grim 1983:132). The published caption reads: "Exterior view of midewiwin lodge at Elbow lake, White Earth reservation, Minnesota, in 1909. Cedar boughs line the lower four feet of the 80-by-20-foot lodge, which was made of overlapping lodge-pole pine. The ritual processional movement follows the east-west orientation." The photograph is from the collections of the National Anthropological Archives, Smithsonian Institution.

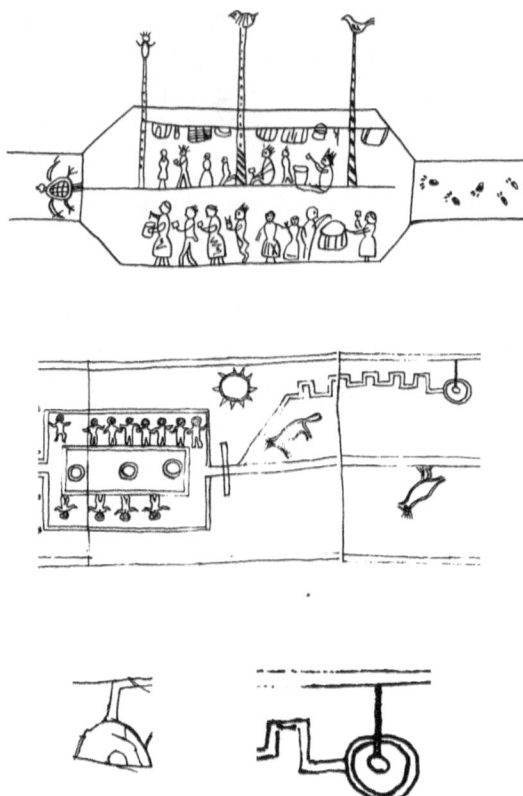

FIGURE 7.14. Images from Ojibwa Midé sacred scrolls: *top*, a portion of the White Earth Scroll (after Dewdney 1967:Fig. 62); *middle*, a portion of a Ghost Lodge scroll (after Dewdney 1967:Fig. 103); *bottom*, an object from the Gallery (*left*) compared with a detail from the Ghost Lodge scroll (*right*).

account for certain features, such as the dome-shaped structure and the petaloid circle that seem to be part of the same composition.

As an alternative, we would suggest that this may be a depiction of a medicine lodge. Note the similarity to the photograph of a medicine lodge ceremony taken at the turn of the last century in Minnesota (Fig. 7.13). We also see a connection to the famous birch-bark scrolls created as ritual guides for the conduct of Midé ceremonies. Beyond the overall similarity to the drawing, there is at least one detailed parallel. The birchbark symbols are not realistic drawings but pathways, and the semicircular object on the Thruston Tablet does not seem so alien when seen in the light of the Midé symbols

(Fig. 7.14).[8] While this reading is far from certain, it is at least as plausible as the canoe.

Background Group 2. The most identifiable elements in this composition are a headless torso and a disembodied head, both apparently human (Fig. 7.12b). The torso wears a kilt and its arms are clearly depicted. In the right hand is an object that is unusual but not unknown in Mississippian art. It has been identified elsewhere as the proboscis of a moth held in the same manner (Knight and Franke 2007). We assigned the disembodied head to the Background but not with great confidence, as it might fit equally well with Foreground Group 2. Differentiating the lines belonging to the kilt and those belonging the Leg (a separate layer described below) was also difficult.

Background Group 3. This is a roughly drawn group of three human heads, a fish, and a small headless human body, connected with a band of lines (Fig. 7.12c). Once again, there seems little to say about this strange composition, except that (as we shall discuss presently) it has numerous parallels in Mississippian art. The meaning of this design is unknown.

THE LEG

This incongruous feature seemingly sits alone, out of scale and out of place relative to the other images on the panel (Fig. 7.15). Holmes was convinced that it was the last element added to the panel. While we could see no direct evidence of it being stratigraphically last, we also saw nothing to contradict Holmes's assertion. Perhaps the matter was clearer in the 1890s, before the

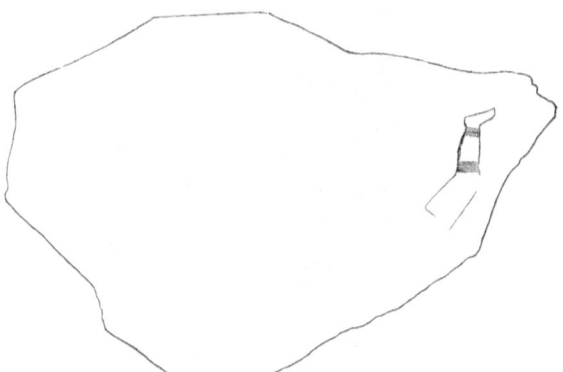

FIGURE 7.15. The Leg on the obverse panel.

tablet's degradation. Be that as it may, we agree with Holmes that this element does not fit comfortably with either the Foreground or the Background and should be treated as a distinct layer. Beyond that, we have little to add.

NINETEENTH-CENTURY ADDITIONS

Before ending our description of the obverse face, it is worth noting the presence of some nineteenth-century additions, which can be seen in Mallery's 1893 photograph and are still visible today. These consist of some initials and a date inscribed just below the roundel border in Foreground Group 3 (Fig. 7.16). As best we can determine based on the old published photograph and our recent examination under strongly raking light, the inscription reads as follows:

H S
P M
1877

The "M" in the second line is very indistinct and may be something entirely different. It is also possible that the date is actually "1879," as a faint line closes the loop on the "9," but we are not sure whether that line is deliberate.

FIGURE 7.16. Enlargement of the lower portion of Mallery's 1893 photograph, showing recent additions to the obverse face. Note the initials "H S," the letter "P," and the date "1877." A faint "M" is also present to the right of the "P" but cannot be seen in the photograph.

FIGURE 7.17. The reverse panel, redrawn from a photograph made in 2005.

The Reverse Panel

The scene on the reverse panel portrays an unidentifiable figure on the left with a bow, possibly shooting an arrow above a roundel border containing a second figure (Fig. 7.17). The activity of the figure (Line Face?) inside the border cannot be discerned. Numerous lines appear in the area immediately above the two figures, but they do not seem to form any recognizable designs. In the upper right, where Parker (1949:16) saw the "man in the moon" and Keeler and Verrill (1962:32) discerned the "head of a dead, ray-eyed 'Viking,'" we also see the possibility of a disembodied head, facing left (just to the right of and silhouetted against Parker's man in the moon). Perhaps this image is a counterpart to the disembodied leg on the obverse, but it is so crudely incised and surrounded by so many other lines that it is difficult to be sure what it represents.

Stylistic examination makes it appear that the reverse panel should be considered a continuation of the three Foreground scenes on the obverse face. The peculiar ways in which the heads, arms, and feet are depicted (as detailed previously) argue for a common artist of the Foreground and reverse scenes. The fact that the storyboard narrative may be continued on the reverse side is probably significant, but what does it mean in regard to function that the tablet must be turned over to see the additional image? It seems more productive to focus speculation on the meaning of the storyboard as a whole.

Possible Mythic Interpretation

A number of previous authors saw the Thruston Tablet as a record of historical events: an "important treaty . . . or tribal event" (Thruston 1890:91), a "war between the prehistoric Indians at Castalian Springs and some other band" (Myer 1928:100), a "historical event of considerable importance" (Parker 1949:16), and last, but not least, a battle between local Indians and marauding Vikings (Verrill and Keeler 1961). We take a different view, based on recent advances in understanding Mississippian imagery (Knight et al. 2001; Reilly and Garber 2007). Specifically, we believe that much of the representational art from this period relates not to historical events but rather to beliefs about the cosmos and the beings that inhabited otherworldly realms. Such imagery often represents "snapshots" of mythic narratives that were widely known throughout eastern North America, some of which survived, perhaps in altered form, into recent times.

As is well known, any attempt to match fourteenth-century images to nineteenth-century texts is faced with almost insurmountable issues, such as the time gap, the radical alteration of the Native societies and belief systems, and the lack of ethnic identifications of archaeological sites. Even so, it seems inadequate to discuss a storyboard without some attempt to delineate a story. In the full recognition that this attempt is speculation, we therefore offer a few reflections on a possible mythic interpretation of the Thruston Tablet storyboard.

Each of the scenes is composed of two males in relation to each other, which immediately suggests a mythic category: the widespread narratives of the Twins. As Paul Radin (1950) pointed out in his discussion of what he termed "the basic myth of the North American Indians," the Twins myths in the Eastern Woodlands and Plains come in two versions. The most widely distributed one is "Lodge-Boy and Thrown-Away" (LBTA), but there are Eastern examples of another one, "Children of the Sun," the version common among the Southwestern tribes. Here are some possible episodes that might be illustrated by the drawings of the tablet scenes. They seem best read in this sequence: Foreground Group 2—Foreground Group 3(—Reverse Panel?)—Foreground Group 1.

Foreground Group 2. If the rayed headdress is interpreted as a solar sign, then Line Face on the right may be identified as closely related to the Sun. The figure on the left may also be related to the Sun, as indicated by the rayed ornament on his chest. If the peculiar multiple arm movements (?) can be taken as greeting or caressing activity (Lankford 1984, 1988), then the scene is one of a meeting between the brothers. The contrast in their clothing—a woven kilt and an animal skin—may indicate the cultural difference between them. In most of the LBTA narratives, the opening episode is the story of the separation of the Twins at their birth, with one of them being brought up by animals or water powers. Even in the Children of the Sun version the two boys are frequently portrayed as only half-brothers, one of them being born from water powers. Both forms emphasize the distinction between them, and the opening episode of LBTA makes a point of the wildness of the more powerful brother, underlined by his capture and domestication. Foreground Group 2 appears to capture at least the spirit of the contrast of the Twins as well as the amity between them. One Winnebago Twins narrative portrays the culture-versus-nature theme as a meeting of a well-garbed boy with a naked boy; after the first gives his clothing to the second and restores his own, the two appear almost identical (Dieterle n.d.b).

Foreground Group 3. In order to determine the truth of the boys' claim that he is their father, the Sun subjects them to some tests. One of the tests is smoking a pipe, a process that will be lethal if they do not possess adequate power. In a Southwestern telling of the Children of the Sun, the Twins survive the test only by the help of a caterpillar, but the same smoking test appears multiple times among the Winnebago in another myth (Matthews 1897:112; Dieterle n.d.a). On the left side Star Eye sits in an enclosure smoking, while on the right Line Face stands arrayed in a peculiar headdress and holds a broken or forked spear, signs that he has already received symbols of his power.

Reverse Panel. Although difficult to read in detail, the roles of Foreground Group 3 appear reversed in this scene. Line Face is now in the enclosure for testing, while his brother stands outside with bow and arrow. The presence of a bow and arrow in both Foreground Group 3 and the reverse panel suggests a possible episode coded in these two scenes: the resuscitation of one deceased brother by the other during their tests; one popular way of accomplishing this in the narratives is by shooting an arrow over the body of the dead boy.

Foreground Group 1. Having survived the tests, the boys have been acknowledged as the Children of the Sun and given weapons befitting their station. Line Face now wields a sacred axe with a woodpecker head and wears a raccoon headdress, while Star Eye now wears the solar headdress originally worn by his brother and bears a spear and shield. It is at this point in the myth, when they are armed with power, that the Twins are charged with their task: to rid the world of the monsters who threaten the existence of human beings.

We offer this speculative reading only as an example of the sort of narrative that probably stands behind the imagery. Nonetheless, it illustrates the kind of search process that needs to be undertaken when the meaning of "storyboard art" is pursued after the structure of the art has been determined, based on empirical examination.

Comparisons and Chronology

The scenes and their details do not stand alone in Mississippian art but show many similarities with images found across the Mississippian world. Indeed, there are enough parallels from other locations to raise the possibility that the Thruston Tablet is a portrayal of stories, characters, and concepts sufficiently well known to have produced multiple attempts at graphic depiction. Here we present a brief survey of examples to illustrate this point.

Let us begin with the level of whole compositions or themes (*sensu* Phillips and Brown 1978:104–105):

- An engraved shell from Spiro—the Lightner Cup (Fig. 7.18)—shows a scene that is strikingly parallel to the Thruston Tablet's Foreground (Phillips and Brown 1978:Pl. 20). There are two figures, differently dressed. One has a woven tunic, while the other has a fringed or skin garment. Note also the fragment of what may be a roundel border across the top. The cup is assigned to the Braden A style. The same contrast in clothing appears on another Spiro cup assigned to Craig A (Phillips and Brown 1984:Pl. 187). There has been little discussion of the Twins mythology in connection with the Spiro art, but the topic seems fruitful, given these parallels with the Thruston Tablet.

- Foreground Group 3 is composed of a figure in an enclosure on the left separated from a figure on the right by a petaloid staff. That same

ICONOGRAPHY OF THE THRUSTON TABLET   165

FIGURE 7.18. The Lightner Cup from Spiro, Braden A style (after Phillips and Brown 1978:Pl. 20).

FIGURE 7.19. Shell cup from Spiro showing an occupied enclosure, petaloid staff, and figure with bow and arrow, Craig A style (after Phillips and Brown 1984:Pl. 165).

composition, in a quite different style, is found on a shell engraving from Spiro (Fig. 7.19; Phillips and Brown 1984:Pl. 165). Two other engravings from Spiro also depict similar enclosures (Phillips and Brown 1984:Pls. 153, 161). All are Craig A in style.

• The humanlike figure holding a rayed spiral seen in Background Group 2 brings to mind comparable scenes in Hightower-style gorgets from northern Georgia and adjacent parts of Tennessee (Fig. 7.20; Phillips and Brown

1978:Figs. 177 [top row], 232; Power 2004:Fig. 16; for a definition of this style, see Muller 1989:20).

- The interlace of heads, torso, and fish in Background Group 3 also has parallels elsewhere (Fig. 7.21). Similar bands of heads occur on Braden B shells at Spiro (Phillips and Brown 1978:Pls. 58, 60), as do fish (Phillips and Brown 1978:Pl. 90). The small headless figures are a feature of Braden C (Phillips and Brown 1978:Pls. 113, 115, 116). Fish also make appearances on shells decorated in the Craig B style (Phillips and Brown 1984:Pls. 234, 234.1, 325). Another Braden-like band of heads is engraved on a monolithic axe from the Wilbanks site in Georgia (Waring 1968a; Phillips and Brown 1978:193; Dye 2004:Fig. 29).

- The Foreground layer on the Thruston Tablet bears a generic resemblance to the wall painting found at the Gottschall Rockshelter in Wisconsin (Fig. 7.22). The latter shows multiple figures with rayed headdresses together with a single "smoker." Dieterle (2005) has argued that the Gottschall imagery represents a story of the Twins, although this interpretation remains in dispute (Salzer 1987; Salzer and Rajnovich 2001).

FIGURE 7.20. Shell gorget from Etowah showing figure holding a rayed spiral, Hightower style (after Penney 1985:Pl. 134).

- The Leg that constitutes a layer by itself has parallels in ceramic leg effigies from both the Middle Cumberland region and the Central Mississippi Valley (Jones 1876:Fig. 28; Thruston 1890:Fig. 43; Power 2004:Pl. 18; Hathcock 1983:Fig. 321, 1988:Figs. 577, 577a, 577b, 578, 578a, 579, 581). Severed

FIGURE 7.21. Interlaced heads from other sites: *left,* shell cup from Spiro, Braden B style (after Phillips and Brown 1978:Pls. 58, 60); *right,* monolithic axe from the Wilbanks site in Georgia (after Waring 1968a: Fig. 17).

FIGURE 7.22. Wall painting from Gottschall Rockshelter, Wisconsin (after Salzer and Rajnovich 2001:Fig. 23).

body parts are known to have served as war trophies (Dye 2004), and we may speculate that this composition was an allusion to that practice.

At a finer-grained level, elements of clothing and regalia also present some fruitful avenues for comparison:

• The head of Line Face in Foreground Group 1 is adorned with a raccoon binding that juts forward. Such headdresses are commonly depicted in shell gorgets of the Hightower style (see Fig. 7.20) (Willoughby 1932:Fig. 29; Phillips and Brown 1978:Figs. 177–178, 232; Power 2004:Fig. 16). They are also found at Spiro on shell engravings assigned to Craig A (Phillips and Brown 1978:154–155).

• The figures on the right in Foreground Groups 1 and 2 both wear a second type of headdress, which consists of a featherlike element arching forward from a bun at the back of the head and a rayed semicircle on top. A similar rayed element is worn by three of the figures at Gottschall Rockshelter (see Fig. 7.22) (Salzer 1987:Figs. 16, 18, 21; Salzer and Rajnovich 2001:Figs. 24, 25, 29). Minus the rayed semicircle, this headpiece closely resembles the headdress on two of the Wehrle copper-repoussé plates from Spiro, both Braden A in style (Phillips and Brown 1978:191, Figs. 249–250).

• The strange bulbous headdress of Line Face in Foreground Group 3 is replicated in a variety of contexts. At Picture Cave in Missouri two identical figures, the mythical Twins, are shown with this headdress, which has been identified as a "bladder" (Fig. 7.23; Duncan and Diaz-Granados 2000:14–15). The same interpretation has been suggested for a rim-effigy design found in large numbers in the Central Mississippi Valley (Lankford and Dye, personal communication). The mythic reference is to the use of bladders by the father of Lodge-Boy and Thrown-Away to prevent the wild boy from escaping to the waters of the Beneath World. It became an element of ritual costume in one version of the Sun Dance.

• The smoker in Foreground Group 3 wears a bilobed-arrow hair ornament. Such head ornaments have been found throughout the Mississippian world, either as artifacts (typically made of sheet copper) or as depictions on pottery, shell, copper-repoussé plates, and rock. The individual instances are too numerous to list. For present purposes, suffice it to say that at Spiro the depictions of such headdresses occur on shells assigned to Braden A and Craig B, and bilobed arrows as stand-alone motifs are found in Braden B

FIGURE 7.23. Wall painting from Picture Cave, Missouri (after Diaz-Granados and Duncan 2000:Fig. 5.48).

(Phillips and Brown 1978:86, 148). Other Braden-style examples include the Castalian Springs Gorget (Fig. 7.24) and the Rogan Plates from Etowah (Phillips and Brown 1978:Figs. 243–244). Hightower gorgets often show bilobed arrows above the central figure's outstretched arms, not as part of the headdress (Phillips and Brown 1978:Figs. 177–178). At Moundville the bilobed arrow is found as a stand-alone motif on Hemphill-style pottery (Steponaitis 1983:59).

- Four of the Foreground's figures and the standing figure on the reverse panel all wear skirts that are broadly similar to those commonly seen in Braden and Craig art at Spiro (Phillips and Brown 1978:95–97). Interestingly, the skirt on the reverse panel and perhaps the one worn by Line Face in Foreground Group 1 are of the "divided" type more typical of Braden imagery (Phillips and Brown 1978:Fig. 126). The loose-fitting tunic on Line Face in Foreground Group 3 has no analogs elsewhere so far as we know. The wide necklaces on many of the Foreground figures may be allusions to the twisted, multistrand necklaces worn by Braden figures, including the one on the Castalian Springs Gorget (Fig. 7.24; Phillips and Brown 1978:180).

FIGURE 7.24. Shell gorgets from Sumner Co., Tennessee: *left,* Castalian Springs Gorget from the site of the same name, Braden A style (after Dye 2004:Fig. 1); *right,* Cushman Gorget from the Rutherford-Kizer Mounds (also known as Saundersville), Hightower style (after Brown 2004:Fig. 22).

- The fan-shaped object behind Line Face in Foreground 2 is a mystery. Phillips and Brown (1984:Pl. 281) call it a "club," but not with great confidence. It is also quite rare, although not unique. The two other examples known to us include a Craig C shell from Spiro (Phillips and Brown 1984:Pl. 281) and the Piasa gorget from Moundville, the stylistic affinities of which are not clear (Phillips and Brown 1978:196–197, Fig. 257).
- In Foreground Group 3, Line Face holds a broken staff or spear. Broken staffs, as well as the closely related broken arrows and broken maces, are common in the Spiro collection and seem to be most commonly associated with Braden shells (Phillips and Brown 1978:148–149, 178–179, 1984:Pl. 149). Only a few marginal examples are known from the Craig corpus.
- Finally, the roundel border occurs in a variety of contexts on the Thruston Tablet: on a shield, a skirt, and a rectangular enclosure. Perhaps the closest analog elsewhere shows up in a set of Moundville pottery designs that characterize Moundville Engraved, *var. Cypress* (Fig. 7.25; Steponaitis 1983:Figs. 18a, 55h, 62d). Even the jagged band within the shield of Foreground Group 1 is found in the Moundville design, where it is more competently drafted as a rayed guilloche. Another instance of the roundel border appears on a wooden spider plaque from eastern Tennessee (Fig. 7.25; Fundaburk and Foreman 1957:Pl. 142).[9] We note that the roundel border is made up of segments similar to those in the "striped panel" of a great many

shell engravings from Spiro (Phillips and Brown 1978:155–156). Such panels also appear as vertical dividers in negative-painted designs on ceramics from Angel (Hilgeman 2000:Figs. 5.21, 5.22).

From a stylistic perspective, the Thruston Tablet is unique. Its manner of depicting human figural elements does not conform to or closely resemble any of the currently defined styles in the Mississippian world. Nonetheless, a few commonalities of style and subject matter help with relationships and dating. The bilobed arrow headdress on the smoking figure in Foreground Group 3 is a highly simplified version in which the lobes are drafted as circles close to the central arrow. This unusual form seems to be a rock-art specialty and is found from eastern Missouri to northern Alabama (Diaz-Granados and Duncan 2000:191–192; Henson 1986:Pl. 28). Simplified bilobed forms with plain circular lobes are also found in shell gorgets of the Hightower style from northern Georgia and eastern Tennessee (Phillips and Brown 1978:Figs. 177–178). The simple rendering of the raccoon hindquarters as a headdress element, without internal details, is also shared with Hightower-style gorgets (Phillips and Brown 1978:Figs. 177–178). The nose-lips-mouth-chin profile line of the human head is drafted as a continuous smooth squiggle, with a weak chin and no teeth. This treatment is most similar to heads in Hightower-style shell gorgets. The figures themselves are stout and stiff, shown in

FIGURE 7.25. Roundel borders from other sites: *left*, ceramic bottle from Moundville, Moundville Engraved, *var. Cypress*; *right*, wooden plaque from eastern Tennessee (after Mellown 1976:Fig. 2).

three-quarters view with avoidance of severe angles. The torsos are parallel-sided, as in Hightower-style shell engraving and to some degree in Craig. This short list of formal similarities leans primarily to the Hightower style centered to the east and south of the tablet's locality, although there are also hints of a relationship to Craig style shell engraving, whose home is far to the west.

All in all, considering both subject matter and style, we see the Thruston Tablet as having many affinities with Hightower and Braden material and fewer with Hemphill and Craig. Indeed, there is perhaps enough in common with Hightower to suggest a comparable date for the tablet: ca. AD 1250–1350 (King 2004:163; Sullivan 2007).[10] The Thruston Tablet probably represents a yet-unnamed style that, like Hightower and Hemphill, is an eastern offshoot or "branch" of the Late Braden style (Brown 2004:108–109).

Discussion

In sum, like many scholars before us, we believe the Thruston Tablet is both a palimpsest and a storyboard. We have presented a separation of the palimpsest's layers—done electronically with image-editing software—and a new interpretation of the story represented in one of these layers. We see this story as mythic rather than historical in character and suggest that has to do with the Twins, supernatural heroes whose many exploits, in countless versions, were recounted by Native storytellers across North America. We also have argued that the Thruston Tablet shows strong thematic and stylistic connections to Mississippian imagery over a wide area. So a question remains: what might account for these connections?

One possible clue is found in a comparison of two artifacts: the Castalian Springs Gorget (see Fig. 7.24; Myer 1917:Pl. 7; Brain and Phillips 1996:53; Dye 2004:Fig. 1), which comes from the eponymous site just a few miles from where the tablet was discovered, and the Lightner Cup from Spiro (see Fig. 7.18) (Phillips and Brown 1978:Pl. 20). Phillips and Brown noted the great similarity in the way the figures are drawn in these two artifacts, likely done by the same hand (Phillips and Brown 1978:180–181). In this context it is interesting to note that the Lightner Cup depicts a Twins scene, reminiscent of the themes depicted on the Thruston Tablet. We are not suggesting that the Lightner Cup was engraved at Castalian Springs or that it was done by the same artist who did the Thruston Tablet. Rather, the presence of the Castalian Springs Gorget nearby suggests that the Thruston Tablet's artist may have had access to the work of the Lightner artist, who was a master of the Braden A or Classic Braden style, which, if Brown (2004) is correct, may have originated in the vicinity of Cahokia. Thus the Lightner artist's work, and the Classic Braden corpus in general, may have provided a canonical model for aspects of the imagery on the Thruston Tablet.

It is also interesting to note that a second well-known shell artifact from Sumner County, the Cushman Gorget (see Fig. 7.24) (Brain and Phillips 1996:51; Brown 2004:Fig. 22), also depicts a possible Twins scene and is engraved in the Hightower style. As with the Lightner Cup, here we see direct evidence of connections with the products of another regional group of artisans, perhaps located in northern Georgia, which also may have provided prototypes for elements of the tablet.

We are also struck by the prevalence of the Twins in the representational art of the Middle Cumberland region. This imagery is seen not only in shell and stone, as we have just discussed, but also in the pottery: Lankford and Dye (2007) have suggested that the "dunce-cap" rim effigies commonly found on bowls in this region are also allusions to the Twins. It may well be that the story cycles involving the Twins had particular importance in the spiritual or political life of the people who lived in this region. This hypothesis does not require that all the artifacts with such imagery be made locally; indeed it is almost certain that the Cushman Gorget was an import. Even if it was made elsewhere, we may speculate that the local people especially sought items from far away that depicted the themes most relevant to them.

These observations also highlight an idea that is becoming ever more widely understood by Mississippian scholars, namely, that there is no single "Southeastern Ceremonial Complex" but rather a series of regional manifestations, each with its own style and thematic emphases. For example, the imagery in this part of Tennessee contrasts strongly with the images at Moundville. At Moundville the Twins are virtually absent (Steponaitis and Knight 2004), but here they are a dominant theme. We hope that this work on the tablet will contribute to delineating some of these regional distinctions in the overall mosaic of Mississippian art.

After more than a century, interpretation of the Thruston Tablet continues to be a work in progress. Our presentation of the imagery and interpretive speculations are obviously not the last word on the subject—and perhaps not even the last word from us. As other aspects of Mississippian art are unraveled and interpreted, they will offer new perspectives for the understanding of the Thruston imagery. So the tablet remains a touchstone to which researchers will continue to return.

NOTES

AUTHORS' ACKNOWLEDGMENTS: Our interest in this tablet was sparked at the Mississippian Iconography Workshop hosted by Kent Reilly at Texas State University in 2005. Stephen Cox subsequently allowed us to examine the tablet at the Tennessee State Museum in Nashville and provided valuable information from the museum's records; David Andrew and Marvin Stewart also greatly facilitated our research at the museum. Thad Wasklewicz, Monica Mihir, and Marcia Taylor aided in recording data on the tablet. Kevin Smith graciously shared his extensive knowledge of Nashville Basin archaeology throughout our investigations. Tracy Brown provided helpful comments on an earlier draft of this chapter, and Christopher Rodning kindly provided copies of relevant documents that reside in the Joseph Jones papers at the Tulane University Library. A preliminary version of this chapter was presented at the 2005 meeting of the Southeastern Archaeological Conference in Columbia, South Carolina; a number of those who heard this presentation offered useful advice. We are very grateful to all these individuals for their help. This research was supported in part by a Reynolds Fellowship and a Research and Study Assignment awarded to the first author by the University of North Carolina at Chapel Hill.

1. It is worth considering the question of exactly where the tablet was found. In his original description, Thruston (1890:91) simply said the tablet was discovered "on Rocky Creek, in Sumner County." Myer, who knew the area well, later added some more detail: "This interesting, somewhat weather-worn engraved slab of local, gray, fossiliferous, close-grained ordovician limestone, was found in the year 1877 on Rocky creek, in Sumner county, Tennessee, probably near where this creek enters Cumberland river" (Myer 1928:99). And again: "Unfortunately no record was kept of the name of the donor, nor any particulars of its discovery. The only information now obtainable is that it was found on Rocky Creek, probably at the old Indian settlement near the mouth of Canoe Branch, about 3 ½ miles from Castalian Springs" (Myer n.d.:485).

Yet only a few years after the original description Thruston changed his story: "In the same mound group, near Nashville, where the Myer gorget was found, an interesting pictograph in stone was discovered and illustrated by the writer, representing a group of Indian warriors—doubtless mound builders—and showing their dress, implements and general appearance" (Thruston 1897:98). Clearly by this time he believed that the tablet had been found at Castalian Springs itself. Later still, Keeler and Verrill offered some support for this alternative view: "After examining the Thruston Tablet, contact was made by telephone with Mr. Robert T. Quarles who was the son of General Thruston's best friend. He had known about the Thruston Tablet since boyhood . . . He declared that the stone had been found in the water of the Creek at the site of the great Mound Builder excavation, as Thruston had said, and it does show marks of water erosion. Since there had been but one small mound on Rocky Creek and this had never been disturbed, and since the place of extensive excavation was on the banks of the next creek, we may feel certain that General Thruston was not quite accurate in his statement as to just where the stone had been found and that it was actually picked up at the famous Bledsoe Lick Creek Mound Builder site" (Keeler and Verrill 1962:32).

Bledsoe Lick is another name for the Castalian Springs site, which Myer himself had excavated (Myer 1917). If that had indeed been the location of the find, one would think that Myer would have heard about it. On the other hand, Thruston got his information closer to the time the tablet was actually found. So it is difficult to judge which version is correct. Either way, the general location of the find is not in dispute, as the two possibilities are only a few miles apart.

2. At least three sources claim that the tablet was discovered in 1874, but the evidence for this assertion is never made clear (Huddleston 1962a; Durham 1969:9; Traxel 2004:Fig. 20).

3. According to Myer (1928:99), the photograph later published by Mallery was actually made by Holmes. Holmes also produced a cast of the Thruston Tablet, which still resides in the National Museum of Natural History (catalog number A135919).

4. As this chapter went to press, an unpublished nineteenth-century illustration of the Thruston Tablet was brought to our attention by Kevin Smith. It resides in the Joseph Jones papers at the Tulane University Library, currently in Box 28. The print is entitled "Engraved Stone from Rock Creek Sumner Co. Tenn. (Medical & Surgical Memory of Joseph Jones M.D.)." At the bottom it is inscribed "J. H. Dowling, Del. N.O."—the last two letters presumably an abbreviation for New Orleans. A brief accompanying manuscript that alludes to the illustration is said by the library's catalog to date to 1895–1896 (Jones 1980:27) and Jones himself died in 1896, which provides a *terminus ante quem*. The illustration appears to be an independent rendering, not based on the images published by Thruston, Holmes, or Mallery. Neither the detail nor the accuracy of the drawing approaches that of Holmes. While having some historical interest, it adds no new information and sheds no new light on the iconographic issues discussed herein.

5. A generally similar discussion of the tablet was included in Myer's manuscript entitled "Stone Age Man in the Middle South" (n.d.), which was never published. The surviving manuscript also lacks the figure showing the reverse face.

6. According to one source (Huddleston 1962b), Lewis never saw the tablet firsthand. Given the faintness of the engraving and the quality of the photographs, it is not surprising that he had difficulty in following the lines with his pen.

7. In a recent book entitled *Footprints of the Welsh Indians*, William Traxel provides yet another photograph and drawing of the Thruston Tablet and suggests that the scenes

depict Welshmen, not Vikings (Traxel 2004:90–92, Fig. 20a–b). We take neither side in this dispute.

8. The dome-shaped object is also similar to a motif that occurs on Menomini bark scrolls (Berres 2001:Fig. 13b [left]; Skinner 1913:Fig 7 [left]). This motif is said to represent a Thunderer or a Thunderer's power (Berres 2001:160; Skinner 1913:75).

9. This wooden plaque resides in the Field Museum in Chicago. It has often been said to come from Moundville (e.g., Fundaburk and Foreman 1957:Pl. 142), but the museum's records indicate that this piece actually was found in eastern Tennessee (Duane Esarey and Ian Brown, personal communication, 2004).

10. Based on recent excavations, Smith and Beahm (2007) date the main occupation at Castalian Springs—where the tablet may have been originally found (see note 1 above)—to ca. AD 1200–1325. Happily, our dates overlap nicely with theirs.

CHAPTER 8

Woman in the Patterned Shawl

Female Effigy Vessels and Figurines from the Middle Cumberland River Basin

Robert V. Sharp, Vernon James Knight, Jr., and George E. Lankford

Excavations at the Averbuch site in Davidson County, Tennessee, in the late 1970s uncovered a remarkably pristine Late Mississippian–period palisaded settlement with three separate cemeteries that together yielded over 600 burials containing over 800 individual human remains as well as artifacts in stone, shell, bone, and ceramic—all carefully documented in a substantial site report (Klippel and Bass 1984). While further assessment of the entire ceramic assemblage from Averbuch (40DV60) is the subject of ongoing research (Moore and Smith 2007), for the present study the archaeological salvage work conducted at this site is notable because among the ceramic items preserved from the site are three hooded female effigy bottles (Klippel and Bass 1984; Reed 1984a). That all three of these figurative vessels depict humpbacked females is not surprising: among the numerous human effigies of the hooded-bottle form throughout the Southeast—and especially in the three most productive regions: northeastern Arkansas, southeastern Missouri, and central Tennessee—humpbacked figures are extremely common (Holmes 1886a:422–426, 1886b:182–186, 1903:Pls. 26–27; Phillips 1939; Phillips et al. 1951:163–165, Tables 2 and 10, Fig. 107a–b; Hathcock 1988:183–209). Instead, what is striking about the Averbuch effigy bottles is that, while all three share stylistic similarities, one of them (Fig. 8.1) was decorated with a particular negative-painted pattern that was first recorded in 1890 on two other effigy vessels from Davidson County in Gates P. Thruston's study *The Antiquities of Tennessee and the Adjacent States* (Fig. 8.2). Since then, works exhibiting this pattern have appeared sporadically in the literature (Cox 1985; Dickens 1982; Myer 1917, 1928; Phillips 1939, 1970:139–141; Phillips et al. 1951), and its existence continues to be noted (Reed 1984a:II.7.25; Brain and Phillips 1996:256–257; Brown 2002/2006).[1]

In our sessions together at the Texas State University Mississippian Iconography Workshops, we initially undertook a broad survey of effigy bottles (with particular emphasis on human hooded-bottle forms) as well as rattles and figurines of pottery depicting kneeling or sitting humans drawn from the Middle Cumberland area, ultimately incorporating over ninety examples from the Peabody Museum of Archaeology and Ethnology at Harvard University, the Tennessee State Museum in Nashville, and miscellaneous published and unpublished sources. As a result of our examination of this substantial corpus of ceramic effigy vessels and figurines from across the Nashville area, we want to draw attention to this effigy figure, who, in more than two dozen examples ornamented with this same pattern or faint traces of it (collected from a seven-county region including Davidson, Montgomery, Robertson, Smith, Stewart, Sumner, and Williamson Counties), is without doubt the single most important subject in the pottery of the Middle Cumberland Culture (Ferguson 1972).[2]

Like many of the humpbacked effigies from the Central Mississippi Valley, the three humpbacked female effigy vessels from Averbuch (and indeed those from across the Cumberland region that are included among the ceramic human effigies at the center of this study) leave no ambiguity about their

FIGURE 8.1. Female effigy bottle with negative-painted ornamentation, photographs taken near the time of excavation 1977–1978, from the Averbuch site, Davidson Co., Tennessee, ceramic, height 15.1 cm, Frank H. McClung Museum, University of Tennessee, Knoxville: *left*, frontal view; *right*, profile view of left side, showing humpback and perforated neck knob.

FIGURE 8.2. Plate 9, Gates P. Thruston, *The Antiquities of Tennessee and the Adjacent States* (1890).

physical condition. They have either a smooth and evenly modeled ridge establishing the line of the backbone and protruding prominently or even dramatically (evident in Fig. 8.1) or a vertical row of knobs showing vertebrae projecting from the center of the spinal column, as depicted on another of the Averbuch effigy vessels (Fig. 8.3). Almost all such figures also display an expanded chest area, created (like their spinal humps) as a bulge in the vessel wall. Although their numbers may well be fewer, straight-backed examples of female effigies are also abundant in the Nashville area, and they contrast markedly with these humpbacked figures. The salient feature of this subgroup is an upright back, with no indication of a backbone. These straight-backed effigies can be somewhat portly, but nonetheless there is no hump. In fact, a vertical groove along the line of the backbone often suggests that the potters creating this feature were eager to emphasize that the character being depicted was emphatically *not* a humpback by showing virtually the opposite feature: an indentation at the spine. Again, though the effigy vessels may sometimes represent large figures—stout or even somewhat bloated through the midsection—we do not believe that they are intended to suggest pregnant females. While the women kneel at rest with their legs bent underneath them and with their hands most often placed against the abdomen or

FIGURE 8.3. Female effigy bottle from the Averbuch site, Davidson Co., Tennessee, ceramic, height 17.7 cm, Department of Anthropology, University of Tennessee, Knoxville: *left*, frontal view; *right*, profile view of left side, showing humpback with protruding vertebrae.

occasionally sit with their knees drawn up before them and their hands resting upon the knees, they certainly show no indication of the full or extended belly of a woman carrying a child late in her term.

Yet, throughout the Cumberland River basin, despite the clearly contrasting aspects of their physique, the humpbacked female effigies and the straight-backed ones are intended to represent the same character, based on our examination. First and foremost, all or nearly all, as far as we know, were recovered from stone-box graves of children (or at the very least subadults) of the Thruston phase, AD 1250–1400, and share similar deposition in mortuary contexts (Breitburg and Moore 2005:130; Broster 1972, 1988; Ferguson 1972; Smith 1991, 1992). In support of our conclusion, we also adduce several essential, fairly emphatic connections between these two groups of effigies. Principal among these characteristics is the depiction of a cloaklike garment that is common to many of these straight-backed and humpbacked effigies, rendered in black-on-white-slip or black-on-buff-paste negative painting, exemplifying the ceramic type known as "Nashville Negative Painted" (Hilgeman 1985, 1991, 2000; Phillips 1970:139–141; Phillips et al. 1951:174–175;

Smith 1992:79–85). This garment bears a common design and is worn in the same manner, strongly suggesting its role as an identity marker for this personage. We see this item of clothing as being worn like a shawl or mantle. It is a rectangular piece of twined fabric that wraps around the figure and may cover the arms, though it allows the hands to be freely shown, perhaps hinting at its twined openwork fabrication. The garment starts at the neckline and has roundels on the shoulders that depict concentric circles, spirals, or a four-dot arrangement that creates a cross-in-circle design. The garment also contains a large-scale pattern of two concentric ovals set against a background of closely spaced diagonal or hatched lines. This design is centered on the right arm and wraps evenly over the front and back of the figure. The decorated field of this design ends at the waist, below which it is replaced by a zone of black pigment denoting a skirt and extending to a skirt line at the knees. Because of the way the design flows in an uninterrupted manner over the chest, arm, and back, we are skeptical of the suggestion that it depicts tattooing of the body rather than a garment with a primary motif imprinted upon it as an identifying attribute.

Indeed, the nature of the design of this cloaklike garment is such that it can best be understood with the aid of a rollout rendering included in Philip Phillips's 1939 dissertation at Harvard (Fig. 8.4) and an oblique perspective produced for his 1970 study of Lower Mississippi Valley ceramics (Fig. 8.5). Against a ground pattern of hatching, or what may be intended as cross-hatching, a curving band of parallel lines begins at the lower left side of the torso, near the waist, rises up the chest along the inside of the left arm, crosses laterally over the upper part of the breasts, and proceeds over the right arm and onto the back before dropping down again at the left arm and terminating at the back of the waist. The curving band describes a large oval as it wraps from the front over to the back; within that oval, also against the hatched ground, is a second, much smaller oval that also wraps from the figure's lower right side, over the right arm, and onto the lower back.

In her review of Mississippian garments known from historical and ethnographic accounts, Penelope Drooker (1992:72–80) has offered valuable confirmation of both the cloaklike shawl or mantle and the knee-length wraparound skirt depicted on these Cumberland effigies. She offers as evidence an alternate-pair-twined rectangular garment from a rock shelter in Morgan County in eastern Tennessee that could have served as either a mantle or skirt, while seven similar fabrics recovered from Spiro are distinguished by

FIGURE 8.4. (*above*) Rollout illustration of a female effigy bottle with negative-painted ornamentation from the cemetery site, Oscar F. Noel's Farm, Davidson Co., Tennessee, ceramic, height 18.0 cm, Peabody Museum of Archaeology and Ethnology, Harvard University, Cambridge, Massachusetts (84-63-10/34286). From Phillips 1939:Fig. 47.

FIGURE 8.5. (*left*) Perspective rendering of a female effigy bottle with negative-painted ornamentation from the cemetery site, Oscar F. Noel's Farm, Davidson Co., Tennessee, ceramic, height 18.0 cm, Peabody Museum of Archaeology and Ethnology, Harvard University, Cambridge, Massachusetts (84-63-10/34286). From Phillips 1970:139; drawing by Eliza McFadden.

their dark red dye; three of them have large-scale geometric designs in yellow, no doubt produced by a resist technique comparable to the negative-painting treatment of ceramics (Drooker 1992:80–83; Willey 1948; Willey and Phillips 1944; Willoughby 1952:115–118, Pls. 145, 147, 148). Drooker (1992:83) believes that these were most likely ceremonial garments, with the large-scale patterns recognizable at a distance. The inclusion of shoulder roundels on these effigy vessels and related figurines may also reflect the ability of the makers of Mississippian textiles to create complex designs that actually contain such concentric elements. A fabric-impressed sherd from the Stone site, a Mississippian settlement in Stewart County, Tennessee (40SW23), demonstrates that a concentric motif like the one exhibited in the shoulder roundels could in fact be contained within an openwork fabric by twining (Drooker 1992:190–192, Figs. 52–53).[3]

Given the fugitive nature of negative painting and the resulting loss of pattern that many effigy vessels have suffered, it is fortunate that a straight-backed effigy from Smith County, Tennessee, has preserved the large-scale pattern almost in its entirety (Fig. 8.6). Certainly rendered here more

FIGURE 8.6. Female effigy bottle with negative-painted ornamentation from Beasley's Bend, near Rome, Smith Co., Tennessee, ceramic, height 22.9 cm, Dr. Arthur Cushman Collection, Old Hickory, Tennessee: *left,* frontal view; *center,* back view; *right,* profile view of right side, showing wraparound patterned garment, shoulder spirals, and perforated neck knob (hair-bun). Photographs by David H. Dye.

completely than on any other known figure, the shawl-like garment with its spiraling roundels is shown to drape nicely around this effigy's neckline and to terminate at the waist, just above the dark, unpatterned skirt. In this case, the negative-painted depiction of patterned fabric wraps around both arms of this very youthful individual like a poncho, from which her hands could emerge.

In addition to the cloaklike mantle and knee-length skirt that these effigies have in common and that we believe are her primary identity markers, other characteristics of her modeling or treatment lend additional support. Among these is a highly prominent feature that we initially chose to call a "neck knob," principally because its significance was not entirely clear to us. This small knob at the back of the neck, generally at its base (visible in Figs. 8.1 [right], 8.3 [right], and 8.6 [right]), is not to be confused with either a humpback itself or the separate protruding vertebrae that appear on some humpbacked effigy vessels (especially since such notched vertebrae can be found on vessels that also show a neck knob). The neck knob can be as simple as a small raised mass or can be more carefully delineated as a flattened rectangular protrusion or a slightly saddle-backed form. Sometimes it is perforated laterally, turning it into a functional handle that could have been used to suspend the image from a cord, but clearly that is not its primary purpose or justification, given the number of times it is negligible in size or unperforated. On the whole, we have come to interpret this element as a hair-bun, suggesting the gathered and folded ends of hair, which yield the saddle-back form on the most explicit or carefully articulated examples. Overall we take it to be one of the markers that this figure's sex is female.[4]

Another aspect directly related to identity markers is hairstyle, and the female vessels and figurines from the Cumberland region depict several distinct hairstyles, shared by a variety of humpbacked and straight-backed effigies. These may prove to be indicators of social or religious significance or may instead reflect the mark of their maker or workshop. One such hairstyle features a prominent pointed node at the crest of the head, with a second, somewhat smaller node lower down toward the forehead and two additional small lobes (one on either side of the first pair) set above each ear. This four-part hairstyle is visible in Figs. 8.3, 8.4, and 8.5. A second hairstyle principally displays a single roach of hair atop the forehead, in line with the nose. This treatment, often combined with a well-defined, raised hairline running in an arc along the top of the forehead, is displayed in Figs. 8.1 and 8.7.

FIGURE 8.7. Female effigy bottle from the Belle Meade site, Davidson Co., Tennessee, ceramic, height 19.5 cm, Mark Clark Collection, Clarksville, Tennessee: *left*, frontal view; *right*, profile view of right side, showing humpback, perforated neck knob (hair-bun), and perforated roach of hair. Photographs by Joseph Mohan.

Finally, it has been the operating assumption of this study—explicit in the title and employed consistently throughout—that these humpbacked and straight-backed figures are female. Although the potters who produced them sometimes depicted their subjects with rather ample breasts, we have found that breast definition or breast size is not an especially coherent or reliable marker of sex in these objects. Instead, we believe that a skirt line indicating a knee-length skirt is a primary marker of sex and in combination with the cloaklike garment forms the foremost determinant and identity marker. In short, although we acknowledge that male effigy figures have been found in the Central Mississippi Valley, with distinct genitals, we have yet to find a single clear example of a male effigy in pottery from the Cumberland region.[5] Posture is another relevant factor. While most of these effigy figures are depicted kneeling, some are seated on their buttocks, with both knees drawn up in front. None is shown with only one knee drawn up or as seated cross-legged, both of these postures being associated with males among the stone temple figures of the same region (Brown 2001; Smith 1991; Smith and

Miller 2009:27–28).[6] In addition, none of the male stone figures show hands placed on the abdomen, as is common among the ceramic effigies. From the combined weight of this evidence, we interpret the entire Cumberland ceramic series as depicting females.[7]

Thus we return to one of our earliest arguments: the two physical forms of these female effigies are intended to represent the same character or individual. Furthermore, this physical dualism is only a reflection of the life span of this female character (the stages of her life, so to speak), from the trim, upright physique of a young woman, through various intermediary stages, to the heavier morphology of an old woman, humpbacked not from disease but simply from advanced age (Diaz-Granados 2004; Diaz-Granados and Duncan 2000; Smith 2001:280–281). The female effigy vessels and figurines examined in this study are primarily distinguished by their decoration with one distinctive negative-painted pattern either on their natural buff earthenware paste or on a white-slipped prepared surface upon which the design is applied. The modeling of this figure's physical and facial features is so consistent, however, that even examples that were apparently left undecorated (Figs. 8.3 and 8.7) but were recovered from similar mortuary contexts as well as ones that have lost all but faint traces of their ornamentation can still be recognized and identified as this female personage.

Cumberland Basin Female Effigies

The identification of a distinct body of ceramic effigy ware from the Nashville area and the broader Cumberland River basin was established in the years just following the Civil War by Joseph Jones, M.D., who himself excavated a number of Mississippian-period settlements, mounds, and earthworks in 1868 and 1869 and at each one "opened" countless stone-box graves. Jones recorded his discoveries and theories in an essay in 1869 in the *American Naturalist* and in a book-length treatise, *Explorations of the Aboriginal Remains of Tennessee*, published by the Smithsonian Institution in 1876. Included in both is his report of his own discovery of a female effigy figure—kneeling with her arms crossed over her chest—in the grave of a child in a burial mound "opposite Nashville," by which he meant the eastern bank of the Cumberland at the heart of the city (Jones 1869:68–70, 1876:44–45, Fig. 9).

In addition to mapping several sites along the Harpeth River, one of the major tributaries of the Cumberland, and illustrating other humpbacked effigy vessels from Brentwood and elsewhere in Williamson County, south of Nashville, Jones described a different grave find that is relevant to the present study: "A small image in my possession, formed of white clay, found in middle Tennessee, painted with the same black pigment as their vases, and dressed in what appears by the markings to be a woven garment, has a cross painted on both shoulders" (Jones 1876:76). Naturally, the "white clay" is an important clue, because the effigies that concern us here are those bearing the pattern imprinted upon their buff or pinkish buff paste or upon a prepared white-slip surface. Jones knew that these should be distinguished from the dark ware that is widespread in the Cumberland for utilitarian vessels and numerous other figural pieces. Based on the drawings reproduced in his study (Jones 1876:76–77, Figs. 44–45; see also Jones 1869:72), this effigy can be identified as one now in the collection of the National Museum of the American Indian (no. 7391): a carefully modeled female effigy bottle, kneeling and tightly skirted, with the remains of a negative-painted design (appearing most prominently across her upper right arm) that bears a strong resemblance to the patterns on other such figures and still shows, with remarkable clarity, the cross-in-circle roundels on her shoulders that Jones described and illustrated. This straight-backed effigy vessel also has pierced ears and a perforated hair-bun at the back of her neck. Her arms are held against her, and her hands meet in front on her stomach. In addition, the figure appears to display an upper garment, which may be the wraparound shawl or mantle, tied together at the base of her throat and overlapping along the left side of her torso.

Following in Jones's footsteps, Gen. Gates P. Thruston owned multiple examples of negative-painted kneeling female effigies and depicted them in three different engraved plates in his 1890 volume. Two light-colored, kneeling female effigies shown in the frontispiece and in Plate 3 appear among an assortment of remarkable head fragments and complete effigy bottles showing a range of sizes (Fig. 8.8). These two effigies (17.1 and 17.8 cm high) are straight-backed and even in 1890 showed little evidence of negative painting, though its presence has been confirmed (Cox 1985:126, nos. 14–15). Both are known to be from stone-box burials on the farm of Oscar F. Noel (40DV3), which at the time lay some 6 km south of Nashville proper. As we have already seen, Thruston depicted two other effigy bottles showing the complete pattern in Plate 9 of his catalogue, setting them among other hooded bottles, animal effigy vessels, and bowls with human and animal heads atop their rims (Fig. 8.2). In presenting this engraved plate he noted the contrast between the lighter-colored ware that would be used for the negative-painted pieces and what he characterized as "the dark, rich, reddish brown ware, the specialty of the Nashville district," that composed the other bottles, bowls, and jars (Thruston 1890:152). Although the precise source of these second two effigies is unknown, it is generally believed that their origin lay in the vast Mississippian-period cemetery discovered on the Noel Farm, for Thruston supervised the excavation of perhaps as many as 3,000 to 4,000 graves at this site in the late 1880s (Phillips 1939:21; Kelly 1985:16).[8] He recorded in connection with the presentation of objects in Plate 9 that he had "obtained more than a hundred . . . specimens of pottery from the Noel cemetery, and other burial grounds in the immediate vicinity of Nashville" (Thruston 1890:152).

The taller of these two effigies (19.2 cm high; Cox 1985:No. 13) is a straight-backed female with modeled hands resting against her thighs (Fig. 8.10). Her facial features are roughly fashioned, with two nodes on the crown of the head representing a hairdress and two large ears, the right one of which is misshapen and strangely drooping. This female has a very well preserved negative-painted pattern that carries over from the front of the figure to her back, clearly displaying the concentric parallel lines that define a large outer

FIGURE 8.8. Frontispiece, Gates P. Thruston, *The Antiquities of Tennessee and the Adjacent States* (1890).

oval and a smaller oval within, all against a background of looped hatching. This pattern ends at the waist and is distinctly separate from the dark-stained skirt. The second of the two effigies (18.1 cm high; Cox 1985:No. 5) depicts a much squatter female, also kneeling and dark skirted, but with several noticeable differences (Fig. 8.9). Foremost among these is the fact that this is a humpbacked figure with several vertebrae appearing raised along the line of the spine. In addition, this figure features a different style in rendering the negative-painted design, with solid oblique lines above and below the parallel band that extends across the chest, and hands rendered in negative painting, instead of being modeled.

Although Thruston knew that Frederic W. Putnam of the Peabody Museum at Harvard University had led an exploration of a number of sites in and around Nashville and the Cumberland River basin in the late 1870s, he seems to have been unaware that two effigy bottles virtually identical to the one just discussed had entered the Peabody's collection as a result of that activity—and from the very same site. The first (PMAE 78-6-10/14218) was discovered by Edwin Curtiss in June 1878, working under Putnam's direction, at the Cain's Chapel site adjacent to Noel Farm.[9] The second, slightly larger effigy (PMAE 84-63–10/34286; 18.0 vs. 16.1 cm high) was recovered in 1884 at the Noel Farm by George Woods—working on behalf of Putnam—from the grave of a child, along with other mortuary goods: a shell spoon, a large shell bead, and over fifty small shell beads. Both of these Peabody effigies have been judged to be the product of the same potter (Phillips 1939; Brown 1990); and given the evident similarities among these buff-colored figures, Thruston's must be attributed to the same maker or workshop. The shape and uneven placement of the ears; the large nose and broad, flattened eyes; the four-part hairstyle and the small hair-bun at the back of the neck that we have described earlier; and even the slightly upturned head all display such consistency of handling that these three female effigy bottles must share common authorship. Indeed, all of these formal aspects exhibit such consistent execution that, with the careful replication of their negative-painted design and their remarkable negative-painted hands, only one thing is surprising: the effigy from Thruston's collection (now in the Tennessee State Museum) is humpbacked, as noted, while the two Peabody effigies are straight-backed. Clearly, on this evidence alone, the identification of this effigy figure—whoever she may be or whatever she may represent—does not hinge upon what would likely appear to most observers to be a determining characteristic: she

FIGURE 8.9. Female effigy bottle with negative-painted ornamentation from Davidson Co., Tennessee, ceramic, height 18.1 cm, Tennessee State Museum, Nashville: *top left,* frontal view; *top right,* back view; *bottom,* profile view of right side, showing humpback, neck knob (hairbun), and four-part hairstyle. Photographs by David H. Dye.

 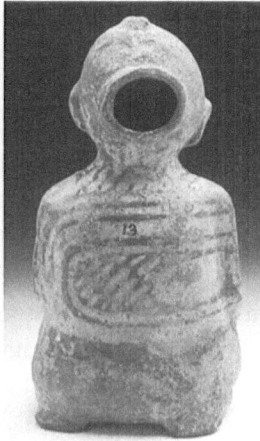 

FIGURE 8.10. Female effigy bottle with negative-painted ornamentation from the cemetery site, Oscar F. Noel's Farm, Davidson Co., Tennessee, ceramic, height 19.2 cm, Tennessee State Museum, Nashville: *left,* frontal view; *center,* back view, showing well-preserved pattern and dark-stained skirt; *right,* profile view of right side, showing straight back. Photographs by David H. Dye.

can be depicted as both straight-backed and humpbacked. She is only one personage, regardless of her size or shape.

It is the larger of these two Peabody effigy bottles (84–63-10/34286) that we have already seen rendered twice for publication (Figs. 8.4, 8.5), and those artistic interpretations serve the figure in the Thruston collection quite well. Although the design on the shoulders of the Thruston effigy is difficult to discern, the two Peabody pieces have maintained the roundels on their shoulders containing four small white circles against a dark-stained background. Again, despite the effacement of the negative-painted design in certain areas of all three effigies, the overall markings remain sufficiently strong that we feel that we know the pattern and can recognize its presence elsewhere, even when only fragments or traces of it appear.

Certainly, fragments of the pattern are all that remain on four remarkably similar effigy bottles from the Gray's Farm site (40WM11) on the Harpeth River in Williamson County—all now in the collections of the Peabody Museum, Harvard (78-6-10/15853, 15870, 15898, and 15983). These female effigies constitute a notable subgroup, in that all four were unearthed by Edwin Curtiss in October 1878 in the course of his excavation of 197 graves at this site, the first three in the mound at Gray's Farm and the fourth in a nearby cemetery, beneath part of the farm's orchard. All four of these female effigies are of substantial girth, close in height (17.2, 20.6, 20.0, and 19.5 cm high, respectively), kneeling, with their hands across their abdomens. Their eyes are apparently closed, though their mouths protrude and their lips are parted. All four have identical small mounds of hair at the rear base of the neck, no doubt representing gathered folds, and they all share with the Noel Farm group the four-part hairstyle described earlier. But in a noticeable departure from the buff-colored Noel cemetery effigies, all four of these female figures were white-slipped before being negative painted. Sadly, this extra step in their production did not guarantee the preservation of the painted pattern; in fact, it seems that the wearing and spalling of the white slip—perhaps from the use of these effigy bottles in mortuary rituals prior to their deposition—may have made these effigies even more vulnerable to the loss of their design.

Overall, the remarkable similarities in form and surface treatment shared by this group prompted Ian Brown (1990, 2002/2006) to suggest that all four are the work of the same potter, a judgment with which we concur. In another striking connection with the Noel Farm group, which presented one humpbacked and two straight-backed effigies of otherwise identical design, the effigies of this Gray's Farm group are mixed as well: three straight-backed, one humpbacked. One of the effigies (78-6-10/15853) was found by Curtiss in a four-foot-long stone-box grave that was almost certainly that of a child, located within the mound and thus perhaps a member of an elite group. And an extraordinary burial it was: this effigy bottle was accompanied by another female effigy example in a different style (78-6-10/15852)—an unslipped and straight-backed figurine/rattle of dark ware, seated with her knees up and her hands on her knees, with a perforated hair-bun at the back of her neck—as well as four other vessels and other grave goods (Brain and Phillips 1996:257), an extraordinary cache for a culture so sparing in other burials (Putnam 1878).

Recent examination and photography of the entire Gray's Farm group of four confirmed that the second of the set (78-6-10/15870), another straight-backed figure, still bears large portions of the negative-painted pattern illustrated above from Phillips's 1939 dissertation (Fig. 8.4), though possibly considerably less "oblique hatching" than Phillips et al. observed (1951: Table 10).[10] Because its original white slip is almost totally gone, along with the design it bore, the third of these Gray's Farm effigies (78-6-10/15898) reveals the natural "pinkish buff" shell-tempered paste that Phillips et al. (1951:174–175) considered to be characteristic of Middle Cumberland ceramics. Despite the undeniable formal consistency of this small group thus far and the necessary inclusion of the final one (78-6-10/15983) on these same stylistic and material grounds, this effigy, which has also suffered the loss of almost all of its slip and pattern, surprisingly presents an enormous humpback. As in the case of the Noel Farm group, with all other attributes being held constant, the representation of this effigy figure transcends what might otherwise be considered to be its principal physiological identifier. She is not by definition a humpbacked figure, but she may be represented as one, just as she may be represented as a female who is straight-backed.

Other female effigy bottles found by Curtiss at Gray's Farm in Williamson County reinforce the central position of this personage. In the burial of a child in the cemetery area, a negative-painted, buff-colored humpbacked figure (Fig. 8.11, left; PMAE 78-6-10/15980) was found with other notable grave goods: two gorgets, one a Cox Mound style and the other showing concentric circles, possibly an unfinished Nashville-style triskele (Brain and Phillips 1996:259). The modeling of this figure (in the shaping of her broad shoulders on a torso that narrows considerably at the waist, the extremely large ears, the protruding nose, and the substantial frontal roach of hair) provides evidence of the style of a maker or workshop clearly different from the group of four just addressed.

This effigy has a very dark stain indicating her skirt; above that, though entirely lost on her back, is our familiar pattern across her upper chest, with evidence of hatching on her right arm and wrist. In addition, a broken but reconstructed cream-colored effigy, also now in the Peabody Museum (78-6-10/15999), is one of the rare negative-painted females depicted in a seated posture, with her knees up in front of her and her arms up against her at her waist. Despite large areas of restoration, the negative-painted pattern remains visible on the upper left side of her chest. This large effigy (height 26.2 cm) has an immense humpback. Once again, her broad shoulders and well-defined waist, her large ears, the raised nodes on her head, her prominent roach, and the clear arc of hair framing her forehead and the upper part of her face suggest that this figure was perhaps crafted in the same workshop as the buff-colored effigy shown in Figure 8.11 and that both were part of a different set than the four white-slipped Gray's Farm effigies discussed

 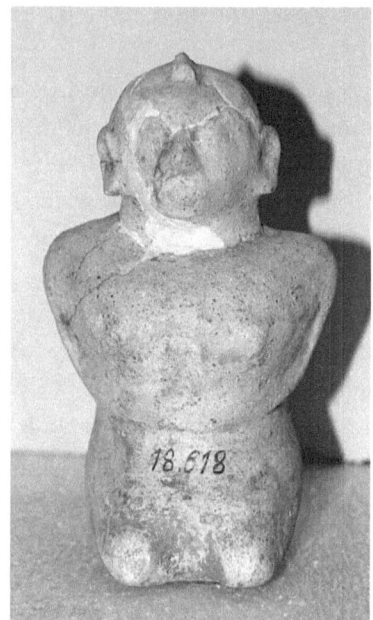

FIGURE 8.11. (*Left*) Female effigy bottle with negative-painted ornamentation from Gray's Farm, Williamson Co., Tennessee, ceramic, height 14.7 cm. Peabody Museum of Archaeology and Ethnology, Harvard University, Cambridge, Massachusetts (78-6-10/15980). Photograph by Vincas P. Steponaitis. (*Right*) Female effigy bottle with negative-painted ornamentation from Mr. Gower's place, Davidson Co., Tennessee, ceramic, height 14.4 cm. Peabody Museum of Archaeology and Ethnology, Harvard University, Cambridge, Massachusetts (79-4-10/18618). Photograph by Vincas P. Steponaitis.

earlier.[11] Another female effigy bottle recovered from a site along the Cumberland River in western Davidson County by Curtiss in May 1879 is a remarkable example of a work that possibly ties together two separate settlements. The characteristics of this effigy figure (Fig. 8.11, right; PMAE 79-4-10/18618)—attributed to the grave of a child at "Mr. Gower's place" in the Peabody Museum ledger—strongly suggest that it is the product of the same maker or the same workshop as the two above: a broad-shouldered torso narrowing dramatically to the waist; cordlike arms held against the sides without evidence of hands; extremely large ears, a receding chin, and a hair roach standing erect above the forehead; and a hair-bun wedged tightly beneath the opening of the bottle in the back of the head. It also displays on its humpback the large oval design against a background of hatching.

Without yet knowing the actual place of origin of these pieces, we can nonetheless recognize that in this instance such female figures were part of ritual beliefs or mortuary practices shared by the Gray's Farm and Gower place communities. This humpbacked figure wears a very dark-stained skirt, most evident across her buttocks. The vessel has been reconstructed with some areas of fill, but a substantial part of her back contains oblique hatching within a curving band that turns at her left arm and arcs down to the rear of her waist—clearly the pattern we have been examining. Its physical features also invite the recognition that we are dealing with a subgroup whose examples are distributed not only between Gray's Farm in Williamson County and the Gower site in western Davidson County but also between one of these locales and the Averbuch site in the northern portion of Davidson County and the Belle Meade site southwest of Nashville. Both the effigy bottle in Fig. 8.1 and the humpback vessel seen in Fig. 8.7 exhibit sufficiently similar characteristics to warrant their inclusion in this same grouping. The negative-painted Averbuch effigy bottle and the unpainted Belle Meade effigy bottle are either the product of the same workshop or remarkably skillful imitations of them, displaying a convincing awareness of that workshop's effigies and their physiological attributes.

Conclusion

The recovery of the six different effigy vessels from Gray's Farm clearly provides an extraordinary opportunity to consider one of the dominant clusters of these figures. While a greater number of such effigy bottles have been recovered from Davidson County, principally from the well-known cemetery on the Noel Farm, the Gray's Farm examples offer not only the second-largest concentration of female effigies (humpbacked and straight-backed) but also evidence of two different stylistic subgroups coexisting within the same settlement. Yet they nonetheless display the same negative-painted pattern, whether on a prepared white slip in the first subgroup of four or on the natural buff or cream surface in the second. And each subgroup was ultimately used to fulfill the same function in funeral rites, especially those of infants and children. Overall, the characteristics of these female effigy vessels —and numerous additional examples from these same counties and others nearby that require further study—unite them as representations of the same possibly supernatural personage who was venerated or invoked in the practices of a mortuary cult complex across the Cumberland River basin (Sharp 2007, 2008).

Seeking the identity of this young/old woman in the patterned shawl is an important task, although it is beyond the limits of this chapter. There are possible candidates for the female divinity in the mythology of Algonkians, Siouans, Iroquoians, and Muskhogeans (see Lankford 2008a:Chapter 2), any of whom may be relevant to the discussion, since the ethnic identity of the Cumberland Mississippians is unknown. Some scholars, for example, have suggested that the related female figurines from the Mississippi Valley should be understood as images of a corn divinity or the Siouan Earth Mother best known from the Mandan and Hidatsa myths (Bowers 1992; Diaz-Granados 2004:143; Diaz-Granados and Duncan 2000:219–220; Duncan and Diaz-Granados 2004; Emerson 1989, 1997a:Chapter 7; Emerson et al. 2003; Prentice 1986). Scholars have called attention to an unusual emphasis on a female divinity by the Shawnees. Their elevation of Grandmother to the role of creator apparently took place in the nineteenth century, but these scholars have suggested that the seedbed for that anomalous religious shift may have been in place for centuries (Voegelin 1936; Voegelin and Voegelin 1944). No one has yet made a case for a single interpretation of the identity of the Cumberland female effigy figure, but these lines of investigation suggest that the quest may not be fruitless. Meanwhile, the stylistic differences that are evident among these effigy vessels sharpen our awareness that we are dealing with intersite and intrasite complexities of interaction. These will also require further examination, along with their relationship to other affiliated grave goods such as ceramic effigy figurines and rattles, animal effigy bowls, negative-painted carafe-neck bottles and owl effigy bottles, and even shell gorgets. As a group these effigy bottles constitute a remarkable example of local ceramic production—indeed, one of the finest discrete bodies of pottery work of the fourteenth century.[12] Within this admittedly modest corpus lies much more to be teased out and understood about the culture that dominated the riverine communities of the Cumberland and its tributaries.

NOTES

1. We are grateful to Ian W. Brown of the University of Alabama for the use of his photographs of artifacts housed in the Peabody Museum of Archaeology and Ethnology at Harvard University, Cambridge, Massachusetts. Dr. Brown also shared with us his

1990 catalogue of this material as well as three unpublished papers offering his insights on both form and interpretation. Additional photographs of the effigy vessels and figurines in the Peabody Museum are accessible online (www.peabody.harvard.edu) and were used in our study as well.

2. The current location of one female effigy figurine exhibiting the full pattern, published twice by William E. Myer (1917, 1928), remains unknown.

3. Mary Spanos of the University of Alabama (personal communication, 2006) has also examined a number of the ceramic female effigy vessels in this study and agrees that what is being depicted in the diagonal patterning of the negative-painted designs is the warp and weft of twined—not woven—fabric. She believes that the garments are essentially shawls or mantles similar to one shown in John White's painting of sixteenth-century coastal Virginia Indians: a twined rectangle of fabric that attaches at the ends at one side of the body (in this case the left); the middle of it would then cover the other arm, though the openwork nature of the twining would allow both arms to be either cloaked by or outside of the garment (Lorant 1965:198; Sloan 2007:125).

4. We are grateful to Kevin E. Smith of Middle Tennessee State University (personal communication and e-mail correspondence, 2006) for his review of our overall analysis of these Cumberland River basin effigy vessels and for sharing with us photographs of stone effigy sculptures from Middle Tennessee that substantiate our interpretation of the neck knob as a hair-bun, whether well defined or only residual (see Smith and Miller 2009:Figs. 2.4c, 2.6, 3.7, 3.34, 3.47, 4.2, and B.3).

5. The small, straight-backed female effigy figurine from the West site on the Cumberland River in Davidson County (40DV12), shown kneeling with her hands on her knees, with pierced ears, two pronounced nodes or topknots, and a perforated hair-bun, is the only known figure from this region with distinctly marked genitalia (Dowd 1972; Brown 2001). This figurine is currently in the Frank H. McClung Museum at the University of Tennessee; we are grateful to Jefferson Chapman for recent photographs of this object.

6. Here again, we are grateful to Kevin E. Smith for comments regarding the corpus of stone effigy sculptures from the Cumberland basin, their frequency as male-female pairs, and the handling of sex-specific characteristics among them (see Smith and Miller 2009).

7. It must be noted that the female effigy vessels addressed in this study, though relatively modest in scale, exist against a background of many small, often roughly fashioned effigy figurines and vessels (some of them solid figures, some rattles) with traits common to the elegantly rendered objects discussed here. These small figurines and effigies, whether straight-backed or humpbacked, are only very rarely decorated with negative painting. Therefore, except where they are directly related to the inclusion of negative-painted pieces in mortuary contexts, they will not be discussed in this chapter but deserve further treatment and analysis separately.

8. As this chapter went to press, a new assessment of Thruston's activities at the Noel Farm by Kevin E. Smith and colleagues (Smith et al. 2009) suggested that, contrary to Thruston's assertion that he became aware of this site only a few years before his 1890 book, he may indeed have known of the vast burial grounds on and around the Noel property by 1885 or 1886.

9. A major study of the Peabody Museum archaeological excavations in the Nashville area appeared as this chapter went to press (Moore and Smith 2009). This work provides a larger, more complete examination of the archaeological contexts that produced the negative-painted female effigy figures that are at the heart of this chapter but does not substantially contradict any of the principal arguments herein.

10. We are grateful to Vincas P. Steponaitis of the University of North Carolina, Chapel Hill, for his examination (and photographs) of this group of effigy bottles at the Peabody Museum, Harvard University, in August 2007, confirming the presence of this pattern on these vessels.

11. In addition to the four female effigy vessels from the Peabody Museum that are part of one Gray's Farm subgroup (78-6-10/15853, 15870, 15898, and 15983) and the two that constitute another stylistic subgroup (78-6-10/15980 and 15999) there is a seventh negative-painted female effigy bottle from Gray's Farm at the Peabody (78-6-10/16000) that bears a significant presence of the pattern we have discussed across its back, but this vessel is too fragmentary to be definitively associated with either subgroup.

12. In addition to the radiocarbon dating of the Averbuch settlement to AD 1310–1367 (Reed 1984b:II.2.7), extremely relevant to the present study is the recent work undertaken at the Gordontown site (40DV6) by the Tennessee Division of Archaeology (TDOA), strongly supporting a dating of this settlement to the Thruston phase. Within that period other forms of decorated ceramics at Gordontown such as Matthews Incised sherds, together with various effigy vessels related to those examined in this chapter, argue for a more restricted assessment of AD 1300–1400 (Smith 1998; Smith and Trubitt 1998; Trubitt 1998:84–89). These estimates have been bolstered by the results of the TDOA's radiocarbon samples from work at Gordontown, the weighted average of which is AD 1315–1414 (at one sigma; Moore and Breitburg 1998:37); more recent calculations using these same samples yielded dates at one sigma of cal AD 1294–1395, cal AD 1326–1348, and cal AD 1392–1443 (Moore et al. 2006:95). Similar calibrated results have appeared in the TDOA's report on the Rutherford-Kizer site in Sumner County (40SU15), which has yielded examples of negative-painted ceramics, including female effigy vessels that are part of the present study (Moore and Smith 2001:73–78). Furthermore, at the closely related Brentwood Library site (40WM210) (Moore 2005; Moore and Smith 2005), all samples returned dates within the Thruston phase and placed the site "between cal A.D. 1298 and 1465" (at one sigma; Moore 2005:119).

REGIONAL STUDIES: MOUNDVILLE

CHAPTER 9
A Redefinition of the Hemphill Style in Mississippian Art

Vernon James Knight, Jr., and Vincas P. Steponaitis

Moundville has long been central to discussions of the Mississippian artistic florescence. Together with Etowah and Spiro, Moundville was once routinely included as one of the "big three" primary centers contributing to the Southeastern Ceremonial Complex, a concept that emphasized unity in Mississippian art and belief. In recent years, though, as individual site histories have come into sharper focus, contrasts rather than commonalities in art and religious expression among major Mississippian centers have moved to center stage. Following on the critique first suggested decades ago by Alex Krieger (1945), we have increasingly appreciated that much of the art once lumped under the heading "Southeastern Ceremonial Complex" does not form a coherent complex at all, either stylistically or thematically. Despite some generalized similarities based on a shared cultural substrate, Mississippian finely crafted art is in fact realized in a number of distinct, inherently local styles, emphasizing different subject matter and different media. The foundation of recent progress along these lines has been an attempt to define these regional styles more explicitly (Brown 1989, 2007c; Muller 1989; Phillips and Brown 1978, 1984).

Definitions

Let us be clear about what we mean by a "style." For us, these are purely formal units expressing fixed conventions of design and execution (see Phillips and Brown 1978). Styles are defined by inferring their rules of depiction, or canons, from a large corpus of examples, with particular attention to how these canons contrast with other styles. In defining styles, we also think it is important to specify a scale that allows the formation of like units in space and time. Specifically, we advocate style definitions that reflect communities of closely interacting artists on a very limited geographic scale. As formal units, styles can be and should be defined independently of considerations of iconographic meaning. In fact, we are convinced that the understanding of style is prerequisite to any comprehension of iconography.

We stress the methodological importance of defining geographically localized styles, because these style units contribute to the solving of puzzles associated with major sites. At each major Mississippian site, it is apparent that the collection of skillfully crafted goods and representational art found there is actually a melange of locally and nonlocally produced goods (Brown 1996, 2004). Objects acquired from afar often express original themes and concepts that are foreign to the context in which they are found. But by using combinations of geological and stylistic criteria, we can distinguish local from nonlocal goods. Removing the "noise" of nonlocal goods results in a much more coherent corpus of images, tied to local circumstances in ways we are beginning to understand.

The stylistic distinctiveness of Moundville engraved art on pottery in relation to the broader compass of Mississippian art was recognized in a number of comments made in the 1970s by Philip Phillips and James Brown (1978). But the name "Hemphill" as applied to Moundville art has its roots in a pottery type and variety, Moundville Engraved, *var. Hemphill*, originally defined to include burnished pottery bearing representational images (Steponaitis 1983). Subsequent exploration of the stylistic coherence of these images on engraved pottery in a series of master's theses written in the 1990s at the

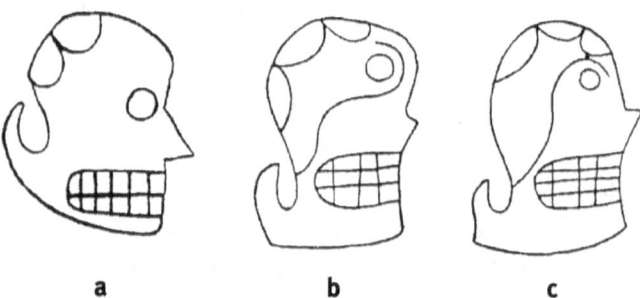

FIGURE 9.1. Hemphill-style skulls in different media: (a) from a stone palette, the Willoughby Disk; (b–c) from an engraved ceramic bottle. (Vessel numbers: b–c, NR9/M5. Collections: a, Peabody Museum of Archaeology and Ethnology, Harvard University [PMAE]; b–c, National Museum of the American Indian [NMAI]. Images: a–c, after Moore 1905:Figs. 5, 147. Moundville vessel numbers follow the conventions described in Steponaitis 1983:11-13.)

University of Alabama by Hyla Lacefield (1995), Kevin Schatte (1997), and Judith Gillies (1998) led to the formal definition of a Hemphill style (Brown 2004; Steponaitis and Knight 2004). In this chapter we suggest an expansion of the Hemphill style concept beyond engraved pottery to incorporate other media, including images on incised and painted pottery as well as certain images on copper, stone, and shell artifacts. We were moved to do this as we examined stylistic cross-ties among various locally crafted goods at Moundville. Broadening the concept to include these other media is parallel to what has already been done with the Classic Braden and Craig styles of the Mississippian Southeast, which were originally defined only for engraved shell at the Spiro site in Oklahoma (Brown 2007c; Brown and Rogers 1989).

For example, Fig. 9.1 juxtaposes two Hemphill-style skulls on engraved pottery (b–c) with a skull taken from the Willoughby Disk (a), a stone palette. Similarities in proportions, the blank circular eyes, the pointed nose, the prominent blocky teeth, the backward-projecting ascending ramus, and the scalloping at the back of the head are all apparent. In fact this stylistic similarity is one of several clues that weigh in favor of the Willoughby Disk as a locally made artifact, despite its raw material (siltstone), which is different from that of other Moundville palettes.

Figure 9.2 compares a series of hand-eye depictions in several media: two Hemphill-style engraved pots (e–f), a trailed-incised pot of the local type Carthage Incised (d), an embossed copper pendant (a), an engraved sandstone palette (b), and an engraved red-claystone pendant (c). In this set, similarities exist in the sagging "eye" motif, the stiff, straight, conjoined fingers, the inclusion of fingernails and thumbnails, the offset finger joints, the shape of the thumb, and the base of the palm.

Figure 9.3 compares skulls and serpent heads in different media. One skull (b) and one serpent head (d) are from Hemphill-style engraved pottery. Another skull (a) is from a Carthage Incised pot, while the second serpent head (c) is from an engraved sandstone palette. Three of these images (a–c) share prominent donut-shaped eyes (repeated in the ear-disk of the Carthage Incised skull [a]), emphatic lips, and ranges of clenched, blocky teeth. We are especially impressed with the similar treatment of two different subjects in different media in images (a) and (c). Note the similarity in the handling of proportions and the almost identical treatment of eyes and teeth. Image (d) is a depiction in engraved pottery of what we believe is the same serpent in (c). The upturned, pointed nose, the short triangular forms on the head just in

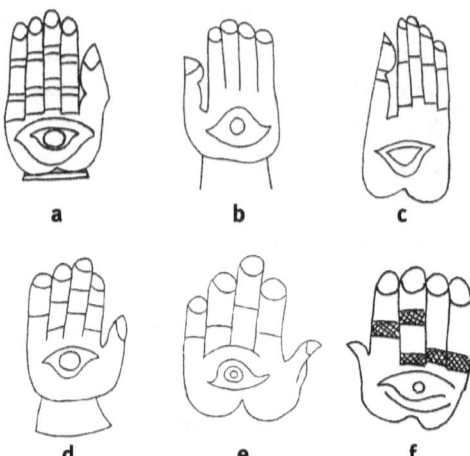

FIGURE 9.2. Hemphill-style hands in different media: (a) from an embossed copper pendant; (b) from an engraved stone palette, the Rattlesnake Disk; (c) from an engraved stone pendant; (d) from an incised ceramic bottle; (e) from an engraved ceramic bowl; (f) from a Moundville Engraved ceramic bottle. (Vessel numbers: d, WR2/M5; e, D4/M5; f, WR10. Collections: a, NMAI, 17/3107; b–c, Alabama Museum of Natural History [AMNH]; d, NMAI. Images: a, after Moore 1907:Fig. 101; b–c, after Krebs et al. 1986:48, 50, 79; d–e, after Moore 1905:Figs. 63, 173.)

front of the more substantial antlers, the form of eye, and the hatched throat indicate a serpent different from the standard winged serpent at Moundville.

Many of the artistic canons that allow us to distinguish Hemphill as a style have been worked out previously for the engraved pottery vessels (Gillies 1998; Lacefield 1995). These rules of depiction have been helpful in discriminating locally made engraved vessels at Moundville from those few found there that are engraved in nonlocal styles. As expanded here to include media other than engraved pottery, general canons of the Hemphill style, as now conceived, include the following:

1. A strong conservatism in composition, execution, and choice of theme. The vast majority of Hemphill compositions fall into a small number of redundantly executed themes. Design structures are few in number. Inventiveness or novelty in composition or in manner of drafting is rare.

2. Multiple elements within a given composition are shown apart from one another in the design field, emblemlike, without overlap and

without obvious interaction among the components. Animate characters are shown stiff and motionless, without fluidity or any indication of activity.

3. Avoidance of overlap extends to the component figures in a larger design; only in rare instances are the elements of a figure depicted as overlying other elements of the same figure.

4. There is a strong tendency for animate figures to be drawn in profile view. Even in-the-round treatments on pottery vessels, which present frontal bodies of serpents and raptors, always depict the head as turned in profile.

5. Cross-hatching is used sparingly for emphasis within figures. The technique is typically used within acute angular spaces, narrow bands, and enclosed semicircles. It is rarely used to create balanced areas of alternating fills, and rarely for background.

Much more specific canons tightly govern the presentation of individual themes.

Such rules of depiction contrast with other regional styles in Mississippian art. Following Gillies (1998), we offer a few examples of these distinctions.

FIGURE 9.3. Hemphill-style heads in different media: (a) skull from an incised ceramic bowl; (b) skull from an engraved pot; (c) serpent head from an engraved stone palette, the Rattlesnake Disk; (d) serpent head from an engraved ceramic bottle. (Vessel numbers: a, SEH9; b, NR25; d, SD805. Collections: a–d, AMNH. Images: a–c, after Krebs et al. 1986:48, 49, 79; d, after Lacefield 1995:Fig. 3.2.)

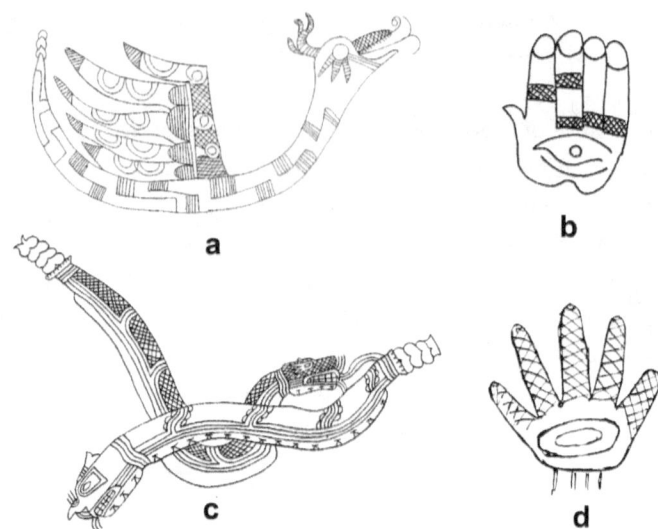

FIGURE 9.4. A comparison of Hemphill and Walls images: (a) Hemphill-style serpent from a Moundville Engraved bottle; (b) Hemphill-style hand from a Moundville Engraved bottle; (c) serpents from a Walls Engraved bottle; (d) hand from a Walls Engraved bottle. Designs (a) and (b) are from Moundville, while (c) and (d) are from sites in the Central Mississippi Valley. (Vessel numbers: a, SD8; b, WR10. Collections: a–b, AMNH. Images: a, after Lacefield 1995:Fig. 4.4; b, after Krebs et al. 1986:79; c, after Phillips and Brown 1978:Fig. 261; d, after Brown 1926:Fig. 279.)

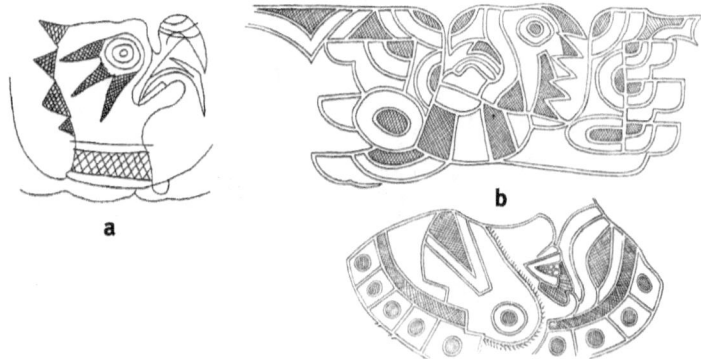

FIGURE 9.5. A comparison of Hemphill and Pensacola images: (a) Hemphill-style raptor from a Moundville Engraved bottle; (b) raptor from a Pensacola Incised bottle. Image (a) is from Moundville and (b) is from a mound near Jolly Bay, Walton Co., Florida. (Vessel numbers: a, SD362. Collections: a, AMNH; b, NMAI. Images: a, after Lacefield 1995:Fig. 4.1; b, after Moore 1901:Figs. 54, 56.)

Figure 9.4 compares a Hemphill serpent and a human hand on Moundville Engraved pottery (a–b) with serpents and a human hand as found on the pottery type Walls Engraved in the Central Mississippi Valley (c–d). Unlike the Hemphill serpent, the Walls snakes interact; they overlap, they contrast with one another in the same composition, and they lack wings; the underlying snake has cross-hatching used to create balanced areas of contrasting fills.[1] Unlike the Moundville hand, the Walls hand has spread fingers without joints and an undifferentiated thumb; the "eye" element is a concentric oval.

A similar contrast can be seen in Figure 9.5, which compares a Hemphill raptor on Moundville Engraved pottery (a) with a raptor on Pensacola Incised pottery (b) from the northern Gulf Coast. Unlike the Hemphill raptor, the Pensacola raptor exhibits cross-hatching in the service of a balanced contrast of positive and negative. Among other differences, it also has something unheard of in Hemphill: the inclusion of composite human-animal subject matter, in this case a Birdman head in profile, superimposed on its tail.

Now let us turn to the Hemphill corpus for an overview of each different medium in turn. Key concepts in this discussion are theme and motif, design structure, and field. *Theme* refers to the subject matter at the level of the composition; themes can be defined by their formal properties without knowing anything about their original referent or meaning. *Motif* also is a formal unit of subject matter but is defined at a smaller scale. A motif is a component of a larger composition that can stand alone as a subject in more than one thematic context. That is, motifs transcend the various forms that serve as identifiers for individual themes. *Design structure* refers to structural rules for organizing and orienting the subject matter within a *field* given by the boundaries imposed by the artifact carrying the design. These usages follow in many respects those of Phillips and Brown (1978).

Engraved, Incised, and Painted Pottery

Definition of the Hemphill style was originally founded on a large corpus of engraved pottery at Moundville with representational imagery. Here, as redefined, we include in the Hemphill corpus certain additional Moundville pottery vessels with representational images executed by trailed incising and painting.

The vast majority of this material falls into five primary themes (Fig. 9.6). The three zoomorphic themes are the winged serpent, the crested bird, and

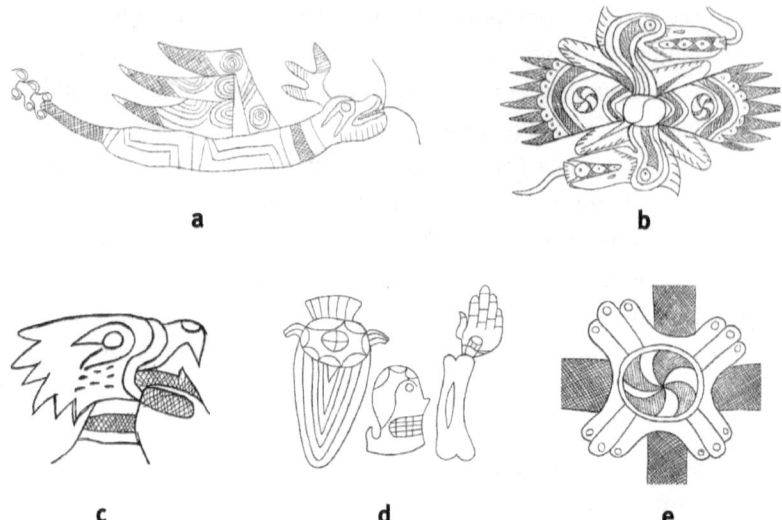

FIGURE 9.6. Five common themes on Hemphill-style pottery: (a) winged serpent; (b) crested bird; (c) raptor; (d) trophy; (e) center symbols and bands. (Vessel numbers: a, NR17/M5; c, SD54/M7; d, NR9/M5; e, SD7/M7. Collections: a, c-e, NMAI; b, AMNH. Images: a-b, d, after Moore 1905:Figs. 9, 147, 152; c, e, after Moore 1907:Figs. 5, 8.)

the raptor. The trophy theme includes compositions with skulls, scalp locks, human hands, and forearm bones, individually or in combination. Finally, the center-symbols-and-bands theme features compositions in which a variety of center symbols are shown intersecting with broad bands. These compositions often include the three-fingers motif, which can be shown to be a *pars pro toto* shorthand for the hand-and-eye concept. Aside from these five dominant themes, a few engraved vessels in the Hemphill style show other subject matter, such as the ogee, bilobed arrows, and (in two cases) human heads. We should note that in general human subject matter other than skulls is extremely rare in Hemphill art, and some subjects that are highly important elsewhere in the Mississippian world, such as the Birdman theme, are entirely absent.

Acceptable design structures are few in number. Among the seven design structures detected by Gillies (1998), the most common is a simple repetition of two identical figures on either side of a vessel. Where more than two figures are shown, they are most commonly arranged in a horizontal band of repeating elements rounding the vessel body. Two or three subjects are sometimes brought together in compositions in which the subjects repeat in an ABAB or ABCABC manner around the vessel. Alternating elements are sometimes inverted. A more complex design structure is the depiction of winged serpents and raptors "in the round," a treatment in which the head and neck are engraved on the front of the vessel, the tail is engraved on the back, and wings appear on opposite sides of the pot between the head and tail.

WINGED SERPENT

The most common theme on Hemphill-style pottery is the winged serpent, whose many variants have been well illustrated (Fig. 9.7a–d; Krebs et al. 1986:77, 79, 96, 97; Mellown 1976:Figs. 44–46, 49; Moore 1905:Figs. 151–152, 160–161, 1907:Figs. 51–62, 63–65). The typical creature who falls into this category has a U-shaped body with no ventral-dorsal distinction, a head with a forked eye surround and antlers, a wing with a vertical leading edge and horizontal feathers, and a tail that ends in rattles. The figure is almost always depicted in profile facing to the right, although a few examples are shown in the round (Fig. 9.7d). These serpents invariably appear on bottles; when in profile they occur in pairs, typically arranged nose to tail, with one on each side of the pot. In a few examples the serpent-in-the-round takes on characteristics of the raptor (see the discussion below). Lankford (2007a) persuasively argues that this theme at Moundville represents the "Great Serpent" in its celestial form, which Native peoples of the Eastern Woodlands associated with the constellation Scorpius.[2]

Schatte (1997) identifies at least eleven stylistic groups within this theme, based on distinctive motifs and the details of execution. He persuasively argues that these groups form a chronological sequence, which in general proceeds from well-executed "naturalistic" forms to poorly drawn "conventionalized" ones. The distinctions are most evident in details of the mouth, antlers, rattles, and body decoration. Interestingly, the depictions at the early end of this sequence show the closest connections to Braden-like art styles elsewhere, while the later depictions are more distinctively local in character.

Serpents are a common subject in Mississippian art; winged serpents are much less so. As a pottery design, the winged version appears outside of Moundville only in the Central Mississippi Valley and the Middle Tennessee Valley. In both regions, these creatures have different body markings and patterns of cross-hatching and punctation than their Hemphill counterparts (Gillies 1998:43–50).

FIGURE 9.7. Moundville pottery decorated in the Hemphill style: (a–d) winged serpent theme; (e–h) crested bird theme; (i–l) raptor theme, including three views (j–l) of a vessel that depicts a raptor in the round. (Vessel numbers: a, NED10; b, NN'38; c, EE25; d, WR81; e, SD472; f, SD472; g, NE60; h, RPB1; i, NE80; j–l, EE416. Collections: a–l, AMNH. Images: a–c, after Mellown 1976:Pls. 44, 45, 46; e–f, j–k, after Krebs et al. 1986:96.)

CRESTED BIRD

The crested bird, sometimes identified as a woodpecker, occurs commonly on engraved bottles and cylindrical bowls at Moundville (Fig. 9.7e–h; Krebs et al. 1986:93, 95–96; Mellown 1976:Fig. 34; Moore 1905:Figs. 8–10, 56–57, 84–85, 112–113, 117–118, 1907:Figs. 34–36, 37–38). The characteristics of this bird include a smooth crest with a hatched edge; a long, sinuous neck; a decorated band that runs along the side of the neck and terminates at the eye; stubby, leaf-shaped wings with a hatched edge and a cross-hatched center; an elongated beak; and an open mouth, sometimes with a protruding "tongue" that resembles a beaded forelock. The head is always shown in profile, facing either left or right (Gillies 1998:50–51; Lacefield 1995:43–46). Elsewhere the crested bird has been identified as a manifestation of "weather powers" that played an important role in Native stories throughout the Eastern Woodlands (Lankford 2007d:24–29); the same may be true of the Moundville images as well.

The usual composition shows two pairs of these birds, each pair seemingly "tied" together with a central knot or medallion in court-card symmetry. As with winged serpents, the pairs are arranged laterally, one on each side of the pot. The tails always occur within each court-card pair, but the heads and wings are optional (e.g., Fig. 9.7h). Hence this composition was previously called "paired tails," but it is clearly part and parcel of the same theme (cf. Steponaitis 1983:61). Crested birds are sometimes accompanied by radial fingers centered on the neck or base—an iconographic link with the trophy theme and with center symbols and bands.

Interestingly, even when the crested bird is depicted in the round, a central element like the medallion always plays an important role in the composition. In two cases the neck of the vessel substitutes for the medallion (another link with center symbols and bands), and in one case the central element is an ogee on the bottom of the vessel, cleverly substituted for the bird's anus (Krebs et al. 1986:93; Moore 1907:Fig. 38; Steponaitis 1983:Fig. 62g).

Based on a limited statistical analysis, Lacefield (1995:57–64) isolates four variants of the designs showing the crested bird. She suggests that these variants may in part represent a chronological sequence, with the most elaborate designs being early. This conclusion echoes Schatte's aforementioned analysis of the winged serpents and may indicate a general pattern, at least in the medium of engraved pots, that certainly bears further study.

A few pots with this theme have been found in the Central Mississippi Valley, associated with the Walls phase. These differ from the Hemphill specimens in details of the head and central medallions (Gillies 1998:52–53).

RAPTOR

A number of engraved vessels at Moundville exhibit the raptor theme, which invariably includes the head of a bird with raptorial characteristics: a hooked beak, a jagged crest, and a forked eye surround (Fig. 9.7i–l; Krebs et al. 1986:83; Moore 1907:Figs. 7–8; Steponaitis 1983:Fig. 62c). The creature is engraved in a variety of ways, either on bottles or on cylindrical bowls. Sometimes it is shown in the round, with wings and a tail. In other cases the four raptor heads are arranged in a band around the vessel's circumference. Rarely, we even find raptors in court-card symmetry, like crested birds (Lacefield 1995:Fig. 4.12; Steponaitis 1983:Fig. 20q). As with winged serpents, the heads are invariably drawn in profile and face to the right. Other common Hemphill features include roundels on the top of the beak, a stepped lower mandible, an open mouth, a barbed tongue, and a banded neck (Gillies 1998:53–55; Lacefield 1995:37–40; Schatte 1998:114–117). Following Lankford (2007b:178), we suspect that these images represent a celestial raptor that was sometimes mentioned in Native stories about the Path of Souls.

The raptor also appears in several designs that show strong ties to other themes. Schatte (1998) identifies three vessels that exhibit what he calls a "pseudo-raptor," a winged serpent with raptor characteristics or vice versa (Moore 1905:Figs. 114–115, 1907:Figs. 10–11). Schatte (1998:122) believes that these are transitional images that indicate "some sort of stylistic and iconographic progression" from raptors to serpents, coincident with some of the chronological changes already described for the latter theme. Similarly, disembodied raptor heads accompanied by either severed tails or hands occur in compositions reminiscent of the trophy theme (Moore 1907:Fig. 9). How these are classified is obviously a matter of preference for now (cf. Lacefield 1995:38–39); a definitive solution must await a better understanding of the iconographic meanings involved. Be that as it may, such ties help establish the coherence of the Hemphill style across thematic boundaries.[3]

Raptors also occur on pottery from the Central Mississippi Valley (Walls), the Middle Tennessee Valley, and the Pensacola area. These differ strikingly from the Hemphill specimens in the way cross-hatching is used, the absence of roundels on the beak, and the nature of the compositions in which the raptors occur (Gillies 1998:53–55, 78–79).

TROPHY

The trophy theme encompasses a diverse set of compositions that have one thing in common: they all feature body parts arranged in a horizontal band around the vessel's circumference, usually on a bottle or cylindrical bowl (Fig. 9.8a–f; Krebs et al. 1986:49, 76, 77, 79, 90, 97, 99; Mellown 1976:Fig. 41; Moore 1905:Figs. 21–22, 62–63, 89–90, 123, 146–147, 153, 157, 173, 1907:Fig. 9). The most common anthropomorphic parts are skulls, forearm bones, and scalps; their zoomorphic counterparts are raptor heads and tails (Lacefield 1995:42–43). A design may consist of a single motif that repeats four to six times or of alternating motifs in repeating pairs or triplets. Sometimes the motifs change their orientation as they repeat. Known designs include skulls, scalps, or hands by themselves; skulls combined with forearm bones and sometimes hands; hands alternating with raptor heads or scalps; and raptor tails by themselves. Radial fingers sometimes occur as a secondary motif. At least one composition discussed previously under the raptor theme—four raptor heads repeating around the vessel—could just as easily be placed in this group. Whether these images represent trophies taken in mythic combat (Knight 2007) or are allusions to stories connected with the Path of Souls (Lankford 2007b), or both, is far from certain. Nevertheless, this seemingly catchall group shows a coherence in composition and substitution that justifies its status as a distinct theme.

The pottery designs of this theme show strong ties to Hemphill representations in copper and stone—particularly to those found on oblong pendants and at least one palette (see Figs. 9.17a, 9.19, 9.22b). Indeed, the shape of the oblong pendants is suggestive of the scalp motif that is a common element in this theme.

Thematically similar compositions occur on pottery from the Central Mississippi Valley (Walls) and the Middle Tennessee Valley, yet stylistically these cannot be confused with the Hemphill corpus. The Walls assemblage provides the best comparative sample, and some of the differences between Hemphill and Walls in the depiction of hands have already been discussed (see Fig. 9.4). As Gillies (1998:56–62) has shown, the same kinds of differences exist in the treatment of heads, forearm bones, and scalps.

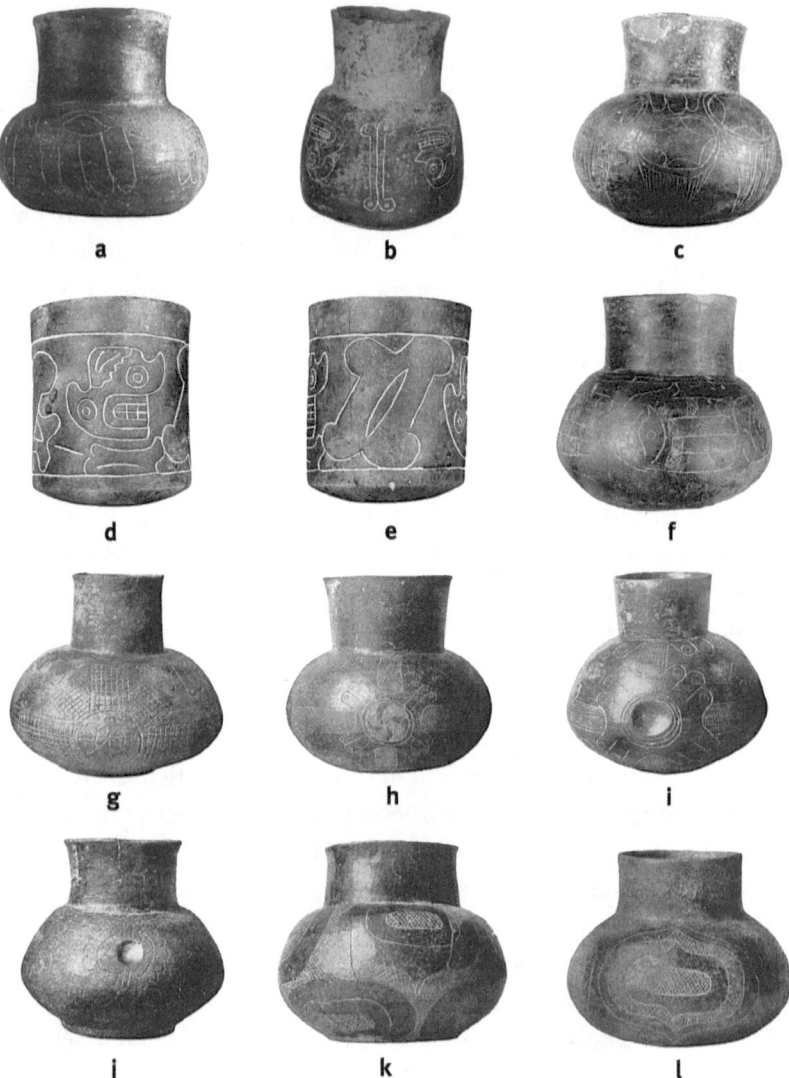

FIGURE 9.8. Moundville pottery decorated in the Hemphill style: (a–f) trophy theme; (g–i) center symbols and bands theme; (j) bilobed arrow theme; (k–l) ogee theme. (Vessel numbers: a, SD32/M7; b, NR25; c–d, SEH9; e, WR10; f, NEC9/M5; g, SD7/M7; h, NR1/M5; i, NR11/M5; j, SD13/M7; k, WR28/M7. Collections: a, f–k, NMAI; b–e, AMNH. Images: g, i–j, after Moore 1905:Figs. 53, 143, 148; h, k–l, after Moore 1907:Figs. 4, 41, 42.)

CENTER SYMBOLS AND BANDS

At first glance, some of the compositions of this theme appear to be geometric rather than representational (Fig. 9.8g–i; Krebs et al. 1986:82, 95; Moore 1905:Figs. 17, 30, 35, 53–54, 64, 125–126, 143–144, 1907:Figs. 4–5, 6, 15). The most common motif consists of a circular medallion, with four or eight cross-hatched bands radiating outward—what was once descriptively termed a "windmill" (Steponaitis 1983:62–63). But a closer look quickly reveals their iconic nature. The most obvious clue is the frequent substitution of radial fingers for the diagonal cross-hatched bands; in one case the same substitution is made with raptor heads and tails. Another is the content of the central medallions, which may be filled with crosses, swirl crosses, or radial T-bars, all common features in other representational images. The main design field on the body of the vessel (usually a bottle) typically contains four of these "windmills" spaced equally around the vessel's circumference—a pattern clearly visible in any two-dimensional rollout. Less obvious is the fact that the neck and base of the vessel are sometimes treated like central medallions, in that they also serve as centers for radial fingers or bands that connect with other medallions. The overall effect is strongly three-dimensional, as if something is being depicted in the round. It is easy to speculate that this theme is some sort of cosmogram, with the medallions marking the six cardinal directions (four horizontal, two vertical) and the bands indicating connections between them.[4]

Outside of Moundville this theme is known on pottery from the Central Mississippi Valley, where it is sometimes seen in the type Walls Engraved, and also from the Lower Mississippi Valley (Weinstein 1984:Fig. 4). The Walls examples differ from the Hemphill ones in a number of ways, including the content of the central medallions and the presence of semicircular elements that depend from the vessel's neck (Gillies 1998:63–64).

Minor Themes

A number of pots at Moundville exhibit themes that are far less common than those just discussed (see Steponaitis 1983:58–63). Many are unique or nearly so. For present purposes we will consider only a few that are of particular comparative interest.

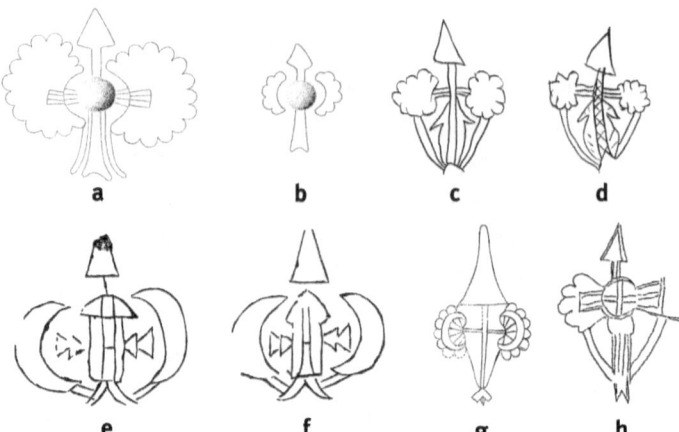

FIGURE 9.9. Images of the bilobed arrow on artifacts from Moundville: (a–b) engraved pottery bottle; (c–d) engraved pottery bowl; (e–f) engraved pottery bowl; (g) Willoughby Disk; (h) Brannon Disk. (Vessel numbers: a–b, F3/M5; c–d, SD48/M7; e–f, SWM5/M7. Collections: a–f, NMAI; g, PMAE; h, AMNH, Mi993. Images: a–b, g, after Moore 1905:Figs. 53, 88; c–f, after Moore 1907:Figs. 40, 44; h, after Brannon 1923:118.)

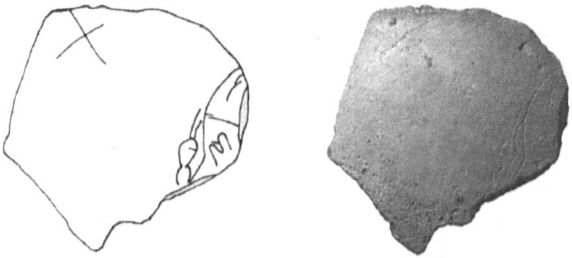

FIGURE 9.10. Drawing (*left*) and photograph (*right*) of a Moundville sherd engraved with a human head. The fragment comes from a bottle with a strongly sloping shoulder, a shape typical of the Moundville II phase. The top of the sherd corresponds to the line where the bottle's neck joins the body. (Collection: AMNH, MPK p 737.)

Four vessels are decorated with the bilobed arrow as a dominant motif (Fig. 9.8j; Moore 1905:Figs. 87–88, 148, 1907:Figs. 49–50). Two of these have simple compositions in which the motif repeats four times around the body, and two have patterns of simple repetition with rotation of the motif. Secondary elements such as crosses, arrows, radial fingers, smaller bilobed arrows, and a rayed cross-in-circle are sometimes added to the composition. Three of the pots have the same kind of bilobed arrow, with petaloid lobes that connect to the central arrow with simple multilinear bands. The fourth vessel's bilobed arrow is different; it has smooth, crescent-shaped lobes connected with bands made of triangular elements. In our view, the first three vessels establish with reasonable confidence that the bilobed arrow was part of the Hemphill repertoire. Indeed, lobes with petaloid margins appear to be an excellent Hemphill marker, as they are found only at Moundville and occur on both ceramics and stone palettes (Fig. 9.9). Whether the fourth vessel is an import or another variant within the local style will only be settled by further study.

The ogee, another classic Mississippian motif, also occurs on Hemphill ceramics (Fig. 9.8k–l; Moore 1905:Figs. 121–122, 1907:Figs. 41–42). The three pots decorated with ogees appear to be local in ware and shape and have a design structure that is consistent with Hemphill norms: simple repetition in a band around the body. Again, we have every reason to believe that this theme, albeit rare, is part of the local style.

Finally, we must consider the rare instances of human heads—not skulls—engraved on Moundville pottery. We know of only two instances. One is a subglobular bottle excavated by C. B. Moore and described by him as follows: "On each of two sides of the body of the bottle is a rude attempt to delineate the human head, now partly weathered away" (Moore 1905:192, Fig. 93). Based on the published photograph, we have little to add to his assessment. The second is a sherd that was found in the Depression-era excavations of the Moundville Roadway (Wilson 2008).[5] It is a bottle fragment, apparently of local ware, that retains a frustratingly small portion of an engraved human head (Fig. 9.10). Only the profile of the forehead and the top of the nose survive, along with the front of the hairline, a beaded forelock, and what may be part of an unusual eye surround. The curvature of the profile, the hairline, and the forelock all have a Braden look to them— insofar as we can tell from such a small piece (cf. Phillips and Brown 1978:Pls. 11–12). If not for the paucity of human figural art at Moundville, we would not even be tempted to venture a guess. But the evidence, fragmentary as it is, suggests that Hemphill potters did occasionally depict human forms, if only in the theme of disembodied heads.

LOCAL EXCEPTIONS AND DISTANT CONNECTIONS

Having set forth some of the canons of the Hemphill style, we can now show examples of representational designs on Moundville pottery that do

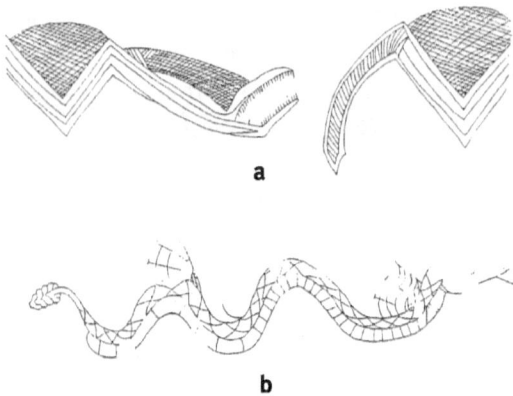

FIGURE 9.11. Images of serpents, not in the Hemphill style, found at Moundville: (a) from an engraved bottle; (b) from another engraved bottle. (Vessel numbers: a, NR99; b, NE63. Collections: a–b, AMNH. Images: a–b, after Lacefield 1995:Fig. 4.13.)

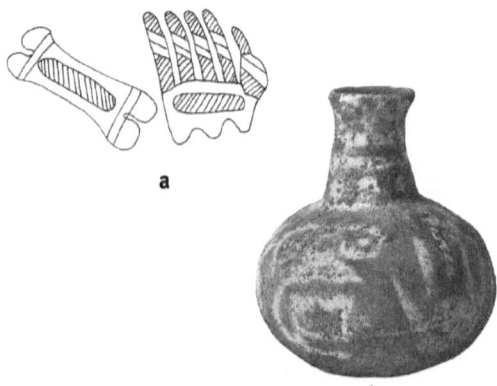

FIGURE 9.12. The trophy theme, not in the Hemphill style, on vessels found at Moundville: (a) from an engraved pot; (b) on a painted pot. Design (a) is rendered in the style of the Walls Engraved, a type most commonly found at sites in the Central Mississippi Valley near Memphis. Vessel (b) is an example of the type Nashville Negative Painted, which is most at home in central Tennessee. (Vessel numbers: a, SD88/M7; b, WR18/M7. Collections: a–b, NMAI. Images: a–b, after Moore 1907:Figs. 20, 45.)

FIGURE 9.13. Hemphill-style pottery found at sites far from Moundville: (a) a crested bird from an engraved vessel found at the Walls site in northwestern Mississippi; (b) an engraved vessel from the Lower Mississippi Valley with a raptor depicted in the round. Both vessels were probably made near Moundville. (Images: a, courtesy of David H. Dye; b, after Holmes 1886a:Fig. 461.)

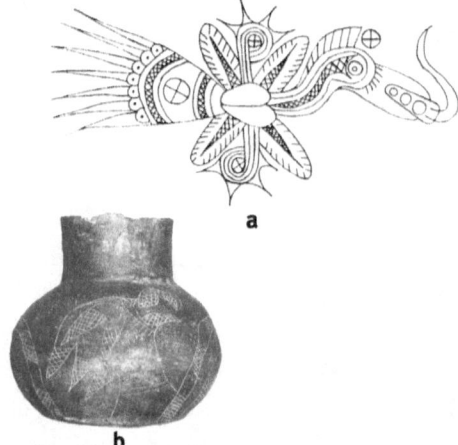

not conform to these canons and therefore are almost certainly *not* locally made. Figure 9.11 shows two snakes, both laid out in non-Hemphill design structures and both including non-Hemphill details such as the crosshatched external filler of the first and the affixed dorsal fins of the second. Figure 9.12 shows two non-Hemphill examples of the trophy theme on pottery found at Moundville, the first a composition of engraved hands and long bones (a) rendered in a style at home in the Central Mississippi Valley and the second (b) a vessel of the type Nashville Negative Painted showing a non-Hemphill skull form and a non-Hemphill hand with spread fingers (see also Mellown 1976:Fig. 27; Moore 1907:Figs. 20, 45–46).

Similarly, we can point to examples of Hemphill-style engraved art on pottery found far outside the Moundville domain. Figure 9.13 shows a Hemphill-style crested bird (a) on a vessel from the Walls site in the Central Mississippi Valley and a Hemphill-style raptor (b) on a vessel from the Lower Mississippi Valley. Both of these were probably made in the Moundville area.

Embossed Copper and Engraved Stone

Moundville has a great diversity of copper and stone items that bear representational art, but much of this diversity has to do with long-distance interaction. When we remove the clutter of nonlocal items in the Moundville corpus, we are left with a remarkably homogeneous set of locally made objects. As is typical of the Hemphill style generally, this set exhibits a strong conservatism in design, despite the diversity of raw materials and functions that are represented. The vast majority of copper and stone items that fall within the Hemphill style at Moundville represent a single theme, which we call "centering." They focus on circular images that function as symbols of the center, with which animate subjects are sometimes combined. Additional themes, numerically much less common but iconographically important, are the human head and mace. Each of these themes is discussed more fully below.

CENTERING

The objects that exhibit this theme all feature a concentric design structure within which various center symbols are featured, often in combination with other motifs. The theme commonly occurs on a number of different artifact types, including copper pendants, stone pendants, and stone palettes. The possible variations can be parsimoniously described by a simple set of

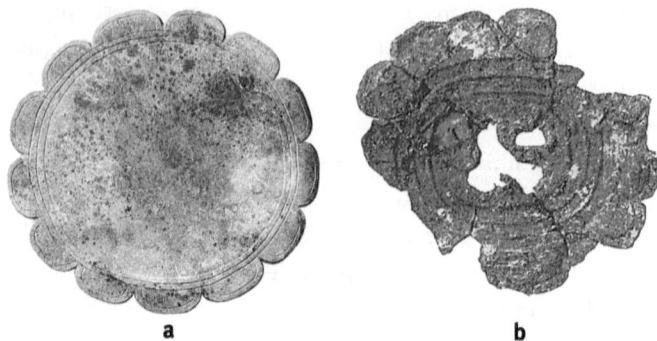

FIGURE 9.14. The centering theme in different media: (a) stone palette; (b) copper pendant. Note the similar design structure. Images not to scale. (Collections: a, NMAI, 17/1474; b, NMAI, 17/3095. Images: a–b, after Moore 1905:Figs. 19, 29.)

TABLE 9.1. Placement of design elements on copper and stone artifacts with centering theme

Design Field	Copper Pendants	Stone Pendants	Stone Palettes
Edge	scalloped undecorated	notched undecorated	scalloped notched undecorated
Rim	multilinear band undecorated	multilinear band	multilinear band hatched band rayed circle ophidian band undecorated
Interior	swirl cross rayed circle ogee hole	swirl cross rayed circle eye hole cross	*on reverse face:* undecorated serpents hand and eye bilobed arrow moth, skull, pole
Dependent triangle	*field may be absent; if present:* V-shaped cutout hand and eye	*field may be absent; if present:* V-shaped cutout hand and eye terrace "shell"/eye bone	*field always absent*

rules that define four design fields, each of which has a limited set of possibilities for substitution (Table 9.1). These simple rules account for a surprisingly wide array of artifacts, including some that are not normally considered to be stylistically related. To illustrate, we need only look at a stone palette and a copper pendant side by side (Fig. 9.14). The similarity in design structure and content is undeniable. We should add that these same design rules also account for a number of small circular pendants of tabular stone and of pottery from Moundville that are often overlooked in discussions of Moundville art (Moore 1905:Fig. 137, 1907:Figs. 91, 93; also see Fig. 9.18 below). We believe that these small artifacts express the same symbolism found in the more elaborate pendants and palettes.

Let us begin by considering the copper pendants. The four design fields are the edge, the rim, the interior, and a dependent triangle which may or may not be present (Fig. 9.15). With the dependent triangle, the pendant is oblong; without the dependent triangle, the pendant is circular.

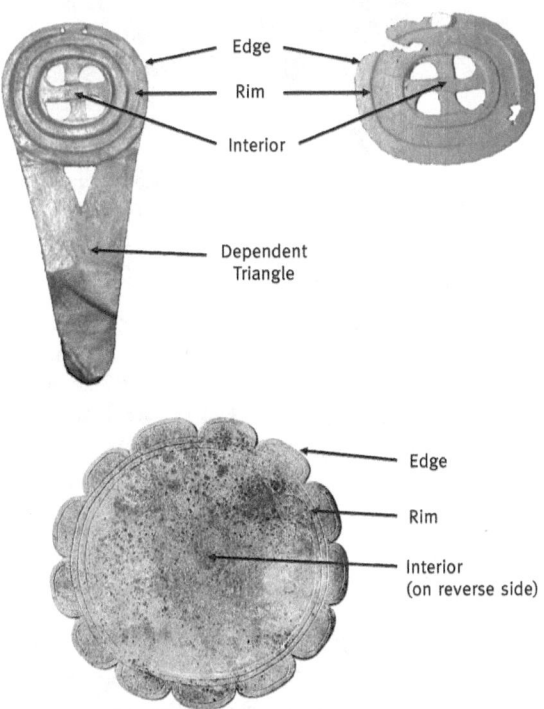

FIGURE 9.15. Design fields on objects exhibiting the centering theme.

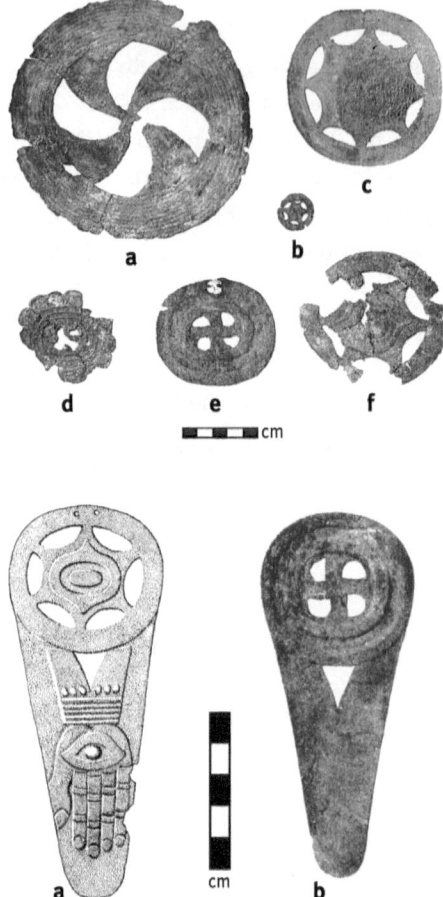

FIGURE 9.16. Circular copper pendants with embossed designs: (a) multilinear band on rim, swirl cross on interior; (b) rayed circle on interior; (c) rayed circle on interior; (d) scalloped edge, multilinear band on rim, swirl cross on interior; (e) multilinear band on rim, swirl cross on interior; (f) rayed circle and ogee on interior. (Collections: a, NMAI, 17/3093; b, NMAI, 17/3097; c, NMAI, 17/202; d, NMAI, 17/3095; e, NMAI, 17/168; f, NMAI, 17/3218. Images: a–d, f, after Moore 1905:Figs. 29, 43, 102, 134, 139; e, after Moore 1907:Fig. 105.)

FIGURE 9.17. Oblong copper pendants with embossed designs: (a) rayed circle and ogee on interior, V-shaped cutout and hand and eye on dependent triangle; (b) multilinear band on rim, swirl cross on interior, V-shaped cutout on dependent triangle. (Collections: a, NMAI, 17/3107; b, NMAI, 17/200. Images: a–b, after Moore 1907:Figs. 101, 102.)

In the corpus of copper pendants (Figs. 9.16, 9.17), we find the following sets of substitutions for each of the design fields (Table 9.1). The edge can be scalloped or plain. The rim can be plain or can be occupied by concentric lines. The interior can be occupied by a swirl cross, a rayed circle, or simply a hole, all usually accented by cutouts. An ogee motif can be combined with a rayed circle in the interior design field. The dependent triangle can feature simply a V-shaped cutout or a V-shaped cutout combined with a hand and eye motif, or the dependent triangle can be absent altogether, as noted. By far the most common composition among the copper pendants has a plain edge, concentric circles on the rim, a swirl cross occupying the interior field, and a

FIGURE 9.18. Circular stone pendants with engraved designs: (a) simple cross, concentric circles, notched rim; (b) central hole and concentric circles. (Collections: a, AMNH, WP59; b, NMAI, 17/2803. Images: b, after Moore 1907:Fig. 93.)

FIGURE 9.19. Oblong stone pendants with engraved designs. (Collection: ANMH. Images: after Webb and DeJarnette 1942:Pl. 58.2.)

dependent triangle with a V-shaped cutout (Fig. 9.17). There are some eleven known specimens of this kind.

The same design features apply to tabular stone pendants, but with somewhat different substitution sets in the four design fields (Figs. 9.18, 9.19, Table 9.1). Among the stone pendants, edges are plain or notched, rims always feature concentric lines, and the interior field can have a swirl cross, a simple cross, a rayed circle, or simply a hole. "Eye" elements are sometimes combined with swirl crosses or rayed circles on the interior. As with the copper artifacts, the dependent triangle can be either present or absent; when present it can feature one or two hand-and-eye motifs or hand-and-eye motifs in combination with terraces, extraneous eyes or "shell" motifs, or forearm bones. It should be noted that all of the stone pendants at Moundville are made of raw materials that are locally available (red claystone or gray micaceous sandstone), which strengthens our belief that these items were locally produced (Steponaitis and Knight 2004; Whitney et al. 2002).

Stone palettes, unlike pendants, are utensils rather than items of personal adornment (Figs. 9.20, 9.21, 9.22). They have a working surface, which we will call the obverse side, in which the central part is usually undecorated because it was subjected to vigorous mixing of substances using a handstone. These artifacts also have a reverse face which can function as a design field and therefore is sometimes decorated, substituting, in a sense, for the interior design field on the pendants. The edge and rim design fields apply to the obverse or working side, whereas the dependent triangle, of course, is always absent.

The following variations occur on the obverse face (Figs. 9.20, 9.21, Table 9.1). Edges can be scalloped, notched, or plain. Rims can feature concentric lines, a narrow band with hatching, a rayed circle or what we are calling an *ophidian band* (Fig. 9.20g). An ophidian band is filled with repeating elements otherwise associated with the bodies of snakes, but these bands connote serpents without manifesting heads or tails.

The designs that occur on the reverse face (or underside) of palettes—the functional equivalent of the interior design field in the stone and copper

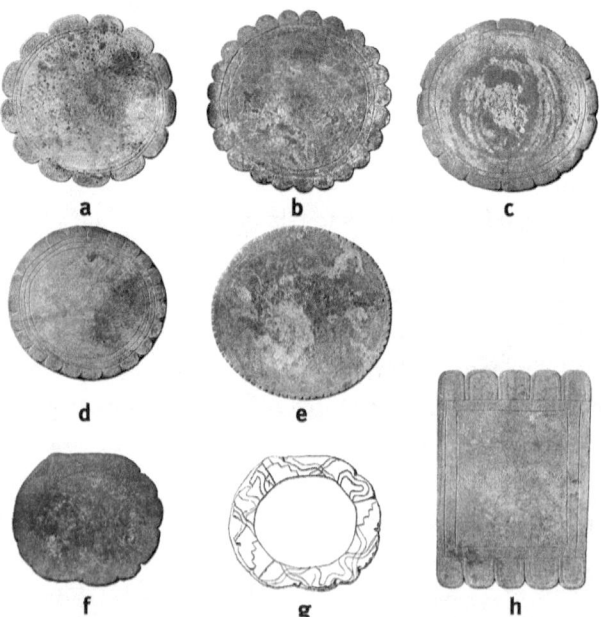

FIGURE 9.20. Stone palettes with engraved designs (obverse face): (a–g) circular palettes; (h) rectangular palette. (Collections: a, NMAI, 17/1474; b, NMAI, 17/1475; c, NMAI, 17/1483; d, NMAI, 17/1476; e, NMAI, 17/1489; f–g, NMAI, 17/1473; h, NMAI, 17/1493. Images: a–e, h, after Moore 1905:Figs. 19, 23, 65, 110, 111, 116; f–g, after Moore 1907:Figs. 87, 88.)

A REDEFINITION OF THE HEMPHILL STYLE

FIGURE 9.21. Stone palette fragments with engraved designs (obverse face). (Collections: a–b, NMAI, 17/2811. Images: a–b, after Moore 1907:Fig. 89).

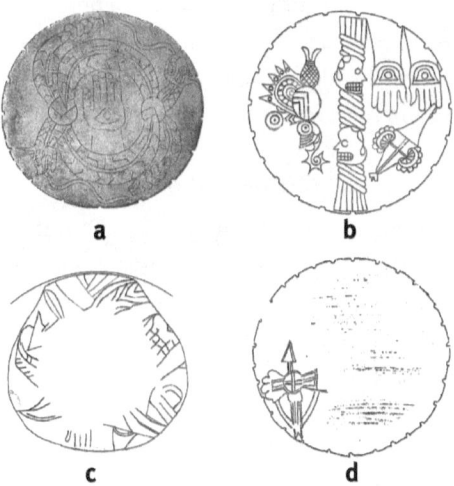

FIGURE 9.22.. Stone palettes with engraved designs (reverse face): (a) Rattlesnake Disk; (b) Willoughby Disk; (c) palette with edges broken and resmoothed; (d) Brannon Disk. (Collections: a, AMNH; b, PMAE; c, AMNH, Rho222; d, AMNH, Mi993. Images: a–b, after Moore 1905:Figs. 5, 7; d, after Brannon 1923:118.)

pendants—include some of the most famous images of Mississippian art (Fig. 9.22). Among these are the Rattlesnake Disk (a) with its dual knotted serpents encircling a perfectly good Hemphill-style hand and eye and the Willoughby Disk (b) with its Hemphill-style skulls on the central axis shown in a broader tableau with paired hand-and-eye motifs, a bilobed arrow, and a moth-based zoomorph (Knight and Franke 2007).

Two other examples are less well known. One is the Brannon Disk (Fig. 9.22d), which has a single bilobed arrow engraved off-center. This palette was published in 1923 with a brief description and sketch (Brannon 1923:118). According to the description, "only one of several drawings remains, the stone apparently having been rubbed to remove them." But the remaining portion of the design does seem consistent with the Hemphill style.

The last example is a palette (Fig. 9.22c) found in the Moundville Roadway excavations during the Great Depression. Here too the central portion of its design has been removed by rubbing. Indeed, the artifact appears to have been recycled: it started as a large palette, presumably circular; the palette was later broken, and the edges were smoothed to form a new, irregular margin. What had formerly been the engraved, reverse face was reground to a slightly concave profile, either through use or in a deliberate attempt to obliterate the design. As a result, only a fragment of the original design remains. It includes Hemphill-style hands and a possible bilobed arrow, but the nature of the other elements and the composition is now hard to decipher.

MINOR THEMES

A theme that occurs rarely in this corpus shows a human head in profile, found on two objects of engraved stone at Moundville. One is a pendant in the shape of a head, carved from red claystone—the same material of which the oblong stone pendants are made (Fig. 9.23a). The eyebrow, nose, lips, and chin are executed by simple marginal notching, resulting in a peculiarly angular style. The neck is notched at the base, communicating, we believe, that the subject is to be understood as a severed head. The surface engraving adds a number of details, including a scalloped line running from the base of the nose to the back of the head and double undulating lines originating at the mouth and running down the center of the neck. Projecting from the top of the head is a rectangular tab, doubly perforated for suspension. The second example is a fragmentary tablet with a lone head in profile engraved on its surface (Fig. 9.23b). This too is made from local stone: the gray micaceous sandstone also used for palettes. Like the pendant just described, it has a nose whose top projects almost laterally outward from the eye, a demarcation of the upper and lower face by a line element, and a blocky treatment of the lips and chin. These two objects hardly constitute an adequate sample for stylistic analysis. Even so, the fact that they share distinctive features of execution *and* are both made of local raw materials gives us reason to assign them to the Hemphill corpus. Their similarity to a shell gorget found at Moundville (discussed below) adds further credence to this assignment.

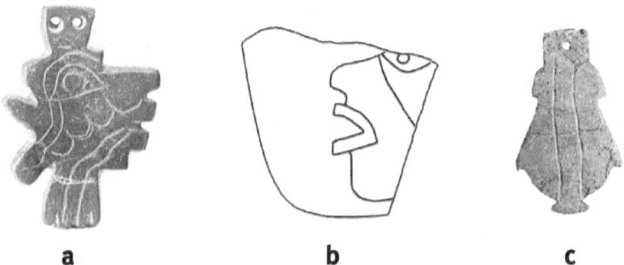

FIGURE 9.23. Stone artifacts with engraved designs exhibiting various themes: (a) red claystone pendant in the shape of a human head; (b) stone tablet with an engraved human head; (c) small stone pendant depicting a mace. (Collections: a–c, ANMH. Images: a, after Krebs et al. 1986:50.)

Yet another subject among engraved stone pendants is the mace (Fig. 9.23c), a standard Mississippian icon of long duration. The mace shape has two short lateral extensions at the midsection, forming a cross with the handle. The mace flares outward at the upper end and bears an apical "button." The surface is engraved with a Greek cross. Only two specimens are known, one complete and the other broken during manufacture. Both are made of local stone: hence their assignment to this local style.

LOCAL EXCEPTIONS AND DISTANT CONNECTIONS

We do not assign many of the other copper and stone items at Moundville to the Hemphill corpus, because there is no strong evidence they were made by local artists. These items are often unique at the site, exhibit no established Hemphill traits, and usually show clear stylistic or geologic connections to other regions.

Examples of such non-Hemphill items in copper include three sheet-copper hair ornaments: a feather (Fig. 9.24d; Moore 1905:Fig. 45), a mace (Fig. 9.24a; Moore 1905:Fig. 105), and a bilobed arrow (Fig. 9.25), which are very similar to more numerous examples at Etowah (cf. Brain and Phillips 1996:134, 136, 150, 153, 155, 158, 160, 373). A copper-clad wooden rattle in the shape of an agnathous human head (Fig. 9.24b) also has an exact counterpart at Etowah (cf. Brain and Phillips 1996:148, 159, 375). A number of sheet-copper "symbol badges" have been found at Moundville (Fig. 9.24c; Moore 1905:Fig. 104), which are stylistically identical with specimens found at Etowah, Lake Jackson, Cemochechobee, and Kogers Island but without the accompanying variety of forms seen at the latter sites (Brain and Phillips 1996:139, 155, 160, 163, 178–179, 372–373; Jones 1982:18; Larson 1959; Schnell et al. 1981:218–226; cf. Webb and DeJarnette 1942:228–229, Pl. 253.1). We suspect that all these items were made elsewhere, probably in regions to the east.

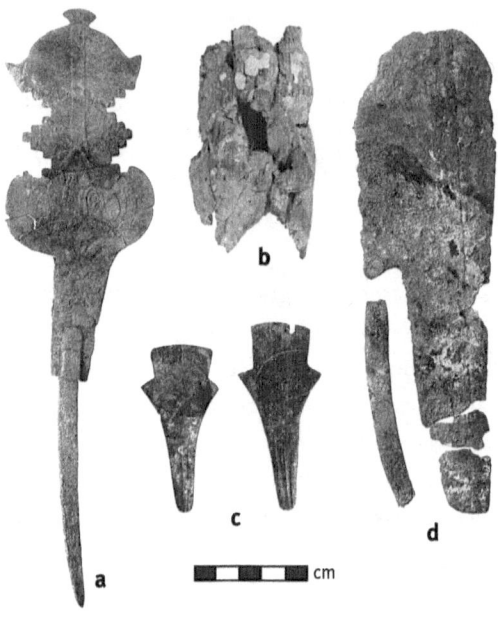

FIGURE 9.24. Copper objects found at Moundville but believed to be nonlocal: (a) headdress ornament in the shape of a mace; (b) agnathous head made of copper-covered wood; (c) sheet-copper "symbol badges"; (d) headdress ornament in the shape of a feather. (Collections: a, NMAI, 17/147; b, NMAI, 17/3; c, NMAI, 17/201; d, NMAI, 17/166. Images: a, c–d, after Moore 1905:Figs. 45, 104, 105.)

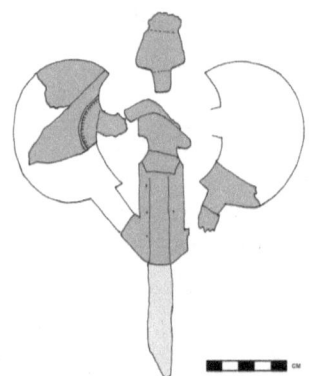

FIGURE 9.25. Bilobed-arrow headdress ornament made of sheet copper, found at Moundville but believed to be nonlocal. The pin at the base of the bilobed arrow is made of bone. (Collection: AMNH, SWG13. Image: redrawn from an illustration by Katherine McGhee-Snow Wilkins.)

A REDEFINITION OF THE HEMPHILL STYLE 229

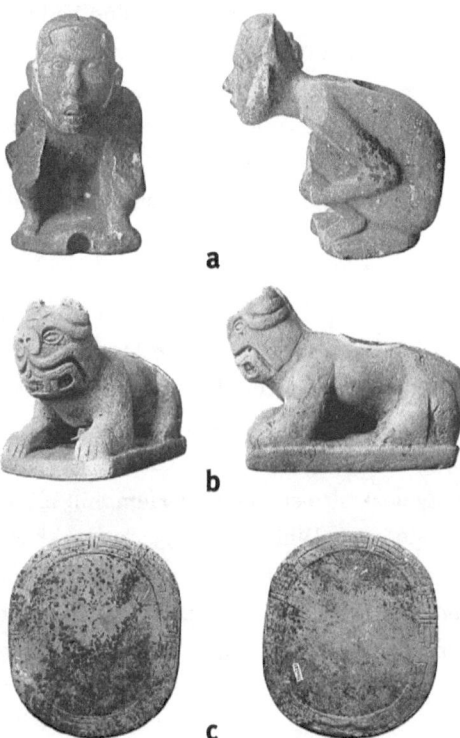

FIGURE 9.26. Stone artifacts found at Moundville but believed to be nonlocal: (a) human-effigy pipe made of Missouri flint clay, probably from Cahokia; (b) Bellaire-style pipe made of Glendon Limestone, probably from the Lower Mississippi Valley; (c) palette with an ophidian band, made of an unusual brown sandstone of unknown source. (Collections: a, NMAI, 17/2810; b, NMAI, 17/893; c, AMNH, Rho119. Images: a–b, after Moore 1905:Figs. 131–132, 165–166.)

At least one stone palette at Moundville is probably nonlocal: an oval, brown-sandstone specimen with an ophidian band on both sides (Fig. 9.26c). Not only is the raw material unusual, but the shape and the presence of a rim band on both sides are strikingly different from Hemphill norms. The style and raw material also mark other well-known Moundville artifacts as imports: several Bellaire-style "cat pipes" are made of a limestone that has been linked to sources in the Lower Mississippi Valley (Fig. 9.26b; Moore 1905:Figs. 1–3, 165–166; Steponaitis and Dockery 1997), a human-effigy pipe made of Missouri flint clay probably originated near Cahokia (Fig. 9.26a; Moore 1905:Figs. 131–132; Emerson et al. 2003), and a small human head carved from fluorite probably came from the Ohio Valley (Moore 1905:Figs. 46–47). The origins of two large stone effigy bowls at Moundville are far less certain, for they have no clear stylistic counterparts and their raw materials remain unsourced (Moore 1905:Figs. 167–171, 1907:Figs. 76–79). Both depict supernatural beings that are bird-serpent composites. One is made of a green metamorphic rock and the other of siltstone. Neither stone appears to be local, but little more can be said until detailed provenance studies are completed.

Understanding the Hemphill style helps us not only to identify foreign artifacts at Moundville but also to recognize Moundville artifacts in distant regions. For example, at least two circular copper pendants at Etowah fit comfortably within the Hemphill corpus (Ga-Brt-E24 and Ga-Brt-E111; Brain and Phillips 1996:140, 158; Willoughby 1932:Fig. 22; cf. Moore 1905:Fig. 134) and a third, although atypical, also shows clear Hemphill influence (Ga-Brt-E25; Brain and Phillips 1996:142; Willoughby 1932:Fig. 23).[6] Hemphill-style pendants of red claystone, undoubtedly made at Moundville, occur at sites along the Tombigbee and Tennessee Rivers (Steponaitis and Knight 2004:176). And a number of Hemphill-style palettes, made of the usual gray micaceous sandstone (Whitney et al. 2002), have been found at sites in the Lower Mississippi Valley.

Especially noteworthy are two Lower Mississippi Valley palettes that present the conundrum of being made of the same material as the Moundville palettes and yet bear images on their reverse sides that are arguably non-Hemphill in style and subject matter. A palette found at the Glass site just south of Vicksburg (Fig. 9.27a) has a triskele as a central element, while the Landrum Disk (Fig. 9.27b) has a spider. Neither subject is otherwise known in the Hemphill corpus; triskeles are more closely associated with shell gorgets in the Nashville Basin, while the spider, particularly with its peculiar hachured motif between the legs, is probably at home somewhere to the west of Moundville. Phillips and Brown (1978:204) have previously noted that apart from the subject matter stylistic ties between the Landrum spider and Moundville are "nonexistent." A fragment from the Rosedale Mound appears to have a human head with a hair roach as part of the reverse design (Fig. 9.28c–e; Weinstein 1984:Fig. 3). Fragments lacking reverse decoration have been found at both Anna and Lake George (Fig. 9.28a, b; Williams and Brain 1983:Fig. 7.41a).[7]

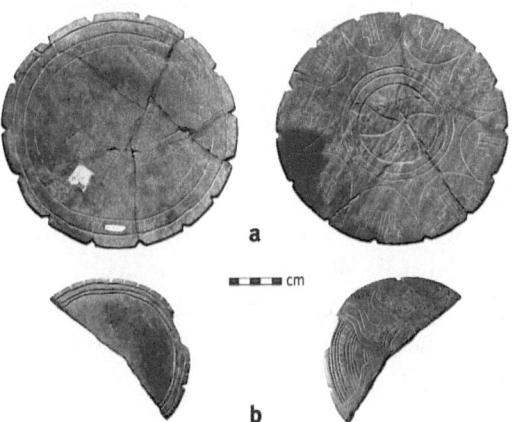

FIGURE 9.27. Palettes found at sites in the Lower Mississippi Valley: (a) Glass site, Warren Co., Mississippi, obverse face (*left*) and reverse face (*right*); (b) Landrum site, Yazoo Co., Mississippi, obverse face (*left*) and reverse face (*right*). The objects are made of the gray micaceous Pottsville Sandstone that outcrops near Moundville. (Collections: a, Ronnie Perkins; b, Mississippi Department of Archives and History, 60.78.)

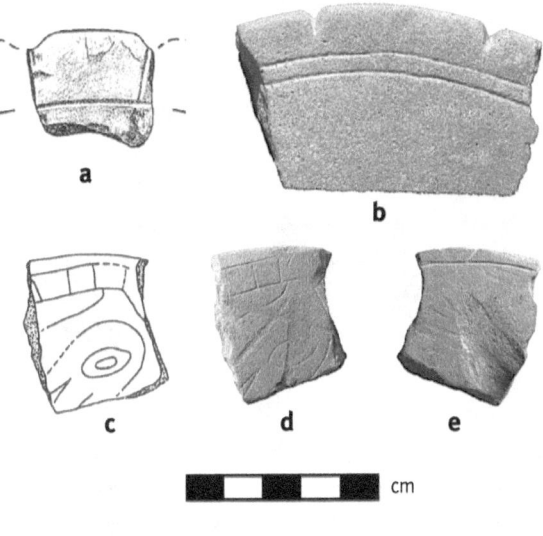

FIGURE 9.28. Hemphill-style palette fragments found at various sites in the Lower Mississippi Valley: (a) Lake George; (b) Anna; (c–e) Rosedale (three views of the same object). All are made of the gray micaceous Pottsville Sandstone. Drawing (c) and photograph (d) show the reverse face of the Rosedale fragment, decorated with a forked eye and a roach, both presumably parts of a human head; (e) is the obverse face of the same fragment. (Collections: a, PMAE; b, Robert Prospere; c–e, Louisiana State University Museum of Natural Science, Anthropology Division, 16lv1-24. Images: a, after Williams and Brain 1983:Fig. 7.41a; c, after Weinstein 1984:Fig. 3.)

Engraved Shell

Although engraved shell is a medium of considerable importance almost everywhere else in the Mississippian world, it is difficult to point to any engraved-shell artifacts at Moundville that are unequivocal Hemphill-style productions. The task of assigning them is complicated, because many are unique, or nearly so, and thus must be considered individually. Certainly some of the engraved shells at Moundville are stylistically nonlocal (Brain and Phillips 1996; Steponaitis and Knight 2004). There are a few candidates for locally produced shell gorgets, although a sufficient stylistic case has not previously been made for any of these.

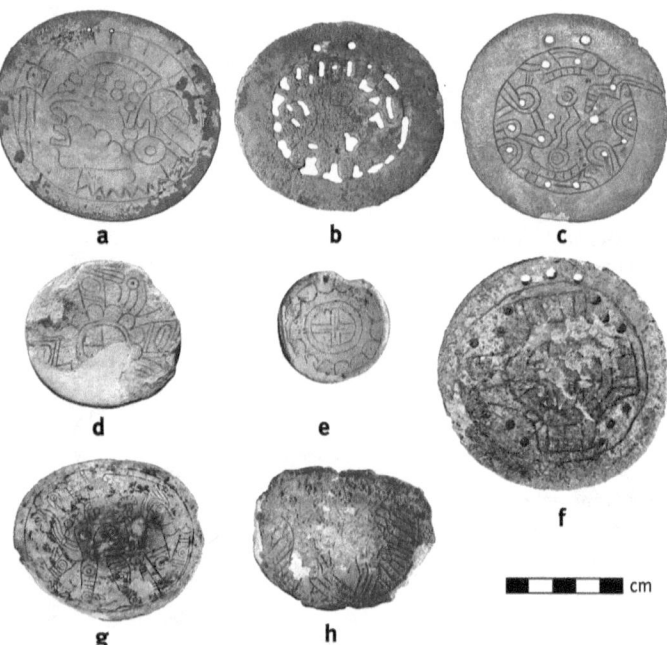

FIGURE 9.29. Shell gorgets from Moundville: (a) human-head gorget in the Hemphill style; (b) "spaghetti" gorget of uncertain style; (c) "spaghetti" gorget of uncertain style; (d) cruciform gorget, possibly Hemphill style; (e) cruciform gorget, possibly Hemphill style; (f) cruciform gorget, possibly Hemphill style; (g) Piasa gorget, probably nonlocal; (h) bird gorget, probably nonlocal. (Collections: a, NMAI, 17/1043; b, AMNH, EE245; c, NMAI, 17/1039; d, NMAI, 17/1041; e, NMAI, 17/1039; f, AMNH, EE330; g, NMAI, 17/1042; h, NMAI, 17/1040. Images: a, c, after Moore 1907:Figs. 95, 97; f, courtesy of AMNH; g, after Steponaitis and Knight 2004:Fig. 21.)

Perhaps the most intriguing possibility in this regard is a gorget featuring a severed human head in profile (Fig. 9.29a; Moore 1907:Figs. 96–97). The theme of the lone human head in profile is extraordinarily rare at Moundville, but it does occur in limited contexts and probably within a tightly constricted time frame. The theme is realized in two stone artifacts already discussed whose credentials as locally made products are unassailable (see Fig. 9.23a and b). The shell gorget exhibits some of the same stylistic features: the lateral projection of the nose, the line across the face, and the blocky lips and chin. Thus if there is such a thing as naturalistic human subject matter rendered in the Hemphill style on shell, we are probably seeing it here.[8]

A distributional and stylistic case can also be made, albeit less strongly, for three gorgets that Brain and Phillips place in their "cruciform genre" (Fig. 9.29d–f; Brain and Phillips 1996:27–28, 32–33, 35, 300–301). Similar gorgets have been found only in northwest Alabama and northeast Mississippi (areas close to Moundville), which suggests the possibility of local manufacture (Brain and Phillips 1996:28, 33). All three represent the centering theme so prominent at Moundville. Two display a cross in a rayed or petaloid circle, rendered in ways that have strong parallels in Hemphill copper and stone (cf. Figs. 9.14–9.21).[9] The crested bird engraved on one of these gorgets is also familiar to Moundville artisans, who depicted this creature on pottery. The placement of the bird's concentric-circle eye and neck band is comparable to Hemphill-style ceramic renderings, and so is the outline of the beak (although the way it articulates with the face is a bit unusual). The third gorget in this set is completely unique and shows a small cross-in-circle design nested within a larger one (Fig. 9.29f). The concept of a center symbol placed within a radiating cruciform of a different kind is comparable to the idea of the center symbols and bands theme as rendered on Hemphill pottery. Hemphill style connections are further suggested by the curvilinear transitions between the arms of the outer cross in the manner of the radial fingers motif (cf. Figs. 9.6d and 9.8h, i).[10]

We are not currently prepared to suggest either of the two "spaghetti style" gorgets from Moundville (Fig. 9.29b, c) as potentially made by Hemphill artisans at Moundville. These belong to a larger thematic group of shell gorgets depicting a highly conventionalized human figure, geographically concentrated in eastern Tennessee and central Alabama, a distribution to which Moundville is peripheral (Brain and Phillips 1996:301–302). Lankford (2008b) assigns the Moundville specimens to two different subcategories based on motif similarities and suggests some comparisons with Hemphill engraved art on pottery, including the court-card symmetry of the specimen in Figure 9.29c. Other tenuous comparisons might be made, but for now we choose to leave the style affiliations of these gorgets open to further discussion, particularly pending the availability of an accurate line drawing of the less intelligible specimen in Figure 9.29b.

We suspect that the remaining two gorgets are nonlocal in origin and therefore non-Hemphill. The one-of-a-kind "Piasa" gorget (Fig. 9.29g) strikes us as thematically and stylistically alien, with its depiction of a human-animal

FIGURE 9.30. Engraved shell cups from Moundville, all presumed to be nonlocal: (a) cup fragment decorated with a human figure with Classic Braden features; (b) cup fragment showing talons and a beaded ankle, probably of the Craig style; (c-k) multiple pieces, likely from a single cup decorated with serpent- and fishlike creatures, probably Braden B in style. (Collections: a-k, NMAI, 17/1044. Images: a, after Moore 1905:Fig. 34.)

composite, a figure seemingly in motion, and no stylistic features that can readily be linked to the Hemphill corpus (Brain and Phillips 1996:298; Moore 1907:Fig. 98; Phillips and Brown 1978:196–197). This piece would seem much more at home in the Mississippi Valley or parts west. A similar argument can be made for a gorget that depicts two birds confronting each other (Fig. 9.29h; Brain and Phillips 1996:300), albeit pointing to a different source. This shell, again unique, has the greatest thematic affinities with the "Hixon style" gorgets of eastern Tennessee and adjacent regions and exhibits no obvious links to the Hemphill repertoire.

Finally, we must take note of at least three engraved conch-shell cups found at Moundville that are definitely nonlocal. The best-known of these is a piece executed in the Classic Braden style that shows a human figure with a raised arm (Fig. 9.30a; Brain and Phillips 1996:298; Moore 1905:Fig. 34; Phillips and Brown 1978:195). Several other fragments, presumably (but not necessarily) from a single shell, show parts of serpent- and fishlike creatures with Braden B characteristics (Fig. 9.30c–k; Brain and Phillips 1996:298–299; cf. Phillips and Brown 1978:Pl. 93). The third cup is represented by a single large fragment that depicts the talons of a bird with shell beads around the ankle (Fig. 9.30b; Brain and Phillips 1996:298–299). Such beaded talons are most commonly seen as subject matter on Craig C shells at Spiro (Phillips and Brown 1984:Pls. 326–332), but in this case the fine treatment of the talons, with the claws drawn as separate objects rather than blending with the rest of the foot, is stylistically closer to Braden (cf. Phillips and Brown 1978:Pls. 33, 90). Whatever the ambiguities, there can be no doubt that all three cups originated elsewhere, probably in the Mississippi Valley or farther west (Brown 2004).

Considerations of Context

Now that the definition of the Hemphill style has been expanded to include painted and incised pottery, copper, stone, and shell artifacts, it remains for us to consider this imagery in a broader cultural and historical context. Let us begin with meaning and use. The imagery is deployed in at least three ways. First, especially on pottery vessels, Hemphill imagery depicts a suite of themes, such as the winged serpent and raptor, that appear to relate to the "Path of Souls," to follow Lankford's (2007b) argument. If these images do refer to the journey of souls in the afterlife, then they are surely an echo of Moundville's remarkable transformation into a regional necropolis after about AD 1350. Second, Hemphill-style imagery as deployed on stone palettes emphasizes the theme of centering, which defines notions of the "center" as a sacred space. We believe that this theme of centering is consonant with the use of stone palettes as portable altars in the preparation of spiritually charged substances, perhaps to be used in ceremonies. Third, Hemphill imagery, especially with the theme of centering, is also found on items of personal adornment: pendants with socially restricted distribution. We think it likely, based on this distribution, that such artifacts were worn as emblems of membership in kinds of organizations whose exact nature is not known.

Let us close with a few observations on the Hemphill style's external relationships. First, a key point is that Hemphill art emerges in the middle of the Moundville sequence, at about AD 1300 or shortly thereafter. Before that time, finely crafted art at Moundville is dominated by an altogether different, more geometric style, especially as realized on engraved pottery with Caddoan stylistic counterparts. Hemphill-style art, once it appears, undergoes an internal stylistic development with a chronology lasting into the fifteenth century. Lacefield (1995) and Schatte (1997) in particular have been successful in seriating Hemphill images on engraved pottery, suggesting that as images are gradually simplified in the 1400s workshops are progressively dispersed, to the detriment of stylistic coherence. Certainly by AD 1500, and possibly earlier, the style had vanished in west-central Alabama.

With regard to the style's origins, it seems abundantly clear that most figural subjects in the earliest Hemphill art are closely related to, and ultimately derived from, what James Brown (2007c) has called Late Braden, although the Moundville artisan's particular take on Late Braden is emphatically subordinated to the local context in the choice of thematic material. The thematic dimensions of Hemphill art are not simply inherited from the art of the Braden tradition. Hemphill's centering theme, which we have emphasized in this chapter, is apparently without Braden precedents and may well be a local carryover from an earlier, local non-Braden artistic expression. Two principal Hemphill images at Moundville, the swirl cross and the rayed circle, have no Braden antecedents.

In this sense the Hemphill art style at Moundville is largely, but not entirely, transplanted. Moundville artisans, once exposed to the powerful images of Braden-style art, selectively "read into" these original images a new set of meanings appropriate to fundamentally different Muskhogean contexts of beliefs and rituals. Dominant among these was a preoccupation with the status of the Moundville center as a geographically propitious place for the deceased to embark on the "Path of Souls." This emphasis might well unite the animate, cosmological, and astronomical themes of Moundville art with the theme of centering, which was so compelling to the elites who both wore these images on their persons and featured them in ceremonies involving stone palettes.

In regard to the obvious Late Braden borrowings, there is nothing unexpected about the process of reinterpreting foreign imagery in a local context by a process of "reading in." As images and their stylistic baggage inevitably cross ethnolinguistic boundaries, the recipients accept what they consider meaningful and discard the rest. As Franz Boas (1928:118–124) long ago understood, what they accept is reinterpreted according to preexisting local cultural models. It is perhaps a special case of what Erwin Panofsky (1960) called "disjunction." To reiterate a point made earlier, perhaps there can be no better demonstration that there is no unitary Southeastern Ceremonial Complex if that concept is taken to imply a pan-Southeastern uniformity of symbols and meanings.

NOTES

AUTHORS' ACKNOWLEDGMENTS: We wish to thank George Lankford, Kent Reilly, and other participants of the annual Mississippian Iconography Workshop for their encouragement, constructive criticism, and patience as the ideas in this chapter took form. We are also grateful to the following individuals who facilitated access to the collections and images that were important to the completion of this study: Mary Bade, Jeffrey Brain, Ian Brown, Patricia Capone, Steven Cox, David Dockery, David Dye, Thomas Evans, Viva Fisher, Eugene Futato, Gloria Greis, Susan Haskell, Kareen Hawsey, James Krakker, Mary Jane Lenz, Pamela Edwards Lieb, Diana Loren, Ann McMullen, Jo Miles-Seeley, Patricia Miller-Beech, Patricia Nietfeld, Ronnie Perkins, Robert Prospere, Rebecca Saunders, Richard Weinstein, and Katherine McGhee-Snow Wilkins. While finishing this paper one of us (Steponaitis) was supported by a Reynolds Fellowship and a Research and Study Assignment from the University of North Carolina at Chapel Hill.

1. David Dye (personal communication, 2007) has reminded us that the well-known pot whose design is shown in Fig. 9.4c is unique in the Walls area and therefore may not be local. But even if this pot turns out not to be an exemplar of the Walls style, our main point here—illustrating the distinctiveness of the Hemphill material—still holds true.

2. Given this interpretation, it is probably no accident that images of the serpent in profile consistently face right. The celestial Great Serpent was said to have a red jewel or eye on its head, represented by the star Antares. When seen in the summer sky, Scorpius consists of a U-shaped line of stars with Antares on the right (Lankford 2007a:Fig. 9.5).

3. Indeed, by using "handwriting" traits (*sensu* Phillips and Brown 1978), we can identify a group of three vessels at Moundville that were clearly engraved by the same person. The first shows only raptor heads, a second shows raptor heads alternating with hands, and a third shows only hands. There could be no better indication that all three thematic variants fall within the same style.

4. It is worth noting that the design of Moundville Engraved, *var. Cypress* may well be another variant of center symbols and bands, perhaps the same cosmogram viewed from a different angle (Knight 2007; Krebs et al. 1986:67; cf. Steponaitis 1983:54–55, Fig. 62d).

5. We are grateful to Greg Wilson for bringing this sherd to our attention.

6. According to Jonathan Leader (2004, 2008; personal communication, 2009), one of the circular, Hemphill-style copper pendants found at Etowah (Ga-Brt-E111; Brain and Phillips 1996:158) was made using very similar tools and techniques as used for its counterpart from Moundville (Moore 1905:Fig. 134). Thus they are alike not only in their imagery but also in their method of manufacture. Another Etowah pendant with Hemphill connections (Ga-Brt-E25; Brain and Phillips 1996:142; Willoughby 1932:Fig. 23) has no exact counterpart at Moundville and so may be from somewhere else. Although its oblong shape is suggestive of the Hemphill pendants, it is unlike the Moundville specimens in its multiple swirl crosses.

7. It is important to note that other decorated stone palettes from the Lower Mississippi Valley—such as the Issaquena Disk and the Almond Disk (see Phillips and Brown 1978:203–204 and references therein)—are not in the Hemphill style; nor are they made of the micaceous, Upper Pottsville Formation sandstone that is typical of Moundville specimens. The Issaquena Disk is made of a brown sandstone, similar to the unusual palette with the ophidian rim band described above. The Almond Disk appears to be made of quartzite.

8. Long ago Phillips and Brown (1978:196) noted the strong similarities between this gorget and the Braden B corpus at Spiro. Later Brown (2007c:235) assigned this piece to his Late Braden style, which subsumed Braden B. Although we have reassigned it, we fully agree with these authors that Hemphill and Late Braden have much in common (Brown 2004; Knight 2006).

9. One difference is that the central elements in the copper and red-claystone pendants (i.e., the ones made of reddish material) are invariably swirl crosses, while those on the shell gorgets or other kinds of stone are almost always straight crosses. Iconographically, this makes perfect sense. Lankford has shown that the swirl cross is a center

symbol associated with the Beneath World in the Native cosmos, while the straight cross was associated with the Middle or Above World (Lankford 2004; see also Reilly 2004:Fig. 2). Red was associated with the Beneath World. Thus the color of the raw material aligns symbolically with the nature of the cross.

10. Muller (1997a:370–374, Fig. 8.5) refers to a "Moundville style" of shell gorgets that he maps but never explicitly defines. Based on its geographical distribution, we guess that this style includes our three cruciform pieces (compare Muller's map with those of Brain and Phillips [1996:28, 33], noting especially the distribution of their Pickett and Tibbee Creek styles). If we are correct, then Muller's terminology provides some independent, albeit implicit, support for our suspicion that these gorgets are local to Moundville.

CHAPTER 10

The Raptor on the Path

George E. Lankford

Several frequently encountered images from Mississippian iconography are illustrations drawn from the widespread mythology of the progress of the soul after death. That argument has been presented in earlier articles on the "Path of Souls" and the "Great Serpent," in which the familiar images of the winged serpent, the hand-and-eye, the skull, and the bone were identified as elements of the celestial journey taken by the free soul after death (Lankford 2004, 2007a, b).

The focus of those studies was the ceramic collection at Moundville, where those particular images from the larger iconographic corpus are found clustered on pottery included in mortuary contexts. Their co-occurrence on bottles and their separation from other images helped identify them as participants in a single area of meaning, at least at Moundville. One other image shares space on a bottle in the Path of Souls cluster: a bird. This figure has been mentioned in the earlier articles but has been reserved for further consideration here, because of some thought-provoking implications of its presence in the iconic group. Thus, while this chapter should be considered an extension of the Path of Souls articles, it will assess the appearance of the raptorial bird at Moundville and some possible lessons in iconographic reasoning that may be drawn from it.

First of all, it should be pointed out that the birds in the iconographic corpus may be of many types. Significant intellectual energy has been spent over the last century in attempting to identify species of various images, an attempt based upon the dual assumption that the images are naturalistic representations and that species identification would permit understanding of the artists' intentions. There has been little agreement on the identifications and even less success in capturing the symbolic dimension via that approach. Part of the problem is the difficulty in measuring both the range of variability permitted within a single artist's work and the variation in representation of the same image, in terms of content, across time and space by different artists. The result is that there is no agreement on how many different birds are depicted in the Mississippian iconographic corpus.

If apparently similar images are examined together to create a serial display of alternate artistic possibilities, then some of the key identifying features of the figure may emerge. An example of this problem was discussed in an earlier examination of the "Crested Bird" (Lankford 2007d). In that study of engraved shell gorgets from the Tennessee Valley region, the two features that seem to be crucial are the feather crest on the head and the straight bill (Fig. 10.1a–d).

Since it seemed advisable to avoid prejudicing the interpretation of the figure by linkage to naturalistic identification, the bird was simply dubbed "Crested Bird." The isolation of the two key identifiers then made it possible to recognize the figure when it appeared in quite different artistic renderings, as happens when the composition changes or when the figure is drawn by a different artist. Use of key identifiers in iconography also makes it possible to assess the breadth of artistic freedom permitted in the creation of these designs. Further, key identifiers permit the researcher to assign images to a separate category, in this case the Crested Bird. The bird on the Moundville pottery collection is not the Crested Bird, as will be seen, and similar iconic

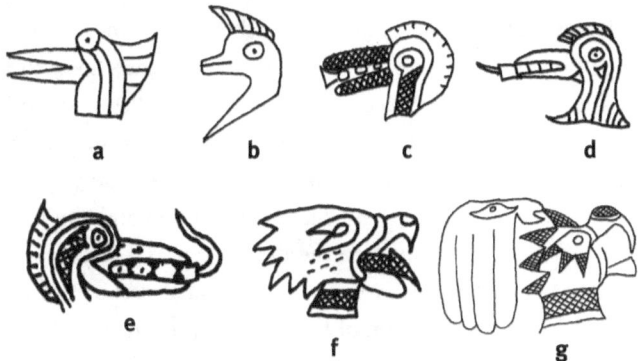

FIGURE 10.1. (a–d) Four examples of the "Crested Bird," two from Tennessee shell gorgets and two from Moundville ceramics, showing a range of artistic renderings (after Moore 1905:Fig. 113 and Moore 1907:Fig. 38); (e, f) a Crested Bird and a Raptor, both from Moundville ceramics (after Moore 1905:Fig. 9 and Moore 1907:Fig. 7); (g) Raptor and Hand-and-Eye on a Moundville pot (Moore 1907:Fig. 9).

identification processes may reveal the same sorts of artistic freedom in the treatment of the Moundville bird. A comparison of the Crested Bird and one of the fairly typical renderings of the Moundville bird permits quick separation of the two (Fig. 10.1e, f).

The key characteristics, at least in distinguishing these two birds from each other, are the jagged feather crest and the hooked beak. The resemblance to the naturalistic class of raptorial birds has long suggested the name "Raptor." In this study that will suffice as a label, with no further attempt at speciation or separation until such time as other iconographic distinctions can be discerned.

This Raptor appears sixteen times on Moundville pottery (both bottles and bowls), according to Steponaitis (1983). It thus has a frequency in the full collection rivaling that of the winged serpent (thirty-three times) and the hand-and-eye design (thirty-one times). The Raptor usually appears as the sole engraved decoration on ceramics, but in one instance it appears in conjunction with the hand-and-eye, thus indicating some connection between the two images. As argued in the earlier studies, this co-occurrence, while unique in the Moundville collection, is enough to bring the Raptor images into the larger five-image cluster that has been interpreted as mortuary symbols (Fig. 10.1g).

Identifying the Moundville Raptor as a mortuary image raises many problems, because a very similar image also appears in other locations (from Etowah to Spiro); it appears in other media, including stone, copper, and shell; and it appears across centuries. Whether those images are all of the same Raptor or whether there are separate figures that need to be distinguished has not been determined. Even if they are all the same Raptor, it seems probable that they are not filling the same social function or symbolic role from one prehistoric group to another, given the wide range of appearances and forms. In any case, these questions are beyond the scope of this chapter, which seeks only to explore the meaning of the Raptor as it appears at Moundville. Any useful insights that may be gathered in this exploration can be applied to the examination of the larger raptorial complex, but that is a different task.

If it is correct that at Moundville the Raptor is part of the Path of Souls mortuary complex, where might it fit? In the earlier presentations I have argued that there was a widespread mythology of death across the Eastern

Woodlands and Plains. That mythology saw the Milky Way as the Path of Souls and provided a description of the skyscape and the details of the journey. The commonality in beliefs, even to details, suggests that the mythological vision was ancient and widespread, but the variations in the ways in which the details are altered or rearranged argue for the development of regional and ethnic variations over time, as might be expected.

One of the recurrent themes of the mythology of death is the necessity for judgment of the soul, an attempt to determine which type of outcome is called for, depending on personal characteristics. In some cases the issue is the social role (warrior? mother? shaman?). In others the judgment is presented as based on moral goodness, but that may reflect more the influence of Christian ethical dualism than traditional values. It does appear that some concept of worthiness is involved in the judgment. Especially for warriors, that assessment might take the form of a test, a frequently encountered theme in Native American myth. In mortuary mythology the outcome of a test may determine the destination of the soul, including whether reincarnation is merited.

This test/decision theme appears in several ways in the full Path of Souls complex, and it seems worthwhile to summarize here the material surveyed in the earlier article (Lankford 2007b). One way in which this idea is symbolized is the image of a fork in the Path of Souls. The naturalistic appearance of the fork is a celestial one—the Milky Way splits, and one path leads to an open gap before the main path can be rejoined. The other path simply continues without hiatus. Deneb, a first-magnitude star, is placed right at the fork in the path and could serve as a marker for the decision point or a figure who would do the deciding.

The decision-making figure takes several forms. One is a fearsome image of a "brain-smasher," usually a woman whose task is to destroy memory (and humanity?) by removing or smashing the brain. Hultkrantz noted that this idea occurs among the Penobscot, Huron, Iroquois, Ojibwa, Menomini, Sauk, Fox, and Winnebago (Hultkrantz 1953:215). The Sauk belief is a good illustration of the image:

> A log serves for a bridge, and this is guarded by a being called Po'kitapawa, "Knocks-a-hole-in-the-head," or "Brain Taker." Brain Taker has a watch dog who barks the alarm whenever a new soul approaches,

and the fleeting spirit must be swift indeed to avoid having his brains dashed out. If this happens, he is destroyed or lost forever, but if he eludes Brain Taker he darts across the log to the abode of the dead, where there is everlasting feasting and rejoicing. (Skinner 1923:36)

This image seems strongly Algonkian, although other linguistic groups were participants in it. The Iroquois and Huron belief was captured early by Jesuit missionaries:

> Another told me that on the same road, before arriving at the Village, one comes to a Cabin where lives one named Oscotarach, or "Pierce-head," who draws the brains out of the heads of the dead, and keeps them. You must pass a river, and the only bridge you have is the trunk of a tree laid across, and very slightly supported. The passage is guarded by a dog, which jumps at many souls, and makes them fall; they are at the same time carried away by the violence of the torrent, and stifled in the waters. (Thwaites 1898:147)

The ethnographic record from the eastern Algonkian and Siouan groups is deficient, but there is a hint that the "brain-smasher" was also part of their imagery. William Byrd reported that an "orator" at a Saponi mortuary ritual told him of their beliefs about the journey of the soul:

> He believ'd that after Death both good and bad People are conducted by a strong Guard into a great Road, in which departed Souls travel together for some time, till at a certain distance this Road forks into two Parts, the one extremely Levil, and the other Stony and Mountainous, ... Near the Entrance into this Blessed Land Sits a Venerable Old Man on a Mat richly woven, who examines Strictly all that are brought before him, and if they have behav'd well, the Guards are order'd to open the Crystal Gate, and let them enter into the Land of Delights ... [The left-hand path goes to an unpleasant, hungry world.] At the End of this Path sits a dreadful old Woman on a monstrous Toad-Stool, whose head is cover'd with Rattle-Snakes instead of Tresses, with glaring white Eyes ... She sends them by buzzard to the bad land, where they eventually are reborn into this world. (Byrd cited in Swanton 1946:750)

At least some of the western Siouan groups believed in the Old Woman as the judge. The Lakota belief was that "She who pushes them over the bank" sat at the fork on the Path of Souls and performed judgment (Brown 1953:29n; Powers 1975:52–53). The Omaha held that there was an Old Man who performed the task:

> It was said that at the forks of the path of the dead (the Milky Way) "there sat an old man wrapped in a buffalo robe, and when the spirits of the dead passed along he turned the steps of the good and peaceable people toward the short path which led directly to the abode of their relatives, but allowed the contumacious to take the long path, over which they wearily wandered." (Fletcher and La Flesche 1911:590)

As has been noted, the eastern Siouan Saponi believed in both the Old Man and the Old Woman.

In some of the Central Algonkian groups the "brain-smasher" is missing, at least in the ethnographic record. They believed in another of the testing motifs, however: the dog. The Miami believed in a Path of Souls that included the log bridge and the dog (Kinietz 1938:52–53). The Shawnee understanding included the fork in the path, the log bridge across the river, and four dogs that attack souls on the bridge (Schutz 1975:95–97). The Delaware belief was similar:

> The bridge along the Milky Way allegedly was guarded by dogs who had died. The dogs allowed passage only to the souls of the good; those who had ever abused a dog were prohibited from crossing. (Kraft 1986:192)
> ... dogs must be treated with respect because they guard the bridge to the afterworld, the bridge that lies at the fork in the Milky Way. (Bruce L. Pearson quoted in Bierhorst 1995:65)

Bierhorst noted in this connection that the motif of the dog that guards the route to the realm of the dead is widespread throughout Mexico and Central and South America as well as being found among the Miami, Ojibwa, Potawatomi, and Shawnee (Bierhorst 1995:65). As has been seen, the dog may be considered a standard feature of the Central Algonkian peoples, and this distribution suggests that it is an ancient motif in this hemisphere. In the light of this very widespread distribution, it is not surprising that the dog also appears in Southeastern belief, although in a slight variation.

For the Cherokee, Stansbury Hagar identified two "dog stars," Sirius and Antares, as guards of the two "opposite points of the sky, where the Milky Way touches the horizon." The souls cross a torrent on a narrow pole, and some fall off. The souls go east then west, following the Milky Way trail to a fork at which a dog must be fed. If they are successful in passing that dog, then they follow the trail to a second dog, which must also be fed. If a soul does not have enough food to feed both of the dogs, then it is trapped between them, a clear warning to the living to make sure they provide ample burial offerings of food for the journey (Hagar 1906:354–356).

The Muskhogean groups seem to have believed in the dog, but not as a guard or antagonist of the soul on the Path of Souls. The Natchez and the Cherokee both tell a myth of the origin of the Milky Way in which a dog was responsible for spilling maize flour across the sky, creating the path (Mooney 1900:259; Swanton 1928:479). This image seems to be backed up by linguistic references to the path of the dogs. The Choctaw term for the Milky Way, for example, is *ofi hata kolofa*, literally "white dog notched or split in two" (Byington 1915:500). Whether such linguistic tags indicate an earlier participation in either of the dog traditions is impossible to determine. Moreover, in the light of the conflicting information from the Cherokee, the prevalence and significance of this apparently trivial story about a dog's maize flour cannot be assessed.

The point of this brief survey of figures is to indicate the variety of ways in which the decision-making or testing theme can be shown. They indicate a functional slot that can be filled by alternate figures, according to the preference of the tribe. It thus comes as no surprise to find important references to a minority view of the judge or antagonist on the Path of Souls. The Alabama and Seminole specified an eagle that was encountered on the path. Swanton learned that among the Alabama "a knife is said to have been put into the hand of an Alabama Indian with which to fight an eagle supposed to beset the spirit trail" (Swanton 1946:724). In 1880 the Seminole burial practices included a piece of burnt wood and bow in the left hand, with an arrow held by the right.

> The fires at the head and feet, as well as the waving of the torches, were to guard him from the approach of "evil birds" who would harm

him. His feet were placed toward the east, that when he arose to go to the skies he might go straight to the sky path, which commenced at the place of the sun's rising . . . He had with him his bow and arrow, that he might procure food on his way. The piece of burnt wood in his hand was to protect him from the "bad birds" while he was on his skyward journey. These "evil birds" are called Ta-lak-i-çlak-o. (MacCauley 1887:521–522)

The Seminole belief that the dead soul must confront a fierce eagle on the Path of Souls is also enshrined in Seminole oral history collections (Judith Knight, personal communication, 1996) and current ritual practice (Mary Johns, personal communication, 1997). The name of the bird recorded by MacCauley as "Ta-lak-i-çlak-o" is almost certainly the Muskhogean term (*tal-aki-thlacco*) for "great eagle," the equivalent of the Alabama *talaktochoba*, of which one modern informant said: "It could pick up humans and carry them off. There are no more of them because they've all been killed" (Sylestine et al. 1993:389).

The distribution list of the variants in the beliefs about the antagonist or judge on the Path of Souls is provocative (Table 10.1). This makes it obvious that the testimony in favor of an eagle as the antagonist is severely restricted. While it is always dangerous to argue from silence, it may be important to note that while Swanton was able to recover the eagle motif from the Alabama, he was not able to do so for other Muskhogean groups for which he had extensive collections and numerous informants. The correlation of this Great Eagle antagonist on the Path of Souls (apparently restricted to the Alabama and Seminole) with the appearance of the Raptor on Moundville mortuary ceramics seems significant. When it is considered that the Alabama are in the group of likely descendants of the Moundvillians, the case is as complete as it is likely to be: for Moundville, the Raptor/Great Eagle was to be found as an antagonist on the Path of Souls, and mortuary ritual would likely have included grave goods which would enable the soul to negotiate or fight with the Raptor on the journey.

If the Raptor on the Path of Souls was the antagonist of choice for the people of Moundville, they would have found the astronomical skyscape ready-made. The first-magnitude star Deneb has already been suggested as the focus of the judgment process, because of both its prominence and its location right at the fork in the Milky Way. Deneb, however, is also the alpha star of the Greek constellation Cygnus, the Swan. It is called that because the major star pattern is a cross, which can readily be seen as a bird (Fig. 10.2). If a swan, why not a Great Eagle?

It thus appears to be a strong possibility that the Raptor on the Moundville pottery, regardless of its meaning in other places and other contexts, was part of a mortuary symbolic complex, related to the celestial realm and linked conceptually to the iconic images of the winged serpent, skull, bone, and hand-and-eye.

If this conclusion is correct, then several cautionary notes may be drawn from the situation. First, the importance of regionalism in understanding

TABLE 10.1. Tribal variants in identity of antagonist/judge

Brain-Smasher/Old Woman	Old Man	Dog	Eagle
Penobscot			
Huron		Huron	
Iroquois		Iroquois	
Ojibwa		Ojibwa	
Menomini			
Sauk		Sauk	
Fox			
Winnebago			
		Potawatomi	
		Miami	
		Shawnee	
		Delaware	
Lakota			
Saponi	Saponi		
	Omaha		
	Osage (?)		
		Cherokee	
		Natchez	
		Chickasaw (?)	
			Alabama
			Seminole

FIGURE 10.2. Part of the Milky Way, containing the Fork and Cygnus, with Deneb.

the meanings of the images is underscored. If Moundville's particular understanding and use of the Raptor are different from those of many other places in which the Raptor appears, then it becomes extremely important to seek meanings in the local context. Scholars may need to speak of the Etowah Raptor, Spiro Raptor, Missouri Raptor, Moundville Raptor, and so on.

Second, since it seems unlikely that the other Raptors in Mississippian iconography are completely unconnected with the Moundville Raptor, the importance of becoming clear about the number and types of meaning that may be embodied in each collection of images is underscored. It is not difficult at this point to suggest a minimum of three that must be sought: a general cognitive meaning, a local application, and the meaning of functional usage. For a quick understanding of the nature of these meaning areas, an appeal to Christian symbolic history is useful. If the general cognitive meaning of a cross is offered, it will focus on the Christ myth, death and resurrection and possibly the theme of cosmic salvation, and so on. In particular regional contexts (such as a Greek monastery) the cross means—in addition to the general cognitive meaning—a particular path of mysticism and spiritual discipline, a "way of the cross" in religious life, so to speak. Further, some artistic styles of crosses (such as Maltese or St. Andrew's) denote specific ethnic or social groups. And some crosses gain added significance from their location on material objects, such as the cross on the back of medieval pilgrims' garments that served to announce that they were returning from the Holy Land. All of these are parts of the total meaning(s) of a cross, and the interpretation of any particular cross cannot really be said to be complete until all those types of meaning have been ferreted out.

By the same token, a Raptor may also have multiple meanings along these lines. It is not difficult to imagine, first, a general Raptor cognitive meaning in the realm of myth, a portrayal of a figure who is an important part of the cosmic structure and the religious life of Native Americans of many different ethnic groups. A second meaning is a local application of the Raptor, with appropriate additions to the local myths, that stresses the mortuary significance of the figure and indicates an eventual personal encounter with the Raptor. A third: objects bearing Raptor symbols that are designed to help in the negotiation with the Raptor and/or indicate a special relationship with it and thus serve as a status or achievement indicator. In such a range of meanings, can any single understanding be considered the "explanation" of the symbol?

From this viewpoint, the task of decoding images such as the Raptor in the Mississippian iconographic corpus will likely prove to be even more difficult than is frequently supposed. It seems unlikely that any of the "meanings" offered by modern scholars will be the total explanation. This study is a good example: the general cognitive meaning of the Raptor has not been explored at all, but I have attempted to gain insight on the regional nature of the Raptor at Moundville and at least one functional use of the image. This study, therefore, does not "explain" the Raptor image, but it is a contribution toward that end. Scholars involved in the decoding project will need to be very careful to avoid treating as competitive interpretations meanings that may be revealed, on examination, not to be mutually exclusive at all.

AUTHOR'S NOTE: An earlier version of this chapter was presented at the 2000 Southeastern Archaeological Conference in Macon, Georgia.

CHAPTER 11

The Swirl-Cross and the Center

George E. Lankford

In the hundreds of artistic designs in the Mississippian iconographic corpus, more than sixty examples of swastikas are known to occur. The Sanskrit label "swastika" used in religious studies has been applied to this image because of its similarity to the ancient Indian symbol. Most of the Mississippian examples, however, are subtler in structure than the right-angle form of the ancient image, for most differ from crosses only in the slight curving bend at the end of the arms of an equal-armed cross. The modern totalitarian connotation attached to the term from its use by the Nazis argues that a more neutral one should be adopted for the Mississippian occurrences. The term that will be used here is "swirl-cross," which seems a descriptive but politically neutral label.

The corpus of swirl-crosses used in this study consists of sixty-two occurrences (see Appendix 11.1). This is not an exhaustive list, however, because more examples occur in the ceramics of both Moundville and the Central Mississippi Valley. The group seems adequate for this examination, though. Seventeen of the sixty-two examples form a group of four copper gorgets and thirteen pendants bearing essentially the same design. The copper emblems are also notable in that almost all of them (fourteen) come from the same site, Moundville in Alabama (Fig. 11.1a, b). The three others are from the nearby chiefdom at Etowah in Georgia.

The other examples of swirl-crosses are found engraved on shell gorgets and ceramics. The locations of the gorgets are distributed across the South, from Spiro in the Arkansas River Valley to the upper Tennessee River. The nineteen ceramic appearances are mostly from the Central Mississippi Valley, with a small sample from Moundville. Although the copper swirl-crosses are essentially the only symbolic figures on those artifacts, the swirl-crosses in the noncopper examples are associated with other symbols.

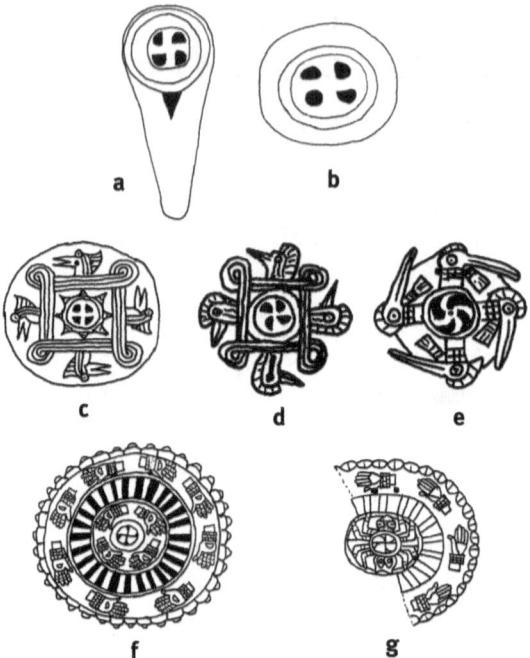

FIGURE 11.1. (a, b) Examples of the copper swirl-cross pendants and gorgets from Moundville (after Moore 1907:Figs. 102, 105); (c) Tennessee Cox Mound gorget; (d) Tennessee Cox Mound gorget (#20), the sole example with a swirl-cross; (e) Four Crested Birds shell gorget from Spiro (#21); (f, g) Hull-style gorgets from Spiro (#25 and #24) (after Phillips and Brown 1984:Pls. 276, 277).

The challenge for the student of iconography is to derive whatever insights may legitimately be gained from examining both the symbolic complex in which swirl-crosses appear and the sparse information regarding their provenience. This chapter will survey the known data then offer some conclusions about the meaning of the symbol and its role in Native American life, particularly at Moundville.

The Swirl-Cross as an Independent Motif

Folklorists have long found it useful in the examination of myth texts to identify "motifs," generally understood to be the simplest identifiable plot elements that have a meaning, a concept similar to the morphemes studied by linguists. As with morphemes, one of the preliminary steps in understanding the usage of motifs is to determine whether a given motif is "free" (it can stand alone as an independent narrative) or "bound" (it has a meaning which makes sense only when it is part of one or more additional motifs). The easiest way to determine this quality is to locate instances of a motif's appearance in which it does indeed stand alone.

If this procedure is applied to visual art forms, then it is easily discernible that the swirl-cross is an independent artistic motif. The examples from Moundville copper, in which the swirl-cross in a circle is the basic motif, are a powerful demonstration of the independence of the image. Two provocative fragments of engraved shell cups from Spiro suggest the same conclusion. Both are examples of the compositional form which, for lack of a better term, might be called "pastiche." Such shell productions have a collection of motifs that are distributed across the surface in a pattern that communicates no clear meaning. Two of those pastiche designs incorporate swirl-crosses (for brevity, references to examples will use the list numbers found in Appendix 11.1; these two designs are #1 and #2). In one (#1), fifteen swirl-crosses float two-dimensionally on the surface alongside a sinuous form of the striped pole, with raccoon bindings tied around it in several places.

In the second engraving (#2), four swirl-crosses-in-circles float alongside four faces (or masks) and nine hollow forms that resemble the shape of the Moundville pendants. The independent appearance of the latter suggests that the pendant form itself may have to be considered an independent motif, which would make the Moundville pendants two-motif artifacts. At Spiro the swirl-cross appears to be an independent motif, reinforcing the conclusion that the Moundville copper gorgets also demonstrate the independent nature of the swirl-cross. Corroborating evidence of the swirl-cross's independence comes from two sites in the Central Mississippi Valley, Beck and Upper Nodena (#48, #58), from which came a bowl and a bottle that bear only a swirl-cross on the base.

The Symbolic Connections

If a motif is bound to specific other motifs with which it is usually or invariably found, then it is possible to see the motif as part of a larger whole that includes the other motifs. With an independent motif, however, there is no larger whole. Fortunately for the examination, even an independent motif can offer more information for analysis. In the present case, many of the swirl-crosses appear as inclusions in more complex compositions which are represented by numerous examples, thus providing a larger comparative collection for study. Earlier students, particularly Madeline Kneberg (1959), Jon Muller (1966a), and Philip Phillips and James Brown (1978), have recognized "types" of designs within the corpus, both stylistic and thematic. Those observations have been summarized and augmented in the compendium of gorget designs by Jeffrey Brain and Philip Phillips (1996). The search for interpretation of those designs has thus been made much easier by the scholarship already accomplished. Here is a survey of the complex swirl-cross appearances, beginning with the shell gorgets then moving to the ceramics. Closer examination of the simple Moundville copper forms will follow in a final section.

SHELL GORGETS

Cox Mound. The Cox Mound style has only twenty-three known examples (Brain and Phillips 1996:9–12). It is a distinctive concentric, balanced design. An earlier study broke the design down into five fields, each of which was discerned to have an independent life, and presumably a meaning, of its own (Lankford 2007d). In field one, at the center of the concentric structure, is a cross (Fig. 11.1c, d, e). Although some of the occurrences are fragmentary, it appears that only one of the examples has any motif other than a cross. That exception is a swirl-cross.

The rayed circle surrounding the cross/swirl-cross has been interpreted by every writer on the subject as the sun, primarily because that is the intuitive meaning to which most observers would leap. Waring treated the sun circle and the cross/swirl-cross as a single motif, considering all variants as equivalents:

> [Cross and Sun Circle] are the motifs most easily identified with a conceptual complex on the historic level, namely the fire-sun-deity complex. Holmes [1906:p. 105] and Willoughby [1932:59] both regarded these motifs as "sun," "cosmic," or "world" symbols . . . The concept of a holy fire identified with the sun and fed by four symbolic logs oriented to the four cardinal points is the most widespread and basic ceremonial concept in the Southeast . . .
>
> In view of the distribution of this complex, of the similarity of its position in the various individual conceptual systems of the Southeast,

and of its association with the symbolic cruciform arrangement of logs, it seems obvious that the Cross and Sun Circle are essential symbols of the fire-sun-deity conceptual complex. (Waring 1968b:33–35)

Waring was followed in this interpretation by James Howard (1968), who emphasized the ritual significance of the four-log structure of the sacred fire that is found at the center of the Creek square grounds.

In earlier iconographic studies I accepted these interpretations of the sun-circle and the cross, since both are plausible and have explanatory value, especially in regard to the Creek practice of centering the sacred fire within a cross in the square grounds. But I did emphasize the separation of the two motifs (sun and fire), thus making the two phenomena the ends of a column which may serve as an axis mundi in the cosmological structure. Further, I identified the striped pole motif as a side view of the same column. In this view, the cross-in-rayed-circle becomes a two-dimensional version of what was understood as a three-dimensional reality (Lankford 2004, 2007d). Even short of that interpretation, however, the cross still seems to be identifiable as a symbol of the Center, just by its form and its location in the center of more complex designs.

With a single exception from the Tombigbee River, the Cox Mound–style gorgets are found only in the Cumberland and lower Tennessee areas, making it almost certain that the center of manufacture and use is to be found in that region. Unfortunately, the single swirl-cross version (#20) has no firmer provenience than "Tennessee," but it is not unreasonable to assume that it too stems from one of the two Cox Mound–style areas. That placement then tightens the focus of the problem of the meaning of substituting the swirl-cross for the cross, since it lessens the probability that the substitution was made by someone outside the community of understanding, altering the design in ignorance of the meaning of the cross. That conclusion leaves a working hypothesis that the swirl-cross was an acceptable substitution for the cross at the center of the Cox Mound–style design, even if only in the one instance. Whether the substitution was one of equivalence or an alteration of the meaning, however, appears to be a distinction that cannot be drawn at this point.

Four Crested Birds. A single shell gorget from Spiro (#21) is readily identified as a creative version of the same cosmological model shown in the Cox Mound style (see Fig. 11.1e). Executed by a Craig artist, as the details suggest, the four Crested Birds surround the central circle, which is a fenestrated swirl-cross with a dotted center. The four birds have straight beaks, feather crests, beads around the neck, and tassels. What has been removed from the Cox Mound design is the looped square, which I identify as the symbol for the earth-island. The Spiro gorget is thus a reduction of the full cosmological design but not necessarily an alteration of its meaning. In this Craig production the emphasis is on the swirl-cross as the center and the four Crested Birds. In this case it cannot even be argued that the swirl-cross is a substitution for the cross, since there is no other example of this design. It can be noted, however, that the swirl-cross is again found in the central position in a cosmological gorget.

Hull. The swirl-cross is found as a standard motif in another design from Spiro, this time in a collection of five gorgets that are remarkably similar, possibly from the same hand or workshop. Called the Hull style by Brain and Phillips (1996:60), the design is basically a set of concentric circles with different motifs in each circle (Fig. 11.1f, g).

The swirl-cross stands in the center, surrounded by a circular band containing four hands-and-eyes. The next circle consists of rayed fenestrations, with no common number of rays. There are twenty-seven fenestrations on two of them (#25 and #28) and eighteen on another (#24). The remainder are too fragmentary to count (#26, #27). The next circular band carries eight hands-and-eyes, apparently the same number on all the gorgets, although only #25 and #28 can be counted with certainty. The final circle is a petaloid border, with the knobbed form on all except #24, which uses a scalloped form with incised lines.

Four of the five gorgets may be by the same hand or workshop and, if they were complete, would probably prove to be identical in design. The fifth (#24), however, is a variant in several ways. For one thing, it appears on the back of a Braden-style gorget, a possible example of recycling of the material (Phillips and Brown 1984:Pl. 276). The different treatment of the petaloid border and the smaller number of fenestrations have already been mentioned. Another change is that the hands in the outer band do not have "eyes" in the palms. The major difference, however, is that the interior band of four hands is replaced by a spider, with the swirl-cross-in-circle resting upon the body of the spider. As Brain and Phillips pointed out, the spider itself is very similar to the spider gorgets from Illinois, which have been labeled the McAdams style (Fig. 11.2a, b). But those thirty gorgets are characterized by

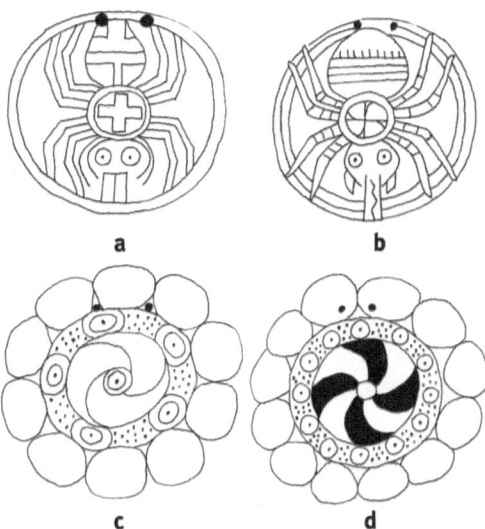

FIGURE 11.2. (a) McAdams spider gorget, III-Sr-X1; (b) McAdams spider gorget, #22 (after Brain and Phillips 1996:107); (c) Nashville II gorget, typical form (Tenn-Hm-W124); (d) Nashville II gorget, swirl-cross variant (#30) (after Brain and Phillips 1996:459, 471).

the spider centered in three or four concentric rings around the edge of the gorget. Brain and Phillips identified two other styles incorporating spiders, the Orton style (four) and Rudder style (two), both found in east Tennessee, on the basis of a different background using concentric bands. In terms of background (concentric bands), the Orton and Rudder spider gorgets are closer to the Hull spider, although the spider design itself seems more similar to McAdams. Moreover, two of the McAdams gorgets also share the swirl-cross in the center on the spider's body. The issue of which is the closer relationship is not unimportant, for the distribution of the spider gorget styles is distinctive (Brain and Phillips 1996:maps on 109 and 111).

When the thirty-five spider gorgets of all three styles are examined together, the differences are telling. As nearly as can be discerned, given the fragmentary state of many of the gorgets, the vast majority bear a cross on the thorax of the spider, with a minority representation of other forms. The count is twenty-four crosses, seven blank spaces (including one with a central dot), one web, one unique bar design, and two swirl-crosses (#22 and #23, both on McAdams gorgets). To these, of course, should be added the Hull spider gorget (#24). Within the spider gorget context, therefore, the swirl-crosses are a minority replacement for crosses in the McAdams style, just as the unique Hull spider variant has a swirl-cross that replaces crosses in the Hull array.

Nashville. The concept of concentric bands seen in the Hull style is manifested distinctively in the Nashville-style series of shell gorgets. There the outer band consists of ovals or ellipses in a circle, producing a scalloped edge. The next band toward the center carries several dotted circles spaced around the band, with the intervening spaces filled with dots. Brain and Phillips (1996) refer to this design as "ophidian," because it suggests a serpent skin reminiscent of the serpent body seen in a number of Southeastern Ceremonial Complex designs, particularly at Spiro. The inner circle usually features a three-armed swirl (a triskele) (Fig. 11.2c, d).

Brain and Phillips separated the Nashville style into two groups, with the second (Nashville II) consisting of all those that did not quite fit the standard set by the putative "master" engraver in the Nashville area. In other words, the point of the distinction is to identify an inner group of the Nashville design (Nashville I) from which the deviance of all the others is measured. The distinction is of little use for this inquiry, however, since the presence of a swirl-cross is the focus here. Of the 108 examples of the Nashville style (including the nearby Springs style), 100 of them have a triskele in the inner circle. One gorget has only two arms; but seven have four arms, thus forming a swirl-cross. Two of the seven swirl-crosses, from Tennessee, are unique forms, although they do have swirl-crosses (#31, #33). The other five are solid swirl-cross variants of the Nashville style.

These five swirl-crosses have a curious distribution: #30 and #32 from Tennessee, #34 and #35 from Arkansas, and #36 from Kentucky. They also have unusual designs. Gorget #30 is an excellent example of Nashville style, except that the center fenestrated whorl opens into an obvious swirl-cross (Fig. 11.2d). Gorget #32, on the other hand, is a Nashville-style gorget from Davidson County that has four tightly wound arms in the center. Technically it is a swirl-cross, because of the four arms, but it takes careful counting to discern the four arms; otherwise, it simply appears to be another triskele gorget. Gorget #36, from the Williams site in Christian County, Kentucky, is a Nashville gorget with four fenestrated arms forming a swirl-cross unconnected at the center. The two Arkansas gorgets are both variants. Gorget #35 is from the Kirkham site in southwest Arkansas and appears to be a poorly done variation on the Nashville style. A small circle with a cross unites the arms of a swirl-cross whorl. Brain and Phillips observed that the idea was derived from the Nashville style, "but the result was a greatly altered production" (Brain and Phillips 1996:121). The other Arkansas swirl-cross (#34) also clearly belongs in the Nashville corpus, but it has large fenestrated arms surrounding a circle and dot. This is an impressive piece of work but stands as a unique gorget. It is from the Foster Place site in Lafayette County in southwest Arkansas.

These variants on the Nashville style, all with swirl-crosses, suggest that the triskele form of the Nashville style may be a local way of executing the swirl-cross, perhaps the result of a single group of allied artists or the distribution of their tradition. Localization of the triskele form does not necessarily indicate that it has the same meaning as the more widespread swirl-cross form; but until a different nuance of meaning can be clarified, the triskele will be treated as simply a local variant of the swirl-cross.

Geometric. Two other gorgets bear swirl-crosses, both of them fitting loosely into the category of the "geometric" gorgets. One (#29) is from the Sanders site in Texas. It is another concentric design, with two circles of fenestrations which produce what may be described as a double solar disk. Inside the two ray bands is a band bearing dotted circles, reminiscent of the Nashville ophidian band. At the center is a fenestrated swirl-cross. The whole gorget is an excellent piece of work, but its classification is problematic. Brain and Phillips (1996) created a "Krieger" style, but there are only two gorgets in the category, the other being La-Ca-B2 from the Belcher site in Louisiana. At its center is a single hole rather than a swirl-cross. The Krieger gorgets are very close in design to two gorgets from the Georgia coast, the only representatives of the Brain and Phillips (1996) category called Claflin (Ga-Cu-SI1 and Ga-MI-CI2). At the center of each of those gorgets is a small cross. The small sample provides only the tentative conclusion that in this group the swirl-cross may substitute for a center hole or cross (Fig. 11.3a, b).

A unique example from the Kellogg site in the Tombigbee drainage in Mississippi (#37) has a distant relationship to these gorgets. It resembles several of the styles already discussed in that it consists of concentric bands, but it differs especially in the sequence of bands. The outer band is crosshatched and bears cymas at the four cardinal positions, with the Crested Birds in the Cox Mound style. The next band toward the interior is a simple one with radial lines crossing the plain band. Next is a petaloid border surrounding a

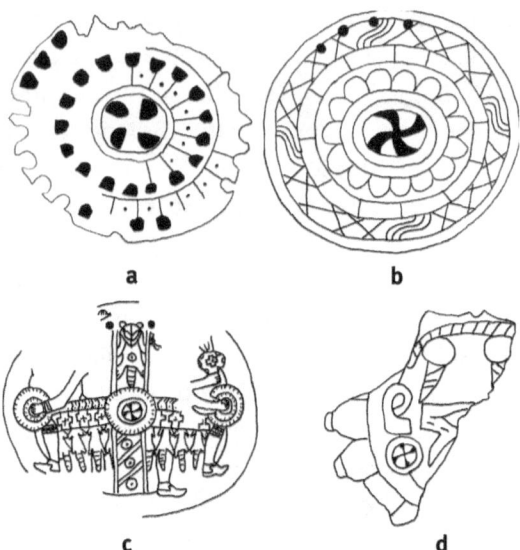

FIGURE 11.3. Two concentric gorgets: (a) Krieger (#29); (b) Kellogg (#37); (c, d) two gorgets from Spiro, #38 and #39.

small plain band. At the center is a fenestrated swirl-cross. While little analysis can be done in regard to a unique gorget, it should be pointed out that the Kellogg gorget belongs in the larger group of concentric design styles and is, at least in that regard, related to the Hull, Cox Mound, and Nashville styles.

Human Figural. Two gorgets from Spiro bear a swirl-cross in the context of human figures. Each has its little bit of insight to add to the mix. Gorget #38 is a shell gorget on which two humanlike figures (they may be divinities) face away from a central vertical column, a pattern frequently encountered in Spiro engravings (Fig. 11.3c, d). Brain and Phillips (1996) place the gorget in the Hamilton style, which is found only at Spiro. "Paired figures are portrayed in ceremonial postures and regalia, and are arranged in a bilaterally symmetrical structure" (Brain and Phillips 1996:55). In nine examples of this style the two figures face away from each other and the central element. The swirl-cross occurs in only one of them (#38), where it is at the center of the central element, within a petaloid border. In this example the petaloid motif is matched by similar motifs (feather fans?) held in the hands of the two figures, although they do not bear swirl-crosses. The two figures are fragmentary, but they seem to be identical, wearing belts with cross designs with raccoons hanging from them, bootees, and rattles also bearing crosses in rayed circles. The central panel is intact, showing a striped pole motif at the bottom, below the swirl-cross, and a raccoon above.

Five of the other gorgets have at least partial remains of the central element. One (Okla-Lf-S111) shows intertwined bands with a raccoon in the center, and another (Okla-Lf-S569) has the same intertwined bands but with the top culminating in a cross in a petaloid border. The central element of Okla-Lf-S219 consists solely of a striped pole, which is present in another form in Okla-Lf-S233. The fifth gorget (Okla-Lf-S225) has a central panel with a unique line decoration, with a petaloid border surrounding a circle in the center. The Hamilton gorgets thus suggest that the swirl-cross may replace a cross in a circle, concentric circles, and possibly a raccoon. The swirl-cross here is also associated with motifs of the center: intertwined bands and striped pole.

The second gorget in this category, #39, is only a fragment. That shell sherd, however, portrays the right side of a humanlike face that bears a forked eye. The ear has a large earspool engraved with a swirl-cross. The head is close to the edge of the gorget, for several elements of a knobbed petaloid border are still attached to the fragment. Phillips and Brown pointed out that even those few clues are sufficient to identify the gorget as Craig B, since the eye-surround details are placed in Craig B on the basis of many other appearances in the Spiro corpus (Phillips and Brown 1984:Pl. 273B). Thus the fragment links the knobbed petaloid border, forked eye surround, and swirl-cross earspool as contemporary, at least at Spiro. It also offers a functional insight—the swirl-cross, used alone as an independent motif, may be worn by someone as an earspool decoration.

Summary. The full corpus of gorgets bearing swirl-crosses has now been examined. If it is fair to assume that the swirl-cross was not a symbol that could be used randomly, then it is worth noting that it has limited symbolic associations. In the collection surveyed, the following additional motifs occur on artifacts in conjunction with the swirl-cross: raccoon binding, raccoon skin, striped pole, masks, pendant forms, Crested Bird, tassel, neck beads, cyma, looped square, cross, concentric circles, rayed circle, spider, forked eye, hand, petaloid border, petaloid fan, paired figures, and rattle. While this appears to be a lengthy list, it is by no means all-inclusive. Missing from the list, for example, are the motifs frequently encountered in connection with the Raptor motif complex, with the exception of the one gorget on which the swirl-cross appears on an earspool worn by a figure with a forked eye.

A much tighter group of motif associations appears when the rules for substitution are examined. On the basis of the survey presented above, it appears that the swirl-cross may substitute in established designs in only a few ways. Here is a summary list:

Cox Mound	style cross
Four Birds	central position
Hull	cross
McAdams	cross
Nashville	triskele
Geometric	central hole or dot
Hamilton	cross, circle, raccoon

The raccoon skin may be removed from the list. It appears in the central position only once. When the swirl-cross is in that position, the raccoon skin hangs above it on the central element. It thus appears that the "substitution" in this case is only a reorganization of the symbols on the central element. That leaves a simple set of occurrences which may constitute design rules:

swirl-cross = cross
swirl-cross = triskele
swirl-cross = circle/hole/dot

As already noted, at present the triskele is understood to be a local equivalent of the swirl-cross, so it can be removed from this list. The substitution list may therefore be condensed into swirl-cross = cross and circle/hole/dot. Does that translate into swirl-cross = cross = circle = hole = dot? The differences in the forms of these motifs appear too great to support the idea that they are synonymous, with the visual choice apparently left to the artist's whimsy. If the proposition that the substitution of these motifs for each other does not indicate equivalence in meaning is accepted, then the nature of the relationship among these allomotifs must be sought along another line.

These instances of substitution have one element in common: they are nearly always located in the center. The majority of the gorgets in the swirl-cross group are concentric cosmograms. The art styles change, but the basic structure remains. The Cox Mound style thus is related to the Krieger, Hull, Nashville, and Geometric gorgets in its very structure, which I have argued is a cosmological image. The substitution of the swirl-cross occurs at the center of those gorgets. I read the center as the column which has the sun at the top and the fire on the earth, symbolized particularly by rayed circle motifs and the cross. The allomotifs should refer to this column or axis that connects worlds, but with a different message. Thus it seems reasonable to hypothesize that the swirl-cross/triskele, and circle/dot/hole are all symbols of the center but make different references.

I have also argued that the Hixon style is a side view of the same cosmological structure shown in the Cox Mound style (Lankford 2004, 2007d). By extension, all the Hamilton-style paired-human designs may also present a central pole or panel which is the side view of the central axis. When the swirl-cross appears on the side of the axis (as in #38), it appears to be performing the same service as in the concentric cosmograms—it indicates a particular place or aspect of the axis. This suggests that the four motifs—swirl-cross, cross, triskele, and circle/hole/dot—are all connected by their participation in the Center. Each must represent a particular aspect of the axis. If the cross represents fire, which is part of the axis on the Earth World, then what are the meanings of swirl-cross, triskele, and circle/dot/hole? To what aspect of the axis do they refer?

CERAMICS

Some answers may come from the ceramic evidence, for the contexts in which swirl-crosses appear are somewhat different from those for swirl-crosses on shell gorgets. In the Central Mississippi Valley are mound centers with associated sites, clusters which are thought of as separate polities even though they seem to have been very close in cultural makeup. Several of them have yielded examples of swirl-crosses, and it seems a safe assumption that many more are yet to be discovered. The swirl-crosses and other SECC imagery appear on ceramic vessels of various forms and decoration. Twenty of them are surveyed here in the hope that they will offer clues to the meaning of the swirl-cross.

Two bottles and two bowls, all Carson Red on Buff, offer more examples of the swirl-cross in a Center placement. Curiously, all four use terrace designs familiar from the Southwest but rare in the Mississippian iconographic corpus (see Lankford 2006).

In the bowl images from Parkin (#55) and Rose Mound (#57), the terraces provide the quadripartite surround that centers the swirl-cross (Fig. 11.4a).

The two bottles from the Hazel site (#53 and #54) place the terraces at the mouth of the vessel, atop the slender neck. The swirl-cross is located on the side in the center of a rayed circle.

Two more vessels, already mentioned, are a plain bowl from Beck (#48) and a plain bottle from Upper Nodena (#58) that are decorated only with a bas-relief swirl-cross in the center of the exterior base. Together, these five vessels serve to continue the shell tradition of using the swirl-cross as a symbol of the Center. Unfortunately, they do not appear to further the search for a meaning of the symbol.

Other examples from the Central Mississippi Valley, however, provide an important clue. Many ceramic effigy bowls from the area incorporate the head of the Great Serpent and its tail, usually curled. Three of them—one

a

b

FIGURE 11.4. (a) Interior of bowl from Parkin (#55). A similar bowl was found at Rose Mound (#57) (Moore 1910:336). (b) Great Serpent effigy bowl bearing a swirl-cross on the head, Belle Meade (#45). Another comes from the Walls site, photograph by David H. Dye.

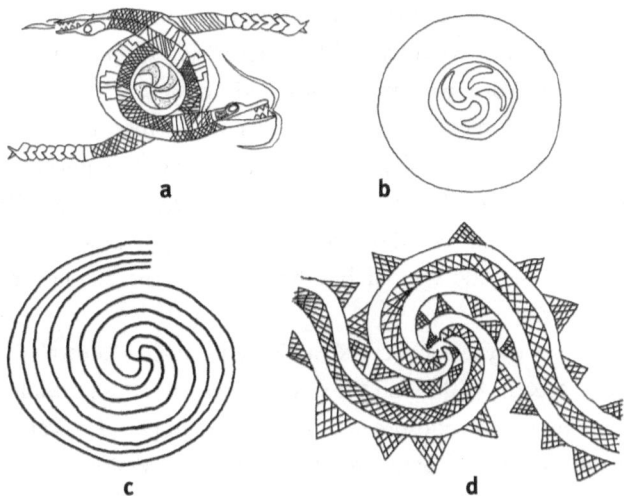

FIGURE 11.5. (a) Design in which the swirl-cross is centered between two serpents (#62, Cagle Lake site, Pemiscot County, Missouri); (b) swirl-cross on the base of a bottle from Upper Nodena (#58); (c, d) simple and complex swirl-crosses in conjunction with the guilloche design: Rose Mound and Walls sites (Moore 1910:Fig. 19).

from Walls (#61) and two from Belle Meade (#45, #47)—are known to bear swirl-crosses upon the back of the head (Fig. 11.4b).

The Great Serpent is a well-known figure in both the mythology and the iconography of the Mississippian peoples (Lankford 1987:Ch. 4, 2007a). Sometimes it appears as a panther, sometimes as a serpent, and sometimes, as in many of these effigy bowls, as a creature bearing characteristics of both. The general concept refers to the amorphous figure(s) of the denizens and the Master of the Beneath World waters. The Beneath World is the lower half of the cosmos, the body of water on which the earth disk floats. A different artistic version of the relationship of Great Serpent and swirl-cross comes from the Cagle Lake site in Pemiscot County, Missouri (Fig. 11.5a).

Why should the swirl-cross, a symbol of the Center, appear on the head of the Great Serpent? In what way is the Great Serpent associated with the Center? Just as the Great Serpent represents all of the water powers, it also is a metaphor for the Beneath World. The Beneath World is the lower realm of the basic three-story universe (which may actually be understood to have many layers as subdivisions of the basic three) and may have a central axis in it. If that axis is the same as the Sun-fire axis—a continuation into the water—the swirl-cross might then represent the Beneath World's portion of it. The swirl-cross thus would stand for a location on the column that connects the Beneath World with the Middle and Above Worlds. From this view, then, the motifs of Sun circle/fire cross/water swirl-cross represent a continuum of points on the cosmological axis, correlating with the three cosmic realms. This does not explain the meaning of the circle/dot/hole, but it suggests that they too might be references to points on the axis. (The circle-dot, for example, may be a star symbol, but that is another project beyond the limits of this chapter.)

More examples of the swirl-cross's appearance in the Central Valley come from the Belle Meade, Walls, and Chucalissa sites. In these examples the guilloche ceramic motif, so widespread in Mississippian pottery, is characterized by obvious swirl-crosses in both simple and complex versions (Fig. 11.5c, d).

The guilloche design itself seems to be derived from Underwater Serpents who support and stabilize the earth disk (Lankford 2007a; see Pauketat and Emerson 1991 for an exploration of this concept as seen in Cahokia pottery). The guilloche sometimes has serpentine characteristics but frequently is conventionalized into a design which defies easy identification with the Beneath World. The swirl-crosses on these pots, however, emphasize the connection. Moreover, the placement of the swirl-crosses at the juncture of serpents—the "corners" of the earth, so to speak—suggests that the swirl-cross may originally have been derived from the lines of the serpentine forms as they come together in those joints. Many of the examples of the guilloche thus preserve the swirl-cross as an integral part of the total design. This hypothesis that the swirl-cross was derived from the guilloche seems unprovable, but it is intriguing that so many "hidden swirl-crosses" are seen in guilloches on Mississippian pottery in various locations.

These examples of the swirl-cross from Central Mississippi Valley ceramics provide a general realm of meaning for the symbol. They point to a connection with the Underwater Serpents who rule the Beneath World, a realm of meaning which can be generalized to refer to the waters or the Beneath World itself. As a symbol of the Beneath World, the swirl-cross can also be used to indicate a location on the world axis, which explains the frequent appearance of the swirl-cross as a symbol of the Center (Fig. 11.5b).

This hypothesis regarding the meaning of the swirl-cross can be tested in the case of two other ceramic instances of the swirl-cross, both of them from Moundville. While there are undoubtedly other ceramic examples at

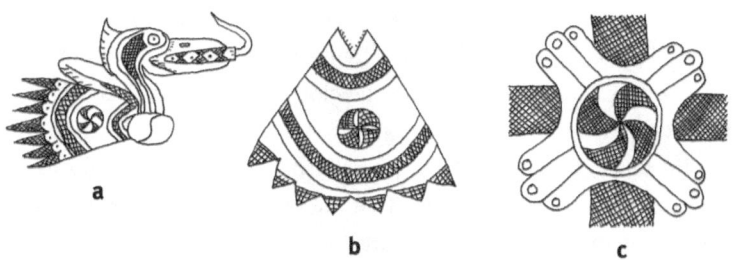

FIGURE 11.6. (a, b) Vessels 4 and 6, Moundville (Moore 1905:Figs. 89 and 90, 9 and 10); (c) Vessel 7, Moundville (Moore 1907:Fig. 4).

Moundville, these are readily available from the illustrations of C. B. Moore. Two of them show the same context, although in different designs. Vessel 4 bears four identical forms, the tail of the Crested Bird. The feathers are banded and bear a swirl-cross in a circle in the center of the tail. Two of the tails are pointed up and two are pointed down (Fig. 11.6a, b). Unfortunately, the bottle bearing this design "lay apart from human remains" (Moore 1905:190), which at the minimum indicates that Moore and his workers were unable to connect the bottle with a specific burial. The design thus stands without context in this instance. The identification of the tails offered so starkly on this bottle is made possible by the design of Vessel 6.

The bottle itself had no context when shown to Moore; it was "said to have been found" at Moundville (Moore 1905:137). The design, however, offers some clarity. It shows two heads of the Crested Bird in court-card symmetry, with two identical tails flanking the column of heads. Feathers (representing wings?) stand between the heads and tails. All are united by an oval shape with a cyma, a motif that may indicate a reduction from a quadripartite structure (V. J. Knight, Jr., personal communication, 2004). The tails again bear swirl-crosses-in-circles, and a fragment shows an identical swirl-cross floating before the crest of the bird head. Vessel 6 thus makes it clear that the swirl-cross is related to the Crested Bird, especially the tail.

If the hypothesis is applied to these two designs, a question arises: "What is the connection between the Crested Bird and the waters of the Beneath World?" It seems unlikely that the Crested Bird could be considered a denizen of the Beneath World, related to the Great Serpent. A myth text may be relevant in addressing this problem. In Swanton's Creek collections, a motif appears several times. It seems to be an etiological motif which explains how the woodpecker got its tail stripes.

"According to one of the fragments collected by myself, water covered everything in the beginning and no living beings existed except two red-headed woodpeckers, which hung to the clouds, with their tails awash in the waters. When the water went down it left marks on their tails which remain today" (Tal mutcasi, medicine maker of Fish Pond and Asilanabi towns, in Swanton 1928:488). Tuggle learned that the bird was the yellowhammer, but Swanton's Alabama informants considered it "a bird a little larger than the common red-headed woodpecker . . . called in their language itka" (Swanton 1928:488). The "larger" specification suggests that the reference is to a pileated or ivory-billed woodpecker. In the version of the flood by Big Jack of Hilibi, "The red-headed woodpecker hung to the sky and the tip of his tail was discolored permanently" (Swanton 1928:488). The Alabama and Koasati versions include the tail motif as part of the flood story: "The flying things flew up to the sky and took hold of it, with their tails half in the water. The ends of their tails got wet. The red-headed woodpecker was flat against the sky and said, 'My tail is half in the water'" (Swanton 1929:121).

This motif is not restricted to the Southeast. Thompson indexed it as "A2211.7: Birds cling to sky in flood (cause of tail colors)," listing only references to it from the Southwest: Navaho, San Carlos Apache, Jicarilla Apache, Sia, and Mohave (Thompson 1929:287). This distribution points to a prehistoric connection between the Southeastern and the Southwestern peoples, a topic explored in a separate article (Lankford 2006).

The existence of this motif in the Southeastern mythic materials does provide a water/Beneath World background for the iconographic emphasis on the tail that bears a swirl-cross. The hypothesis of the Beneath World meaning of the swirl-cross says that there should be a connection between the Crested Bird's tail and water, so it is gratifying that a myth provides information about a tail marked by Beneath World water.

The final example of the usage of the swirl-cross on Moundville ceramics is a more abstract design. It was found on Vessel 7, a bottle recovered from the ground south of Mound D (Fig. 11.6c). The swirl-cross appears at the center of fingerlike projections which form a cross, a design which was also found as a single decoration on Vessel 28 from south of Mound D (Moore 1907:349). On Vessel 7 it appears four times around the perimeter, at the junction of cross-hatched bands. The "fingers" motif is frequently encountered on Moundville ceramics, and the appearance of the swirl-cross in conjunction with it opens another area for testing of the swirl-cross-water hypothesis. Unfortunately, that examination must wait until the "fingers" motif has been subjected to iconographic analysis. It is enough at this point to say that these few additional examples do not disprove the hypothesis that the swirl-cross points to the Beneath World, its waters, and its inhabitants.

The Moundville Copper Pendants and Gorgets

In this hypothesis the Moundville gorgets and pendants are emblems of the Great Serpent's realm or the column which connects the earth with that realm. When we recall the role of the Great Serpent in the founding of medicine societies (such as the Midé among the Central Algonkians and Siouans), a further hypothesis is suggested: the Moundville copper emblems may be marks of membership in a medicine society which derives its powers from the Underwater Powers. Alternatively, they may be lineage indicators, suggesting a totemic relationship to the powers of the Beneath World. It is possible to do a limited test of both hypotheses, for the grave contexts of the copper emblems should be totally adult if the gorgets and pendants are shamanic in nature; if the emblems are found in children's graves, they are more likely to refer to inherited identity or status. As it happens, most of the Moundville swirl-crosses come from graves which were carefully excavated, both by C. B. Moore a century ago and by several archaeologists since. A survey of the known provenience data yields answers to two important questions. What kinds of people owned copper pendants/gorgets? What other objects were associated with the swirl-cross items in the burials?

Table 11.1 lists the copper swirl-cross artifacts—first gorgets then pendants—together with what is known of the burial context (compiled from Brain and Phillips 1996:296–355; Moore 1905; and Steponaitis 1983). Several observations can be made regarding this list. First, a swirl-cross gorget and pendant can both be found in a single grave (M151 and M251, Mound C Burial 31). Second, multiple swirl-cross pendants can be found in a single grave (Mound C Burial 31). Third, while most of the swirl-cross coppers were found with adults, four were found with two children. An infant burial south of Mound D (148) contained a swirl-cross pendant, probably on a thong or cord with a few shell beads, placed around the neck of the child. Burial 31 in Mound C was a child with two swirl-cross pendants and one swirl-cross gorget. While it is possible that the coppers were gifts from adults who were the actual owners, the hypothesis that the swirl-cross emblems were related

TABLE 11.1. Moundville swirl-cross copper gorgets and pendants

#	Identification	Location	Additional Information
	Five copper gorgets		
18	Ga-Brt (Etowah)	No data	
19	Ga-Brt (Etowah)	No data	
4	Ala-Tu-M22	Mound C, Burial 31	2 swirl-cross pendants and pearls [child]
13	Ala-Tu-M72	Mound O, Burial 40	wrist beads, galena, bottle, bowl, pot
11	Ala-Tu-M151	S of Mound D, Burial 162	swirl-cross pendant (= M251)
	Thirteen copper pendants		
3	Ala-Tu-M17	Mound C, Burial 9	"encased in wood"
5	Ala-Tu	Mound C, Burial 32	copper-covered wooden earplug
6	Ala-Tu-M24	Mound C, Burial 37	scalp gorget (M23), annular gorget (M14), copper plume (M25), copper axe (M173), 45 copper-covered wooden beads & pearls at ankle, pearls at neck, amethyst effigy head (M180)
17	Ga-Brt-E25	Mound C, W. K. Moorehead	pearl & shell beads, copper headdress, Burial 96 (stone box), mica, tortoiseshell strips, 2 chert swords
7	Ala-Tu-M148	S of Mound D, Burial 65	(not fenestrated), galena, ear plug, beads
9	Ala-Tu-M149	S of Mound D, Burial 132	pearl
11	Ala-Tu-M251	S of Mound D, Burial 162	swirl-cross gorget (M151), shell beads at shoulder & pelvis, pearl
12	Ala-Tu-M	S of Mound D, Burial 163	shell beads at knees
8	Ala-Tu-M	S of Mound D, Burial 66	pearl, copper disk (ear plug?), shell beads at wrist & forearm & between thighs, Moundville Engraved, var. Hemphill winged serpent bowl (M128) [Moundville III]
10	Ala-Tu-M150	S of Mound D, Burial 148	beads, shell beads at neck
14	Ala-Tu-M	Rhodes, Burial 1927	
15	Ala-Tu-M	Rhodes, Burial 1928	
16	Ala-Tu-M	Rhodes, Burial 1936	

to adult participation in a medicine society seems seriously weakened. Nevertheless, the multiplicity of coppers in Burial 31 suggests that they were bestowed at death, since it seems unlikely that a child would wear more than one. This possibility also provides support for the view that such gifts at death had meaning and power for life beyond the grave.

The child of Burial 31 was not the only person buried with multiple coppers. The adult in Burial 162 south of Mound D had both a swirl-cross pendant and a swirl-cross gorget. The adult in Burial 37 in Mound C bore a treasure on his body: a swirl-cross pendant (M24), "scalp" gorget (M23), annular gorget (M14), copper plume (M25), copper axe (M173), forty-five copper-covered wooden beads and pearls at his ankle, and pearls around his neck accompanying an amethyst effigy head (M180). If his dress in death was the same as his ritual dress in life, he must have made a brilliant figure with all the copper.

A similar well-dressed adult provides the final observation. The man in Burial 66 south of Mound D had shell beads at his wrist and forearm and between his thighs. The latter, and possibly the former, may have been attached to apparel. Burial 66 also wore a swirl-cross pendant with a pearl and another copper disk, possibly an earspool. Beside him was a Moundville Engraved var. Hemphill bowl incised with a winged serpent. In the light of the hypothesis that the swirl-cross is related to the Beneath World, it seems significant that the bowl bears the image of the Great Serpent, the master of the Beneath World (Lankford 2007a). The man in Burial 66 thus has two separate artifacts, copper and ceramic, that are related to the Master of the Beneath World.

Conclusion

This comparative examination of the known examples of the swirl-cross symbol has ranged from Georgia to Texas and looked at swirl-crosses in copper, clay, stone, and shell. The result is an identification of the swirl-cross as a symbol for the Beneath World, water, and the Underwater Serpent. This hypothesis, derived from and dependent on other hypotheses about the cosmological meaning of other Mississippian symbols, has the virtue of explaining the different ways in which the swirl-cross appears in the ancient art. The plausibility of the model must be assessed by the observer, of course, since none of these hypotheses is subject to scientific proof.

On the basis of this set of identifications, further speculations about the patterns of distribution and usage are possible. The geographic distribution of the symbol—particularly if the guilloche itself was understood to embody the swirl-cross—indicates that the Beneath World symbolism was widespread, possibly one of the Mississippian universals. At the same time, it must be noted that there were "hot spots" of swirl-cross usage. In the Central Mississippi Valley effigy pots of the Great Serpent were part of an array of specialized pottery, including items such as head pots. The symbols of the Beneath World were apparently just part of the iconographic corpus and the social structure producing it, important but not dominant. In the Cumberland region the emphasized symbol was a triskele, which has been treated here as a regional style variant of the swirl-cross, with three arms instead of four.

By contrast, the Moundville focus of swirl-cross symbolism in copper emblems, along with other symbols of death (Lankford 2007b), suggests a different function or social organization. It is tempting to think of Moundville or its leaders as having a special relationship with the Beneath World and its Powers. More than that cannot be said at this point. Even so, the unusual nature of the swirl-cross symbolism at Moundville—location on copper, emblematic form, role as personal ornament, dominance in the array of symbols—calls for closer examination of its local significance.

All together, these observations of three areas with different emphases in the iconography of the swirl-cross serve to underscore the importance of regional examination of such symbols. While the total corpus lists examples of swirl-crosses from a wide geographic area, creating the illusion of universality, there appear to be three focal zones with different uses and perhaps different meanings for the symbol. The swirl-cross is thus an excellent illustration of a widely known artistic icon that has lent itself to regional adaptation.

AUTHOR'S NOTE: Few materials for the examination of the appearance of the swirl-cross symbol in the Central Mississippi Valley have been published, apart from the early reports of C. B. Moore. For years, however, information and photographs have been patiently gathered by David Dye and Charles McNutt, University of Memphis anthropology faculty members, and their students. I have benefited greatly by access to that photographic archive, which has been generously shared by Dr. Dye.

An earlier version of this chapter was delivered in 2002 at the Southeastern Archaeological Conference meeting in Biloxi, Mississippi.

APPENDIX 11.1. Known examples of swirl-crosses

		Shell Cups	
1	shell cup	Craig A (Spiro) interlace: raccoon binding, striped pole, s-c	P&B, Pl. 167
2	shell cup	Craig B (Spiro) floating: masks (gorget?) on shell bend line, pendant, s-c	P&B, Pl. 266
		Copper	
3	s-c pendant	Md. C, Bur. 9 "encased in wood"	B&P, Ala-Tu-M17
4	s-c gorget	Md. C, Bur. 31 2 s-c and pearls	B&P, Ala-Tu-M22
5	s-c pendant	Md. C, Bur. 32	B&P, Ala-Tu
6	s-c pendant	Md. C, Bur. 37 "Big Man": + scalp gorget, annular gorget, plume, axe	B&P, Ala-Tu-M24
7	s-c pendant	S of Md. D, Bur. 65, not fenestrated + galena, ear plug, beads	B&P, Ala-Tu-M148
8	s-c pendant	S of Md. D, Bur. 66 + pearl	B&P, Ala-Tu-M
9	s-c pendant	S of Md. D, Bur. 132 not fenestrated + galena, ear plug, beads	B&P, Ala-Tu-M149
10	s-c pendant	S of Md. D, Bur. 148, infant: + beads	B&P, Ala-Tu-M150
11	s-c pendant	S of Md. D, Bur. 162 + scalp gorget (= M151)	B&P, Ala-Tu-M251
12a	s-c pendant	S of Md. D, Bur. 163 + shell beads at knees	B&P, Ala-Tu-M
12b	s-c pendant	S of Md. D, Bur. 164, fenestrated scalp gorget, repoussé ogee, hand & eye	B&P, Ala-Tu-M147
13	s-c gorget	Md. O, Bur. 40 + beads, galena	B&P, Ala-Tu-M72
14	s-c pendant	Rhodes, Bur. 1927	B&P, Ala-Tu-M
15	s-c pendant	Rhodes, Bur. 1928	B&P, Ala-Tu-M
16	s-c pendant	Rhodes, Bur. 1936	B&P, Ala-Tu-M
17	pendant (4 s-c)	Md. C, WKM Bur. 76 stone-box grave + pearl & shell beads, head-dress of copper, mica, tortoiseshell strips, 2 chert swords	B&P, Ga-Brt-E25
18	s-c gorget		B&P, Ga-Brt
19	s-c gorget		B&P, Ga-Brt
		Shell Gorgets	
20	gorget	Cox Mound w/ s-c at center	B&P, Tenn-X
21	gorget	Craig (Spiro) 4 birds (crest, tassel, beads) around s-c w/ center hole	B&P, Okla-Lf-S352

APPENDIX 11.1. Known examples of swirl-crosses, *continued*

22	gorget	McAdams style spider in rings, lightning palpi, s-c on body	B&P, Ill-Sr-X2
23	gorget	McAdams style, Madison Co., IL spider in rings, s-c on body [see Tenn-Je-F12]	B&P, Ill-Ms-X1
24	gorget	Craig B (Spiro), in style of McAdams Hull: concentric hands, spider, s-c on spider, scalloped border (= P&B, Pl. 276)	B&P, Okla-Lf-S679
25	gorgets	Craig B (Spiro)	P&B, Pl. 277A (= B&P, Okla-Lf 389)
26	gorget frag.	Hull: concentric hand and eye (2 circles)	P&B, Pl. 277B
27	gorget frag.	beads, s-c at center, knobbed petaloid	P&B, Pl. 277C
28	gorget	Craig (Spiro) Hull: hand and eye, beads, knobbed petaloid border	B&P, Okla-Lf-S390
29	gorget	Sanders site, geometric, s-c	B&P, Tex-La-S18
30	gorget	Nashville II, s-c, dotted band, petaloid oval border	B&P, Tenn-Ch-X1
31	gorget	s-c, lines on petaloid border	B&P, Tenn-Hu-X
32	gorget		B&P, Tenn-Da-CF4
33	gorget	s-c lines on Nashville-like gorget: dotted band, petaloid border	B&P, Tenn-Me-X2
34	gorget	Foster Place, Red River concentric: dotted petaloid surround, s-c (Nashville var.?)	B&P, Ark-La-FP1
35	gorget	Kirkham site, Clark Co., AR	B&P, Ark-Cl-K1
36	gorget	Williams site, Christian Co., KY	B&P, KY-Ch-W1
37	gorget	Kellogg Site, Clay Co., MS concentric: 4 cymas, petaloid surround, s-c	B&P, Miss-CY-K2
38	gorget	Craig A (Spiro) paired figures, raccoon, striped pole, s-c	B&P, Okla-Lf-S242
39	gorget	Craig B (Spiro), human w/ s-c earspool (eye surround, border, earspool = Craig B)	B&P, Okla-Lf-S16
Ceramics			
40	bottle	Moundville, south of Mound D (Fig. 5) s-c in fingers and bands	B&P, Ala-Tu-M7?
41	bottle	S of Md. D (Fig. 6) single large s-c in finger cross	B&P, Ala-Tu-M28
42	bottle	S of Md. D (no burial) (Fig. 89/90) 4 CB tails w/ s-c	B&P, Ala-Tu-M4

APPENDIX 11.1. Known examples of swirl-crosses, *continued*

43	bottle	no context (Fig. 9/10) CB heads and tails: s-c on tails & crest	B&P, Ala-Tu-M6
44	jar	Ark-Armorel (3MS23), guilloche w/ floating s-c (Childs 1993)	
45	bowl	Ark-Belle Meade (3CT30), HWS effigy: s-c in circle on head	
46	bottle	Ark-Belle Meade (3CT30) : s-c in center of barbell cross	
47	bowl	Ark-Belle Meade (3CT30) , HWS effigy: s-c in circle on head	
48	bowl	Ark-Beck (3CT8): s-c bas-relief on base	
49	bowl	Ark-Beck (3CT8): guilloche and 8 floating s-cs	
50	jar	Ark-Beck (3CT8): 4 guilloche corners surrounding s-c	
51	bottle	Ark-Friends (3MS6): s-c in guilloche corners; terrace on rim	
52	bottle	Ark-Friends (3MS6): s-cs around rayed disk (neck missing)	
53	bottle	Ark-Hazel (3PO6): Carson Red on Buff: rayed circle w/ s-c	
54	bottle	Ark-Hazel (3PO6): Carson Red on Buff: rayed circle w/ s-c	
55	bowl	Ark-Parkin (3CS29): Red on Black: s-c in center of four terraces	
56	bottle	Ark-Rose Mound (3MS15): s-c in guilloche corners; rim terrace	
57	bowl	Ark-Rose Mound (3MS15): s-c in bowl, terraces (Moore 1910:336)	
58	bottle	Ark-Upper Nodena (3MS4): s-c bas-relief on base	
59	bottle	MS-Lake Cormorant (22DS501): hand and s-c	
60		MS-Walls area (22DS?): guilloche and 2 s-c	
61	bowl	MS-Walls (22DS1): serpent effigy, s-c on head	
62		MO-Kersey (Pemiscot Co.): looped snakes, s-c in center	

NOTE: s-c: swirl-cross; P&B: Phillips and Brown; Md.: Mound; Bur.: Burial; B&P: Brain and Phillips; WKM: W. K. Moorehead; HWS: Horned Water Serpent; CB: Crested Bird.

REGIONAL STUDIES: ETOWAH AND UPPER TENNESSEE VALLEY

CHAPTER 12

Iconography of the Hightower Region of Eastern Tennessee and Northern Georgia

Adam King

The overarching goal of this volume is to begin to understand the regional variation in Mississippian iconography. In this chapter I hope to contribute to that effort by discussing the unique elements of iconographic expression found in eastern Tennessee and northwestern Georgia and then placing the history of representational art creation in the region within a broader social and political context.

The decision to treat eastern Tennessee and northwestern Georgia as a single unit for analysis is not an arbitrary one. Years of archaeological research have shown that sites between the Etowah River Valley in Georgia and the Tennessee River in eastern Tennessee share a great many elements of material culture ranging from architectural styles to burial practices (Hally and Langford 1988; Hally and Rudolph 1986; King 2003). Most importantly for this chapter, particular artistic styles and iconographic themes are unique to the representational art of this region (Muller 1989).

Although archaeologists have recognized the existence of this region for a long time, there is no name that is universally used to refer to it. Here I propose the term "Hightower" to designate this region. This is the name that Muller (1989) chose to designate a particularly well-defined artistic style recognized as having its home in eastern Tennessee and northern Georgia. "Hightower" is likely an anglicized version of a Cherokee word used to designate an important trail that ran through northwestern Georgia and also a name applied to the Etowah site.

Representational Art of the Hightower Region

Representational art is found almost exclusively in two media in the Hightower region: engraved shell and embossed copper. In this section I will discuss the themes represented in the region's art and, where defined, the decorative styles that have been recognized. Within each medium, style and theme will be discussed chronologically.

ENGRAVED SHELL

Engraving shell, particularly for gorgets made of marine shell, has a long tradition in the Hightower region. It appears to begin in the Early Mississippian period and continues into the early Protohistoric period. Unfortunately, outside of Muller's (1966a) pioneering work and more recent analyses by Johann Sawyer (2009), the kinds of detailed structural analyses needed for a concrete definition of the decorative styles in the Hightower region have not been completed. As a result, not all shell gorget themes can be assigned to defined styles.

Centering Themes. The earliest engraved shell in the Hightower region appears in the form of gorgets exhibiting various versions of the cross-in-circle theme (Fig. 12.1). This theme is fairly widespread across the Mississippian area and appears prominently in the Hightower region during the Early and Middle Mississippian periods. Lankford (2004) has suggested that the cross-in-circle motif may represent the earth or This World in the Eastern cosmology, with the cross defining the center as well as an axis mundi connecting This World to the Above and Beneath Worlds. Howard (1968) has also linked this motif to the sacred fire of the Green Corn ceremony.

In the Hightower region the cross-in-circle is sometimes expressed as a simple engraved or excised cross enclosed within one or two concentric circles, while in still other cases the cross-in-circle is represented as an excised filfot cross enclosed within one or more concentric circles. Although gorgets with each of the variants are found in eastern Tennessee (see Brain and Phillips 1996:30, 33), to date no formally defined local styles have been recognized. Therefore it is unclear if a local gorget engraving tradition existed at this time.

The Bennett Style. In the Hightower region, the cross-in-circle appears most commonly enclosed by a square, referred to as the crib (Brain and Phillips 1996:21–24) or the square cross design (Kneberg 1959:5). Sawyer (2009) has recognized the earliest version of this theme in his Bennett style, which dates from AD 1150 to 1250 and has its presumed center of production at the Hixon site (Fig. 12.1a).

The Hightower Style. By AD 1200 there is another recognizable shell engraving tradition in the Hightower region producing shell gorgets decorated in

FIGURE 12.1. Cross-in-circle gorgets: (a) Bennett style, drawing by Johann Sawyer; (b) Moorehead style, drawing by Johann Sawyer.

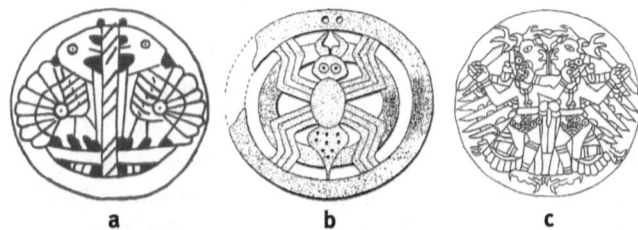

FIGURE 12.2. Hightower-style gorgets: (a) Turkey Cock theme, drawing by George Lankford; (b) spider theme (Moorehead 2000:Fig. 32); (c) anthropomorphic theme, drawing by Jack Johnson.

what Muller (1989) has defined as the Hightower style (Fig. 12.2). At this point, Hightower-style gorgets exhibit two recognizable themes. The most common theme is known as the Turkey Cock and depicts two birds with tails fanned standing on a flat surface (Figure 12.2a). The birds are positioned facing one another with a striped pole between them. Lankford (2004) has constructed a convincing case that this theme actually shows the three worlds of Eastern cosmology viewed from the side. The birds represent the Above World, the flat surface This World, and the open space below the Beneath World. The striped pole is the axis mundi that extends from the sun in the Above World through This World into the Beneath World.

The second theme, which is much less common, depicts a spider (Figure 12.2b). Although this theme has not received the attention given to the Turkey Cock, it may be related to This World symbolism. It shares many design elements with the much more abundant spider theme of the Eddyville style (Muller 1989) of the Central Mississippi Valley. The Eddyville spiders always have the circle-in-cross motif on the dorsal surface of their thorax,

FIGURE 12.3. Facial markings on the Hightower anthropomorphic gorgets: (a) Mask in Dances with Mothra; (b) Fork Mouth in Dances with Mothra, drawing by Jack Johnson.

connecting it to This World as well as the renewal implied by the new fire symbolism. The Hightower spider does not have the circle-in-cross motif on its back. Instead the cut-out spider is superimposed over a circle, itself creating the circle-in-cross motif. Therefore the Hightower spider probably refers to the same This World and potentially renewal themes alluded to by the Eddyville spiders.

Based on stratigraphic evidence and a radiocarbon date from the Hixon site (Sullivan 2001), a third theme in the Hightower style appears slightly later, possibly after AD 1250 (Fig. 12.2c). This is the anthropomorphic theme, which includes several different variants. All of the anthropomorphic variants depict some version of the Birdman theme and might even refer to different points in a narrative (see Chapter 13). It is likely that the Birdman depicted here is thematically connected to the same supernatural shown on the Classic Braden–style copper plates found in Etowah's Mound C (discussed below).

While clearly referring to the Birdman theme, these gorgets also show paired figures and two distinct individuals, who are distinguished based on differences in treatment of the face. One individual has a distinctive forked treatment surrounding the mouth (Fork Mouth) (Fig. 12.3a), while the other has what appears to be a mask covering the eyes but exposing the jaw and mouth (Mask) (Fig. 12.3b). These treatments are not present on the figures shown in the Dancing Warriors theme, but they are found in all of the other themes. In fact, with the exception of the Dances with Snake theme (only one example), all the other themes show both figures in the same poses.

Paired individuals or Hero Twins figure prominently in epic narratives throughout the ethnographic literature of the eastern United States. In many of the Twins narratives, they go through a series of adventures or trials before

12.4. Hixon-style gorget (Muller 2007:Fig. 2.14).

ascending to the Above World. Reilly and Garber argue that the Hightower anthropomorphic gorgets represent moments in just such a narrative (see Chapter 13). Significantly, both Fork Mouth and Mask appear doing the same kinds of things in the Hightower narrative. Following Lankford's (2008b) arguments discussed below, all of this leads me to suggest that the paired figures on the Hightower anthropomorphic gorgets are an early version of the same mythic figures recorded historically as Lodge-Boy and Thrown-Away.

The Hixon Style. By the middle of the thirteenth century, around the same time that the anthropomorphic theme of the Hightower style appears, a new decorative style also appears in the region. This is the Hixon style as defined by Muller (1989). Gorgets of the Hixon style currently are known to depict only the Turkey Cock theme (Fig. 12.4). The theme is clearly carried over from the Hightower style, likely with the same meaning, but is executed in what Muller (1989) calls the more conventionalized Hixon style.

The Moorehead Style. At this same time, AD 1250 to 1350, the Moorehead style replaces Bennett as the carrier of the cross-in-circle motif in the Hightower region (Sawyer 2009:141) (Fig. 12.1b).

The Lick Creek Style. Sometime near the end of the fourteenth century, two new styles with new themes appear to supplant the Hightower and Hixon styles with their Turkey Cocks and anthropomorphic figures. One of these is the Lick Creek style (Muller 1989), which depicts a wide-eyed, open-mouthed rattlesnake (Fig. 12.5a). It is no doubt important that the excised portions of the gorget create a cross-in-circle, with the snake forming the cross. In Eastern cosmology (Hudson 1976:165; Lankford 1987:83), snakes are associated with the Beneath World, so this theme combines Beneath World symbolism with a reference at least to the centered axis mundi that connects the three worlds.

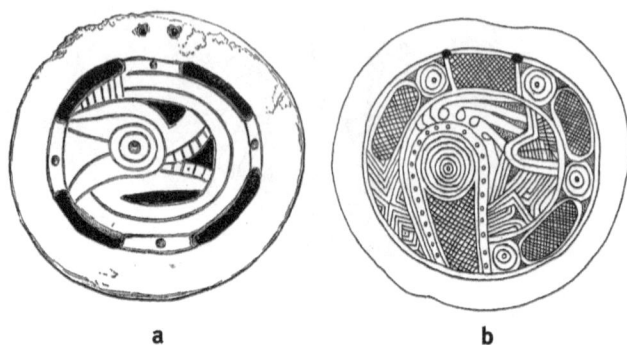

FIGURE 12.5. Rattlesnake gorgets: (a) Lick Creek style (Hally 2007:Fig. 10.1); (b) Citico style (Hally 2007:Fig. 10.1).

FIGURE 12.6. Williams Island–style gorget, drawing by George Lankford.

The Williams Island Style. The second new style is called Williams Island by Muller (1989). Sometimes referred to as spaghetti gorgets, these depict an anthropomorphic theme with two general variations (Fig. 12.6). One variation has only one figure, while others have two figures side by side. Usually the figures appear to be in motion among a maze of swirls. Lankford (2008b) has argued that this theme is related to Lodge-Boy and Thrown-Away, the historically known Twins. In recorded versions of Creek mythology, the Twins have a series of adventures and eventually leave This World to reside in the Above World, where they are associated with natural forces like wind, thunder, and lightning. A detailed examination of the imagery reveals that the figures have swirls rather than feet, which Lankford argues represent wind, and lightning bolts appear to pass behind their heads.

The Citico Style. Somewhat later, probably in the sixteenth century, the Citico style (Muller 1989) develops out of and supplants the Lick Creek style

ICONOGRAPHY OF THE HIGHTOWER REGION

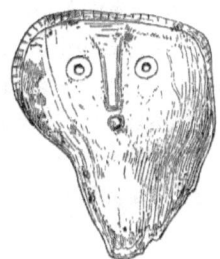

FIGURE 12.7. Shell face mask gorget (Hally 2007:Fig. 10.1).

(Fig. 12.5b). The only theme continues to be the coiled rattlesnake, which becomes more conventionalized and more complex. The excised areas are eliminated from the gorget structure, thereby obscuring the reference to the cross-in-circle motif.

Face Mask. Possibly at about this same time engraved shell face masks also appear (Fig. 12.7). Most of these masks are too small to have been worn as masks, and they often are found in burial contexts on the deceased's chest rather than on the face. These probably were gorgets simply made into the form of a face, sometimes with a forked eye surround or what appears to be lightning emanating from the eyes. Marvin Smith and Julie Smith (1989) have argued that these are likely the faces of Above World supernaturals or the Thunderers—another version of the Twins depicted in the Hightower and Williams Island gorgets. These mask gorgets are fairly widespread throughout the Deep South but are most common and clearly cluster in eastern Tennessee (see Brain and Phillips 1996:76, 79, 81), suggesting that at least some were made in the Hightower region.

EMBOSSED COPPER

The history of representational art created in copper is much shorter in the Hightower region and also less clearly understood. Current information suggests that copper artifacts did not appear in the region until after AD 1250 and largely disappeared by AD 1400. In fact the use of copper artifacts appears to be limited entirely to the Middle Mississippian period and corresponds very closely to Etowah's rise to power.

The Classic Braden Style. The earliest copper artifacts found in the region were recovered from the earlier stages of Etowah's Mound C. Most prominent among those artifacts are the embossed copper plates excavated by John P.

Rogan in 1884 (Fig. 12.8a). These depict the Birdman theme and are executed in the Classic Braden style, whose place of origin is the American Bottom (Brown and Kelly 2000). Brown (2007b) has made the case that the Birdman is connected thematically to a supernatural recorded among Siouan speakers of the upper Midwest known as Morning Star, He-Who-Wears-Human-Heads-on-His-Ears, or Red Horn. Clearly the Classic Braden plates carried a foreign style and mythology to the East and the Etowah site. In addition to the Birdman, other motifs executed in the Classic Braden style found at Etowah include the bilobed arrow and various elements of falcon imagery. An

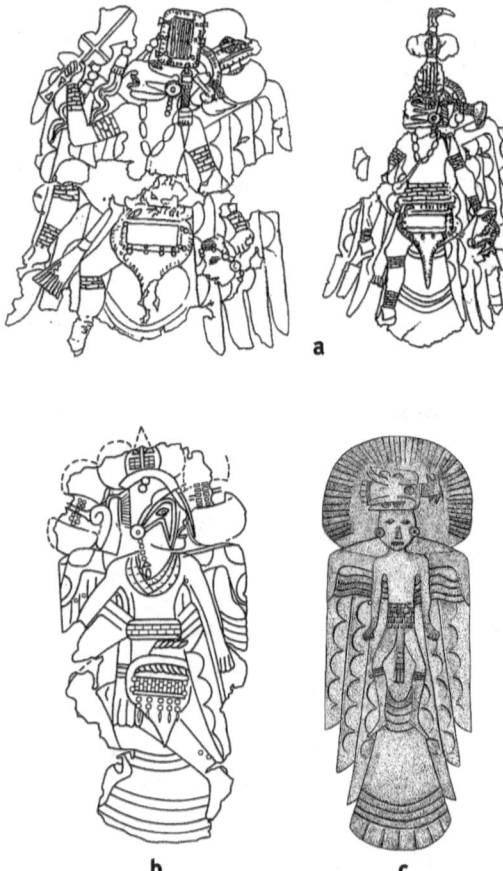

FIGURE 12.8. Birdman copper plates from Mound C at Etowah: (a) Classic Braden Rogan Plates (Moorehead 2000:Figs. 14, 15); (b) Late Braden Birdman plate (Brown 2007b:Fig. 4.2b); (c) "stack" plate, drawing by George Stuart.

FIGURE 12.9. Hemphill-style copper gorget from Mound C at Etowah, photograph by David H. Dye.

argument can be made that both of these themes are elements of the broader Birdman theme.

The Late Braden Style. In addition to Classic Braden, other decorative styles are represented in copper artifacts from Mound C. Some of these pieces may fit in the Late Braden style (Brown 2007c). This is particularly the case with the Birdman themed copper plate (Fig. 12.8b) excavated from Etowah's Mound C by Warren Moorehead (Brown 2007b).

The Hemphill Style. Other pieces conform to the stylistic rules of the Hemphill style (see Chapter 9), centered on Moundville. This applies to the two copper gorgets exhibiting the swirling cross (Fig. 12.9), the single copper gorget with the cross-in-circle, and the copper pendant with the scalp motif, all found in Etowah's Mound C. Consistent with their presumed Moundville origin, most of these pieces reference the Beneath World.

A Potential Local Copper Style. Despite the presence of nonlocally produced copper artifacts in the region, particularly in Etowah's Mound C, evidence suggests that a local copper-working tradition developed in the Hightower region, and probably at Etowah, by the fourteenth century. In his exploration of copper-working throughout the East, Jonathan Leader (1988) found what appear to be some of the tools and implements needed to create copper cutouts and embossed plates. In Mound C burials he discovered what appear to be tortoiseshell templates for making cutouts, embossing tools, and cut scraps of sheet cooper.

The imagery of a series of copper plates and other objects from the Hightower region (mainly Etowah) does not comfortably fit in any of the known extraregional styles (Fig. 12.8c). These represent a corpus potentially created in a local copper-working style.

Included in this corpus are the same kinds of themes often associated with Classic and Late Braden imagery found elsewhere, such as the Raptor, the Birdman, the ogee, and the Piasa (see Brain and Phillips 1996:132–175). Interestingly, these copper objects make reference to beings of the Above and Beneath Worlds as well as a means of traveling from one to the other. As noted above, the Raptor and the Birdman refer to inhabitants of the Above World and possibly even a particular resident of that world. The Piasa, on the other hand, with its mixture of feline, human, snake, and bird characteristics, is likely a representation of the Underwater Panther who lives in the Beneath World. The ogee, as Reilly (2004) has argued, is a portal through which it was possible to pass between these worlds.

Political Geography and the History of Imagery

Some interesting patterns emerge when the appearance of these styles and the themes associated with them are viewed against the backdrop of the political history of eastern Tennessee and northern Georgia. These patterns provide an important context for understanding regional variation in Mississippian imagery.

EARLY MISSISSIPPIAN (AD 1000–1250)

What we think are chiefdom capitals begin to appear fairly early in the Hightower region in the Early Mississippian period. Mound centers like Etowah and Sixtoe Field in northern Georgia were established around AD 1000, while Davis in eastern Tennessee was occupied by AD 1100. Interestingly, very few burials have been found at habitation sites, with or without platform mounds, throughout the region in these early contexts. Gerald Schroedl et al. (1990) have argued, I think persuasively, that at least in eastern Tennessee most people were buried in communal burial mounds located away from habitation sites, representing a continuation of the Late Woodland Hamilton burial practices. People buried in these mounds usually are interred with few if any grave goods. Consequently imagery executed in shell, copper, or any other medium has not been found in these early contexts.

Sometime late in the twelfth century, gorgets with the crib and other cross-in-circle and centering motifs begin to appear. According to Sawyer's (2009) work, at least some of these gorgets were made in the Hightower region, likely in eastern Tennessee. Evidence from complicated stamped pottery motifs in the region makes it clear that centering motifs like the crib have a deep history in the area. Centering motifs like the cross-bar diamond and the filfot cross appear in the area as early as AD 1100 and have predecessors that go back as early as AD 900 (Hally and Langford 1988).

By AD 1200 both the political landscape and imagery of the region had changed. In Georgia the Etowah site and all other mound centers in the Etowah River Valley became abandoned and occupation on the Coosawattee River shifted a few kilometers from Sixtoe Field to Bell Field. In eastern Tennessee Davis was abandoned and occupation began at Hixon and in the Chickamauga Basin and likely also at Hiwassee Island and Citico. Also at this time Muller's Hightower style, with its Turkey Cock and spider themes, is recognizable as a distinct decorative style at home in eastern Tennessee.

The symbolism found on these Early Mississippian gorgets refers to themes that I will call universalizing. As discussed above, the centering motifs, the Turkey Cock, and possibly even the spider theme all make reference to the same general conception of the structure of the cosmos. This kind of symbolism and the ideas behind it, such as fertility and a proper and orderly world, are not exclusive but instead refer to themes in which all people in Mississippian society likely had a stake.

MIDDLE MISSISSIPPIAN (AD 1250-1400)

By the beginning of the fourteenth century yet another political change had dramatically transformed the political and crafting landscape. Sometime after AD 1250 Etowah was reoccupied and experienced a quick rise to regional dominance. A surge in the construction of monuments occurred at the site, as existing Mounds A and B were expanded and construction began on a new and particularly special mound, Mound C. In the immediate vicinity of the site as many as five secondary capitals appeared, indicating that populations were drawn to the emerging center. The initiation of construction of Mound C is particularly significant, because it clearly functioned as a specialized mortuary facility. Included in those Mound C burials were shell gorgets, copper plates, and many other elaborate objects.

One of the interesting aspects of Etowah's reoccupation and ascent to regional political prominence is that it effectively involved the creation of a new chiefdom with its own justification for a ranked social order. It appears that the charter for that new ranking system appealed to beliefs, imagery, and artwork that were foreign to the Hightower region. As noted above, in the earliest stages of Etowah's Mound C copper plates and cutouts were found executed in the Classic Braden style. As Brown (2004; Brown and Kelly

2000) has argued, that Classic Braden style had its roots in the American Bottom and the cultural milieu that saw the dramatic emergence of Cahokia as the primatial Early Mississippian center. Therefore the charter on which Etowah's new chiefdom was based not only was rooted in foreign ideas but also alluded to what may have been thought of as a mythical place of great power in the Mississippian world.

The introduction of this new style, with its new decorative themes (mainly the Birdman and associated symbols like the bilobed arrow and Raptor imagery), correlates nicely with the creation of a new theme in the Hightower gorget style: the anthropomorphic theme depicting a variant of the Birdman. In the gorget sequence of the Hixon mound, those Hightower-style anthropomorphic gorgets appear later than the Turkey Cock and spider themes, sometime after AD 1250 (Sullivan 2001). This happens to be around the same time that Etowah was reoccupied and the earliest of the Braden plates were buried in Mound C. Given the apparent importance of the Birdman in chartering the new social order of Etowah, it should not be surprising that the theme found its way into the local gorget-crafting tradition of the Hightower region. The Hightower anthropomorphic gorgets represent a melding of a foreign theme—the Birdman—with a local artistic style. Since the Birdman does not appear as Twins in the Classic Braden style, it seems reasonable to suggest that the Birdman was grafted onto an existing Twins narrative and thereby made more relevant to local populations of the Hightower region.

Undoubtedly, the appearance of the Classic Braden imagery on the Rogan Plates had something to do with the transfer of the Birdman to shell engraving. However, the Hightower anthropomorphic gorgets show some clear stylistic, thematic, and structural affinities with the Classic Braden Eddyville gorgets of the confluence region. These affinities are indicative of a level of sustained interaction between the two areas that must also have played an important role in the melding of the Birdman theme with the Twins theme.

Muller (1989) has argued, and I think most accept, that eastern Tennessee is the locus of production of the Hightower style. Although it has not been investigated, eastern Tennessee gorget crafters were most likely trained and worked at Citico, Hixon, or both. There are reasons to believe that the anthropomorphic theme of the Hightower style may actually have been made at Etowah. First, more anthropomorphic Hightower gorgets were found at Etowah than at all other sites combined. A more compelling reason is because the Birdman theme is later in the Hightower sequence than the spider and

Turkey Cock and makes its appearance shortly after the Birdman shows up at Etowah in Classic Braden imagery. It is clear that the Birdman plays a critical role in the reestablishment of Etowah as a chiefdom capital by chartering the newly established ranking system.

At about the same time that the anthropomorphic theme appeared in the Hightower style, a new style appeared in the region. This is Muller's Hixon style, which carried the same Turkey Cock theme from the Hightower style but in a simpler, more conventionalized form. The appearance of this conventionalized form of the Hightower style may represent an attempt by people in eastern Tennessee to maintain a gorget-crafting tradition that was distinct from the one associated with the new dominant center in the region—Etowah.

After the Classic Braden imagery inspired a new theme in the Hightower style, it also may have initiated a new local copper-working tradition. As noted above, there is no evidence of copper working in the Hightower region before AD 1250. After the introduction of Braden imagery, however, other decorated copper plates appear that may be part of an Etowah copper-working tradition. Leader (1988) has found evidence that some people buried in Etowah's Mound C had the tools, raw materials, and templates to make copper symbol badges cut into the form of maces, arrows, and avian features such as talons and plumes. The plates may have been another aspect of that local copper working. The dominant themes in both the plates and the symbol badges reference the Birdman and the Raptor, both of which are also key themes in the Braden imagery.

With the dramatic rise of Etowah and the introduction of Braden artwork and Braden-inspired themes, the symbolism found on shell and copper artwork in the Hightower region shifted from universalizing to more individualizing in nature. Rather than referring to universal themes, the Birdman on the Rogan Plates seems to allude to a specific figure and is particularly suited to serving as a charter for the status of individuals or at least an individual corporate group. I think the same argument can be made for the Hightower anthropomorphic gorgets, although in a slightly different way. Those gorgets depict the Twins in what appear to be very specific moments of a longer narrative. That narrative seems to parallel the historically recorded Twins narratives, where they go through a series of trials to prove themselves before taking their place in the Above World (Lankford 2008b). In essence, the gorgets serve as reminders of why those Twins are supernaturals and what they have done for humanity. They emphasize becoming a supernatural and therefore provide the same opportunity as the Rogan Plates do to charter the status of individuals or social groups.

The introduction of Braden imagery and associated beliefs brought new themes and artwork into the Hightower region. It also served as a catalyst for change in the nature of the messages being communicated by the artwork and the purpose to which it was likely put. The Birdman and related images depicted on copper, along with images of the Twins coming of age as supernaturals shown on gorgets, were suited to chartering the elevated-status positions of individuals or corporate groups.

LATE MISSISSIPPIAN (AD 1400–1600)

The Etowah site was again abandoned sometime before AD 1400, and its associated polities fell apart. With the fall of Etowah, the Little Egypt site on the Coosawattee River emerged as a key center in northwestern Georgia. Hixon was abandoned in favor of Dallas in eastern Tennessee, and it seems that Citico remained an important place. Overall, across the Hightower region this was a period of political decentralization, as the large Middle Mississippian centers were abandoned in favor of a larger number of smaller centers scattered more widely across the landscape.

With this decentralization came some notable changes in imagery. By the end of the fifteenth century the Hightower and Hixon gorget styles were replaced by the Williams Island and Lick Creek styles, while copper working as an art all but disappeared. These new styles introduced new themes into the region. The Lick Creek and later Citico styles introduced a new universalizing theme, the rattlesnake, with its allusion to water, fertility, and the powers of the Beneath World. The Williams Island gorgets exhibited a version of the Twins that differs in some important ways from the Twins depicted on the Hightower gorgets. The Hightower Twins are shown proving themselves as supernaturals. The Williams Island Twins are already supernaturals and seem to represent the Above World powers they control rather than proving they belong there. This particular take on the Twins emphasizes their role in the order of the universe—something a broader segment of society has a stake in understanding and maintaining. Interestingly, with the demise of the more individualizing Middle Mississippian polities the local crafting traditions returned to the universalizing themes.

Etowah (reoccupied late in the fifteenth century) was a shadow of its former greatness by the early sixteenth century. The Hightower region was dominated by another polity, centered on the Coosawattee River at the Little Egypt site (Hally et al. 1990) and was described by Hernando de Soto and later Spanish explorers as the paramount chiefdom of Coosa (Hudson et al. 1985). Despite the Spaniards' depiction of a centralized chiefdom (see Muller 1997b for a critique), the artwork left to archaeologists exhibits universalizing themes. As in the previous century the rattlesnake remained an important figure dominating the Citico-style gorgets. In addition, still another version of the Twins appeared in the form of the face mask gorgets. Here the depictions of the Twins become even more conventionalized, and their nature as individuals is subordinated to their role as Above World powers.

Conclusion

Three important observations can be drawn from a look at the nature and history of representational art in the Hightower region. The first of these is that shell engraving emphasizing universal themes appears to be the norm or staple of the Hightower region's representational art. The shell engraving has the longest history in the region and persists even after Braden-inspired imagery and copper working fall away.

The second observation is that copper working and individualizing themes were brought to the Hightower region and in a sense superimposed over the existing local artistic tradition. Ultimately, the change in the nature of the themes represented extended into the local shell-working industry with the emergence of the anthropomorphic theme of the Hightower style. With the fall of Etowah and creation of a more decentralized landscape, however, the shell-working tradition reverted to the more common universal themes.

The third observation is that changes in the media used and themes emphasized in representational art were brought about by political changes affecting the entire region. The Braden imagery and copper-working industry appear with the reoccupation of Etowah after AD 1250. The individualizing theme emphasized in the Braden artwork paralleled the clearly more individual-focused approach to the Middle Mississippian chiefdom centered on Etowah. With the collapse of that polity, and others similarly organized, the media used and themes represented reverted to those more "traditionally" found in the Hightower region.

CHAPTER 13

Dancing in the Otherworld
The Human Figural Art of the Hightower Style Revisited

F. Kent Reilly III and James F. Garber

Introduction

Hightower-style gorgets are beautifully executed human figural or anthropomorphic carvings on marine shell. The first reported Hightower anthropomorphic gorget was recovered from the Toqua Mound in Tennessee (Wilson 1896). Forming a corpus of approximately twenty-eight known examples, the majority of the Hightower-style human figural objects originate in the Upper Tennessee and Coosa River Valleys, with the largest concentration found at Etowah.

Since their early publication in the last quarter of the nineteenth century, Hightower-style objects have continued to be a focus of research for archaeologists and art historians alike (Brain and Phillips 1996; King 2003, 2004; Kneberg 1959; Marceaux and Dye 2007; Muller 1966a,b, 1989; Phillips and Brown 1978; Sullivan 2001, 2007; Chapter 12). Except for two examples, the occurrences of the Hightower style are limited to a relatively restricted geographical range of the Upper Tennessee and Coosa River Valleys (see Map 1 in the Introduction). Because of this limited distribution, Hightower gorgets are an excellent example of related objects that support the argument for the existence of regionalism within the overall temporal boundaries of Mississippian art.

Methodology

"Style" by its very definition is most easily understood as the formal qualities of a work of art that link it to other works of art. Additionally, style in its various definitions is understood to have a point of origin. It has been shown repeatedly that the best way to identify a style and its origins as well as themes and their meaning is through the methodology of structural analysis.

Structural analysis is best defined as understanding a composition or work of art by separating the object under study into its component parts.

Structural analysis is one step in a process of iconographic interpretation that was pioneered by the art historian Erwin Panofsky (1939:3–32). Currently "Panofsky's Method" is usually shortened into a series of organizational steps: (1) assembling a corpus of imagery; (2) grouping these images within "like" subgroups that reveal patterning; (3) dissecting all or specific examples of the imagery corpus; and (4) offering interpretation when possible. It should be noted that the basis of all symbolic interpretation is patterning. Patterning is the recognition of relationships among subgroups in terms of their compositional divisions such as elements, symbols, motifs, and themes.

Using this methodology as a primary foundational focus, the purpose of this chapter is to introduce a previously unrecognized theme or motif set of the human figural Hightower-style gorgets (Brain and Phillips 1996:44). We will propose a relationship of this new theme set to the rest of the corpus and suggest a possible structure of interpretation based on a "storyboard" layout. Art and symbolism are often used as visualizations of ideology in those non-technologically complex societies that lack written forms of expression (Earle 1997; Helms 1979, 1993; Reilly 2004).

The Hightower Style: Identification and Temporal Placement

Few styles have gone through as many name changes as the Hightower style. As previously mentioned, the "type object" for the Hightower style was unearthed at what was then called the Big Toco site, now referred to in the literature as the Toqua site located near Chattanooga, Tennessee (Brain and Phillips 1996:44). Jon Muller analyzed this Toqua gorget and other gorgets of the human figural corpus. He chose the name "Mound C Tentative Style" because the largest number of these gorgets had been recovered from Mound C at Etowah (Brain and Phillips 1996:44). Subsequently he would change the style designation to "Hightower" (Muller 1989:20, 67–70). His expanded definition, however, included "turkey cock" and "spider" theme gorgets under his Hightower designation.

Jeffrey P. Brain and Philip Phillips dropped the "Hightower" designation in favor of the original "Big Toco" designation and placed this style, with others, within a late archaeologically discernible period of AD 1400–1650 (Brain and Phillips 1996:395-397). Despite the expanded corpus of the Hightower style proposed by Muller, this chapter deals exclusively with the human figural examples. Human figural gorgets are usually found in elite mortuary context.

In fact, King has shown that their placement in Mound C at Etowah is closely associated with the highest level of elite burials (King 2007a:107-133). Mortuary studies reveal that carved shell gorgets exhibiting cosmological or creation themes are more numerous and available or perhaps accessible to the nonelite population in the same geographical area. For example, Lankford (2004:206–217, 2007d) has presented a cosmological interpretation for the more numerous turkey cock/crested bird theme and notes that it is found in the same geographical area as the human figural Hightower-style gorgets. A similar argument could be made for the spider theme displayed on gorgets. Spiders figure prominently in many Native American creation stories.

Big Toco/Hightower Style Dates

A few words should be said about the temporal association for the origin of the human figural gorgets and the designation used in this chapter. Madeline Kneberg (1959) published a chronology for the totality of the Hightower human figural gorget corpus that derived from the Chickamauga Basin of eastern Tennessee (AD 1000–1750). Certainly the eighteenth-century date proposed by Kneberg as the termination of the Hightower style is much too late for what we currently know about both this art style and the system within which it existed. In a reevaluation of Kneberg's data made possible by new radiocarbon dates from the Hixon Mound, however, Lynne Sullivan (2001, 2007) has convincingly argued for a new temporal bracketing of these representations (AD 1250–1350). Because the designation "Big Toco style" is closely associated in the literature with a much later temporal period, it seems best to revert to Muller's (1989:20) label "Hightower style."

The Hightower Style: The Stylistic Attributes or Formal Qualities of the Human Figural Representations

A close investigation of the Hightower-style figural representations reveals figures that are finely and closely executed in a naturalistic composition that identifies them as products of the Greater Braden style (Brown 2004; Brown and Kelly 2000; see Chapter 3).

Like other human figural representations in the Greater Braden style, the arms and legs of the Hightower human figures are proportional in the relationship between head and torso. The head is shown in profile. The shoulder line does not cross the full torso. The eyes are often presented as diamond shaped and open with a dot pupil but without eyelids. The mouth is shown as partially open, as if the figure is speaking or perhaps singing. The upper and lower lip as well as the chin are prominent. The nose is rendered either naturalistically or as the curved beak of a raptor. When a limb is shown in a bent posture, the depiction again is naturalistic, not awkward. Hands that grasp objects are depicted with the opposable thumb placed over the fingers. The figures are also posed in positions that reflect motion—perhaps running or more probably dancing.

These anthropomorphic representations in most instances appear by themselves, but in one thematic grouping they are paired. This pairing may perhaps be best understood as a representation of twins. In most of the human figural representations the head of the central figure is turned to the viewer's left. In the case of the paired figures the heads face each other in a left/right mirrored opposition (Marceaux and Dye 2007).

All of the Hightower gorgets are carved on the concave shell surface except in one instance where the carved image is executed on the convex side. It should be noted that in every instance the figural design overlaps the circular border. This border in itself functions as a cartouche that frames the figure, perhaps providing a locative or symbolic locator function.

We believe that Etowah was the location of a *taller* or workshop that produced the majority of Hightower human figural gorgets (Reilly 2007b). A *taller* can exist in a specific location and time. Such *talleres* are generally composed of several artists or craftspersons supervised and instructed by a master (Reilly 2007b). In any culture, scattered *talleres* are responsible for distinctive but not identical styles. Typically, artists from other locations come to learn from the artists of a distinctive *taller* and then return to their points of origin, bringing their stylistic skills with them. Thus an argument can be made for the spread of styles over large areas as a product of learned crafting as opposed to a dependence on the movement of objects (Helms 1979, 1993).

Regalia

Either individually or paired, the Hightower anthropomorphic figures are elaborately garbed. The specifics of regalia are determined by theme, however, as discussed below. Generally speaking, most Hightower anthropomorphic figures hold ritual accoutrements such as severed heads, supernatural insects and snakes, and long blades or swords. The upraised or extended positioning of the hands emphasizes our conclusion that these figures are engaged in activity. Although the nature of this activity has been a matter of speculation, a recent study convincingly argues that some form of ritualized or actual combat may have been a major focus (Marceaux and Dye 2007).

Individual costume details include headdresses composed of antlers and raccoon hindquarters, wings and avian tail assemblages, beaded loincloths or short skirts, and in at least one instance a bellows-shaped apron. The figures wear a necklace of large shell beads with a columella pendant. In several instances these figures are depicted with either clawed feet or hands. The rendition and placement of these differs according to theme (see the discussion below).

The Placement of Hightower Style Gorgets in Etowah Mound C

Adam King (2004:156) developed a hypothesis proposing that Etowah Mound C was constructed entirely in the Wilbanks phase (AD 1250–1400) in a series of seven construction phases. The placement of Hightower gorgets in Mound C interrments is limited primarily to the three construction phases of the Early Wilbanks phase (AD 1250–1325). However, at least two exceptions date to the Late Wilbanks phase (AD 1325–1375) (King 2004).

King's research has further revealed that while gorget categories such as the Annular, Triskele, Cruciform, and Turkey Cock appear to be restricted to specific areas of Mound C, Hightower anthropomorphic gorgets are recovered in all areas of the mound (King 2004:160). King explains gorget placement as an indication of social organization in death as well as life. For instance, the placement of Turkey Cock gorgets in the northwest corner of Mound C and the Annular-Cruciform-Triskele gorgets in the southwest corner may reflect clan or lineage organization (King 2001). Burials containing Hightower human figural gorgets are located throughout Mound C (particularly in the north side), which may reflect the status of a ruling lineage that transcends ordinary lineage or clan limitations (King 2001, 2004).

Hightower-Style Themes within the Etowah Gorget Corpus

Several researchers have recognized that the corpus of Hightower-style figural gorgets could be grouped or subdivided into thematic categories. Phillips and Brown recognized similarities between their "Birdman" and "Eagle Dancers" originally classified by Kneberg (1959:9) within the corpus of the shell from the Great Mortuary in the Craig Mound at Spiro. The Hightower gorgets were later organized into four themes (Brain and Phillips 1996:44): (1) "Buddha," a seated figure; (2) "headsman," a knife-wielding dancing figure; (3) "Morning Star," a standing figure; and (4) "mortal combat," two facing figures with knives reaching for each other's throats. Brain and Phillips (1996:44) saw this organization as having little or no utility and as an impediment in terms of explaining or understanding the "structural integrity" of what for them is the Big Toco style.

Rejecting the Brain and Phillips hypothesis that theme has little to add to our understanding of the Hightower human figural gorgets, a subgroup of the Mississippian Iconographic Workshop at Texas State University–San Marcos in 2001 explored the human figural Hightower-style gorgets from Mound C at Etowah in terms of the categories of theme and context. Those investigations resulted in the identification of several thematic categories, some of which closely reassembled those proposed by Brain and Phillips (1996:41): "Dances with Mothra," "Dances in Mortal Combat," "Dances with Heads," and "Seated in Display." We should add that the designation "Dances" is used in all themes because the placement of the feet and the positioning of the raised legs appeared strikingly similar to dance steps.

Dances with Mothra

Three Dances with Mothra gorgets were recovered from Mound C (Burials L-137, L-223, and L-27) at Etowah (Fig. 13.1a). In all three cases the minimal investigation of the skeletal remains listed the grave occupants as adult females. In only one case (Burial L-223), a stone-box grave, was the tomb type recorded. Burials L-137 and L-223 date to the Early Wilbanks phase (AD 1250–1325), while Burial L-27 dates to the Late Wilbanks phase (AD 1325–1375). All the Dances with Mothra gorgets are buried with adult females, indicating the potential for associating specific grave objects with a specific sex.

The Dances with Mothra thematic category consists of gorgets carved on the concave surface of a shell. The figure overlaps the circular border of the gorget on all sides. The fenestrations are not as large as in some other examples. The composition of the central figure presents the face in profile, as is the case with the other Hightower human figural gorgets, wearing

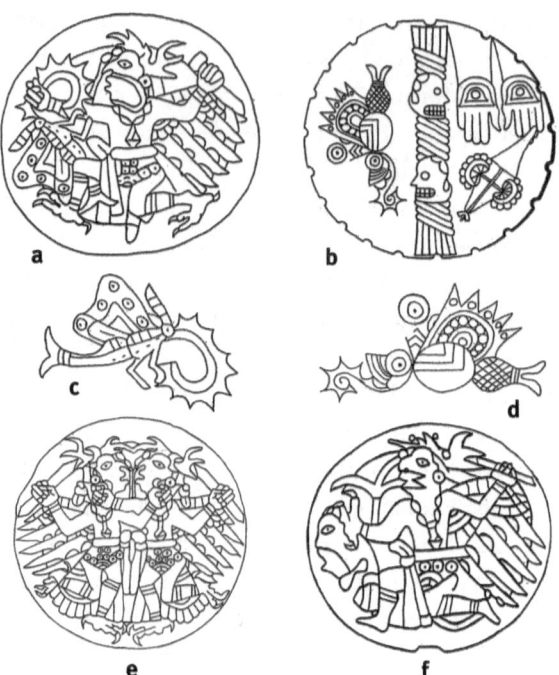

FIGURE 13.1. (a) Dances with Mothra gorget, drawing by Jack Johnson from a photograph by David H. Dye; (b) Willoughby Disk, drawn from a rubbing by Barbara Page (Phillips and Brown 1978:Fig. 208); (c) Mothra from Dances with Mothra gorget, drawing by Jack Johnson; (d) Mothra from Willoughby Disk, drawing by Jack Johnson; (e) Dances in Mortal Combat gorget, drawing by Jack Johnson; (f) Dances with Heads gorget, drawing by Jack Johnson.

a headdress composed of antler tines and raccoon hindquarters. The nose is carved like the beak of a raptor. The figure's hair is not visible, except for the braided and beaded forelock. The eye is diamond shaped and lacks an eye-surround. A narrow ellipsoidal stripe surrounds the open mouth. The lips and chin are clearly visible, as is the case in most Greater Braden anthropomorphic representations. The figure is adorned with a circular ear flare. The chest is frontal and bears a shell bead necklace from which descends a columella pendant. In the left hand the figure grasps a Dover Flint Sword or Blade (Marceaux and Dye 2007). In the right hand the figure grasps the curling proboscis of a forked-tailed supernatural insect. The insect's visible wing is bordered by a band of circles and dots, and it closely resembles the supernatural insect that is carved on the Willoughby Disk a Moundville palette (Knight and Franke 2007) (Fig. 13.1b, d). Around the anthropomorphic figure's waist is tied an elaborate knotted sash that secures a beaded kilt. Both of the anthropomorphic figure's legs end in feet consisting of taloned claws. The figure exhibits a set of avian wings and an avian tail. It would appear that the combination of wings and other avian features with anthropomorphic figures is a Greater Braden trait that in the Hightower corpus functions as a locative that places the figure in the Above World or celestial realm (Lankford 2004, 2007d; Reilly 2004, 2007c).

The relationship of the humanoid figure to the supernatural insect it holds or controls is certainly hostility. The Mothra supernatural is further threatened by the Dover Flint Blade brandished in the left hand. This hostility is in contrast to the depiction of this same supernatural insect at Moundville. In the case of the Moundville representations the insect either appears in a series of *pars pro toto* representations or in a larger design such as the Willoughby Disk. We cannot help wondering if this difference in presentation might be a reflection of a larger, combative political hostility.

Dances in Mortal Combat

A Dances in Mortal Combat gorget (GA BRT M-K5) has been recovered in only one Etowah Mound C burial (Fig. 13.1e), although another example was recovered from a burial in the Etowah village area (Brain and Phillips 1996:45). In each case no age or sex could be determined for the grave occupant.

The mortal combat theme has been elegantly described and interpreted by Shawn Marceaux and David Dye (2007). As they observed, these combat-theme gorgets show two figures in a mirror-image composition. Each figure is dressed similarly to its Dances with Mothra counterpart and is also equipped with wings and an avian tail, suggesting that the action is taking place in the Above World. Both figures also stand on clawed feet. Unlike the Dances with Mothra counterpart, these paired figures assault each other rather than some form of insect supernatural. Each figure holds and threatens its "twin" with a Dover Flint Sword while assaulting it with a closed fist.

Dances with Heads

Dances with Heads gorgets have been recovered from three Etowah Mound burials (Fig. 13.1f). Burial R-g dating to the Early Wilbanks phase was recorded as a child of indeterminate sex. Rogan did not record the form of the burial. Burial M-37 was recorded as an adult of indeterminate sex. The burial form was a stone-box grave. Burial L-179 contained an adult male in a partial stone-box grave. If Rogan had recorded the form of burial R-9 as the stone-box variety then we would have another sex/gender pattern, like the female association of Dances with Mothra. In this case it would be a linkage of the Dances with Heads gorgets and stone-box graves.

There are strong similarities between the regalia worn by the human figural representation on the Dances with Heads gorgets and on the two types of gorgets already described. But the presentation of Dances with Heads is distinctly different. The figure has a raptor beak, avian wings, and a tail. Whereas all three of the anthropomorphic figures in the first two gorget types are equipped with clawed feet, however, Dances with Heads has distinctly human feet and a clawed right hand. This clawed hand grasps a severed anthropomorphic head. The back of this head has a projection that is tied off with either a cord or a band. The left hand of the figure holds what appears to be a Dover Flint Sword, as do the other representations.

The Dances with Heads figure lacks any form of eye-surround and instead has a forked surround about the mouth (Marceaux and Dye 2007:169–171). Since the view of this mouth or painted "buccal surround" is limited by the profile presentation, we suggest that the mouth-surround in its entirety would take the form of a rectangular painted boxlike structure with a forked indentation at either end.

Seated in Display

Three Seated in Display gorgets were recovered from Mound C burials at Etowah (Burials M-13, M-223, and L-57). Burial M-13 contained an adult of indeterminate sex in a stone-box context dating to the Early Wilbanks phase. Burial M-23, also of the Early Wilbanks phase, contained an adult male. Its burial form was not recorded. Burial L-57 contained an adult male from the Late Wilbanks phase and was found in an unusual roofed and log-lined tomb located in a projection on Mound C's north side. If in the future the sex of the adult in M-13 can be determined to be male then another important pattern emerges: an association of Seated in Display gorgets with elite male burials.

The regalia elements as well as the posture of the anthropomorphic figure centered on the Seated in Display gorgets are dramatically different from those of its Hightower counterparts (Fig. 13.2a, b). Unlike the other anthro-

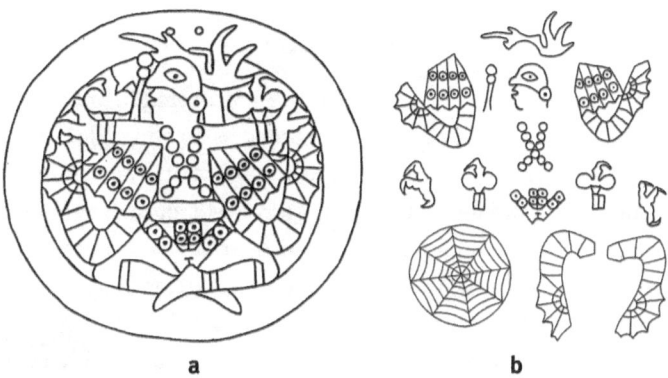

FIGURE 13.2. (a) Seated in Display gorget, drawing by Jack Johnson; (b) Seated in Display individual regalia elements, drawing by F. Kent Reilly III.

pomorphic figures, which are standing, Seated in Display is seated in a cross-legged posture, as its thematic name implies. The figure wears the antler-tine and raccoon-skin headdress and exhibits a beaded forelock. Like its anthropomorphic counterparts, Seated in Display has a pair of wings emerging from his outstretched arms. They are not the wings of the celestial raptor avian, however, resembling more the wings of an insect or perhaps a bat. Behind the seated figure emerges a pair of tail elements that also resemble the split tails of certain insects. The motifs at the end of these tail elements, when combined, form the spiderweb motif (Phillips and Brown 1978:155).

Attached to each outstretched arm are bilobed arrow motifs. Instead of a shell bead necklace with a columella pendant the torso bears shell beads worn in crossed bandolier fashion (Fig. 13.2a, b). Both of the figure's hands are shown as clawed. The kilt or loincloth appears to be identical to those worn by the other anthropomorphic figures. The figure also appears to wear a tight-fitting cap that resembles the cap/mask worn by many wrestlers on television.

Seated in Display is a unique image bearing certain regalia elements that project an overall feel of Beneath World power and authority. It seems clear that Seated in Display is a transformed supernatural, as in the case of the raptor avian imagery of the previously discussed gorgets. It may well be that in these two types of wings we are dealing with a metaphorical set of opposing supernaturals who represent the Above World and day and the Beneath World and night.

Morning Star

A Morning Star gorget (GA BRT-E-139) has been recovered in only one Etowah Mound C burial (#223). This burial is recorded as a young adult female in a flexed posture reposing on a layer of split cane. But another example of the Morning Star gorget was found in the St. Marys, Missouri, assemblage (MacCurdy 1913). The human figural representation in this Morning Star category is the most human of any of the figures under discussion (Fig. 13.3a). Unlike the other gorget images, Morning Star has no clawed appendages. No loincloth is depicted, but the figure wears a shell bead necklace with a columella pendant, knotted sash, and antler-tine and raccoon-skin headdress as well as ear flares.

Four regalia elements connect this image to a previously examined gorget and one other element to a yet undiscussed example. The eye of the

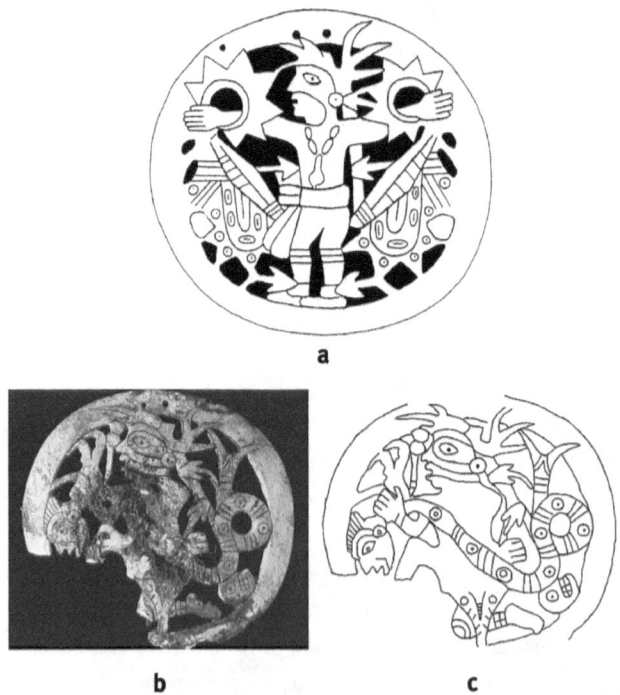

FIGURE 13.3. (a) Morning Star gorget from the St. Marys assemblage, drawing by Jack Johnson; (b) Dances with Snakes gorget, photograph by David H. Dye; (c) Dances with Snakes gorget, drawing by F. Kent Reilly III.

Morning Star anthropomorphic figure is diamond shaped and lacks an eye-surround. The Morning Star figure has a painted or perhaps tattooed narrow ellipsoidal stripe surrounding the open mouth. This is identical to the mouth-surround of the Dances with Mothra figure. Whereas Dances with Mothra's right hand grasps the curling proboscis of a forked-tailed supernatural insect, the Morning Star figure grasps the proboscis of a Mothra supernatural in both hands. As in the case of the supernatural held by Dances with Mothra, this insect's wings are bordered by a band of circles and dots and in this instance a horseshoe-shaped cartouche containing barred oval motifs. Unlike the Dances with Mothra example, the split tails of these supernatural insects are not visible. Behind the figure's left shoulder is a staff with two raccoon-skin bindings, and each ankle of this figure also has a raccoon skin binding. The Morning Star gorget category is linked not only to Dances with Mothra but to the central actor of the Dances with Snakes gorget discussed below.

Dances with Snakes

In 2004 our attention was drawn to another potential human figural Hightower gorget theme that we have titled Dances with Snakes. Unfortunately, our proposed thematic division is represented by a single Etowah gorget (GA-BRt-E50) recovered in Burial L-179 on the southwest corner of Mound C. The grave is recorded as that of a probable extended adult male in a partial stone box. Additional burial goods included a large number of shell beads, a bone hairpin, and a copper gorget with an embossed cruciform design (Brain and Phillips 1996:146).

The lips and chin of the anthropomorphic figure are prominent and clearly distinguished, reflecting a very important Greater Braden attribute. Unlike those of the other gorgets in the Etowah Hightower corpus, the design was carved on the convex rather than the concave surface of the shell. Such a carving effort is a difficult task indeed and perhaps represents the artist's effort to emphasize the Beneath World theme of the gorget.

A break along the wearer's righthand corner of the gorget has caused the loss of the anthropomorphic figure's foot and right leg below mid-calf and part of the skirt and sash that surrounds the figure's waist. We believe that this breakage also destroyed a skull that would complement the skull seen behind the figure's right foot.

The gorget imagery is damaged by a line of rot or decay that runs from the right shoulder across the chest and down through the bellows-shaped apron (Brown 2007a). This apron is only identifiable because a very small portion was outside the decay line. While the bead-bordered kilts worn by other members of the Hightower thematic corpus have been identified as bellows-shaped aprons, only Dances with Snakes clearly wears one. Unfortunately, this gorget also has a green discoloration in its mid-section that further obscures some of the finer details of the carving and incising. This green stain is the result of being in contact with the copper cruciform gorget found in the same grave. Because of the decay and staining, the only recorded image of the gorget was a black-and-white photograph. Little could be learned about the regalia details and the objects held by the anthropomorphic figure.

In 2005 David Dye traveled to Etowah and spent considerable time photographing the Dances with Snakes gorget. His photographs revealed hitherto-unseen details of the overall figural composition. They showed enough detail for a line drawing of these previously unknown details to be made (Fig. 13.3b, c).

This line drawing revealed an anthropomorphic figure that lacks wings, unlike the figures in the other four thematic categories. It appears that the combination of wings and other avian features with anthropomorphic figures is a Greater Braden trait that in the Hightower corpus has been modified from its original association with Morning Star and become a locative (as previously stated) that places the figure in the Above World or celestial realm (Lankford 2004, 2007d). Where, then, is the action taking place in the case of Dances with Snakes? The skull located behind the left foot undoubtedly gives the answer. In terms of the overall composition of this gorget, an identical skull would most likely have been placed behind the right foot, as noted. The placement of skulls on either side of the central figure indicates that the skulls are functioning as a locative identifying the location of the action as the realm of the dead. Mississippian-period art of the Greater Braden style is replete with locatives. Until now the majority of those locatives have served to identify celestial locations (Lankford 2007d; Reilly 2007c). It seems only logical that locatives for the other realms would also exist in the Greater Braden–style artistic corpus.

The central figure wears a headdress composed of antler tines and raccoon hindquarters. The hair is not discernible except for the beaded and braided forelock. An eye-surround in the ellipsoidal or water-moccasin form surrounds the diamond-shaped eye. The open mouth has a stripe of facial paint an old canister filled with clippings from a 1920s silent film in the attic of the house that is being cleaned out. Unfortunately, the images of the actors on the individual film cells are not recognizable. But the costumes, ten-gallon hats, and hand-held objects such as six-guns and lariats leave no doubt that the film in question was a Western. The edited clips in several instances contain enough cells for the viewer to recognize some of the film sequences even if the full story is not evident.

The clues necessary to organize the human figural Hightower-style gorgets sequentially, like the 1920s film, are most likely represented by regalia and hand-held objects. Thus the gorgets can almost certainly be organized on a storyboard, like the cell sequences from the film, using the regalia and hand-held objects as a guide.

The most obvious placement of an overlapping relationship or gorget sequence on our storyboard is provided by the relationship between Dances with Mothra and Morning Star (Fig. 13.6, Vignette 1). Both of these gorgets depict anthropomorphic figures dominating supernatural insects and carry the same ellipsoidal motif around the mouth. A second possible sequence is the relationship between Dances with Snakes and Dances with Heads, who appears to hold the head severed from the human-headed snake depicted on the Dances with Snake gorget (Fig. 13.6, Vignette 2).

Another possible sequence or vignette is a grouping composed of the three gorgets that are equipped with avian locatives: Dances with Mothra, Dances in Mortal Combat, and Dances with Heads (Fig. 13.6, Vignette 3). These three gorgets are further linked through their clawed appendages. The figures in Dances with Mothra and Dances in Mortal Combat have clawed feet, while Dances with Heads has a clawed right hand. Even though all the anthropomorphic figures are undoubtedly supernaturals, the Seated in Display figure is unique as a figure of power who is only linked to the other figures through his clawed hands. A final vignette sequence is suggested by the depiction of the figures in Dances with Mothra, Dances with Heads, Morning Star, and Dances with Snakes in the act of overcoming a nonhuman actor in the manner of the "Labors of Hercules" (Fig. 13.6, Vignette 4).

It has been suggested that the series of events depicted in the gorget sequence may have chartered specific aspects of elite Mississippian ritual and behavior (Marceaux and Dye 2007:183; Reilly 2004:136–137, 2007a). It has also been suggested that these objects, regalia, and themes were linked to performances of creation stories through which the elite, as the principal actors, publicly validated their status and power (Marceaux and Dye 2007:183; Reilly 2001, 2004:136–137, 2007a). Perhaps more of our missing sequences will be recovered through archaeological investigation and the examination of the many public and private collections that exist throughout the eastern United States. This evidence may provide the missing elements that will allow scholars to reconstruct the ancient ideology of the thriving Native American culture of the Mississippian period that once dominated the geographical and political landscape of eastern North America.

AUTHORS' ACKNOWLEDGMENTS: Many of the conclusions reached in this chapter are not ours alone. They are the product of at least three years of interaction (2001–2003) with fellow scholars during the Mississippian Iconography Workshops held at Texas State University–San Marcos. Among those scholars are David Dye, Carol Diaz-Granados, Adam King, Richard Townsend, Bill Johnston, George Lankford, Jim Knight, Vin Steponaitis, and Robert Sharp. Mistakes in this manuscript are completely our own and do not reflect on the knowledge and scholarly precision of the individuals mentioned above.

CHAPTER 14

Raptor Imagery at Etowah

The Raptor Is the Path to Power

Adam King and F. Kent Reilly III

Raptors, Raptor parts, and human/Raptor composite figures are some of the most enduring elements of Mississippian imagery. In fact, as Lankford acknowledges in Chapter 10, they also are some of the most widespread motifs and themes in Southeastern iconography. Lankford explores the place of the Raptor in the iconography of Moundville and in the narratives of the western Muskogean speakers of the historic period. In this chapter we examine the role of the Raptor in the imagery recovered from the Etowah site. Ultimately, what we find is that the Raptor figures quite differently in the history of Etowah and crafting in the region than at Moundville. Additionally, we speculate that the difference in the way the Raptor is used actually reflects aspects of the relationship between Etowah and Moundville.

The Raptor at Etowah

Unlike Moundville, where the Raptor is quite rare, at Etowah the Raptor in its various forms dominates figural imagery. It appears as full representations of Raptors, either as individuals or paired, on embossed copper plates. Raptor imagery (for example, as talons or wings) also seems to be present in the so-called copper cutouts or ornaments found decorating headdresses buried in Mound C. Most famous are the embossed copper plates depicting a human with Raptor elements, including wings and tail, hooked beak, and forked eye-surround (Fig. 14.1a, b). This same figure appears in various poses on the Hightower-style gorgets of the anthropomorphic theme (Fig. 14.1c).

Brown (Brown 2004, 2007b; Brown and Kelly 2000) has called this figure the Birdman, and it is distributed widely across the Southeast and Midwest. We think it is possible, at least at Etowah, to make the case that this Birdman and the images of Raptors and Raptor body parts are elements of a larger Raptor or Birdman theme. The case for this is best made through the imagery

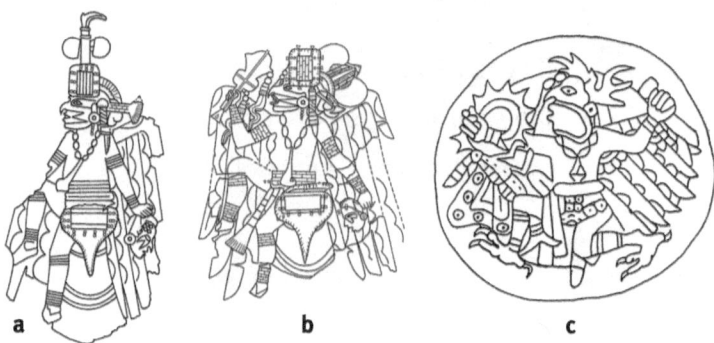

FIGURE 14.1. (a, b) the Rogan Plates; (c) Hightower anthropomorphic gorget.

present on the Malden Plates, a series of embossed copper plates depicting Raptors. In one of these images, the Raptor has a human head but a body that matches all the other Raptor images in the cache.

Brown (2004, 2007b) has argued that the Birdman was likely a supernatural figure with thematic associations like those of the historically recorded Morning Star of the Osage or Red Horn of the Winnebago. These individuals were great warriors who fought on behalf of humanity in wars of the supernatural. They were beings of the Above World and often were associated with the Thunderers (birdlike supernaturals) and the falcon. Thematically, these individuals were linked to the triumph of life over death and day over night as well as fertility and the recycling of the souls of the dead into the souls of the newly born.

The most famous images of the Birdman at Etowah are found on the embossed copper plates excavated by Rogan in 1884 (Thomas 1894). Brown (Brown 2004; Brown and Kelly 2000) has argued that the Birdman was a central theme in the Classic Braden style that developed at Cahokia in the twelfth and thirteenth centuries. In fact, based on stylistic grounds and crafting techniques, it is clear that the Rogan Plates actually were decorated in the Classic Braden style. This means that the plates functioned as heirloomed objects of power and that the images they carried were foreign to Etowah as well as being at least a century old by the time they were interred in the Early Wilbanks phase (AD 1250–1325) stages at Etowah's Mound C. Undoubtedly, as heirloomed items, the Rogan Plates functioned as significant objects of power that helped to visualize and validate the elite position of Etowah's ruling lineage.

As King discusses in Chapter 12, those Classic Braden images appear at an interesting and critical time in the history of Etowah. The Early Wilbanks phase is a time when Etowah was reoccupied after a short abandonment. Just as the abandonment represented an end to the ranked social form at Etowah, the reoccupation of the site involved the reestablishment of a ranked social order. It appears that this new social order, complete with a new definition and materialization of eliteness, was chartered by a foreign ideology represented by the Rogan Plates. In a real sense, the Birdman became the path to power, as the charter for leadership in the newly reestablished Etowah chiefdom. The arrival of Raptor imagery, in both its zoomorphic and anthropomorphic forms, at Etowah signals the arrival of elite cult bearers as well as a new "cult" that was manifested in a specific avian iconography and through the medium of copper.

Interestingly, with the appearance of the Birdman in the Classic Braden imagery at Etowah, the Birdman also appeared as a new theme in the local Hightower shell-engraving style. This appears to be an interpretation of the Birdman theme imported from the Classic Braden style to a locally produced artistic tradition. Those Hightower-style gorgets of the anthropomorphic theme depict a Birdman in various poses. A closer examination of the figures on those gorgets reveals that there actually are two distinct Birdman figures repeating the same poses. King argues in Chapter 12 that these two figures represent Hero Twins possibly historically related to Lodge-Boy and Thrown-Away of the later Creek narratives. This argument is based on one constructed by Lankford (2008b) for the Williams Island figures, who also appear to be twins of some kind. Reilly and Garber argue in Chapter 13 that the Hightower anthropomorphic gorgets appear to constitute vignettes in a longer narrative. That narrative may have parallels to the Native American narratives featuring the Twins that are common throughout the East.

The archaeology of Etowah demonstrates that the Birdman and other Raptor-related images are found only during the Early and Late Wilbanks phases. Sometime in the Late Wilbanks phase (AD 1325–1375) Etowah was again abandoned, this time possibly due to armed attack (Dye and King 2008; King 2003). The regionally dominant polity associated with the site collapsed and was never resurrected. With the disappearance of Etowah from the political landscape, the Birdman and Raptor-related imagery disappeared from the crafting landscape of northern Georgia.

Based on Waring's (1968b) exploration of ethnographic information from the records of Muskhogean speakers, the Raptor may have disappeared from the crafting record but not from the sacred narratives of those people. Among the Creeks, the eagle (or the Raptor more generally) was seen as the king of birds and even as an intermediary between people and the creator. It was associated with warfare and also with healing and was a prominent symbol associated with the annual Busk (Waring 1968b:46).

On the basis of these associations, Waring (1968b:46) argues for a connection between Raptors and what he calls the Yahola-Hayuya concept. One of Swanton's most important informants, Jackson Lewis, stated that Yahola and Hayuya were "two important male deities supposed to reside together in the air without any other companionship" (Swanton 1928:485). Their names figure prominently in medical songs; they were appealed to in sickness and could endow individuals with strength and clear vision and thought. They also figure prominently in the Busk and ceremony surrounding the black drink. As Waring (1968b) notes, their capabilities and associations are very similar to those of the Raptor—both are associated with healing and figure prominently in the Busk. If we add to this the apparent pairing of the Birdman figures on the Hightower anthropomorphic gorgets, then the connection between Raptors and the paired "air spirits" becomes clearer. Interestingly, the paired air spirit deity or preternatural entity survives in areas outside of the lower South. The Osage speak of an avian creator spirit who is the combined essence of two supernatural eagles and who represents regenerative powers in both the natural order and the souls of those soon to be reborn.

While the Raptor trappings disappear from the crafting of the Hightower region after the demise of Etowah in the Middle Mississippian period, the Twins continue to appear in the iconographic record (see Chapter 12 and Lankford 2008b). When the Twins become supernatural they are understood to be creatures of the Above World and maintain an avian identity, often as the Raptor. Despite its absence from the imagery of the region, the connection between the Raptor and the Twins apparently continued in the sacred narratives of the area. This disappearance of the visual imagery may be linked to the disappearance of the members of the ranked social order that wore this imagery as regalia items in ceremonies that publicly validated their elite position at Etowah during the Wilbanks phase.

Waring (1968b) makes another interesting suggestion regarding the Raptor, particularly the eagle. He states that eagle feathers were a key component in the Calumet ceremony of the Muskhogean area. According to Waring, the Calumet in this area was not associated with a pipe but instead functioned as something of a royal standard, as described by William Bartram (1794:149–150). James Adair discussed this standard in the following context: "The Indians cannot shew greater honour to the greatest potentate on earth, than to place him in the white seat—invoke Yo He Wah [Yahola], while he is drinking the Cussena, and dance before him with the eagle tails" (Adair 1775:168–169). He further noted that "waving the eagles tail over the head of a stranger is the strongest pledge of good faith" (Adair 1775:60).

Waring's choice of the word "Calumet" could be misleading in this context. But it calls to mind Robert Hall's (1997) arguments about the use of the Calumet in the Mississippi Valley as the means through which deceased souls were brought back to life as part of adoption ceremonies. Both Hall (1997) and Brown (2007b) argue that the historically known figures like Morning Star, Red Horn, and He-Who-Wears-Human-Heads-as-Earrings had this same ability to bring dead souls back to life. If Brown's (2007b) argument that those figures are descendants of the Birdman is correct, it is possible that the Birdman of the Classic Braden style also possessed the same ability. To the extent that the Creek eagle and the eagle feather "standard" were connected to the Birdman and his presumed associations, then they may have served the same purpose as the Calumet of the Mississippi Valley. In other words, the honor and pledge of good faith showed to visitors by waving the eagle tail standard over them (as described by Adair 1775) may actually have been an adoption ceremony where some deceased person was brought to life in the body of the honored guest. In the same way that the gifts of Morning Star lived on through the Calumet of the Mississippi Valley, the abilities of the Birdman lived on through the Creek eagle's tail.

Speculations on the Use of the Raptor at Etowah and Moundville

In contrast to the case at Moundville, at Etowah the Raptor, most visible as the Birdman, is a culture hero and not a villain on the Path of Souls. Rather than being a test to pass on the Path, the Birdman was the path to power.

This contrast, and the speculations we derive from it, hinges on the assumption that the Raptor at Moundville is intended to be the same being as the Birdman/Raptor imagery at Etowah. Lankford is correct in pointing out that the form the representation takes at each site (such as the curve of the beak and shape of the wings) cannot be used to argue for or against the notion that they are the same being. Such similarities or differences may simply be conventions of different stylistic traditions. It is potentially more important that the images at the two sites share some key features, including the distinctive talons, hooked beak, and forked eye surround.

If we make the interpretive leap that they are the same being, we are led down an interesting but speculative path. Based on indications of exchange of material goods, it seems apparent that Etowah and Moundville were not in close contact. Citing the distribution of finished goods and important raw materials, Brown et al. (1990) infer that Etowah and Moundville were centers of two distinct interaction spheres. That separation is confirmed by the lack of evidence for contact between the sites, as seen in everything from domestic pottery to artistic styles and elaborate display goods (Welch 1991). In the Mississippian Iconography Workshop this divide has been dubbed the Cane Curtain. While the separateness of the spheres does not necessarily indicate animosity or hostility, it is reasonable to infer that it does indicate a certain amount of competition in the larger region to attract labor, raw materials, and finished goods.

Reilly (2007a) has suggested that the long-nosed supernatural that appears infrequently at Moundville could be interpreted as an important symbol for the visualization of elite power at the Moundville site. Knight and Franke (2007) have tentatively identified the complement from the natural world on which this supernatural image is constructed as the sphinx or hawk moth—both members of the Sphingridae family. Members of this species come out at dusk and feed on and pollinate plants of the Solonaceae family, such as tobacco, potatoes, tomatoes, and datura. While certainly unsubstantiated, its nighttime association might fit with a site whose primary identity appears to have become a portal to the Path of Souls visible in the night sky (Lankford 2007b).

In the artifact assemblage from Moundville the supernatural hawk moth or Mothra with curled proboscis and feathery antenna is found on a long-necked bottle in the form of a *pars pro toto* representation in which the wings of the Mothra and its curled proboscis figure prominently (Fig. 14.3). Several sherds from similar bottles also carry fragments of the *pars pro toto* representation. Mothra also appears on Hightower gorgets (Fig. 14.1c). The most dramatic image of Mothra, however, is on the Willoughby Disk (Fig. 14.2). This disk is carved from slate, unlike the other Moundville disks or palettes,

FIGURE 14.2. The Willoughby Disk and Mothra.

FIGURE 14.3. A Moundville bottle with Mothra imagery (*pars pro toto*).

which were carved from sandstone. Mothra imagery has also been found in Missouri. A bottle decorated with Mothra imagery executed in the Nashville Negative Painted style was recovered in Scott County, Missouri (Fig. 14.3). Just as the Birdman imagery at Etowah signals the arrival of new elites and their accompanying ideologies, the Mothra imagery at Moundville may very well signal a similar change in authority or belief.

An argument can be made that the ruling lineages of different Mississippian sites may have legitimized their authority by linking their descent to a prominent supernatural on the Path of Souls or other preternaturals from a series of stories that deal with important human issues such as the balance in nature that allows the world and its inhabitants to function properly.

Furthermore, the Path of Souls story may be one fragment out of a larger ancient mythological matrix that included the exploits of Morning Star in his avian identity. There may be a bit stronger evidence to argue that Etowah's identity was symbolized by the Birdman. This being the case, placing the Raptor as gatekeeper on the Path of Souls may have been a way of "othering" Moundville's nearby rival, Etowah. Similarly, depictions on Hightower-style gorgets of the Birdman holding Mothra's proboscis in one hand and a weapon in another might be a similar sort of expression from Etowah. In this case the Birdman (possibly associated with the Morning Star and certainly the rescuer of life from death) is depicted holding Mothra (associated with the night sky and the pollination of the critical ritual item tobacco) in a scene that depicts the triumph of day over night.

Regionalism in the Meaning of the Raptor

In the use of the Raptor and Raptor imagery at Etowah and Moundville we see a clear expression of the regionalism inherent in Mississippian iconographic systems. Raptors and Raptor-related images are common features of Mississippian art, especially art impacted by the development and spread of the Greater Braden style. As those images were taken from their original context (the American Bottom) and traveled to other areas they in all likelihood gained new meanings or in some cases emphasized certain aspects of a shared belief system that were more locally informed and better suited local needs and systems of elite validation.

Just as clearly, distinct symbol sets were emphasized in different places and different settings. The choice of the symbols featured in local art traditions depended on the messages to be communicated. The Birdman clearly played a foundational role in Etowah's rise to regional importance. Not unexpectedly, the Birdman and associated imagery are featured during the Middle Mississippian period. This situation has no parallel at Moundville. Instead Moundville took on a role as portal to the Path of Souls. Predictably, much of the symbolism prominent at Moundville appears to be related to the rituals of death and the journey along the Path of Souls that was undoubtedly a concern for all Native Americans during the Mississippian period whatever their regional affiliation, just as it is for all human beings of any time or place.

BIBLIOGRAPHY

Adair, J.
   1775   *The History of the American Indians*. Edward and Charles Dilly, London.

Baerreis, D. A.
   1957   The Southern Cult and the Spiro Ceremonial Complex. *Bulletin of the Oklahoma Anthropological Society* 5:23–28.

Bailey, G. (editor)
   1995   *The Osage and the Invisible World: From the Works of Francis La Flesche*. University of Oklahoma Press, Norman.

Bailey, G., and D. C. Swan
   2004   *Art of the Osage*. St. Louis Art Museum/University of Washington Press, Seattle.

Baird, D. A.
   1980   *The Quapaw Indians*. University of Oklahoma Press, Norman.

Barnes, R. H.
   1984   *Two Crows Denies it: A History of Controversy in Omaha Sociology*. University of Nebraska Press, Lincoln.

Bartram, W.
   1794   *Travels through North and South Carolina, Georgia, East and West Florida, the Cherokee Country, the Extensive Territories of the Muscoguleges or Creek Confederacy, and the Country of the Choctaws*. 2nd ed. Joseph Johnson, London.

Beck, R. (editor)
   2007   *The Durable House: Architecture, Ancestors, and Origins*. Occasional Paper No. 35. Southern Illinois University, Carbondale.

Berenson, B.
   1902   The Rudiments of Connoisseurship. In *The Study and Criticism of Italian Art*, 111–148. George Bell, London.

Berres, T. E.
   2001   *Power and Gender in Oneota Culture: A Study of a Late Prehistoric People*. Northern Illinois University Press, DeKalb.

Bierhorst, J.
   1995   *Mythology of the Lenape*. University of Arizona Press, Tucson.

Blitz, J. H.
   1993   *Ancient Chiefdoms of the Tombigbee*. University of Alabama Press, Tuscaloosa.

Boas, F.
   1928   *Primitive Art*. Harvard University Press, Cambridge, Mass.

Bowers, A. W.
- 1950 *Mandan Social and Ceremonial Organization.* University of Chicago Press, Chicago.
- 1965 *Hidatsa Social and Ceremonial Organization.* University of Nebraska Press, Lincoln.
- 1992 *Hidatsa Social and Ceremonial Organization.* Reprint. University of Nebraska Press, Lincoln.

Brain, J. P., and P. Phillips
- 1996 *Shell Gorgets: Styles of the Late Prehistoric and Protohistoric Southeast.* Peabody Museum of Archaeology and Ethnology, Harvard University, Cambridge, Mass.

Brannon, Peter A.
- 1923 The Moundville Group. *Arrow Points* 7(6):105–108, 111, 115, 118.

Breitburg, E., and M. C. Moore
- 2005 Mortuary Analysis. In *The Brentwood Library Site: A Mississippian Town on the Little Harpeth River, Williamson County, Tennessee,* edited by M. C. Moore, 123–142. Research Series No. 15. Tennessee Division of Archaeology, Nashville.

Brooks, R. L.
- 1996 The Arkansas Valley: A New Paradigm, Revisionist Perspectives and the Archaeological Record. *Caddoan Archaeology Newsletter* 7(1):17–27.

Brose, D. S., J. A. Brown, and D. W. Penney
- 1985 *Ancient Art of the American Woodland Indians.* Abrams, New York.

Broster, J. B.
- 1972 The Ganier Site: A Late Mississippian Village on the Cumberland River. In *The Middle Cumberland Culture,* edited by R. B. Ferguson, 51–78. Publications in Anthropology No. 3. Vanderbilt University, Nashville.
- 1988 Burial Patterns for the Mississippian Period in Middle Tennessee. *Tennessee Anthropologist* 13(1):1–15.

Brown, C. S.
- 1926 *Archaeology of Mississippi.* Reprint. AMS Press for Peabody Museum of Archaeology and Ethnology, Harvard University, Cambridge, Mass., 1973.

Brown, I. W.
- 1990 Catalog of the Human Effigy Vessels in the Collections of the Peabody Museum of Archaeology and Ethnology, Harvard University. Unpublished paper.
- 2002/ The Hunchbacks of Tennessee: Ceramic Human Effigy Vessels in the
- 2006 Collections of the Peabody Museum of Archaeology and Ethnology, Harvard University. Paper presented at the annual meeting of the Southeastern Archaeological Conference, Biloxi, Miss., 2002 (revised 2006).

Brown, J. A.
- 1976 The Southern Cult Reconsidered. *Midcontinental Journal of Archaeology* 1:115–135.
- 1985 The Mississippian Period. In *Ancient Art of the American Woodland Indians,* by D. S. Brose, J. A. Brown, and D. W. Penney, 93–145. Abrams, New York.
- 1989 On Style Divisions of the Southeastern Ceremonial Complex—A Revisionist Perspective. In *The Southeastern Ceremonial Complex, Artifacts and Analysis:*

The Cottonlandia Conference, edited by P. K. Galloway, 183–204. University of Nebraska Press, Lincoln.
1991   *Aboriginal Cultural Adaptations in the Midwestern Prairies*. Garland Publishing, New York.
1996   *The Spiro Ceremonial Center: The Archaeology of Arkansas Valley Caddoan Culture in Eastern Oklahoma*. 2 vols. Memoirs of the Museum of Anthropology No. 29. University of Michigan, Ann Arbor.
1997   The Archaeology of Ancient Religion in the Eastern Woodlands. *Annual Review of Anthropology* 26:465–485.
2001   Human Figures and the Southeastern Ancestor Shrine. In *Fleeting Identities: Perishable Material Culture in Archaeological Research*, edited by P. Ballard Drooker, 76–93. Center for Archaeological Investigations, Southern Illinois University, Carbondale.
2002   Forty Years of the Southeastern Ceremonial Complex. In *Histories of Southeastern Archaeology*, edited by S. Tushingham, J. Hill, and C. McNutt, 26–34. University of Alabama Press, Tuscaloosa.
2004   The Cahokian Expression: Creating Court and Cult. In *Hero, Hawk, and Open Hand: American Indian Art of the Ancient Midwest and South*, edited by R. F. Townsend and R. V. Sharp, 105–123. Art Institute of Chicago and Yale University Press, New Haven.
2005   Beyond Red Horn: Where Ethnology Meets History. Paper presented at the 70th Annual Meeting of the Society for American Archaeology, Salt Lake City.
2007a   Chronological Implications of the Bellows-Shaped Apron. In *Chronology, Iconography, and Style: Current Perspectives on the Social and Temporal Contexts of the Southeastern Ceremonial Complex*, edited by A. King, 38–56. University of Alabama Press, Tuscaloosa.
2007b   On the Identity of the Birdman within Mississippian Period Art and Iconography. In *Ancient Objects and Sacred Realms: Interpretations of Mississippian Iconography*, edited by F. K. Reilly III and J. F. Garber, 56–106. University of Texas Press, Austin.
2007c   Sequencing the Braden Style within Mississippian Period Art and Iconography. In *Ancient Objects and Sacred Realms: Interpretations of Mississippian Iconography*, edited by F. K. Reilly III and J. F. Garber, 213–245. University of Texas Press, Austin.

Brown, J. A., and D. H. Dye
2007   Severed Heads and Sacred Scalplocks: Mississippian Iconographic Trophies. In *The Taking and Displaying of Human Trophies by Amerindians*, edited by R. J. Chacon and D. H. Dye, 274–294. Kluwer Academic/Plenum Publishers, New York.

Brown, J. A., and J. Kelly
2000   Cahokia and the Southeastern Ceremonial Complex. In *Mounds, Modoc, and Mesoamerica: Papers in Honor of Melvin L. Fowler*, edited by S. R. Ahler, 469–510. Scientific Papers 55. Illinois State Museum, Springfield.

Brown, J. A., R. A. Kerber, and H. D. Winters
1990   Trade and the Evolution of Exchange Relations at the Beginning of the Mississippian Period. In *The Mississippian Emergence*, edited by B. D. Smith, 251–280. Smithsonian Institution, Washington, D.C.

Brown, J. A., and J. D. Rogers
  1989   Linking Spiro's Artistic Styles: The Copper Connection. *Southeastern Archaeology* 8:1–8.
Brown, J. A., and R. F. Sasso
  2001   Prelude to History on the Eastern Prairies. In *Societies in Eclipse: Archaeology of the Eastern Woodlands Indians, A.D. 1400–1700*, edited by D. S. Brose, C. W. Cowan, and R. C. Mainfort, Jr., 205–228. Smithsonian Institution, Washington, D.C.
Brown, J. E. (editor)
  1953   *The Sacred Pipe*. Penguin Books, Baltimore.
Brown, T. L.
  2005   *Ceramic Variability within the Parkin Phase: A Whole Vessel Metric Analysis From Northeast Arkansas*. Research Report No. 32. Arkansas Archeological Survey, Fayetteville.
Buchner, C. A., II
  2003   Ceramic Analysis. In *Mississippian Transitions at John's Lake*, edited by C. A. Buchner. Research Series 60. Arkansas Archeological Survey, Fayetteville.
Burnett, E. K.
  1945   *The Spiro Mound Collection in the Museum*. Contributions from the Museum of the American Indian, vol. 14:9–47. Heye Foundation, New York.
Burns, L. F.
  1985   *Osage Indian Customs and Myths*. Ciga Press, Fallbrook, Calif.
  1989   *A History of the Osage People*. Ciga Press, Fallbrook, Calif.
  1994   *Symbolic and Decorative Art of the Osage People*. Ciga Press, Fallbrook, Calif.
  2005   *Osage Indian Customs and Myths*. University of Alabama Press, Tuscaloosa.
Byers, A. M.
  2006   *Cahokia: A World Renewal Cult Heterarchy*. University Press of Florida, Gainesville.
Byington, C.
  1915   *A Dictionary of the Choctaw Language*. Bureau of American Ethnology Bulletin 46. Government Printing Office, Washington, D.C.
Catlin, G.
  1844   *Letters and Notes on the Manners, Customs and Condition of North American Indians*. 4th ed. 2 vols. David Bogue, London.
Childs, T.
  1993   Variations of Walls Engraved and Rhodes Incised Pottery. *Arkansas Archeologist* 32:139–152.
Childs, T. H., and C. H. McNutt
  2002   A Comparison of Designs and Moundville Engraved, *var.* Hemphill and Mississippi Valley Varieties of Walls Engraved Ceramics. Paper presented at the annual meeting of the Southeastern Archaeological Conference, Biloxi, Miss.
Conant, A. J.
  1879   *Foot-prints of Vanished Races in the Mississippi Valley: Being an Account of Some of the Monuments and Relics of Pre-historic Races Scattered over Its Surface, with Suggestions as to Their Origin and Uses*. C. R. Barns, St. Louis.

Cox, S. D.
  1985 Catalogue of the Gates P. Thruston Collection. In *Art and Artisans of Prehistoric Middle Tennessee: The Gates P. Thruston Collection of Vanderbilt University Held in Trust by the Tennessee State Museum*, edited by S. D. Cox, 65–163. Tennessee State Museum, Nashville.
Cox, S. D. (editor)
  1985 *Art and Artisans of Prehistoric Middle Tennessee: The Gates P. Thruston Collection of Vanderbilt University Held in Trust by the Tennessee State Museum*. Tennessee State Museum, Nashville.
DeMallie, R. J., and D. R. Parks
  2001 Tribal Traditions and Records. In *Handbook of North American Indians, Volume 13: Plains*, edited by R. J. DeMallie, 1062–1073. Smithsonian Institution, Washington, D.C.
Dewdney, S.
  1967 *The Sacred Scrolls of the Southern Ojibway*. University of Toronto Press, Toronto.
Diaz-Granados, C.
  1993 The Petroglyphs and Pictographs of Missouri: A Distributional, Stylistic, Contextual, Temporal, and Functional Analysis of the State's Rock Graphics. 2 vols. Ph.D. dissertation, Department of Anthropology, Washington University, St. Louis.
  2004 Marking Stone, Land, Body, and Spirit: Rock Art and Mississippian Iconography. In *Hero, Hawk, and Open Hand: American Indian Art of the Ancient Midwest and South*, edited by R. F. Townsend and R. V. Sharp, 138–149. Art Institute of Chicago and Yale University Press, New Haven.
Diaz-Granados, C., and J. R. Duncan
  2000 *The Petroglyphs and Pictographs of Missouri*. University of Alabama Press, Tuscaloosa.
  2004 Reflections of Power, Wealth, and Sex in Missouri Rock-Art Motifs. In *The Rock-Art of Eastern North America*, edited by C. Diaz-Granados and J. R. Duncan, 145–158. University of Alabama Press, Tuscaloosa.
Diaz-Granados, C., M. W. Rowe, M. Hyman, J. R. Duncan, and J. R. Southon
  2001 AMS Radiocarbon Dates for Charcoal from Three Missouri Pictographs and Their Associated Iconography. *American Antiquity* 66(3):481–492.
Dickens, Roy C., Jr. (editor)
  1982 *Of Sky and Earth: Art of the Early Southeastern Indians*. Georgia Department of Archives and History, Atlanta.
Dieterle, R. L.
  2005 Gottschall: A New Interpretation. In *The Encyclopedia of Hočąk (Winnebago) Mythology*. http://www.hotcakencyclopedia.com/ho.Gottschall.html (accessed 22 May 2009).
  n.d.a Bluehorn (Evening Star). In *The Encyclopedia of Hočąk (Winnebago) Mythology*. http://www.hotcakencyclopedia.com/ho.Bluehorn.html (accessed 22 May 2009).
  n.d.b Redhorn's Father (Young Man and Naked One). In *The Encyclopedia of Hočąk (Winnebago) Mythology*. http://www.hotcakencyclopedia.com/ho.RedhornsFather.html (accessed 22 May 2009).

Dorsey, G. A.
  1902 The Osage Mourning-War Ceremony. *American Anthropologist* 4:404–411.
  1906 *The Pawnee Mythology, Part 1.* Carnegie Institution, Washington, D.C.
Dorsey, J. O.
  1884 *Omaha Sociology.* Bureau of American Ethnology, Third Annual Report. Government Printing Office, Washington, D.C.
  1885 *Osage Traditions.* Bureau of American Ethnology, Sixth Annual Report. Government Printing Office, Washington, D.C.
  1886 Migrations of Siouan Tribes. *American Naturalist* 20:211–222.
  1894 *A Study of Siouan Cults.* Bureau of American Ethnology, Eleventh Annual Report. Government Printing Office, Washington, D.C.
Dowd, J. T.
  1972 *The West Site: A Stone Box Cemetery in Middle Tennessee.* Miscellaneous Paper No. 10. Tennessee Archaeological Society, Nashville.
Drooker, P. B.
  1992 *Mississippian Village Textiles at Wickliffe.* University of Alabama Press, Tuscaloosa.
Duffield, L. F.
  1964 *Engraved Shells from the Craig Mound at Spiro, LeFlore County, Oklahoma.* Memoirs No. 1. Oklahoma Archaeological Society, Oklahoma City.
Duncan, J. R.
  1981 Central Missouri Prehistoric Ceramics: Types and a Proposed Local Sequence. M.A. thesis, Lincoln University, Jefferson City, Missouri.
Duncan, J. R., and C. Diaz-Granados
  2000 Of Masks and Myths. *Midcontinental Journal of Archaeology* 25:1–26.
  2004 Empowering the SECC: The "Old Woman" and Oral Tradition. In *The Rock-Art of Eastern North America: Capturing Images and Insight,* edited by C. Diaz-Granados and J. R. Duncan, 190–215. University of Alabama Press, Tuscaloosa.
Durham, W. T.
  1969 *The Great Leap Westward: A History of Sumner County, Tennessee from Its Beginnings to 1805.* Sumner County Public Library Board, Gallatin, Tenn.
Dye, D. H.
  1998 An Overview of Walls Engraved Pottery in the Central Mississippi Valley. In *Changing Perspectives on the Archaeology of the Central Mississippi Valley,* edited by M. J. O'Brien and R. C. Dunnell, 80–98. University of Alabama Press, Tuscaloosa.
  2004 Art, Ritual, and Chiefly Warfare in the Mississippian World. In *Hero, Hawk, and Open Hand: American Indian Art of the Ancient Midwest and South,* edited by R. F. Townsend and R. V. Sharp, 190–205. Art Institute of Chicago and Yale University Press, New Haven.
  2007 Ritual, Medicine, and the War Trophy Iconographic Theme in the Mississippian Southeast. In *Ancient Objects and Sacred Realms: Interpretations of Mississippian Iconography,* edited by F. K. Reilly III and J. F. Garber, 289–320. University of Texas Press, Austin.
Dye, D. H., and A. King
  2008 Desecrating the Sacred Ancestor Temples: Chiefly Conflict and Violence in the American Southeast. In *North American Indigenous Warfare and Ritual*

Violence, edited by R. J. Chacon and R. G. Mendoza, 160–181. University of Arizona Press, Tucson.

Earle, T.
1997   *How Chiefs Come to Power: The Political Economy in Prehistory.* Stanford University Press, Palo Alto.

Eggan, F. R.
1952   The Ethnological Cultures and Their Archaeological Backgrounds. In *Archaeology of the Eastern United States,* edited by J. B. Griffin, 35–45. University of Chicago Press, Chicago.

Emerson, T. E.
1982   *Mississippian Stone Images in Illinois.* Circular 6. Illinois Archaeological Survey, Urbana.
1989   Water, Serpents, and the Underworld: An Explanation into Cahokia Symbolism. In *The Southeastern Ceremonial Complex: Artifacts and Analysis,* edited by P. Galloway, 45–92. University of Nebraska Press, Lincoln.
1997a   *Cahokia and the Archaeology of Power.* University of Alabama Press, Tuscaloosa.
1997b   Cahokian Elite Ideology and the Mississippian Cosmos. In *Cahokia Domination and Ideology in the Mississippian World,* edited by T. R. Pauketat and T. E. Emerson, 190–228. University of Nebraska Press, Lincoln.
2003   Crossing Boundaries between Worlds: Changing Beliefs and Mortuary Practices at Cahokia. *Wisconsin Archeologist* 84:73–80.

Emerson, T. E., R. E. Hughes, M. R. Hynes, and S. U. Wisseman
2003   The Sourcing and Interpretation of Cahokia-Style Figurines in the Trans-Mississippi South and Southeast. *American Antiquity* 68(2):287–313.

Ensor, B. E.
2001   Disproportionate Clan Growth in Crow-Omaha Societies: A Kinship-Demographic Model for Explaining Settlement Hierarchies and Fissioning in the Prehistoric U.S. Southeast. *North American Archaeologist* 23:309–337.
2003   Kinship and Marriage among the Omaha, 1886–1902. *Ethnology* 42:1–14.

Esarey, D.
1987   Mississippian Spider Gorgets. Paper presented at the Thirty-second Annual meeting of the Midwest Archaeological Conference, Milwaukee.
1990   Style Geography and Symbolism of Mississippian Spiders. Paper presented at the annual meeting of the Southeastern Archaeological Conference, Mobile, Ala.

Ferguson, R. B.
1972   The Arnold Village Site: Excavations of 1965–1966. In *The Middle Cumberland Culture,* edited by R. B. Ferguson, 1–49. Publications in Anthropology No. 3. Vanderbilt University, Nashville.

Fisher-Carroll, R.
2001   Environmental Dynamics of Drought and Its Impact on Sixteenth-Century Indigenous Populations in the Central Mississippi Valley. Ph.D. dissertation, University of Arkansas, Fayetteville.

Fletcher, A. C., and F. La Flesche
1911   *The Omaha Tribe.* Bureau of American Ethnology 27. Government Printing Office, Washington, D.C.
1992   *The Omaha Tribe.* Reprint. University of Nebraska Press, Lincoln.

Fletcher, R.
  1891   Review of *The Antiquities of Tennessee and the Adjacent States. American Anthropologist* 4(1):83–86.
Foster, M. K.
  1996   Language and the Culture History of North America. In *Handbook of North American Indians: Languages*, vol. 17, edited by I. Goddard, 64–110. Smithsonian Institution, Washington, D.C.
Fowler, M. L.
  1996   The Mound 72 and Woodhenge 72 Area of Cahokia. *Wisconsin Archeologist* 77:36–59.
  2003   Cahokia: Circles, Calendars, Corn, and Cosmology. *Wisconsin Archeologist* 84:57–73.
Fundaburk, E. L., and M. D. Fundaburk Foreman (editors)
  1957   *Sun Circles and Human Hands: The Southeastern Indians—Art and Industries.* Privately printed, Luverne, Ala. (Reprint: American Bicentennial Museum, Fairhope, Ala., 1985.)
Galloway, P. (editor)
  1989   *The Southeastern Ceremonial Complex: Artifacts and Analysis.* University of Nebraska Press, Lincoln.
Gartner, W. C.
  1996   Archeoastronomy as Sacred Geography. *Wisconsin Archeologist* 77:128–150.
Gill, S. D., and I. F. Sullivan
  1992   *Dictionary of American Mythology.* Oxford University Press, New York and Oxford.
Gillies, J. L.
  1998   A Preliminary Study of Moundville Hemphill Representational Engraved Ceramic Art Style. M.A. thesis, Department of Anthropology, University of Alabama, Tuscaloosa.
Goddard, I.
  1996   The Classification of the Native Languages of North America. In *Handbook of North American Indians: Languages*, vol. 17, edited by I. Goddard, 290–323. Smithsonian Institution, Washington, D.C.
Grant, C.
  1981   *Rock Art of the American Indian* (1967). Reprint: Promontory Press, New York.
Greenblatt, S.
  1989   Towards a Poetics of Culture. In *The New Historicism*, edited by H. A. Vesser, 1–14. Routledge Press, New York.
Griffin, J. B.
  1944   The De Luna Expedition and the "Buzzard Cult" in the Southeast. *Washington Academy of Sciences* 34(42):99–303.
  1952   An Interpretation of the Place of Spiro in Southeastern Archaeology. *Missouri Archaeologist* 14:89–106.
  1961   Relationships between the Caddoan Area and the Mississippi Valley. *Bulletin of the Texas Archeological Society* 31:27–37.
  1981   The Acquisition of a Little Known Haul from the Lower Mississippi Valley. *Geoscience and Man* 22:51–55.

1995   A Search for Oneota Cultural Origins: A Personal Retrospective Account. In *Oneota Archaeology: Past, Present, and Future*, edited by W. Green, 9–18. Office of the State Archaeologist, Report 20. University of Iowa, Iowa City.

Grim, J. A.
1983   *The Shaman: Patterns of Siberian and Ojibway Healing*. University of Oklahoma Press, Norman.

Hagar, S.
1906   Cherokee Star Lore. In *Boas Anniversary Volume: Anthropological Papers Written in Honor of Franz Boas*, 354–366. G. E. Stechert, New York.

Hall, R. L.
1989   The Cultural Background of Mississippian Symbolism. In *The Southeastern Ceremonial Complex, Artifacts and Analysis: The Cottonlandia Conference*, edited by P. Galloway, 239–278. University of Nebraska Press, Lincoln.

1997   *An Archaeology of the Soul: North American Indian Belief and Ritual*. University of Illinois Press, Urbana.

2004   The Cahokia Site and Its People. In *Hero, Hawk, and the Open Hand: American Indian Art of the Ancient Midwest and South*, edited by R. F. Townsend and R. V. Sharp, 92–103. Art Institute of Chicago and Yale University Press, New Haven.

2005   Contradictions as a Source of Historical Perspective: Examples from the Symbolism of Camp Circle and Sacred Poles. Native Symbolic Expression around the Great Lakes and Beyond, edited by W. A. Fox and R. J. Pearce. Special issue of *Ontario Archaeology* 79/80:115–126.

Hally, D. J.
2007   Mississippian Shell Gorgets in Regional Perspective. In *Southeastern Ceremonial Complex: Chronology, Content, Context*, edited by A. King, 185–231. University of Alabama Press, Tuscaloosa.

Hally, D. J., and J. B. Langford, Jr.
1988   *Mississippi Period Archaeology of the Georgia Valley and Ridge Province*. Laboratory of Archaeology Series Report 25. University of Georgia, Athens.

Hally, D. J., and J. Rudolph
1986   *Mississippian Period Archaeology of the Georgia Piedmont*. Laboratory of Archaeology Series, Report 24. University of Georgia, Athens.

Hally, D. J., M. T. Smith, and J. B. Langford
1990   The Archaeological Reality of De Soto's Coosa. In *Columbian Consequences*, edited by D. H. Thomas, 121–138. Smithsonian Institution Press, Washington, D.C.

Hamilton, H.
1952   The Spiro Mound. *Missouri Archaeologist* 14:17–86.

Hamilton, H. W., J. T. Hamilton, and E. F. Chapman
1974   *Spiro Mound Copper*. Memoir No. 11. Missouri Archaeological Society, Columbia.

Hathcock, R.
1976   *Ancient Indian Pottery of the Mississippi River Valley*. Hurley Press, Camden, Ark.

1983   *The Quapaw and Their Pottery: A Pictorial Study of Proto-Historic Pottery of the Quapaw Indians, 1650–1750 A.D.* Hurley Press, Camden, Ark.

1988 *Ancient Indian Pottery of the Mississippi River Valley: A Pictorial Study of Prehistoric Pottery of the Mississippian Culture, 1000–1650 A.D.* 2nd ed. Walsworth, Marceline, Mo.

Helms, M.
1979 *Ancient Panama: Chiefs in Search of Power.* University of Texas Press, Austin.
1993 *Craft and the Kingly Ideal: Art, Trade, and Power.* University of Texas Press, Austin.

Henning, D. R.
2001 Plains Village Tradition: Eastern Periphery and Oneota Tradition. In *Handbook of North American Indians: Plains*, vol. 13, part 1, edited by R. J. DeMallie, 222–233. Smithsonian Institution, Washington, D.C.
2005 The Evolution of the Plains Tradition. In *North American Archaeology*, edited by T. R. Pauketat and D. D. Loren, 61–186. Blackwell, Hoboken.
2007 Continuity and Change in the Eastern Plains, A.D. 800–1700: An Examination of Exchange Patterns. In *Plains Village Archaeology: Bison-Hunting Farmers in the Central and Northern Plains*, edited by S. A. Ahler and M. Kay, 67–82. University of Utah Press, Salt Lake City.

Henson, B. B.
1986 Art in Mud and Stone: Mud Glyphs and Petroglyphs in the Southeast. In *The Prehistoric Native American Art of Mud Glyph Cave*, edited by C. H. Faulkner, 81–108. University of Tennessee Press, Knoxville.

Hilgeman, S. L.
1985 Lower Ohio Valley Negative Painted Ceramics. *Midcontinental Journal of Archaeology* 10(2):195–213.
1991 Angel Negative Painted Design Structure. *Midcontinental Journal of Archaeology* 16(1):3–33.
2000 *Pottery and Chronology at Angel.* University of Alabama Press, Tuscaloosa.

Holley, G. R., and J. A. Koepke
2003 Harmony in the Cahokian World. *Wisconsin Archeologist* 84:155–164.

Hollinger, R. E.
2005 Conflict and Culture Change in the Late Prehistoric and Early Historic American Midcontinent. Ph.D. dissertation, University of Illinois, Urbana-Champaign.

Holmes, W. H.
1883 Art in Shell of the Ancient Americans. Bureau of American Ethnology, Annual Report 2, pp. 185–305. Government Printing Office, Washington, D.C.
1885 Ancient Pottery of the Mississippi Valley: A Study of the Collection of the Davenport Academy. *Proceedings of the Davenport Academy of Natural Sciences* 4:123–196.
1886a Ancient Pottery of the Mississippi Valley. Bureau of American Ethnology, Annual Report 4, 361–436. Government Printing Office, Washington, D.C.
1886b Ancient Pottery of the Mississippi Valley: A Study of the Collection of the Davenport Academy of Sciences. *Proceedings of the Davenport Academy of Natural Sciences* 4:123–196.
1891 The Thruston Tablet. *American Anthropologist* 4(2):161–196.
1903 *Aboriginal Pottery of the Eastern United States.* Bureau of American Ethnology Annual Report 20. Government Printing Office, Washington, D.C.

1906　Certain Notched or Scalloped Stone Tablets of the Moundbuilders. *American Anthropologist* (n.s.) 8:101–108.

Howard, J. H.
  1968　*The Southeastern Ceremonial Complex and Its Interpretation*. Memoir No. 6. Missouri Archaeological Society, Columbia.

Huddleston, E.
  1962a　Viking Stone's Defacement Deplored. *Nashville Banner*, 16 August 1962.
  1962b　Vikings on Cumberland? Tablet Hints It Is So. *Nashville Banner*, 16 September 1962.

Hudson, C. M.
  1976　*The Southeastern Indians*. University of Tennessee Press, Knoxville.

Hudson, C. M., M. Smith, D. Hally, R. Polhemus, and C. DePratter
  1985　Coosa: A Chiefdom in the Sixteenth-Century Southeastern United States. *American Antiquity* 50(4):723–737.

Hultkrantz, Å.
  1953　*Conceptions of the Soul among North American Indians*. Monograph Series 1. Ethnological Museum, Stockholm, Sweden.
  1973　*Prairie and Plains Indians*. Brill, Leiden.

Jones, B. C.
  1982　Southern Cult Manifestations at the Lake Jackson Site, Leon County, Florida: Salvage Excavation of Mound 3. *Midcontinental Journal of Archaeology* 7:3–44.

Jones, J.
  1869　The Aboriginal Mound Builders of Tennessee. *American Naturalist* 3(2):57–73.
  1876　*Explorations of the Aboriginal Remains of Tennessee*. Smithsonian Contributions to Knowledge 22(2). Smithsonian Institution, Washington, D.C.

Jones, K. R.
  1980　The Archaeological Work of Joseph Jones: Manuscript Materials in the Tulane University Library. *Human Mosaic* 14(1):22–35.

Keeler, C., and L. R. Verrill
  1962　The Viking Boat Finale. *Bulletin of the Georgia Academy of Sciences* 20(3–4):29–36.

Kehoe, A. B.
  2007　Osage Texts and Cahokia Data. In *Ancient Objects and Sacred Realms: Interpretations of Mississippian Iconography*, edited by F. K. Reilly III and J. F. Garber, 246–261. University of Texas Press, Austin.

Kelly, J. C.
  1985　Gates P. Thruston and His Collection. In *Art and Artisans of Prehistoric Middle Tennessee: The Gates P. Thruston Collection of Vanderbilt University Held in Trust by the Tennessee State Museum*, edited by S. D. Cox, 3–18. Tennessee State Museum, Nashville.

Kelly, J. E.
  1991　The Evidence for Prehistoric Exchange and Its Implications for the Development of Cahokia. In *New Perspectives on Cahokia: Views from the Periphery*, edited by J. B. Stoltman, 65–92. Prehistory Press, Madison.
  1996　Redefining Cahokia: Principles and Elements of Community Organization. *Wisconsin Archeologist* 77:97–119.

2003 The Context of the Post Pit and Meaning of the Sacred Pole at the East St. Louis Mound Group. *Wisconsin Archeologist* 84:107–125.

Kelly, J. E., J. A. Brown, and L. S. Kelly

2008 The Context of Religion at Cahokia: The Mound 34 Case. In *Religion in the Material World*, edited by L. Fogelin, 297–318. Occasional Paper No. 36. Southern Illinois University, Carbondale.

King, A.

2003 *Etowah: A Political History of a Chiefdom Capital*. University of Alabama Press, Tuscaloosa.

2004 Power and the Sacred: Mound C and the Etowah Chiefdom. In *Hero, Hawk, and Open Hand: American Indian Art of the Ancient Midwest and South*, edited by R. F. Townsend and R. V. Sharp, 150–165. Art Institute of Chicago and Yale University Press, New Haven.

2007a *Southeastern Ceremonial Complex: Chronology, Content, Context*. University of Alabama Press, Tuscaloosa.

2007b The Southeastern Ceremonial Complex: From Cult to Complex. In *Southeastern Ceremonial Complex: Chronology, Content, Context*, edited by A. King, 1–14. University of Alabama Press, Tuscaloosa.

2007c Whither SECC? In *Southeastern Ceremonial Complex: Chronology, Content, Context*, edited by A. King, 251–258. University of Alabama Press, Tuscaloosa.

Kinietz, V. (editor)

1938 *Meearmeear Traditions: C. C. Trowbridge's Account*. Occasional Papers of the Museum of Anthropology No. 7. University of Michigan, Ann Arbor.

Klippel, W. E., and W. M. Bass (editors)

1984 *Averbuch: A Mississippian Manifestation in the Nashville Basin*. 2 vols. Department of Anthropology, University of Tennessee, Knoxville.

Kneberg, M.

1959 Engraved Shell Gorgets and Their Associations. *Tennessee Archaeologist* 15(1):1–39.

Knight, V. J., Jr.

1986 The Institutional Organization of Mississippian Religion. *American Antiquity* 51:675–687.

1989 Some Speculations on Mississippian Monsters. In *The Cottonlandia Conference*, edited by P. Galloway, 205–210. University of Nebraska Press, Lincoln.

2006 Farewell to the Southeastern Ceremonial Complex. *Southeastern Archaeology* 25(1):1–5.

2007 A Preliminary Assessment of Moundville Engraved "Cult" Designs from Potsherds. In *The Southeastern Ceremonial Complex: Chronology, Content, Context*, edited by A. King, pp. 151–164. University of Alabama Press, Tuscaloosa.

Knight, V. J., Jr. (editor)

1996 *The Moundville Expeditions of Clarence Bloomfield Moore*. University of Alabama Press, Tuscaloosa.

Knight, V. J., Jr., J. A. Brown, and G. E. Lankford

2001 On the Subject Matter of Southeastern Ceremonial Complex Art. *Southeastern Archaeology* 20:129–141.

Knight, V. J., Jr., and J. A. Franke
- 2007 Identification of a Moth/Butterfly Supernatural in Mississippian Art. In *Ancient Objects and Sacred Realms: Interpretations of Mississippian Iconography*, edited by F. K. Reilly III and J. F. Garber, 136–151. University of Texas Press, Austin.

Knight, V. J., Jr., and V. Steponaitis (editors)
- 1998 *Archaeology of the Moundville Chiefdom.* Smithsonian Institution Press, Washington, D.C.

Kraft, H. C.
- 1986 *The Lenape.* New Jersey Historical Society, Newark.

Krebs, W. P., P. Futato, E. M. Futato, and V. J. Knight, Jr.
- 1986 *Ten Thousand Years of Alabama Prehistory: A Pictorial Resume.* Bulletin 8. Alabama State Museum of Natural History, Tuscaloosa.

Krieger, A. D.
- 1945 An Inquiry into Supposed Mexican Influence on a Prehistoric "Cult" in the Southern United States. *American Anthropologist* 47:483–515.

Lacefield, H. L.
- 1995 A Preliminary Study of Moundville Engraved Pottery. M.A. thesis, Department of Anthropology, University of Alabama, Tuscaloosa.

La Flesche, F.
- 1918 Researches among the Osage. *Smithsonian Miscellaneous Collections* 70:110–113.
- 1921 *The Osage Tribe: Rite of the Chiefs; Sayings of the Ancient Men.* Bureau of American Ethnology. Annual Report 36. Government Printing Office, Washington, D.C.
- 1925 *The Osage Tribe: Rite of Vigil.* Bureau of American Ethnology. Annual Report 39. Government Printing Office, Washington, D.C.
- 1932 *A Dictionary of the Osage Language.* Bureau of American Ethnology Bulletin 109. Government Printing Office, Washington, D.C.
- 1939 *War Ceremony and Peace Ceremony of the Osage Indians.* Bureau of American Ethnology Bulletin 101. Government Printing Office, Washington, D.C.
- 1975 *A Dictionary of the Osage Language* (1932). Reprint. Indian Tribal Series, Phoenix, Ariz.

Lankford, G. E.
- 1984 Saying Hello to the Timucua. *Mid-America Folklore* 12(1):7–23.
- 1987 *Native American Legends.* August House, Little Rock.
- 1988 Saying Hello in the Mississippi Valley. *Mid-America Folklore* 16(1):24–39.
- 2004 World on a String: Some Cosmological Components of the Southeastern Ceremonial Complex. In *Hero, Hawk, and Open Hand: American Indian Art of the Ancient Midwest and South*, edited by R. F. Townsend and R. V. Sharp, 207–217. Art Institute of Chicago and Yale University Press, New Haven.
- 2006 Some Southwestern Influences in the Southeastern Ceremonial Complex. *Arkansas Archeologist* 45:1–26.
- 2007a The Great Serpent in Eastern North America. In *Ancient Objects and Sacred Realms: Interpretations of Mississippian Iconography*, edited by F. K. Reilly III and J. F. Garber, 107–135. University of Texas Press, Austin.

2007b The "Path of Souls": Some Death Imagery in the Southeastern Ceremonial Complex. In *Ancient Objects and Sacred Realms: Interpretations of Mississippian Iconography*, edited by F. K. Reilly III and J. F. Garber, 174–212. University of Texas Press, Austin.

2007c *Reachable Stars: Patterns in the Ethnoastronomy of Eastern North America.* University of Alabama Press, Tuscaloosa.

2007d Some Cosmological Motifs in the Southeastern Ceremonial Complex. In *Ancient Objects and Sacred Realms: Interpretations of Mississippian Iconography*, edited by F. K. Reilly III and J. F. Garber, 8–38. University of Texas Press, Austin.

2008a *Looking for Lost Lore: Studies in Folklore, Ethnology, and Iconography.* University of Alabama Press, Tuscaloosa.

2008b Riders in the Sky. In *Looking for Lost Lore: Studies in Folklore, Ethnology, and Iconography*, 139–162. University of Alabama Press, Tuscaloosa.

Lankford, G. E., and D. H. Dye

2007 Conehead Effigies: A Distinctive Artform of the Northern Part of the Lower Mississippi Valley. Paper presented at the Mississippian Iconographic Workshop, Texas State University, San Marcos.

Larson, L.

1959 A Mississippian Headdress from Etowah, Georgia. *American Antiquity* 25(1):109–112.

Leader, J. M.

1988 Technological Continuities and Specialization in Prehistoric Metalwork in the Eastern United States. Ph.D. dissertation, Department of Anthropology, University of Florida, Gainesville.

2004 The Evidence for Copper Working at Etowah. Paper presented at the annual meeting of the Southeastern Archaeological Conference, St. Louis, Mo.

2008 Copper Working at Etowah: Continuing Analyses of Manufacture, Repair and Reuse at a Major Site in the Mississippian Southeast. Paper presented at the annual meeting of the Southeastern Archaeological Conference, Charlotte, N.C.

Liberty, M. P., W. R. Wood, and L. Irwin

2001 Siouan Languages. In *Handbook for North American Indians, Volume 13–Plains*, edited by R. J. DeMallie, 399–415. Smithsonian Institution, Washington, D.C.

Lorant, S. (editor)

1965 *The New World: The First Pictures of America.* Revised ed. Duell, Sloan and Pearce, New York.

MacCauley, C.

1887 *The Seminole Indians of Florida.* Bureau of American Ethnology Annual Report No. 5:469–532. Smithsonian Institution, Washington, DC.

MacCurdy, G. G.

1913 Shell Gorgets from Missouri. *American Anthropologist* 15:395–414.

Mainfort, R. C., Jr.

1999 Late Period Phases in the Central Mississippi Valley: A Multivariate Approach. In *Arkansas Archaeology: Essays in Honor of Dan and Phyllis Morse*, edited by R. C. Mainfort, Jr., and M. D. Jeter, 143–167. University of Arkansas Press, Fayetteville.

2001 The Late Prehistoric and Protohistoric Periods in the Central Mississippi Valley. In *Societies in Eclipse: Archaeology of the Eastern Woodlands Indians, A.D. 1400–1700*, edited by D. S. Brose, C. W. Cowan, and R. C. Mainfort, Jr., 173–189. Smithsonian Press, Washington, D.C.

2004 Arkansas History and Prehistory in Review. *Arkansas Archeological Society, Field Notes* 318:3–10.

Mallery, G.
1886 *Pictographs of the North American Indians: A Preliminary Paper.* Bureau of American Ethnology Annual Report 4. Smithsonian Institution, Washington, D.C.

1893 *Picture-Writing of the American Indians.* Bureau of American Ethnology Annual Report 10. Smithsonian Institution, Washington, D.C.

Marceaux, S., and D. H. Dye
2007 Hightower Anthropomorphic Marine Shell Gorgets and Duck River Sword-Form Flint Bifaces, Middle Mississippian Ritual Regalia in the Southern Appalachians. In *Southeastern Ceremonial Complex: Chronology, Content, Context*, edited by A. King, 165–183. University of Alabama Press, Tuscaloosa.

Mathews, J. J.
1961 *The Osages: Children of the Middle Waters.* University of Oklahoma Press, Norman.

Matthews, W.
1897 *Navaho Myths.* Houghton, Mifflin, Boston. (Reprint: University of Utah Press, Salt Lake City, 1994.)

Mellown, R. O.
1976 *The Art of the Alabama Indians.* University of Alabama Art Gallery, Tuscaloosa.

Mochon, M. J.
1972 Language, History and Prehistory: Mississippian Lexico-Reconstruction. *American Antiquity* 37(4):478–503.

Mooney, J.
1900 *Myths of the Cherokee.* Bureau of American Ethnology Annual Report 19. Government Printing Office, Washington, D.C.

Moore, C. B.
1901 Certain Aboriginal Remains of the Northwest Florida Coast: Part I. *Journal of the Academy of Natural Sciences of Philadelphia* 11:419–497.

1905 Certain Aboriginal Remains of the Black Warrior River. *Journal of the Academy of Natural Sciences of Philadelphia* 13:125–244. (Reprinted in *The Moundville Expeditions of Clarence Bloomfield Moore*, edited by V. J. Knight, Jr., 21–142. University of Alabama Press, Tuscaloosa, 1996.)

1907 Moundville Revisited. *Journal of the Academy of Natural Sciences of Philadelphia* 13:337–405. (Reprinted in *The Moundville Expeditions of Clarence Bloomfield Moore*, edited by V. J. Knight, Jr., 143–224. University of Alabama Press, Tuscaloosa, 1996.)

1910 Antiquities of the St. Francis, White, and Black Rivers, Arkansas. *Journal of the Academy of Natural Sciences of Philadelphia* 14:253–364. (Reprinted in *The Lower Mississippi Valley Expeditions of Clarence Bloomfield Moore*, edited by D. F. Morse and P. A. Morse, 293–402. University of Alabama Press, Tuscaloosa, 1998.)

Moore, M. C. (editor)
　2005　*The Brentwood Library Site: A Mississippian Town on the Little Harpeth River, Williamson County, Tennessee.* Research Series No. 15. Tennessee Division of Archaeology, Nashville.

Moore, M. C., and E. Breitburg (editors)
　1998　*Gordontown: Salvage Archaeology at a Mississippian Town in Davidson County, Tennessee.* Research Series No. 11. Tennessee Division of Archaeology, Nashville.

Moore, M. C., E. Breitburg, K. E. Smith, and M. B. Trubitt
　2006　One Hundred Years of Archaeology at Gordontown: A Fortified Mississippian Town in Middle Tennessee. *Southeastern Archaeology* 25(1):89–109.

Moore, M. C., and K. E. Smith
　2005　Ceramic Artifact Descriptions. In *The Brentwood Library Site: A Mississippian Town on the Little Harpeth River, Williamson County, Tennessee,* edited by M. C. Moore, 143–182. Research Series No. 15. Tennessee Division of Archaeology, Nashville.
　2007　Mississippian Mortuary Pottery from the Nashville Basin: A Reanalysis of the Averbuch Site Ceramic Assemblage. Paper presented at the Southeastern Archaeological Conference, Knoxville, Tenn.
　2009　*Archaeological Expeditions of the Peabody Museum in Middle Tennessee, 1877–1884.* Research Series No. 16. Tennessee Division of Archaeology, Nashville.

Moore, M. C., and K. E. Smith (editors)
　2001　*Archaeological Excavation at the Rutherford-Kizer Site: A Mississippian Mound Center in Sumner County, Tennessee.* Research Series No. 13. Tennessee Division of Archaeology, Nashville.

Moorehead, W. K. (editor)
　2000　*Exploration of the Etowah Site in Georgia: The Etowah Papers.* University Press of Florida, Gainesville. (Reprint of 1932 edition by Yale University Press.)

Morelli, G.
　1892　*Italian Painters: Critical Studies of Their Works.* Translated by C. J. Foulkes. John Murray, London.

Morse, D. F.
　1990　The Nodena Phase. In *Towns and Temples along the Mississippi,* edited by D. H. Dye and C. A. Cox, 69–97. University of Alabama Press, Tuscaloosa.

Morse, D. F., and P. A. Morse
　1983　*Archaeology of the Central Mississippi Valley.* Academic Press, New York.
　1989　The Rise of the Southeastern Ceremonial Complex in the Central Mississippi Valley. In *The Southeastern Ceremonial Complex: Artifacts and Analysis,* edited by P. Galloway, 41–44. University of Nebraska Press, Lincoln.
　1990　Emergent Mississippian in the Central Mississippi Valley. In *The Mississippian Emergence,* edited by B. D. Smith, 153–173. Smithsonian Institution Press, Washington, D.C.
　1996a　Changes in Interpretation in the Archaeology of the Central Mississippi Valley since 1983. *North American Archaeologist* 17:1–35.
　1996b　Northeast Arkansas. In *Prehistory of the Central Mississippi Valley,* edited by C. H. McNutt, 119–135. University of Alabama Press, Tuscaloosa.

2000 Social Interaction between the American Bottom of Cahokia and the Crowley's Ridge Lowland Division of the Lower Mississippi River A.D. 800–1200. In *Mounds, Modoc, and Mesoamerica: Papers in Honor of Melvin L. Fowler*, edited by S. R. Ahler, 347–360. Scientific Papers, vol. 28. Illinois State Museum, Springfield.

Muller, J.
1966a Archaeological Analysis of Art Styles. *Tennessee Archaeologist* 22:1:25–39.
1966b An Experimental Theory of Stylistic Analysis. Ph.D. dissertation, Department of Anthropology, Harvard University, Cambridge, Mass.
1979 Structural Studies of Art Styles. In *The Visual Arts, Plastic and Graphic*, edited by J. M. Cordwell, 139–212. Mouton Publishers, The Hague.
1989 The Southern Cult. In *The Southeastern Ceremonial Complex: Artifacts and Analysis*, edited by P. Galloway, 11–26. University of Nebraska, Lincoln.
1995 Regional Interaction in the Later Southeast. In *Native American Interactions: Multiscalar Analyses and Interpretations in the Eastern Woodlands*, edited by M. S. Nassaney and K. E. Sassaman, 317–340. University of Tennessee Press, Knoxville.
1997a *Mississippian Political Economy*. Plenum Press, New York.
1997b Review of *Shell Gorgets: Styles of the Late Prehistoric and Protohistoric Southeast*, by Jeffrey P. Brain and Philip Phillips. Peabody Museum of Archaeology and Ethnology, Harvard. *Southeastern Archaeology* 16(2):176–178.
1999 Southeastern Interaction and Integration. In *Great Towns and Regional Polities in the Prehistoric American Southwest and Southeast*, edited by J. E. Neitzel, 143–164. Amerind Foundation, Dragoon, Ariz.
2007 Prolegomena for the Analysis of the Southeastern Ceremonial Complex. In *Southeastern Ceremonial Complex: Chronology, Content, Context*, 15–37. University of Alabama Press, Tuscaloosa.

Müller, W.
1956 *Die Religionen der Waldlandindianer Nordamerikas*. Dietrich Reimer, Berlin.

Murdock, G. P.
1955 North American Social Organization. *Davidson Journal of Anthropology* 1:85–97.

Myer, W. E.
1917 The Remains of Primitive Man in Cumberland Valley, Tennessee. *Proceedings of the 19th International Congress of Americanists (1915)* (Washington, D.C.): 96–102.
1928 Pictograph Slabs of America. *Proceedings of the 20th International Congress of Americanists (1922, vol. 2)* (Rio de Janeiro):97–105.
n.d. Stone Age Man in the Middle South. MS 2566, National Anthropological Archives, Smithsonian Institution, Washington, D.C.

Myers, T. P.
1992 *The Birth and Rebirth of the Omaha*. University of Nebraska State Museum, Lincoln.

O'Brien, M. J.
1994 *Cat Monsters and Head Pots: The Archaeology of Missouri's Pemiscot Bayou*. University of Missouri Press, Columbia.

O'Brien, M. J., and R. C. Dunnell
   1998   *Changing Perspectives on the Archaeology of the Central Mississippi Valley.* University of Alabama Press, Tuscaloosa.
Orr, K.
   1951   Change at Kincaid: A Study of Cultural Dynamics. In *Kincaid: A Prehistoric Illinois Metropolis,* edited by F.-C. Cole, R. Bell, J. Bennett, J. Caldwell, N. Emerson, R. MacNeish, K. Orr, and R. Willis, 293–359. University of Chicago Press, Chicago.
Panofsky, E.
   1939   *Studies in Iconology: Humanistic Themes in the Art of the Renaissance.* Oxford University Press, Oxford.
   1960   *Renaissance and Renascences in Western Art.* Stockholm, Sweden.
Parker, M.
   1949   A Study of the Rocky Creek Pictoglyph. *Tennessee Archaeologist* 5(2):13–17.
Pauketat, T. R.
   2004   *Ancient Cahokia and the Mississippians.* Cambridge University Press, Cambridge.
Pauketat, T. R., and T. E. Emerson
   1991   The Ideology of Authority and the Power of the Pot. *American Anthropologist* 93:919–941.
   1997   Cahokian Political Economy. In *Cahokia: Domination and Ideology in the Mississippian World,* edited by T. R. Pauketat and T. E. Emerson, 30–51. University of Nebraska Press, Lincoln.
Payne, C.
   2007   Middle-Period Mississippian in the St. Francis Basin. Paper presented at the Annual Meeting of the Midsouth Archaeological Conference, Memphis.
Penney, D. W.
   1985   Continuities of Imagery and Symbolism in the Art of the Woodlands. In *Ancient Art of the American Woodland Indians,* D. S. Brose, J. A. Brown, and D. W. Penney, 147–198. Abrams, New York.
Perino, G.
   1960   The Piasa Design in Arkansas. *Central States Archaeological Journal* 7:146–150.
Phillips, P.
   1939   Introduction to the Archaeology of the Mississippi Valley. Ph.D. dissertation, Harvard University, Cambridge, Mass.
   1940   Middle American Influences on the Archaeology of the Southeastern United States. In *The Maya and Their Neighbors,* 349–367. D. Appleton Century, New York.
   1970   *Archaeological Survey in the Lower Yazoo Basin, Mississippi, 1949–1955.* Papers of the Peabody Museum of American Archaeology and Ethnology, vol. 60. Harvard University, Cambridge, Mass.
Phillips, P., and J. A. Brown
   1978   *Pre-Columbian Shell Engravings from the Craig Mound at Spiro, Oklahoma, Part 1* (paperback edition). Peabody Museum Press, Cambridge, Mass.
   1984   *Pre-Columbian Shell Engravings from the Craig Mound at Spiro, Oklahoma, Part 2* (paperback edition). Peabody Museum Press, Cambridge, Mass.

Phillips, P., J. A. Ford, and J. B. Griffin
　1951　*Archaeological Survey in the Lower Mississippi Alluvial Valley, 1940–1947*. Papers of the Peabody Museum of Archaeology and Ethnology, vol. 25. Harvard University, Cambridge, Mass. (Reprint: University of Alabama Press, Tuscaloosa, 2003.)

Ponziglione, P. M., S.J.
　1897　The Osages and Father John Schoenmakers, S.J. Interesting Memoirs Collected from Legends, Traditions and Historical Documents. 4 vols. Handwritten manuscript on file at Midwest Jesuit Archives, St. Louis, Mo.

Power, S. C.
　2004　*Early Art of the Southeastern Indians: Feathered Serpents and Winged Beings*. University of Georgia Press, Athens.

Powers, W. K.
　1975　*Oglala Religion*. University of Nebraska Press, Lincoln.

Prentice, G.
　1986　An Analysis of the Symbolism Expressed by the Birger Figurine. *American Antiquity* 51(2):239–266.

Price, J. E., and C. R. Price
　1979　*An Inventory and Assessment of the Leo Anderson Collection of Archaeological and Historical Specimens*. Reports of Investigations No. 256. Center for Archaeological Research, Southwest Missouri State University, Springfield.

Putnam, F. W.
　1878　Archaeological Explorations in Tennessee. *Eleventh Annual Report of the Trustees of the Peabody Museum* 2(2):305–360.

Radin, P.
　1948　*Winnebago Hero Cycles: A Study in Aboriginal Literature*. Indiana University Publications in Anthropology and Linguistics, Bloomington.
　1950　The Basic Myth of the North American Indians. *Eranos-Jahrbuch* 17:359–419.

Rankin, R. L.
　1988　Quapaw: Genetic and Areal Affiliations. In *In Honor of Mary Haas: From the Haas Festival Conference of Native American Linguistics*, edited by W. Shipley, 629–650. Mouton de Gruyter, Berlin.

Reed, A.
　1984a　The Averbuch Ceramic Assemblage: Description and Interpretation. In *Averbuch: A Mississippian Manifestation in the Nashville Basin*, edited by W. E. Klippel and W. M. Bass, vol. 2, chap. 7, 1–50. Department of Anthropology, University of Tennessee, Knoxville.
　1984b　Radiocarbon Dates. In *Averbuch: A Mississippian Manifestation in the Nashville Basin*, edited by W. E. Klippel and W. M. Bass, vol. 2, chap. 2, 1–8. Department of Anthropology, University of Tennessee, Knoxville.

Reents-Budet, D.
　1984　The Averbuch Ceramic Assemblage: Description and Interpretation. *In Averbuch: A Mississippian Manifestation in the Nashville Basin*, edited by W. E. Klippel and W. M. Bass, vol. 2, chap. 7, 1–50. Department of Anthropology, University of Tennessee, Knoxville.
　1994　Classic Maya Pottery Painting. In *Painting the Maya Universe: Royal Ceramics of the Classic Period*, edited by D. Reents-Budet, 2–35. Duke University Press, Durham.

Rees, M. A.
- 1997 Coercion, Tribute and Chiefly Authority: The Regional Development of Mississippian Political Culture. *Southeastern Archaeology* 16:113–133.

Reilly, F. K., III
- 2001 Gorget Imagery as Evidence for Specific Ritual Activity at Etowah, Georgia. Paper presented at the annual meeting of the Society for American Archaeology, New Orleans.
- 2004 People of Earth, People of Sky: Visualizing the Sacred in Native American Art of the Mississippian Period. In *Hero, Hawk, and Open Hand: American Indian Art of the Ancient Midwest and South*, edited by R. F. Townsend and R. V. Sharp, 125–137. Art Institute of Chicago and Yale University Press, New Haven.
- 2007a By Their Vestments Ye Shall Know Them: Ritual Regalia and Cult-Bearers in Mississippian Art. Paper presented at the Annual Meeting of the Southeastern Archaeological Conference, Knoxville, Tenn.
- 2007b Crafting the Sacred: Mississippian "Talleres" and the Acquisition of Esoteric Knowledge. Paper presented at the Annual Meeting of the Southeastern Archaeological Conference, Knoxville, Tenn.
- 2007c The Petaloid Motif: A Celestial Symbolic Locative in the Shell Art of Spiro. In *Ancient Objects and Sacred Realms: Interpretations of Mississippian Iconography*, edited by F. K. Reilly III and J. F. Garber, 39–55. University of Texas, Austin.

Reilly, F. K., III, and J. F. Garber (editors)
- 2007 *Ancient Objects and Sacred Realms: Interpretations of Mississippian Iconography*. University of Texas, Austin.

Revard, C.
- 1987 Traditional Osage Naming Ceremonies: Entering the Circle of Being. In *Recovering the Word, Essays on Native American Literature*, edited by B. Swann and A. Krupat, 446–466. University of California Press, Berkeley.

Ridington, R.
- 1987 Omaha Images of Renewal. *Canadian Journal of Native Studies* 7(2):149–164.

Ridington, R., and D. Hastings (In'aska)
- 1997 *Blessing for a Long Time: The Sacred Pole of the Omaha Tribe*. University of Nebraska Press, Lincoln.

Roberts, M. N., and A. F. Roberts
- 1996 *Memory, Luba Art and the Making of History*. Museum of African Art, New York.

Sabo, G., III
- 1993 Indians and Spaniards in Arkansas: Symbolic Action in the Sixteenth Century. In *The Expedition of Hernando de Soto West of the Mississippi, 1541–1543: Proceedings of the De Soto Symposia 1988 and 1990*, edited by G. A. Young and M. P. Hoffman, 192–209. University of Arkansas Press, Fayetteville.
- 1995 Rituals of Encounter: Interpreting Native American Views of European Explorers. In *Cultural Encounters in the Early South: Indians and Europeans in Arkansas*, compiled by J. Whayne, 76–87. University of Arkansas Press, Fayetteville.

Sabo, G., III, and D. Sabo (editors)
- 2005 *Rock Art in Arkansas*. Popular Series No. 5. Arkansas Archeological Survey, Fayetteville.

Salzer, R. J.
   1987   Preliminary Report on the Gottschall Site (47IA80). *Wisconsin Archaeologist* 68(4):419–472.
   2005   The Gottschall Site: 3,500 Years of Ideological Continuity and Change. Native Symbolic Expression around the Great Lakes and Beyond, edited by W. A. Fox and R. J. Pearce. Special issue of *Ontario Archaeology* 79/80:109–114.

Salzer, R. J., and G. Rajnovich
   2001   *The Gottschall Rockshelter: An Archaeological Mystery*. Prairie Smoke Press, St. Paul.

Sawyer, J. A.
   2009   The Mississippian Period Crib Theme: Context, Chronology, and Iconography. M.A. thesis, Department of Anthropology, Texas State University, San Marcos.

Schambach, F.
   1993   Some New Interpretations of Spiroan Culture History. In *Archaeology of Eastern North America: Papers in Honor of Stephen Williams*, edited by J. B. Stoltman, 187–230. Archaeological Report No. 25. Mississippi Department of Archives and History, Jackson.

Schatte, K. E.
   1997   Stylistic Analysis of the Winged Serpent Theme at Moundville. M.A. thesis, Department of Anthropology, University of Alabama, Tuscaloosa.
   1998   Identification of Some Thematic Variation in the Iconography of Moundville, Alabama. *Journal of the Steward Anthropological Society* 2(1–2):113–127.

Schnell, F. T., V. J. Knight, Jr., and G. S. Schnell
   1981   *Cemochechobee: Archaeology of a Mississippian Ceremonial Center on the Chattahoochee River*. University Press of Florida, Gainesville.

Schroedl, G. F., C. C. Boyd, Jr., and R. P. S. Davis, Jr.
   1990   Explaining Mississippian Origins in East Tennessee. In *The Mississippian Emergence*, edited by B. D. Smith, 175–196. Smithsonian Institution, Washington, D.C.

Schutz, N. W.
   1975   The Study of Shawnee Myth in an Ethnographic and Ethnohistorical Perspective. Ph.D. dissertation, Indiana University, Bloomington.

Sears, W.
   1964   The Southeastern United States. In *Prehistoric Man in the New World*, edited by J. D. Jennings and E. Norbeck, 259–287. University of Chicago Press, Chicago.

Sharp, R. V.
   2007   Iconographical Investigation of a Female Mortuary Cult Figure in the Ceramics of the Cumberland Basin. Paper presented at the Southeastern Archaeological Conference, Knoxville, Tenn.
   2008   Mississippian Regalia: From the Natural World to the Beneath World. Paper presented at the Southeastern Archaeological Conference, Charlotte, N.C.

Skinner, A. S.
   1913   *Social Life and Ceremonial Bundles of the Menomini Indians*. Anthropological Papers of the American Museum Of Natural History 13(1). Trustees of the American Museum of Natural History, New York.

1923   *Observations on the Ethnology of the Sauk Indians.* Public Museum of Milwaukee Bulletin 5. Trustees of the Museum of Milwaukee, Milwaukee. (Reprint: Greenwood Press, Westport, Conn., 1970.)

Sloan, K.
2007   *A New World: England's First View of America.* University of North Carolina Press, Chapel Hill.

Smith, K. E.
1991   The Mississippian Figurine Complex and Symbolic Systems of the Southeastern United States. In *The New World Figurine Project, Volume 1,* edited by T. Stocker, 123–138. Research Press, Provo.
1992   The Middle Cumberland Region: Mississippian Archaeology in North Central Tennessee. Ph.D. dissertation, Department of Anthropology, Vanderbilt University, Nashville.
1993   Archaeology at Old Town (40WM2): A Mississippian Mound-Village Center in Williamson County, Tennessee. *Tennessee Anthropologist* 18(1):27–44.
1998   Gordontown in Historical Perspective. In *Gordontown: Salvage Archaeology at a Mississippian Town in Davidson County, Tennessee,* edited by M. C. Moore and E. Breitburg, 13–19. Research Series No. 11. Tennessee Division of Archaeology, Nashville.
2001   Human Figurines as Messengers Communicating with Past, Present, and Future Cultures. In *The New World Figurine Project, Volume 2,* edited by T. Stocker and C. L. Otis Charlton, 271–286. Research Press, Provo.

Smith, K. E., and E. L. Beahm
2007   Placing the Castalian Springs Chiefdom in Time and Space. Paper presented at the 64th annual meeting of the Southeastern Archaeological Conference, Knoxville.

Smith, K. E., and J. V. Miller
2009   *Speaking with the Ancestors: Mississippian Stone Statuary of the Tennessee-Cumberland Region.* University of Alabama Press, Tuscaloosa.

Smith, K. E., M. C. Moore, and S. T. Rogers
2009   The Enigma of the Noel Cemetery: Thruston's "Ancient Metropolis of the Stone Grave Culture." Paper presented at the annual meeting of the Southeastern Archaeological Conference, Mobile, Ala.

Smith, K. E., and M. B. Trubitt
1998   The Gordontown Ceramic Assemblage from a Regional Perspective. In *Gordontown: Salvage Archaeology at a Mississippian Town in Davidson County, Tennessee,* edited by M. C. Moore and E. Breitburg, 129–131. Research Series No. 11. Tennessee Division of Archaeology, Nashville.

Smith, M. T., and J. B. Smith
1989   Engraved Shell Masks in North America. *Southeastern Archaeology* 8(1):9–18.

Smith, T. S.
1995   *The Island of the Anishnaabeg: Thunderers and Water Monsters in the Traditional Ojibwe Lifeworld.* University of Idaho Press, Moscow.

Spinden, H. J.
1931   Indian Symbolism. In *Introduction to American Indian Art* (2):1–18. Exposition of Indian Tribal Arts, New York.

Stahle, D. W., M. K. Cleveland, and J. G. Hehr
  1985   A 450-Year Drought Reconstruction for Arkansas, United States. *Nature* 316:530–532.
Stahle, D. W., E. R. Cook, M. K. Cleveland, M. D. Therrell, D. M. Meko, H. D. Grissino-Mayer, E. Wilson, and B. H. Luckman
  2000   Epic 16th Century Drought over North America. *EOS* 81:121–125.
Steelman, K. L., M. W. Rowe, R. F. Boszhardt, and J. R. Southon
  2001   Radiocarbon Age Determination of a Rock Painting at Arnold/Tainter Cave, Wisconsin. *Midcontinental Journal of Archaeology* 26(1):121.
Steponaitis, V. P.
  1983   *Ceramics, Chronology, and Community Patterns: An Archaeological Study at Moundville.* Academic Press, New York.
  2007   Foreword. In *Ancient Objects and Sacred Realms: Interpretations of Mississippian Iconography,* edited by F. K. Reilly III and J. F. Garber, ix–x. University of Texas Press, Austin.
Steponaitis, V. P., and D. T. Dockery III
  1997   The Geological Source of the Emerald Effigy Pipes and Its Implications for Mississippian Exchange. Paper presented at the annual meeting of the Southeastern Archaeological Conference, Baton Rouge, La.
Steponaitis, V. P., and V. J. Knight, Jr.
  2004   Moundville Art in Historical and Social Context. In *Hero, Hawk, and Open Hand: American Indian Art of the Ancient Midwest and South,* edited by R. F. Townsend and R. V. Sharp, 166–181. Art Institute of Chicago and Yale University Press, New Haven.
Sullivan, L. P.
  2001   *Dates for Shell Gorgets and the Southeastern Ceremonial Complex in the Chickamauga Basin of Southeastern Tennessee.* Research Notes No. 19. McClung Museum, University of Tennessee, Knoxville.
  2007   Shell Gorgets, Time, and the Southeastern Ceremonial Complex in Southeastern Tennessee. In *Southeastern Ceremonial Complex: Chronology, Content, Context,* edited by A. King, 88–106. University of Alabama Press, Tuscaloosa.
Swanton, J. R.
  1928   *Religious Beliefs and Medical Practices of the Creek Indians.* Bureau of American Ethnology Bulletin 43. Government Printing Office, Washington, D.C.
  1929   *Myths and Tales of the Southeastern Indians.* Bureau of American Ethnology Bulletin 88. Government Printing Office, Washington, D.C.
  1946   *The Indians of the Southeastern United States.* Bureau of American Ethnology Bulletin 137. Government Printing Office, Washington, D.C. (Reprint: Smithsonian Institution Press, Washington, D.C., 1979.)
  1995   *Myths and Tales of the Southeastern Indians* (1929). University of Oklahoma Press, Norman.
Sylestine, C., H. K. Hardy, and T. Montler (editors)
  1993   *Dictionary of the Alabama Language.* University of Texas Press, Austin.
Tavaszi, M. M.
  2004   Stylistic Variation in Ceramic Mortuary Vessels from Upper Nodena (3MS4) and Middle Nodena (3MS3). M.A. thesis, University of Arkansas, Fayetteville.

Thomas, C.
  1894   Report on the Mound Explorations of the Bureau of Ethnology. Twelfth Annual Report, Smithsonian Institution. Bureau of Ethnology, Washington, D.C.
Thompson, S.
  1929   Tales of the North American Indians. Indiana University Press, Bloomington.
Thruston, G. P.
  1890   The Antiquities of Tennessee and the Adjacent States. Robert Clarke, Cincinnati.
  1897   Engraved Shell Gorgets and Flint Ceremonial Implements. American Antiquarian and Oriental Journal 19:96–100.
Thwaites, R. G. (editor)
  1898   The Jesuit Relations and Related Documents. Vol. 120. Burrows Brothers, Cleveland. (Reprint: Pageant, n.p., 1959.)
Tixier, V.
  1940   Tixier's Travels on the Osage Prairies. Edited by J. F. McDermott. University of Oklahoma Press, Norman.
Townsend, R. F., and R. V. Sharp (editors)
  2004   Hero, Hawk, and Open Hand: American Indian Art of the Ancient Midwest and South. Art Institute of Chicago and Yale University Press, New Haven.
Traxel, W. L.
  2004   Footprints of the Welsh Indians: Settlers in North America before 1492. Algora Publishing, New York.
Trubitt, M. B.
  1998   Ceramic Artifact Descriptions. In Gordontown: Salvage Archaeology at a Mississippian Town in Davidson County, Tennessee, edited by M. C. Moore and E. Breitburg, 61–128. Research Series No. 11. Tennessee Division of Archaeology, Nashville.
Van Straten, R.
  1994   An Introduction to Iconography. Translated by Patricia de Man. Gordon and Breach, Langhorne, Pa.
Verrill, L. R., and C. Keeler
  1961   A Viking Saga in Tennessee? Bulletin of the Georgia Academy of Sciences 19(4):78–82.
Voegelin, C. F.
  1936   The Shawnee Female Deity. Yale University Publications in Anthropology No. 10. Yale University Press, New Haven.
Voegelin, C. F., and E. W. Voegelin
  1944   The Shawnee Female Deity in Historical Perspective. American Antiquity 46(3):370–375.
Walker, C. P.
  2004   Prehistoric Art of the Central Mississippi Valley. In Hero, Hawk, and Open Hand: American Indian Art of the Ancient Midwest and South, edited by R. F. Townsend and R. V. Sharp, 219–230. Art Institute of Chicago and Yale University Press, New Haven.
Wallace, A. F. C.
  1956   Revitalization Movements. American Anthropologist 58:264–281.
Waring, A. J., Jr.
  1948   Brief on Symposium on the "Southern Cult." American Antiquity 14(2):151–153.

1968a An Engraved Monolithic Axe from Georgia. In *The Waring Papers: The Collected Works of Antonio J. Waring, Jr.*, edited by S. Williams, 78–80. Papers of the Peabody Museum of Archaeology and Ethnology, Harvard University. Peabody Museum, Cambridge, Mass.

1968b The Southern Cult and Muskhogean Ceremonial: General Considerations. In *The Waring Papers: The Collected Papers of Antonio J. Waring, Jr.*, edited by S. Williams, 30–69. Papers of the Peabody Museum of Archaeology and Ethnology, Harvard University. Peabody Museum, Cambridge, Mass.

1968c Summary of the 1954 Moundville Meeting. In *The Waring Papers: The Collected Papers of Antonio J. Waring, Jr.*, edited by S. Williams, 90–92. Papers of the Peabody Museum of Archaeology and Ethnology, Harvard University. Peabody Museum, Cambridge, Mass.

Waring, A. J., Jr., and P. Holder
1945 A Prehistoric Ceremonial Complex in the Southeastern United States. *American Anthropologist* 47(1):1–34. (Reprinted in Williams 1968:9–29.)

Warren, R. E.
2007 Thunderbird Effigies from Plains Village Sites in the Northern Great Plains. In *Plains Village Archaeology: Bison-Hunting Farmers in the Central and Northern Plains*, edited by S. A. Ahler and M. Kay, 107–125. University of Utah Press, Salt Lake City.

Webb, W. S., and R. S. Baby
1957 *The Adena People No. 2*. Ohio Historical Society, Columbus.

Webb, W. S., and D. L. DeJarnette
1942 *An Archaeological Survey of the Pickwick Basin in the Adjacent Portions of the States of Alabama, Mississippi, and Tennessee*. Bureau of American Ethnology Bulletin 129. Government Printing Office, Washington, D.C.

Weinstein, R. A.
1984 The Rosedale and Shellhill Discs: "Southern Cult" Evidence from Southeastern Louisiana. *Louisiana Archaeology* 11:65–88.

Welch, P. E.
1991 *Moundville's Economy*. University of Alabama Press, Tuscaloosa.

Wellmann, K.
1979 *A Survey of North American Indian Rock Art*. Akademische Druck- u. Verlagsanstalt, Graz, Austria.

Welsch, R. L.
1981 *Omaha Tribal Myths and Trickster Tales*. Swallow Press, Chicago.

Wesler, K. W.
1991 Ceramics, Chronology, and Horizon Markers at Wickliffe Mounds. *American Antiquity* 56:278–290.

Whitney, C., V. P. Steponaitis, and J. J. W. Rogers
2002 A Petrographic Study of Moundville Palettes. *Southeastern Archaeology* 21:227–234.

Willey, G. R.
1948 The Cultural Context of the Crystal River Negative-Painted Style. *American Antiquity* 13(4):325–328.

1964 *An Introduction to American Archaeology, Volume 1: North and Middle America*. Prentice-Hall, Englewood Cliffs, N.J.

Willey, G. R., and P. Phillips
   1944   Negative-Painted Pottery from Crystal River, Florida. *American Antiquity* 10(2):173–185.
Willey, G. R., and J. A. Sabloff
   1993   *A History of American Archaeology.* 3rd ed. W. H. Freeman, New York.
Williams, S.
   1980   Armorel: A Very Late Phase in the Lower Mississippi. *Southeastern Archaeological Conference Bulletin* 21:72–81.
Williams, S. (editor)
   1968   *The Waring Papers: The Collected Works of Antonio J. Waring, Jr.* Papers of the Peabody Museum of Archaeology and Ethnology, Harvard University. Peabody Museum, Cambridge, Mass.
Williams, S., and J. P. Brain
   1983   *Excavations at the Lake George Site, Yazoo County, Mississippi, 1958–1960.* Peabody Museum of Archaeology and Ethnology No. 74. Harvard University, Cambridge, Mass.
Williams, S., and J. M. Goggin
   1956   The Long-Nosed God Mask in the Eastern United States. *Missouri Archaeologist* 18:1–72.
Willoughby, C. C.
   1932   Notes on the History and Symbolism of the Muskhogeans and the People of Etowah. In *Etowah Papers: Exploration of the Etowah Site in Georgia,* edited by W. K. Moorehead, 7–105. Yale University Press, New Haven.
   1952   Textile Fabrics from the Spiro Mound. The Spiro Mound, edited by H. W. Hamilton. Special issue of *Missouri Archaeologist* 14:107–118.
Wilson, G.
   2008   *The Archaeology of Everyday Life at Early Moundville.* University of Alabama Press, Tuscaloosa.
Wilson, T.
   1896   *The Swastika: The Earliest Known Symbol and Its Migrations, with Observations on the Migration of Certain Industries in Prehistoric Times.* U.S. National Museum, Annual Report for 1894, 757–1011. U.S. Federal Printing Office, Washington, D.C.
Wimberly, S. B.
   1956   A Review of Moundville Pottery. *Southeastern Archaeological Conference Newsletter* 5(1):17–20.
Wissler, C.
   1914   Material Cultures of the North American Indians. *American Anthropologist* 16:447–505.
Yelton, J. K.
   1998   A Different View of Oneota Taxonomy and Origins. *Wisconsin Archaeologist* 79(2):268–283.
Zurel, R.
   2002   Signature Theory and Meaning of Hopewell Icons. Paper presented at the Annual Meeting of the Midwest Archaeological Conference, Columbus, Ohio.

CONTRIBUTORS

James A. Brown is a professor of anthropology at Northwestern University.

Carol Diaz-Granados is a research associate in the Department of Anthropology, Washington University.

James R. Duncan is past director, Missouri State Museum, teaching at Lindenwood University in St. Louis.

David H. Dye is a professor of archaeology, Department of Earth Sciences, University of Memphis.

James F. Garber is a professor of anthropology at Texas State University, San Marcos.

Adam King is a research associate professor in the South Carolina Institute of Archaeology and Anthropology at the University of South Carolina.

Vernon James Knight, Jr., is a professor of anthropology at the University of Alabama.

George E. Lankford is a professor emeritus of folklore at Lyon College in Batesville, Arkansas.

F. Kent Reilly III is a professor and director of the Center for the Study of the Arts and Symbolism of Ancient America, Department of Anthropology, Texas State University, San Marcos.

Robert V. Sharp is executive director of publications at the Art Institute of Chicago.

Vincas P. Steponaitis is a professor of anthropology and director of the Research Laboratories of Archaeology at the University of North Carolina.

INDEX

NOTE: *Italic page numbers refer to illustrations and tables.*

Alabama people, 31, 246, 247
Algonkian cosmology, 18, 63n.1, 244, 245
Anheuser site, Missouri, *81, 82*
Anna site, 230, *231*
anthropomorphs: Braden art style, 300–301, 305, 306, 309; and ceramic art, 127–128; and engraved shell, 282–283, *282, 284,* 290–291; and rock-art, 67, 79–80, *79*
Averbuch site, Tennessee, 177–180, *178, 180,* 195
axis mundi, 20, 25–26, 27, 31

Belle Meade site, Tennessee, *185,* 195, 264–265, *264*
Bennett style, 280, *281*
Berry site, Missouri, 126–127, *126*
bilobed arrow emblem: and Dhegiha Sioux cosmology, 54–55; and embossed copper, 286; Hemphill style, 169, 172, *214,* 216–217, *216;* Hightower style, 303, *303;* and rock-art, 66, 67, 68, 72, 84, *85, 88,* 89, 92, 94, 171; and Thruston Tablet, 168–169, *171*
Birdman: and Braden art style, 38; and Cahokia, 73, 75, 314; and ceramic art, 128; and Dhegiha Sioux cosmology, 52, 53, 60, 61–62; and Etowah, 319, 320; Hightower style, 282, 286, 288, 290–291, 292, 299, 315, 316; and Raptors, 313–314, 316, 317–318; in rock-art, 50, 67, 75–76, 92; and Rogan Plates, 66, 290, 314, 315
birds: iconography of, 240–241; and rock-art, 75–76; Thunderbirds, 6, 47, 60–61. *See also* Crested Bird; hawk; Raptors
Birger Figurine, 27, 50–51, 56, 91, *91*
Braden art style: anthropomorphs, 300–301, 305, 306, 309; and Dhegiha Sioux cosmology, 18, 51–52, 62, 63; individualizing theme, 293; and Muskogean cosmology, 18, 39; and Spiro engraved shells, 37, 38, 203; and Thruston Tablet, 164, 166, 168, 169, 172, 173. *See also* Classic Braden style
Brain, Jeffrey, 94, 233, 254, 256–260, 295, 299
Brannon Disk, 225–226, *225*
Brown, Ian W., 192, 196–197n.1
Brown, James, 9, 10–11, 12, 13, 66, 89, 146, 153, 170, 172, 173, 202, 207, 230, 236, 254, 261, 286, 289–290, 299, 308, 313, 314, 317, 318
Buchner, C. Andrew, 101, 107
Burns, Louis, 57, 58, 83–84
Bushnell Ceremonial Cave, Missouri, 67, 82, *82, 83, 84, 85,* 86
Bushnell-Meissner site, Missouri, 83, *84, 85,* 86

Cagle Lake site, Missouri, 265, *266*
Cahokia: beaker, *85,* 86; and Birdman, 73, 75, 314; and ceramic art, 105–106, 107, 108, 118; and Classic Braden style,

28, 38, 39; and depiction of deities, 51; and Dhegiha Sioux people, 20, 41; iconography of, 67, 84, 87, 93; mounds of, 27–28, 66, 68, 71, 74; stone figurines, 37–38; Woodhenge, 43
calumet ceremony, 50, 317
Carson Red on Buff ceramics, 102, 263
Castalian Springs, Tennessee: iconography of, 67, 68, 87, 88; and Thruston Tablet, 139, 169, 174–175n.1, 176n.10
Castalian Springs Gorget, 169, 170, 172–173
Castalian Springs Tablet, 143
centering theme: Hemphill style, 219, 220, 221–226, 221, 222, 223, 224, 225, 233, 236; Hightower style, 280, 281, 288–289
center-symbols-and-bands theme, Hemphill style, 208, 208, 214, 215, 233, 238n.4
ceramic art: and Classic Braden style, 99–100; and effigies, 105, 106, 107, 110, 112, 113–114, 114, 173, 177–179, 178, 179, 180; and Great Serpent, 110, 112, 118, 120, 125, 129–130; Holmes's classification of, 101–102, 103; motifs of, 104, 107, 109–110, 111, 113, 114, 115, 116, 124, 125, 127, 242; and Moundville, 170, 171, 207–215, 208, 236, 251, 266–269, 267; Phillips's classification of, 102–103; and swirl-cross, 86, 130, 131, 251, 263–269, 264, 265, 267, 274–275; and Underwater Panther, 125–126, 126, 128–129, 129, 130, 131, 133; and utilitarian ritual ware, 100–101, 107–110, 113, 116–117, 120, 122
Cherokee people, 28, 246
Children of the Sun epic, 31, 76, 163, 164
Childs, Terry, 123, 127
circle motifs, 83–84, 84, 110
Citico style, 284–285, 284, 290, 292, 293
Classic Braden style: and Cahokia, 28, 38, 39; court-card design in, 31; defining, 203; and embossed copper, 285–286, 291; and Etowah, 290; and Moundville, 234, 235; and ogee motif, 90; and Osage cosmology, 27, 28; and regionalism, 99–100; and rock-art, 76; and Rogan Plates, 66, 290, 314, 315; and Southeastern Ceremonial Complex, 16; and Thruston Tablet, 173. *See also* Braden art style
Commerce Eagle petroglyph, 67, 75
copper: Hemphill style, 213, 219, 220, 221–223, 221, 222, 287, 287; Hightower style, 279, 285–288, 286, 289, 291; local exceptions, 227–228, 228, 230; Moundville pendants and gorgets, 253, 269, 270, 271; and swirl-cross, 222, 222, 251, 252, 253, 269–271, 273, 287, 287
Cox Mound, Tennessee, 252, 254–255, 262, 263
Craig Mound, Oklahoma, 9, 89, 132, 133
Craig style: and Braden art style, 39; defining, 203; and Moundville, 234, 235; and Path of the Souls Cycle, 59; and serpents, 307, 308; and swirl-cross, 255–256, 261; and Thruston Tablet, 164, 165, 166, 168, 169, 170, 172
Crested Bird: Hemphill style, 207, 208, 210, 211–212, 218, 219, 233; and shell gorgets, 241, 241, 252, 255–256; and swirl-cross, 252, 255–256, 267–268, 267
cross-in-circle motifs: and ceramic art, 108, 110, 187; and engraved shell, 280, 281; and rock-art, 66, 67, 68, 72, 84, 85, 86–87, 94
cult, use of term, 4–12, 15
cupules motif, and rock-art, 84, 85
Curtiss, Edwin, 189, 191–192, 193, 194
Cushman Gorget, 170, 173

Deer Run Shelter site, Missouri, 79, 80, 80, 91
de Soto, Hernando, 8, 293
Dhegiha Sioux cosmology: and Braden art style, 18, 51–52, 62, 63; cosmograms in imagery, 52–62, 53; and earth-sky division, 37, 45–50, 62–63; iconographic representations of, 20; and rock-art, 92–93; Sacred Camp Circle as repre-

sentation of, 43–45, *44*, 49–50; and star people, 25, 26, 28, 29; and success in war, 41–42; symbolism of, 50–52, 60, 63. *See also* Osage cosmology
Dhegiha Sioux people, 19–20, 37, 39–41, 42, 43–50
Diaz-Granados, Carol, 41, 54, 72
Donnell site, Missouri, *81*, 82
Dorsey, George, 28
Dorsey, J. Owen, cosmic chart of, 19, 21, 23–24, 30, 32n.1, 42, 49
Douglass Gorget, Missouri, 87, *88*
Drooker, Penelope, 146, 181, 183
Duncan, James, 41, 54, 61–62, 72
Dye, David, 173, 237n.1, 301, 306

Earth and Fertility Cycle, 51–52
Earthmother: and Braden art style, 38; and Dhegiha Sioux cosmology, 50–51, 53, 55–56, 60, 61, 62, 63; in rock-art, 50; and spider, 57
Eddyville-style shell gorgets, 37, 281–282, 290
elites, 28, 100–101, 120, 311–312, 315, 316, 318, 319
elite women: Mark of Honor tattoo, 47, *48*; and spider tattoos, 29–30, 33n.6, 38, 57, 58, *58*
Emerson, Thomas, 12, 51, 107
Etowah, Georgia: Hemphill style, 230, 238n.6; Hightower style, 285–286, 288–289, 292–293, 294, 298–309; iconography of, 66, 67, 68, 72, 84, 87; Malden Plates, 314; and Raptors, 249, 313–320, *314*; and regionalism, 7–10; Rogan Plates from, 10, 28, 66, 67, 68, 72, 73, 74, 75–76, 87, 88, 92, 169, 286, *286*, 290, 292, 314, *314*; shell gorget, 166; social changes in, 116; and swirl-cross, 251
Evening Star, 24–25, 26, 31
face mask, 285, *285*
female effigy vessels/figurines: and Averbuch site, 177–179, *178*, *180*; cloaklike garment, 180–181, 183–184, 196, 197n.3; hairstyles, *178*, *180*, *182*, *183*, 184, *185*, 189, 192; humpbacked versus straight-backed, 179–180, 184, 185, 186, 187, 189, 191, 192, 193; neck knob, *178*, *180*, *183*, 184; negative-painted pattern, 177, *178*, 179, 180, *182*, 183–184, *183*, 186, 187–189, *190*, 191, *191*, 192, 193, *194*, 195, 198n.12; renderings of, 181, *182*; sex-specific characteristics, 185–186, 197nn.5,6,7
Fletcher, A. C., 25, 42, 43, 48, 49, 56
foot motifs, 81–82, *81*, 84, *85*, 92
Foreman, Mary Fundaburk, 64, 144
Frumet site, Missouri, 83, *84*
Fundaburk, Emma Lila, 64

Garber, James F., 283, 315
Geometric style, 259–260, *260*, 262
Ghost Dance, 5–6
Gillies, Judith, 203, 205, 208, 213
Glass site, Mississippi, 230, *231*
Gottschall Rockshelter, Wisconsin, 38, 73, 166, *167*, 168
Gower site, Tennessee, *194*, 195
Gray's Farm site, Tennessee, 191–195, *194*, 198n.11
Great Panther, 119
Great Serpent: and ceramic art, 110, *112*, 118, 120, 125, 129–130; and cosmology, 119, 240; and eye-surrounds, 126–127; and Hemphill style, 121, 122, *122*, 123, 209, 238n.2; and Osage cosmology, 29; and swirl-cross, 264–266, *264*, *265*, 269, 272
Great Sky Serpent, 29
Griffin, James, 5, 8, 9, 19
Grizzlyman, 53, 57

hafted celt, 84, *85*, 92
Hall, Robert, 12, 47, 49, 54, 317
hand/arm motifs: and ceramic art, 124, 242; Hemphill style, 203, *204*, *206*, *207*, 208, *208*, 213, 223, 226; and rock-art, 80–81, *80*
hawk: as animal form of Morning Star, 52, 55, 63; and Osage cosmology, 26, 55; and rock-art, 67, 72–73, *73*, 75–76, 86, 92; and Rogan Plates, 66, 67; and symbolism, 60–61

He'dewachi ceremony, and Omaha people, 43–49, *44*, *47*, 63n.2
Hemphill style: and bilobed arrow, 169, 172, 214, 216–217, *216*; context of, 235–237; and cross-in-circle, 86; defining, 202–205; design structures, 208–209; embossed copper, 213, 219, 220, 221–223, *221*, *222*; engraved, incised, and painted pottery, 207–215, *208*, *210*, *214*, *218*, *236*; engraved shell, 232–235, *232*, *234*; engraved stone, 213, 219, 220, 221, 223–227, *223*, *224*, *225*, *227*, *231*; and Great Serpent, 121, 122, *122*, *123*, 209, 238n.2; hands, 203, 204, 206, 207, 208, *208*, 213, 223, 226; human heads, *216*, *217*, 226, *227*, *232*, *233*; local exceptions, 217, *218*, 219, 227–230, *228*, *229*; and Path of the Souls Cycle, 59, 122–123, 212, 213, 235–236; Pensacola images compared to, *206*, *207*; Raptors, 206, 207, 208, *208*, *210*, 212–213, *218*, 219, 238n.3; serpent heads, 203–204, *205*; skulls, 202, 203, 205, 208, 213, 225; and Underwater Spirit, 91, *91*; Walls images compared to, *206*, *207*, 212, 213, 215, 237n.1; winged serpents, 207, *208*, 209, *210*
Hero Twins: and Gottschall Rockshelter, 166; and Hightower style, 282–283, 284, 285, 290, 291–292, 293, 315; and Osage cosmology, 26–27, 28; and Raptor, 316; and Thruston Tablet, 162–164, 168, 172, 173
Hidatsa people, 25, 28, 29, 196
Hightower style: Dances in Mortal Combat, 300, 301, *310*, 311; Dances with Heads, 300, 301–302, *307*, *310*, 311; Dances with Mothra, 299–301, *300*, 305, *310*, 311, 318; Dances with Snakes, 304, 305–309, *308*, *310*, 311; defining, 294–295; embossed copper, 279, 285–288, *286*, *289*, *291*; engraved shell, 279, 280–285, *281*, *282*, *283*, *284*, *285*, 293; human figural representations, 295–309, 311; Morning Star, 304–305, *304*, *306*, *310*, 311; political geography and history of, 288–293; and regalia, 297–298, 302–303, *304*, *311*; Seated in Display, 302–303, *303*; shell gorgets, 165, *166*, 168, 169, *170*, 171–172, 173, 281, *281*, 294, 295, 298–309, *300*, *303*, *304*, *310*, *311*, *314*, *318*; temporal placement of, 295–296; vignettes, 309, *310*, *311*, 315
Hixon style, 263, 283, *283*, 290, 291, 292
Holder, Preston, 4, 5, 6–7, 10, 11, 12, 13, 14, 18, 65, 66, 81, 94
Hollywood Mound, Georgia, *307*, 308
Holmes, William Henry: classificatory work of, 101–102; and swirl-cross, 254; and Thruston Tablet, 139–142, *140*, *143*, *144*, *146*, *147*, *148*, *150*, *151*, *152*, 159–160, 175nn.3,4
Hon-ga A-hiu-ton, 22, 25, 26, 27, 32n.2
Howard, James, 7–8, 94, 255, 280
Hull style, 252, 256–258, 262
Hultkrantz, Åke, 45–46, 243–244
human figurals: and Hightower style, 295–309, 311; and swirl-cross, 260–261, *260*. *See also* anthropomorphs
Huron people, 244

iconographic art: diversity in, 3, 4, 6, 7–8, 9, 10–11, 13, 16; and regionalism, 7–8, 9, 11, 12, 14–15, 16, 17; unity in, 3–7, 8, 9, 12, 15, 16, 17

Jones, Joseph, 175n.4, 186–187

Kansa people, 18, 20, 26, 39, 40, 92
Keeler, Clyde, 144, 147, 148, 161, 174n.1
Kent site, Arkansas, 128–129, *129*
Kersey site, Missouri, 124, *125*
King, Adam, 15, 296, 298, 315
Kneberg, Madeline, 254, 296, 299
Knight, V. J., Jr., 12, 13, 15, 16, 120, 318
Krieger, Alex, 4, 39, 70, 201

Lacefield, Hyla, 203, 211, 236
La Flesche, Francis, 22, 25, 33n.3, 39, 42, 43, 48, 49, 56, 57
Lake George site, 230, *231*
Lankford, George, 18, 30, 49, 58, 59, 103, 119, 122, 124, 133, 173, 209, 212, 233–

234, 235, 238–239n.9, 280, 281, 283, 284, 296, 313, 315, 317–318
Leader, Jonathan, 238n.6, 287, 291
Lévi-Strauss, Claude, 45
Lewis, T. M. N., 143, 175n.6
Lick Creek style, 283, *284*, 292
Long-Nosed God maskettes, 52, 54, 72, 74, 76, 318
Lost Creek site, Missouri, *66*, *85*, *86*, 89
Lower Mississippi Valley: ceramic art of, 99–117, 118, 123–130, 133–134; Hemphill style, 230, *231*; population of, 101, 116, 123; social changes in, 104–105, 116; stone palettes, 230, *231*, 238n.7; stone sculpture of, 131, 133

mace, 87, *88*, 89, 92, 227, *227*
Maddin Creek site, Missouri, motifs of, *66*, *67*, *77*, 77, 79, *79*, 80, *80*, 81, 82, 83, 84, *85*, *88*, 89–90, *90*, 92
Mallery, Garrick, 139, 142, 143, 144, 147, 148, 175nn.3,4
Mandan people, 25, 28, 76, 196
Mathews, John Joseph, 28, 29–30
Matthews, William, 21, 22, 23–24, 25, 26, 30, 32n.1, 33n.4
McAdams style, 256–258, *257*
McKern, W. C., 5, 6
Middle Mississippi Valley, 64, 65, 92, 94, 102
Mississippian Ideological Interaction Sphere (MIIS), 31, 64, 65, 71–72, 93, 94
Mississippian period, archaeological sites of, *xii*
Mitchell site, Missouri, 79, *79*
Moore, C. B., 217, 267, 269
Moorehead, Warren, 287
Moorehead style, *281*, 283
Morning Star: abilities of, 317; and Dhegiha Sioux cosmology, 26, 51, 52, 54–55, 56, 62, 63; Hightower style, 304–305, *304*, 306, *310*, *311*; and Osage cosmology, 24, 27, 31, 38, 42, 49, 314; and rock-art, 72, 73, 79
Morning Star Cycle, 51–52, 54–55, 56
Morse, Dan, 12, 104, 105–108, 109

Morse, Phyllis, 12, 104, 105–108, 109
Mortar Figure pipe, 56
Moundville, Alabama: bottle with Mothra imagery, 319, *319*; and ceramic art, 170, 171, 207–215, 208, 236, 251, 266–269, *267*; copper pendants and gorgets, 253, 269, *270*, *271*; and Great Serpent, 120–123; motifs of, 66, 67, 68, 77, 80, 84, 86, 87, *88*, 89, 90, 92, 169, 170, 173; and Raptors, 240, 241, 242, 247–250, 313, 317, 318, 320; social changes in, 116; style definitions in, 201–205, 207; and swirl-cross motif, 252, 253, 266–269, *267*, *270*, *271*; and winged serpent motif, 118–119, 121–125, *122*, 130, 133; wooden spider plaque from, 170, 176n.9. *See also* Hemphill style; Rattlesnake Disk, Moundville; Willoughby Disk, Moundville
Muller, Jon, 12, 15, 239n.10, 254, 279–281, 283, 284, 289–291, 295, 296
Muskogean cosmology: and Braden art style, 18, 39; and cult-bringers, 7; and Hemphill style, 236–237; and Path of Souls Cycle, 246, 247; and Raptors, 313, 316–317; and Rogan Plates, 28
Myer, William, 142–143, 144, 149, 174–175nn.1,3,5, 197n.2

Nashville style, 257, 258–259
Natchez people, 18, 28, 246
Noel, Oscar F., 187–188, 189, 192, 193, 195, 198n.8

ogee motif: and ceramic art, 110, 124, *125*, *127*; Hemphill style, 214, 217, 222; Hightower style, 288; and rock-art, 84, *85*, 89–90, *90*
Ojibwa Midé people, *157*, 158–159, *158*, 176n.8
Old-Woman-Who-Never-Dies: and ceramic art, 110, *112*; and deer, 79; and Dhegiha Sioux cosmology, 55; and Osage cosmology, 28–29, 31, 50–51; and rock-art, 70–71; and vulva motifs, 77, 83. *See also* Earthmother
Omaha people: as cognate tribe, 20, 26,

39, 40, 42, 92; and earth-sky division, 23, 46, 49; and He'dewachi ceremony, 43–49, 44, 47, 63n.2; and Mississippi River Valley, 40; and Path of Souls Cycle, 245; Pipe of the Sacred Pole, 52, 54, 54; reconstructed cosmogram of, 47; as representative of Dhegiha Sioux people, 62; Sacred Camp Circle of, 43–45, 44, 49–50; sacred poles of, 25; symbolism of, 51, 56, 60; visual imagery of, 18

oral traditions: and Dhegiha Sioux cosmology, 51, 60; encoding of, 120; and Muskogean cosmology, 18; and Omaha cosmology, 56–57, 61; and Osage cosmology, 18, 28, 31, 61; and rock-art, 65, 72–74, 76, 77, 79–80, 81, 93, 94–95

Osage cosmology: characters in chart, 23–30; Dorsey chart, 19, 21–22, 23–24, 25, 26, 30, 42; iconographic representations of, 19, 20–23, 21, 44, 49, 55, 56, 57, 60, 84; prayers to the sun, 47; RedCorn chart, 21, 21, 22, 23, 26, 30; as representative of Dhegiha Sioux, 62; synthesis of Dorsey and RedCorn charts, 23, 24, 24; tripartite universe in, 42–43; unified dualism as theme of, 31; visual imagery of, 18. *See also* Dhegiha Sioux cosmology

Osage people, 39, 40, 92, 93
Osage Tribal Museum, 27, 29
Otoe people, 39, 40

Panofsky, Erwin, 237, 295
Parker, Malcolm, 143–144, 145, 146, 147, 148, 161
Parkin site, Arkansas, 127, 128, 263, 264
Path of the Souls Cycle: and Birdman, 317, 319–320; and Braden art style, 52; fork in Milky Way, 243, 247–248, 249; and Great Serpent, 119; and Hemphill style, 59, 122–123, 212, 213, 235–236; and Morning Star, 320; and Moundville disk palettes, 87; and ogee, 92; and Raptors, 240, 242, 247, 318, 320; regional variations in, 243, 248–249; rituals associated with, 134; test/decision theme in, 243–247; tribal variants in identity of antagonist/judge, 243–247, 248; and winged serpent, 59–60, 240

Pawnee people, 39, 51, 55, 58
Paydown Deer site, Missouri, 78, 78
Pecan Point site, Arkansas, 127, 128, 129, 130
Peene-Murat site, Missouri, 80, 80, 89, 90
Pemiscot County, Missouri, 90, 90, 91
Perrault winged serpent pipe, 131, 132, 133
Peter Bess Fort, 67, 73, 75
Phillips, Philip, 4, 5, 6, 9, 10, 11, 61, 89, 94, 102, 146, 153, 170, 172, 181, 192–193, 202, 207, 230, 233, 254, 256–261, 295, 298–299, 308

Piasas (water spirits), 59–60, 87, 170, 288
Picture Cave, Missouri: Black Warrior, 74, 76; and Braden art style, 38; dating of, 70, 74, 81; motifs at, 67–68, 73, 73, 76, 78, 78, 80–81, 80, 83, 84, 87, 88, 91, 91, 94; and Osage cosmology, 27, 31; Raptors of, 22; and Thruston Tablet, 168, 169; Underwater Spirit, 70, 76

Pipe of the Sacred Pole, 52, 54, 54, 55
pit and groove motifs, and rock-art, 82–83, 82, 86
Plattin Creek site, Missouri, 77, 77
Pole Star, 27, 49, 63n.2
Ponca people, 18, 20, 26, 39, 40, 92
pottery vessels: bilobed arrow, 88, 89; cross-in-circle, 85, 86; and Underwater Spirit, 90–91, 91. *See also* ceramic art

quadrupeds, and rock-art, 78–79, 78
Quapaw/Arkansas people: as cognate tribe, 20, 39, 40, 92, 93; creation story of, 29; and earth-sky ideology, 23, 44; and Mississippi River Valley, 40; visual imagery of, 18
Quarles, Robert T., 174–175n.1

Radin, Paul, 28, 162
Raptors: and Birdman, 313–314, 316, 317–318; and Etowah, 249, 313–320,

314; Hemphill style, 206, 207, 208, 208, 210, 212–213, 218, 219, 238n.3; Hightower style, 287, 288; and Moundville, 240, 241, 242, 247–250, 313, 317, 318, 320; and Muskogean cosmology, 313, 316–317; in Osage cosmology, 22–23, 25, 316; and Path of the Souls Cycle, 240, 242, 247, 318, 320; and swirl-cross, 261
Rattlesnake Bluff site, Missouri, 76, 77, 87, 88
Rattlesnake Disk, Moundville, 122, 124, 204, 205, 225, 225
RedCorn, Andrew E. "Bud," 19, 21, 21, 23, 24, 26, 30, 33n.4
RedCorn, Jim, 19, 21, 21, 23, 24, 30, 33n.4
Reilly, Kent, 13–14, 51, 56, 57, 59, 61–62, 283, 288, 315, 318
Ridington, Robin, 43, 49–50
Riviera site, Missouri, 81, 82
rock-art: anthropomorphic imagery of, 67, 79–80, 79; Birdman in, 50, 67, 75–76, 92; and Braden art style, 38; contextual aspects of, 65, 68–69; iconography of, 65; motifs of, 70, 71–72, 74–91, 92, 171; and mound sites, 66–68, 93, 94; and oral traditions, 65, 72–74, 76, 77, 79–80, 81, 93, 94–95; and regionalism, 65, 71–72, 75; and Southeastern Ceremonial Complex, 64, 65; temporal aspects of, 69–70, 73, 74
Rocky Hollow site, Missouri, 77, 77, 80
Rogan, John P., 285–286, 301–302, 314
Rosedale Mound, 230, 231

St. Louis Mound Group, 68, 74
St. Louis Riverfront site, Missouri, 81, 82
St. Mary Common Field, Missouri, 67
St. Marys, Missouri, 30, 304, 304, 308
Sawyer, Johann, 280, 288
Schatte, Kevin, 121, 203, 209, 211–212, 236
Schneider site, Missouri, 80, 80
Seminole people, 28, 246–247
serpents: and ceramic art, 118, 123–126, 125; Dances with Snakes, 304, 305–309, 308; and Dhegiha Sioux cosmology, 58–60; Hemphill style, 206, 207; human-headed serpents, 307, 308, 308, 309; Lick Creek style, 283, 284; and Moundville, 67, 218, 219; and rock-art, 76–77, 77; winged serpents, 59–60, 118–119, 121–125, 122, 127–130, 129, 131, 132, 133, 207, 208, 209, 210, 240. See also Great Serpent
Sharp, Robert, 124
Shawnee people, 196, 245
shell gorgets: "balanced" composition in, 31; and Braden art style, 38, 50; and Crested Bird, 241, 241, 252, 255–256; and cross-in-circle motif, 68, 71; Hemphill style, 232–235, 232, 238–239n.9, 239n.10; Hightower style, 165, 166, 168, 169, 170, 171–172, 173, 281, 281, 294, 295, 298–309, 300, 303, 304, 310, 311, 314, 318; and spider iconography, 30, 38; and swirl-cross, 251, 252, 254–263, 257, 260, 273–274
Smith, Kevin, 175n.4, 176n.10, 197nn.4,6, 198n.8
Southeastern Ceremonial Complex (SECC): and Braden art style, 37, 39; centers contributing to, 201; and cult, 4, 6; definition of, 3, 10, 11–14, 15, 16; and regionalism, 16–17, 39, 65, 173; and rock-art, 64, 65, 67, 71–72, 73, 74–75, 81, 84, 86, 93, 94; and Rogan Plates, 66; sites of, 9; transmission of, 7–8
Spanos, Mary, 197n.3
spider: and Dhegiha Sioux cosmology, 57–58, 60; gorgets, 84, 85; Hightower style, 281–282, 281, 289, 290–291, 295, 296; and Osage cosmology, 29, 30; and swirl-cross, 256–258, 257; tattoos, 29–30, 33n.6, 38, 57, 58, 58; wooden plaque from Moundville, 170, 176n.9
Spinden, Herbert, 4
Spiro, Oklahoma: and Classic Braden style, 16; Craig Mound, 9, 89, 132, 133, 299, 307, 308, 309; and female effigy

vessels/figurines, 181, 183; iconography of, 59, 67, 68, 77, 80, 87; mounds of, 66; and Raptors, 249; and regionalism, 7, 8, 9, 10; Resting Warrior pipe, 73–74; and swirl-cross, 251, 252, 255–256

Spiro engraved shells: and Braden art style, 37, 38, 203; Crouching Warrior effigy pipes, 56; and cult, 10, 11; Lightner Cup, 164, 165, 172, 173; motifs of, 73, 75, 84, 85, 88, 89; and skirts, 153; themes of, 39; and Thruston Tablet, 146, 164–165, 165, 167, 168–171; and Underwater Panther, 129, 130, 132, 133; and winged serpent, 133

stone, engraved: Cahokia figurines, 37–38; Hemphill style, 213, 219, 220, 221, 223–227, 223, 224, 225, 227, 231; local exceptions, 229–230, 229; palettes, 87, 219, 220, 221, 223–225, 224, 225, 226, 229, 229, 230, 231, 238n.7; sculpture, 131, 133. *See also* Rattlesnake Disk, Moundville; Willoughby Disk, Moundville

Sullivan, Lynne, 15, 296

Sun Dance, 168

Swanton, John R., 18, 28, 247, 267–268, 316

swirl-cross: and ceramic art, 86, 130, 131, 251, 263–269, 264, 265, 267, 274–275; and copper, 222, 222, 251, 252, 253, 269–271, 273, 287, 287; as independent motif, 252–253; meaning of, 252, 255, 261–263, 264, 266–267, 271–272; and shell cups, 251, 273; and shell gorgets, 251, 252, 254–263, 257, 260, 273–274; and stone, 223; symbolic connections of, 124, 127, 130, 253–269

Thousand Hills State Park petroglyphs, Missouri, 78, 78, 79, 91

Three Hills Creek, Missouri, 67, 80, 80, 82, 82, 85, 86

Thruston, Gates P.: effigy vessels, 177, 179, 187–188, 188, 189, 191, 198n.8; Thruston Tablet, 137–139, 138, 141, 142, 144, 174–175n.1, 175n.4

Thruston Tablet: background layer of obverse panel, 151, 155–159, 155, 156, 165–166; comparisons and chronology of, 164–174; descriptions of, 137, 138, 139, 140–144, 148, 175–176n.7; discovery of, 137, 175n.2; foreground layer of obverse panel, 150, 151–155, 152, 153, 154, 158, 161–162, 163, 164–165, 166, 169, 170, 171; Holmes's drawing of, 140, 146, 147, 148; leg layer of obverse panel, 159–160, 159, 167–168; location of, 139, 174–175n.1; Mallery's photograph of, 142, 142, 147, 148, 160, 175n.3; mythic interpretation of, 162–164, 172; nineteenth-century additions, 160; obverse panel analysis, 149–160; obverse panel based on Holmes, 148, 149, 150, 159; Parker's photographs of, 144, 145, 146, 147, 148; photograph with raking light, 147, 149, 160, 161; previous studies of, 137–144, 146; recent investigations of, 146–149; reverse panel, redrawn from photograph, 148–149, 161; reverse panel of, 161–164, 161; Thruston's published illustration of, 138, 139–140

Thunderbirds, 6, 47, 60–61

Toqua Mound, Tennessee, 294, 295

Traxel, William, 175–176n.7

trophy theme: Hemphill style, 208, 208, 213, 214; Walls Engraved style, 218, 219

Tsi-Zhu: clan, 26, 30; tattoo, 19, 19, 23, 30

Turtleman, 53, 56–57

Underwater Panther: and ceramic art, 125–126, 126, 128–129, 129, 130, 131, 133; and eye-surrounds, 126–127; Hightower style, 288; and shell fragments, 132, 133

Underwater Spirit, 70, 72, 73, 76, 79, 90–91, 91

Upper Mississippi Valley, 37, 38, 40

Vavak, Floyd, 75

Venerable Man, 25–26, 27

Verrill, Ruth, 144, 147, 148, 161, 174n.1

Virgin Mary, imagery of, 121

vulva form motifs: and Earthmother, 55; and Old-Woman-Who-Never-Dies, 77, 83; and rock-art, 82, 83, 84, 85, 86, 90, 92

Walker, Chet, 123, 130
Waring, A. J., Jr., 4, 5, 6–7, 10, 11, 12, 13, 14, 18, 65, 66, 81, 94, 254–255, 315–317
Washington State Park A, Missouri, 67, 77, 77, 79, 82, 83
Washington State Park B, Missouri, 67, 79, 79, 81, 82, 87, 88
Wellmann, Klaus, 64, 69–70
White, John, 197n.3
Wilbanks site, Georgia, 166, 167
Willenberg Shelter, Missouri, 71, 87, 88

Williams, Stephen, 4, 18, 86
Williams Island style, 284, 284, 292, 315
Willoughby, C. C., 254
Willoughby Disk, Moundville: and bilobed arrow, 68, 88, 89; and Mothra, 300, 300, 301, 318–319, 319; and skulls, 202, 203, 225, 225
Winnebago people: cosmology of, 40, 51, 56, 60; ethnographic information from, 27, 28; Hero Twins narrative, 163; and Red Horn, 77, 79, 314
Wulfing Plate, Missouri, 73, 75

Yahola-Hayuya concept, 316

Zebree site, Arkansas, 105, 106

www.ingramcontent.com/pod-product-compliance
Lightning Source LLC
Chambersburg PA
CBHW030126240426
43672CB00005B/38